PAUL

PAUL
THE PAGANS'
APOSTLE

—◆—

Paula Fredriksen

Yale
UNIVERSITY
PRESS
New Haven & London

Published with assistance from the Louis Stern Memorial Fund and from the
Ronald and Betty Miller Turner Publication Fund.

Yale University Press books may be purchased in quantity for educational,
business, or promotional use. For information, please e-mail sales.press@yale.edu
(U.S. office) or sales@yaleup.co.uk (U.K. office).

Set in PostScript Electra type by IDS Infotech, Ltd.
Printed in the United States of America.

Library of Congress Control Number: 2017931450
ISBN: 978-0-300-22588-4 (hardcover : alk. paper)

A catalogue record for this book is available from the British Library.

This paper meets the requirements of ANSI/NISO Z39.48-1992 (Permanence of
Paper).

10 9 8 7 6 5 4 3 2 1

This is for Krister.

The past is gone; and the truth of what is past lies in our own judgment, not in the past event itself.

Augustine of Hippo, *Contra Faustum* 26.5

CONTENTS

PREFACE

The Kingdom of God, Paul proclaimed, was at hand. His firm belief that he lived and worked in history's final hour is absolutely foundational, shaping everything else that Paul says and does. And this conviction is all the more remarkable when we consider that, by the time that we hear from him, mid-first century, the Kingdom is already late.

We easily lose sight of this fact. Our historical perspective obscures it. We look backward, and for good reason see Paul's epistles as "early," a mere couple of decades after Jesus's execution. But while history is always done backward, life is lived only forward, one day at a time. This means that our view of Paul's circumstances and experience can never be the same as Paul's. When the god of Israel revealed his son to Paul (c. 34 C.E.?), Paul had understood what it meant: the establishment of God's Kingdom could not be far behind. But Paul gives this interpretation in letters addressed to his gentile community in Corinth some twenty long years after the event (1 Cor 15.12–52). Why—how—can he still be so sure? And in another letter, written even later, we find him yet again asserting the nearness of the End: "You know what hour it is, how it is full time now for you to awake from sleep. Our salvation is nearer *now* than when we first believed. The night is far gone; the day is at hand" (Rom 13.11–12). How many years, by this point, stood between Paul and his call to proclaim this good news? Why—how—after the passage of so much time, can Paul still be so sure that he knows the hour on God's clock?

This is the question that drives the present study. It will lead us into a Jewish world incandescent with apocalyptic hopes: that God verged on realizing his ancient promises to Israel; that the messiah had come, and would soon come again; that the dead were about to be raised and, together with the living, transformed; that the nations and even the nations' gods would shortly turn to worship the god of Israel. And it will propel us into a Mediterranean world thick with ancient actors: pagans and Jews; healers and prophets; angels and demons; Greeks and Romans; and, not least, angry superhuman forces, divine powers, and hostile cosmic gods. Both worlds are Paul's, and his convictions about the first shaped his actions in the second.

Paul held these convictions as a committed Jew, and he *enacted* them as a committed Jew. In brief, so this study will argue, Paul lived his life entirely within his native Judaism. Later traditions, basing themselves on his letters, will displace him from this context. Through the retrospect of history, Paul will be transformed into a "convert," an ex- or even an anti-Jew; indeed, into the founder of gentile Christianity. But Paul did not know and could not know what these later generations, looking backward, did know: that his mission would end without the return of the messiah. That shortly after his lifetime, Rome would destroy his god's temple and his city, Jerusalem. That new gentile movements independent of and hostile to Judaism would crystallize around his letters, claiming their theologies as Paul's own.

But Paul lived his life—as we all must live our lives—innocent of the future. As historians, we conjure that innocence as a disciplined act of imagination, through appeals to our ancient evidence. Only in so doing can we begin to see Paul as Paul saw himself: as God's prophetic messenger, formed in the womb to carry the good news of impending salvation to the nations, racing on the edge of the End of time.

INTRODUCTION

THE MESSAGE AND THE MESSENGER

> Paul, slave of Jesus Christ, called to be his messenger, set apart for God's good news—promised beforehand through his prophets in the sacred scriptures—concerning his son, from the seed of David according to the flesh, and declared son of God in power according to the spirit of holiness by the resurrection of the dead: Jesus Christ our lord, through whom we have received grace and apostleship in order to bring the obedience of faithfulness on behalf of his name to all the nations, including to you.
>
> Romans 1.1–6

This is Paul's self-introduction, midcentury, to a community that he did not yet know: former pagans, now followers of Christ, gathered in the empire's capital city, Rome. His opening lines reveal much about the dramatic transformations of this upstart Jewish movement in the decades following Jesus's death. Jesus himself, teaching in Aramaic, had gone to fellow Jews in the Galilee and in Judea. Moving between villages and his people's sacred citadel, the temple in Jerusalem,[1] Jesus had proclaimed the message of his own slain mentor, John the Baptizer: God's Kingdom, they both taught, was at hand.[2]

Paul, Jesus's "slave" (*doulos*) and "messenger" (*apostolos*), continued to proclaim this message; but he lived and worked in a much bigger world. Paul taught, thought, and heard scripture in Greek, the English of

Mediterranean antiquity. Paul traveled widely, ranging along the *via Egnatia*, the great East–West highway that connected the cities of Asia Minor and of Greece to Rome. And Paul took the "good news" of God's approaching Kingdom not to fellow Jews, but to a much larger population: Paul preached to pagans.[3]

In the time between Jesus and Paul, more than the ethnicity of their respective audiences had shifted. The content of their message, this "good news," had altered too. Jesus, if we can trust the later gospel portraits of him, had summoned his Jewish audiences to repent of their sins in preparation for the Kingdom's coming. "The Kingdom of God is at hand: Repent, and trust in the good news!" (Mk 1.15). Within its original intra-Jewish context, this call to repentance had specific content. *Metanoeite*, the Greek word that the gospels used for Jesus's summons, implies a change of mind (*nous* means "mind" in Greek). But this idea rests on the Hebrew word *tshuv*, "turn," hence the later rabbinic term for repentance, *tshuvah*. "Turning" from sin within a Jewish context meant, specifically, returning to the covenant between God and Israel, that is, to the teachings of the Torah.[4]

Other traditions about John the Baptizer and about Jesus also point in this direction of linking Torah-observance/*tshuvah* to preparation for the Kingdom. Josephus, contemporary with the gospel writers, relates that the Baptizer urged his hearers to "purify themselves by right conduct," specifically by practicing justice (Greek *dikaiosynē*) toward each other and piety (Greek *eusebeia*) toward God (AJ 18.116–19). "Justice" and "piety" in this context are not pious abstractions: they are a two-word code for a core tradition of the Sinai covenant, the Ten Commandments. The first five commandments comprise the first table of the Law, *eusebeia*, governing relations with God (exclusive worship; no images; no abuse of God's name; keeping the Sabbath; honoring parents). The second five, or second table of the Law, *dikaiosynē*, govern relations between people (thus, forbidding murder, adultery, theft, lying, and coveting).

This same theme of keeping (especially) the Ten Commandments echoes in gospel traditions about Jesus. When asked what were the greatest of the commandments, the Jesus of the Synoptic tradition answers by quoting Deuteronomy 6.4 (love of God, that is, *eusebeia*) and Leviticus 19.18 (love of neighbor, that is, *dikaiosynē*, Mk 12.29–31 and parallels).

Elsewhere he cites these forthrightly. "You know the commandments: 'You shall not murder. You shall not commit adultery. You shall not steal. You shall not bear false witness. You shall not defraud. Honor your father and your mother'" (Mk 10.19). And again like John, Jesus evidently linked the message of the Kingdom's coming and his call to repentance with threats of eternal punishment, the dire consequences of apocalyptic judgment: by such, both men focused their listeners' attention on God's burning anger toward sinners, the better to spur them to repentance.[5]

Paul's *evangelion* did and did not continue in this vein. He too spoke of the Kingdom's rapid approach, and he warned his listeners of God's wrath against sinners. And from time to time he too urged them to conduct their lives according to the standard of the commandments, and specifically of (most of) the Ten Commandments (e.g., 1 Cor 7.19; Rom 13.8–10). But his letters are also filled with what might seem like the opposite message: warnings against the Law, demands that his congregations *not* observe it, claims that the Law languished under the power of sin and of death (e.g., Rom 7.7–25).

Most dramatically changed in the period between Jesus and Paul, however, is the figure of Jesus himself. In Paul's *evangelion*, Jesus has become a main feature of the message. Jesus is the *Christos*, God's "son" and his messiah.[6] In 1 Thessalonians, 1 Corinthians, and Romans, Paul connected Jesus intimately with a dramatic and definitive End-time event, the resurrection of the dead (1 Thes 4.13–18; 1 Cor 15 passim; Rom 1.4 and 11.15). And finally, and momentously, and most surprisingly—another significant change from the message and the mission of Jesus of Nazareth—Paul declared that the good news about the establishment of Israel's messiah and of the Kingdom of Israel's god as forespoken by Israel's prophets in Israel's scriptures was meant as well to go to the *ethnē*, the "nations," that is, to pagan hearers.

To understand these few lines of Paul's brief self-introduction in Romans, then, we need to skip back almost three decades, to a prehistoric (that is, prerecorded) moment of this movement, the time before we have any writings from its members. The origins of Paul's gospel trace not only to the mission and message of Jesus of Nazareth (27–30 C.E.?), but even more dramatically and specifically, to traditions about his resurrection.

◆◆◆

What happened then is now impossible to say. Our different sources tell different stories; only the broadest outlines are clear. Absolutely certain that Jesus of Nazareth had died, some of his followers began to perceive, and then to proclaim, that Jesus lived again. God, they said, had raised him from the dead.

Paul, mid-first century, is our earliest source for this tradition, and he implies that these experiences were visual: Christ "was seen" (*ōphthē*), he says, first by Peter ("Cephas"), then by "the twelve" (the inner group of Jesus's followers). Then he "was seen" (same verb again, *ōphthē*) by almost 500 followers; thereafter by James (Jesus's brother); and then finally "by all the apostles" (1 Cor 15.5–7). "Last of all," Paul concludes this passage, Christ appeared to him (*ōphthē* again, v. 8; cf. 9.1: "Have I not seen Jesus our lord?").

Where did all these visions occur? Paul says nothing about the venues of the original community's experiences, but he implies in his letter to the Galatians that his vision came to him in Damascus (Gal 1.15–17). A generation or two after Paul, the evangelists will situate the initial resurrection appearances variously in the Galilee (thus Mark and Matthew), or in or around Jerusalem (Luke, John), and they will name different initial witnesses, whether female followers, Peter, or anonymous disciples.[7] What did they see? Christ in a spiritual body, Paul insists, and definitely *not* in a body of flesh and blood (1 Cor 15.44, 50). Christ in a flesh-and-blood body, some later evangelists insist no less strongly (Lk 24.39–40; Jn 20.27).[8]

At what point did the risen Christ appear? According to the gospels, shortly after Jesus's crucifixion. But Acts recounts that the risen Christ appeared continuously for forty days in and around Jerusalem after Jesus's resurrection (Acts 1.3–12). And Paul's chronology suggests that his own vision came to him quite a while thereafter, in distant Damascus (thus c. 34? The movement needed time to consolidate, to organize enough to spread out from Jerusalem, and to reach Syria). Clearly, "the" resurrection was not a single event, but a protracted series of visionary experiences occurring variously and in widely different places over an extended period—in Paul's case, several years after Jesus's crucifixion.

Despite the confusions and contradictions of our sources and the uncertainties about what they recount, this conviction that God had raised Jesus from the dead opens up onto an entire world of ancient Jewish biblical and extrabiblical traditions and fiercely held expectations and commitments. And these in turn all cohere with Jesus's inaugural proclamation, "The Kingdom of God is at hand" (Mk 1.15).

This foundational prophecy provided much of the content of the early movement's message as well as its motivation. Yet by itself, it probably would not have sufficed to posthumously propel Jesus's followers out of Jerusalem to Caesarea and to Jaffa, thence to Damascus, to Antioch, and eventually to Rome. Other visionary Jews, centuries to either side of Jesus's lifetime, had uttered similar prophecies and also gathered their own groups of committed followers; but no sustained missionary movements had grown in the aftermath of their deaths.[9]

What distinguishes Jesus from his mentor John the Baptizer, or from the Dead Sea sectarians' Teacher of Righteousness, or from the signs prophets described by Josephus, or from the authors of apocalypses whether canonical or apocryphal, is this singular claim that some of his followers made *about* him—namely, that he had been raised from the dead.

That claim tells us nothing directly, of course, about the historical Jesus himself. Nor, as we have just seen, does it help us much in reconstructing the actual experience of his earliest disciples: the written traditions are too late and too various. What this claim does provide, however, is a strong index of the degree to which Jesus's followers lived, thought, and worked within a framework of apocalyptic expectations—or, rather, within *two* apocalyptic frameworks. The first was older and traditional, the second recent and particular.

The older framework drew upon Jewish convictions about God's Kingdom as an event at the End of Days, the historical realization of God's promises of redemption to Israel. (Christ had come, explained Paul to his gentile readers in Rome, precisely in order to confirm these promises: Rom 15.8; cf. 1.2–3.) Within this older context, as we shall see, the resurrection of the dead had come to be anticipated as one of a number of God's saving final acts. As such, resurrection was imagined as an event that would be both eschatological (that is, occurring at or as the

End-time) and communal (see Ezek 37.11, "the whole house of Israel"; cf. 1 Cor 15.12–16).

As measured by these older traditions, then, claims about Jesus's own resurrection would have been doubly anomalous: they concerned not a collective, but an individual; and thereafter, time and the quotidian had continued. But the disciples also functioned within a second apocalyptic framework, the recent and particular teaching of Jesus himself: not just that the Kingdom was coming, but that it was coming *very soon.* If we can trust a theme present in the later gospels (which were written probably sometime between c. 70 and c. 100), Jesus had taught that his own activities—healings and exorcisms—themselves demonstrated or enacted the Kingdom's kinetic proximity.[10] In other words, it was less the content of Jesus's message as such that had distinguished it from that of so many others, but rather its urgent timetable, his insistence that the eschatological future impinged *now,* upon the present. And the pressing urgency of his good news combined with the degree to which Jesus forged his immediate followers into a community utterly committed to himself, to his prophecy, and to his singular authority in announcing it. Indeed, his followers' insistence that Jesus had been raised measures the intensity of their commitment: his death neither disillusioned (many of?) them nor, in their view, could it disconfirm his prophecy.[11]

These two apocalyptic frameworks, ancient and proximate, combined powerfully, mutually reinforcing each other, as the disciples sought the significance of their own experience of a raised Jesus. Jesus's individual resurrection, they reasoned, reinforced his original message by itself heralding the eschatological End-time, thus the coming general resurrection and the establishment of God's Kingdom. (Decades later, Paul would encourage his gentile communities by teaching similarly, 1 Thes 4.13–18; 1 Cor 15.12–24.) For these disciples, Jesus's resurrection supported and even vindicated the foundational gospel prophecy: the Kingdom truly was at hand. The risen Jesus was thus in a sense the first swallow of the impending eschatological spring.

But why should these resurrection experiences have supported an identification of Jesus as "messiah"? Why would such a conviction lead his apostles to continue, and even to expand, Jesus's original mission to

Israel? What prompted their extending this idiosyncratically Jewish message even further, to pagans? By what criteria would these pagans be included in this movement? And what about this mission and its message would provoke the hostility of other Jews, of other pagans, of Roman magistrates, and even, as Paul will complain, of pagan gods (e.g., 2 Cor 4.4; 11.25–28)?

To understand all of these developments, and to see more clearly Paul's important place within them, we need to situate Paul's letters within their two generative contexts, the scriptural and the social. The first, the sacred texts and traditions of Israel and the ways that late Second Temple Jews would have interpreted these especially in light of apocalyptic hopes, represents an explicitly and idiosyncratically Jewish context, though one in which the idea of the non-Jewish nations played various prominent roles. The second, the world of the Greco-Roman city, which was Paul's apostolic ambit, represents a wide-flung and explicitly pagan social context, though one into which Jewish populations had been comfortably settled for centuries by Paul's lifetime. We begin, then, with scriptural stories, before turning to social institutions and behaviors.

1

ISRAEL AND THE NATIONS

We think of the Bible as a book. It begins at the beginning, with Genesis, and it proceeds to its closing—2 Chronicles for Jews, Revelation for Christians—tucked neatly between two covers. But the Greek term that stands behind the modern English equivalent—*ta biblia*, "the books"—conveys more accurately the manifold nature of these ancient texts. This collection comprises a multitude of individual writings, whose period of composition stretches for well over a millennium. And its discrete writings are themselves composite documents, containing within their seeming unity a diachronic multitude of voices, literary genres, religious and political visions, local oral traditions—the work of countless now-lost authors, editors, and scribes. The Bible is not a book: it is a library.

No one in Paul's period would ever have seen a "Bible." Individual texts or discrete collections (such as Psalms, or Proverbs, or various prophets) were bound together as separate scrolls. The scriptural texts in themselves, further, were unstable: Qumran's library of twenty-one Isaiah manuscripts, for example, preserves over 1,000 individual textual variants. Other books, noncanonical now but authoritative for different Jewish communities then, recast, updated, or expanded the earlier biblical stories. (Jubilees, an extremely important apocryphon from the second century B.C.E., retells in accents peculiar to itself the older stories from Genesis and Exodus; other important traditions, associated with the figure of Enoch, retail visions of fallen angels, of an apocalyptic Jerusalem, and of the coming judgment of a heavenly "Son of Man.")[1] Finally, significant differences and textual variations measure the distance between Hebrew texts and Hellenistic-period Greek versions. Our modern ideas of "book" or of "canon" or of "*the* Bible" simply do not capture this fluid aspect of ancient textuality.[2]

In the crucible of apocalyptic hope, in the course of the late Second Temple period to the high Roman Empire (roughly 200 B.C.E. to 200 C.E.), the documentary montage preserved in these scriptures achieved, for some Jews, a new kind of notional unity. Their many different elements, themes, and traditions coalesced to support various master narratives of Israel's impending redemption. This genre of master narrative—"apocalyptic eschatology," in academic parlance[3]—filled a gap perceived between lived experience and the promises, covenants, and hopes that shaped Jewish scriptures.[4] Apocalyptic eschatology corrects history. It promises a speedy resolution of history's moral dissonances: good triumphs over evil, peace over war, life over death.

Apocalyptic hope, the vibrant matrix of Jesus's mission to Israel, is also the interpretive context for understanding the gentile mission of Paul. Tracing its development—and Paul's understanding of his own role in realizing its promises—means tracing as well the dynamic interactions between Jewish scriptures and Jewish history that would have shaped both these biblical traditions and the sensibilities of their first-century readers and hearers. In the chapter that follows, I will comment from time to time on issues of redaction (that is, how a given segment of scripture might have been edited into the story as it now stands) and of historical provenance (when such a piece of tradition, generated by what historical context, might have entered into the biblical text). But I am not interested in biblical criticism as such. Rather, I want to survey the stories in the Jewish Bible, attending to both its Hebrew and its Greek voices, in order to trace the themes shaping Roman-period hopes for the coming of God's Kingdom. Understanding that story of redemption requires having a grasp of the characters of its three chief dramatis personae: God, the nations, and Israel.

BEGINNINGS

God and Cosmos

Without explanation, without introduction, evidently unaccompanied, the god of Genesis simply appears "in the beginning." He commands light and darkness, shapes order out of chaos, and in six days makes the heavens, the earth, and everything in them, including, finally, humanity "both male and female" (Gen 1.1–30). A special intimacy connects this god with his human creatures: them he makes after his own "image and likeness," and he grants them dominion over the earth (1.28–30). Finishing his work, God himself then rests on the seventh day, the Sabbath, and blesses it (2.1–4).

This god is a solitary and universal deity, these elegant verses imply. Yet Creation conceals complications: who are the others whom God addresses once he proposes to create humanity (Gen 1.26)? The text does not say.[5] Another complication of this god's unique and universal status is his resting on the seventh day (2.2–3): by writing the Sabbath and the divine observance of it into the very structure of the universe, these same verses render this god "Jewish": keeping the Sabbath on the seventh day of the week will eventually unite this god with his people Israel (Exod 31.13–17).[6] How Jewish, then, is God? Different ancient authors, commenting on these verses, answered this question differently. But as we will see, Paul himself affirms this ethnic identification. His god is the universal deity, superior to all other divine personalities; the god of all humanity, "the god of the nations also" (Rom 3.29). Yet at the same time and in particular ways he is also the god specifically of Israel, the god of "the forefathers" (that is, of Abraham, Isaac, and Jacob, Rom 15.8), the god of Jewish history, the "father" both of Israel and of its messiah (Rom 9.4–5 and passim). The universal high god's "Jewishness," and his fidelity to those promises that he makes (later on in the book of Genesis) to the patriarchs of Israel, is the pivot upon which Paul's vision of universal redemption will turn.

(Divine ethnicity may seem a strange idea; but gods in antiquity tended to share in the ethnicity of the peoples who worshiped them. The Jewish god was no exception: Roman gods were particularly invested in the future and the well-being of Rome: Athena in Athens, Aphrodite in Aphrodisias, and so on. And ancient gods and humans—we will see how in the next chapter—tended to cluster in family groups. In this regard, then, the biblical god's "Jewishness" simply marks him as an ancient deity. What *was* odd, in the perspective of their non-Jewish contemporaries, was the Jews' insistence that their particular god was *also* the universal, highest god—a claim that Paul himself affirms, but a claim that later gentile interpreters of Paul, as we shall see, will deny.)

The god of the Bible does not long remain in the magnificent isolation of this creational week. Jewish scriptures teem with other supernatural personalities. The "sons of God" who mate with human women seem to have some sort of superhuman status (Gen 6.1–4; cf. Job 1.6): according to Enoch, they were fallen angels, their progeny evil spirits.[7] God avails himself of divine intermediaries (Exod 3.2, 14.19); he converses with Satan (Zech 3.1–2; Job); he is attended by cherubim (Ps 80.1; Ezek 10.20) and seraphim (Isa 6.2–6); he presides over a heavenly angelic court (1 Kgs 22.19; Job 1.6). According to Jubilees, the two highest orders of angels in God's presence were circumcised (15.27), and they keep the Sabbath with him (2.17–20). All of these divine entities are elevated, superhuman powers. In the biblical narratives, however, they are also clearly God's subordinates.

But another category of supernatural beings, more independent than subordinate, also populates ancient Israelite scriptures: other *elohim*, "gods." Sometimes Israel's god battles (and bests) these forces, or he "executes judgment" on them (Exod 12.12); at other points he takes these gods captive (Jer 43.12), or punishes them (46.25), or sends them into exile (49.3). Sometimes these gods are mentioned as matter-of-fact: "All the peoples walk, each in the name of its god," observes the prophet Micah, "but we will walk in the name of the Lord *our* god forever and ever" (Mic 4.5). "God stands in the divine council; in the midst of the gods he gives judgment" (Ps 82.1). At other times, these gods are overpowered by Israel's god (as Ps 82.6–8, asserting God's "international" or transethnic power and authority), or they are scorned because of the worship that foreign peoples tender to their images (Ps 95.5, 97.7; Isa 44.6–20). Often, they serve as the inferior contrast to Israel's god. ("Who is like you, O Lord, among the gods?" sings Moses, Exod 15.11; "All gods bow down before him," Ps 97.7.) The point to note for now, however, is that some passages of scripture speak simply of these other gods: they *are*.[8]

Scriptures' acknowledgment of other gods can come as a surprise to modern readers. Were ancient Jews not "monotheists"? Yes and no. Earlier scholarship came up with the term "henotheism" as a way to accommodate the Bible's other divinities. "Henotheism" means the worship of only one god, without denying the existence of other gods; "monotheism" indicates the conviction that only one god exists. Henotheism was supposedly a prior developmental stage along the evolutionary road to monotheism: eventually, monotheism triumphs. The Bible, according to this way of thinking, preserves traces of the "more primitive" phase (multiple gods, with one god supreme) within an essentially monotheistic (one god only) text.[9]

The problem with all of this terminological finesse is the way that it obscures a simple historical observation: in antiquity, "monotheists" were polytheists. That is to say, no matter how fiercely loyal to their own chief deity ancient Jews and, eventually, Christians might have been, their world view still left scope for many other gods. As we will see, Paul himself speaks of these gods, complains about their activities, bemoans their effects, and predicts their coming destruction or defeat or submission to the returning, triumphant Christ; but their existence is a given. Well into the fifth century C.E., in *City of God*, Augustine will sound much the same way. The difference between pagans and Christians, he notes there, is not their respective beliefs in the existence or in the powers of these other divine entities, but what they *name* them. Christians call these gods "demons"; pagans call these demons "gods" (*City of God* 9.23). This distinction between "gods" and "demons" will be introduced, as we will see, once Hebrew scripture transitions to Greek; but it is not a distinction native to these ancient Hebrew writings themselves. In antiquity, "monotheism" is a species of polytheism.[10]

Eventually, what are now extrabiblical traditions will fill in perceived gaps in the biblical narrative, explaining how these other gods—errant angels? heavenly rebels?—came to be. But before we can further frame this issue of other gods, we need to consider the humans who honored them. Where did the nations who honored these other gods come from, and what is their relation to Israel, and to Israel's god?

God and Humanity

The stately creational days of Genesis 1 yield abruptly to a different (and probably older) story of beginnings in Genesis 2. Here, human history unwinds as a tale of disobedience and punishment, striving and failure. The first couple defies the divine command, bringing pain, hard labor, and death into the world (Gen 2–3). Cain kills his younger brother Abel in humanity's second generation (4.1–13). Within ten generations, human wickedness is so great, corruption and violence so rampant, that the Lord regrets having created them at all ("And the Lord was sorry that he had made humankind upon the earth, and it grieved him to his heart," 6.6). Unleashing the waters of chaos that he had pent up on Creation's second day (1.6–8), God obliterates life from the earth, saving only one family, that of Noah, "a righteous man, blameless in his generation" (6.9). "I am going . . . to destroy from under heaven all flesh in which there is the breath of life," God tells Noah, "but I will establish my covenant [*brit*] with you" (6.17–18; cf. 8.21–9.17, for its terms). The waters come and consume all life. "Only Noah was left, and those who were with him in the ark" (7.23).

Once the waters recede, God has an insight about the creature that he made in his own image (an idea recalled in Gen 9.6): "the inclination of the human heart is evil from youth" (8.21). Vowing never again to annihilate all life because of humanity's moral failures, God sets a rainbow in the sky to remind both him and them of their covenant (9.15). Humanity now begins again with the families of Noah's three sons, Shem, Ham, and Japhet, and the children and grandchildren born to them after the flood: in Jewish tradition, some seventy different "nations" (Hebrew *goyim*, Greek *ethnē*; 10.1–32). All humanity descends from Adam and Eve; but more precisely, all humanity—seventy nations by this count—descend from Noah.[11]

The "Table of Nations" in Genesis 10, and the primacy of Noah, express a foundational biblical concept, the idea of the totality of the family of man. The word *goyim*, "nations," occurs for the first time in the Hebrew Bible here. The three founding kinship units—those of Shem, Ham, and Japhet—are listed according to "their genealogies, their languages, their lands, and their nations" (on Shem, 10.31; cf. 10.5 on Japhet and 10.20 on Ham). These ethnic identifiers—kinship group (shared "blood"), language, and locality ("land")—quite commonly cluster in ancient writings. The Greek historian Herodotus, famously, will define "Greekness" (*to hellēnikon*) in much the same terms (see below, p. 35). Conspicuous by its absence in the Table of Nations, however, is one of the most important and basic of ancient ethnic identifiers: Genesis does *not* say, "according to their gods" (though cf. Deut 32.8). The gods of the nations are not listed with this first tabulation. Other gods *qua* narrative characters have yet to appear in the story.[12]

For now, it is enough to note that this way of saying "all humanity," referring to the plenum of nations descended from Noah, will reverberate throughout scripture, echoing in the prophets, especially Isaiah; in later Second Temple writings (Jubilees, Qumran texts, the Sibylline Oracles); continuing on in Josephus, the rabbis, and the later Aramaic Targumim.[13] Paul too will think with this idea, alluding to the Table of Nations at the crescendo of his argument in Romans 11:25–26. All human families look back to Noah, in this tradition; thus all human families, later Jewish traditions will say, likewise look back to Noah's covenant with God.[14]

God and Israel

The god of the Bible makes the universe by divine fiat. He preserves Noah because of Noah's righteousness (Gen 6.9), giving humanity its second chance to "be fruitful and multiply, and fill the earth" (9.1). But God creates Israel by an unexplained choice,[15] over time, through a promise:

> Now the Lord said to Abram, "Go out from your country and your kindred and your father's house to the Land that I will show you. I will make of you a great nation [*goy gadol*], and I will bless you and make your name great, so that you will be a blessing. I will bless those who bless you, and the one who curses you I will curse. And in you all the families of the earth will be blessed. (Gen 12.1–3)

The promise of coming into the land—*the* Land, in biblical narrative; the Land of Israel—combined with the promise of progeny/"nationhood" and of universal blessing for all the earth's families, exerts a gravitational pull over the rest of Abram/Abraham's story and, indeed, over the rest of the book of Genesis. God subsequently makes a covenant with Abraham, again pledging the Land (15.12–21) and foretelling Abraham and Sarah's status as progenitors of "many nations" (17.5–6, 15–16). More signally, Abraham and Sarah will produce Isaac, whose children will inherit the Land "for a perpetual holding; and I will be their god" (17.8). Abraham for his part must "walk before [God] and be blameless" (17.1; cf. 18.19), circumcising all the males of his house as "a sign of the covenant between me and you throughout your generations . . . an everlasting covenant" (17.10–14, esp. 17.12, which specifies circumcision "on the eighth day"). From Abraham through Isaac to Jacob (named "Israel," 32.28) and thence to Jacob's sons and grandsons, the eponymous fathers of Israel's twelve tribes, this covenant is affirmed and repeated. Joseph, dying in Egypt, surrounded by his brothers, closes the book of Genesis by recalling God's promise: "God will surely come to you, and bring you up out of this land to the Land that he swore to Abraham, Isaac, and Jacob" (50.24). When Paul speaks in Romans of "the promises given to the fathers" (Rom 15.8), it is passages like these that he has in mind.

The next four books of the Torah, from Exodus through Deuteronomy, narrate the stages through which God shapes the children of Israel into the foretold *goy gadol*, a great nation. Liberating them from Pharaoh with great signs and wonders, contesting against the gods of Egypt, leading the people out into the wilderness of Sinai, God reveals his plan to Moses:

> Thus you shall say to the house of Jacob and tell to the Israelites: You have seen what I did to the Egyptians, how I bore you on eagles' wings and brought you to myself. Now therefore, if you obey my voice and keep my covenant, you shall be my treasured possession out of all the peoples. Indeed, the whole earth is mine, but you shall be for me a kingdom of priests and a holy nation. (Exod 19.4–6)

Thereafter, an enormous body of legislation fills the rest of these "five books of Moses." Cultic and ethical instruction; agricultural regulations and statutes protecting the poor; sacrificial protocols and rules for animal husbandry; food ways, sexual codes, criminal and property law and torts; rules for distinguishing between pure and impure; the establishment of community holy days and especially rules for observing the Sabbath; measurements for the sanctuary and specifications for everything from priestly garments to curtain rings: God's commandments comprise the content of his *torah*, his "instruction" or "teaching" to Israel, setting the terms of their covenant.[16] Part of the reason for God's mandating these practices is specifically to set Israel apart from other peoples ("You shall faithfully observe all my laws and all my regulations. . . . I, the Lord, am your god, who has set you apart from other peoples," Lev 20.22, 24). And included in this revelation are prescriptions for repairing the relationship between God and the individual Israelite when, whether deliberately or inadvertently, the human partner to the covenant erred (e.g., Lev 26.41–42). To the whole nation, further, God gives a "fast of atonement," Yom Kippur (16.1–34), "an everlasting statute for you, to make atonement for the people of Israel once a year for all their sins." God builds a relationship meant to last.

Fundamental to this god's covenant, emphasized repeatedly, are his twin demands for exclusive and aniconic worship. No other gods, and no images. (These are the first two of the Ten Commandments, Exod 20.3–5; Deut 5.7–8.) Accustomed as we are to these two provisos, we can easily fail to see how odd they were in their historical context. In cultures where all gods exist—a social reality that Israel's god does not deny—worshiping only one god to the *exclusion* of others can seem at least incautious, if not downright impious. By definition, any god is more powerful than any human; and gods as a group tended to be sensitive to human slights, and quick to let their displeasure be known. (The humans who worshiped them were no less sensitive. Later Greek and Latin ethnographers, as we shall see, will complain about Jewish "atheism," that is, the Jews' refusal to honor the gods of the majority.) But Israel's god was particularly adamant on these two points: his people may not worship him by making an image (e.g., Deut 4.15–16), nor may they make and bow down to an image of any humans, birds, or animals (4.16–18; the story of the Golden Calf, Exod 32, provided a standing cautionary tale). What about worshiping objects not made by human hands, such as natural phenomena? Other nations worship stars and planets; Israel may not (Deut 4.19). More: when they come into the Land, Israel must eradicate the peoples who dwell there, because they have practiced linked abominations: idol-worship and infanticide.

> When the Lord *your* god has cut off before you the nations whom you are about to enter to dispossess them, when you have dispossessed them and live in their land, take care that you are not snared into imitating them, after they have been destroyed before you. Do not inquire concerning *their* gods, saying, "How did these nations worship their gods? I also want to do the same." You must not do the same for the Lord your god, because every abhorrent thing that the Lord hates they have done for their gods. They would even burn their sons and daughters in the fire to their gods. (Deut 12.29–31)

Closing with blessings and with curses—blessings if Israel keeps the covenant, curses if they do not; punishment promised for waywardness, compassion and forgiveness for rededication—Deuteronomy brings the five books of the Law to its close (Deut 30–33). Moses dies. The twelve tribes stand on the east bank of the Jordan River, poised to come into the Land; ready, finally, to realize God's ancient promises to Abraham, Isaac, and Jacob.

KINGDOM AND EXILE

David's House, and God's

Once settled in the land of Canaan, the different tribes worshiped at various altars scattered throughout the countryside. Priests and judges regulated cultic and social life. Persisting in this way for several centuries, this loose confederacy of tribes and clans eventually reorganized under a monarch, first Saul (c. 1020–1000 B.C.E.), and after him, David (c. 1000–961) and then David's son, Solomon (c. 961–922).

Both in his own lifetime and later, in the perspective of biblical tradition, David was the key figure. He united the tribes and defeated local enemies (such as the Philistines). He shut down regional sanctuaries. And he consolidated both political and military power and traditional cult in his capital city, Jerusalem. Biblical tradition voiced ambivalence about these arrangements, (retrospectively) warning the tribes in the wilderness about some of the questionable consequences of kingship (Deut 17.14–19; cf. 1 Sam 8.10–18). But these same scriptures also embraced and endorsed David and his dynasty, asserting that God himself had loved the king and promised eternal dominion to the sons of his line:

> The Lord declares to you [David] that the Lord *will make you a house.* When your days are fulfilled and you lie down with your ancestors, I will raise up your offspring after you . . . and I will establish his king-dom. *He shall build a house for my name,* and I will establish the throne of his kingdom forever. *I will be a father to him, and he will be my son.* When he commits iniquity, I will punish him . . . but I will not take my steadfast love away from him. . . . And your house and your kingdom shall be made sure forever before me. *Your throne will be established forever.* (2 Sam 7.11–17)

In the ancient world, divinity localized in two prime ways: it attached to places (sacred groves, mountains, altars, temples) and it attached to peoples (hence the idea of gods' ethnicities, mentioned above). The dynamics of the story that stretches from Genesis through Deuteronomy articulate the Jewish refractions of this idea in continually asserting the binding relationship between Israel's god, his people, and the Land. And the people's relationship with God is frequently expressed in the language of family descent: "Israel is my first-born son," God declares in Exodus 4.22, and this image of Israel's sonship, thus of God's "paternity," recurs throughout Jewish scriptures (e.g., Jer 31.9, 20; Paul repeats this idea of Israel's sonship in Rom 9.4). God, further, dwells *with* his people (as do other gods with theirs), and God's proximity is one of the reasons for and requirements of Israel's dedication to "holi-ness," that is, separateness. (When Paul calls his gentiles away from their gods to his own, he too will insist on their "separation" or "sanctity," *hagiasmos.*)

The messianic-Davidic traditions about these two houses, however—the genealogical-biological house (David's) and the sanctified house of the temple (God's)—intensified for Israel these two ways of expressing divinity's locality, in people and in places. God remains Israel's "father"; but in a special way he is father to the kings of David's line. "You are my son; today I have begotten you," God says on the coronation day of an Israelite king (Ps 2.7). "I have found David, my servant," sings the Psalmist; "With my holy oil I have anointed him; . . . He shall cry to me, 'You are my father'" (Ps 89.20, 26). "I will be a father to him," God through the prophet Samuel tells David about David's son (2 Sam 7.14, cited above). And since kings are "crowned" in Israelite tradition by being anointed with oil, this means that the "anointed one" (Hebrew *mashiach*, Greek *christos*), David's heir, is in this special way God's "son" (cf. Rom 1.3). This idea would have a long future in later Christianity.

The divine aspect of Davidic royalty, unlike Egyptian or Greek or Roman expressions of this idea, did not imply literal divine descent. David's offspring are normally human. Individual kings are mortal; it is their *succession* that is immortal. The messiah's divine sonship in these Hebrew texts articulated a special relationship with God; it did not mean that the messiah himself (unlike Pharaoh, or Alexander the Great, or the emperors of Rome) was a god in his own right. The message that formed around the memory and mission of Jesus of Nazareth will draw on all of these themes while enlarging them; eventually, Jesus's messianic "son-ship" will indeed imply a divine status, one that Paul himself will affirm and articulate. Those developments lie off in the late Second Temple period, however; the ancient scriptural texts seem to distinguish between Davidic descent and actual divinity.

What about that other aspect of ancient, localized divinity, the sanctity of God's "house"—that is, of the temple in Jerusalem—that David's son would build? Israel's god, Jews insisted, was the lord of the whole universe, the god of all other gods, the "god of the nations also" (Paul again, Rom 3.29). "The heavens to their uttermost reaches belong to the Lord your god," God tells Israel in the wilderness, "the earth and all that is on it" (Deut 10.14). God had framed everywhere and everything, and no place was far from him. But because of David's consolidation of the cult in Jerusalem, and especially because of Solomon's construction of a temple and an altar on *har bayit-Adonai*, "the mountain of the Lord's House" (Isa 2.2), God was thought to "live" particularly in Jerusalem, within his *mishkan*, his "dwelling place." (Paul repeats this idea too, Romans 9.4; so too Jesus in the gospel of Matthew 23.31.)

Jerusalem thus became the pilgrimage center for the three annual holidays that had been introduced as part of the covenant during Israel's period of wandering in the desert: Sukkot (in the fall, eventually commemorating the desert wandering), Passover/Unleavened Bread (in early spring, commemorating the redemption from Egypt), and Shavuot (in late spring/early summer, eventually associated with the Sinai revelation). The laws pertaining to sacrifices, framed in biblical narrative as relating to the mobile tabernacle, were "transposed" to this regal new setting. The temple and Jerusalem, God's presence therein, the eternal dominion of David's line: these aspects of David's consolidation of authority and of military and political power entered into Israel's construction of covenant. The city and the temple, too, pronounced prophets and psalms, would abide forever.

But David's throne and God's temple in fact did not abide. History battered Israelite prophecy. After Solomon's death (c. 922 B.C.E.?), the kingdom split in two, ten tribes living in the northern region ("Israel") and two tribes in the south ("Judah"). Regional cultic sites again sprang up, while the old indigenous deities once again made their presence felt. Within two centuries, the north capitulated to Assyrian expansion (c. 722 B.C.E.). Some of its people were deported, scattered, and resettled within the Assyrian empire: these ten "lost" tribes would forever after haunt Jewish memory.[17] Once Assyria fell to Babylon, the newer imperial power consolidated its control over the southern kingdom of Judah. But in 586 B.C.E., following an ill-advised rebellion, Judah too fell. The temple was destroyed, the city laid waste; and the king Zedekiah, blinded and battered, was taken into exile in Babylon with many of his people (2 Kgs 25.1–12).

Only after Babylon fell in its turn to the growing power of Persia were the Judean exiles allowed to go home (c. 538 B.C.E.; 2 Chr 36.22–23). Those who returned rebuilt the temple, but it was a small and humble affair compared to the remembered grandeur of Solomon's. Governors and high priests who reported to Persia served in the stead of defunct Davidic kings. The trickle of returning Judeans nonetheless made a tremendous effort at reconsolidation. They were helped in this effort by a vital legacy: the traditions of their prophets.

Prophecy and Promise

Our English word *prophet* rests on the Greek *prophētēs.* A Greek *prophētēs* (*pro-*, for; *phanai*, to speak) was someone who spoke for a god, interpreting an oracle. Since the question taken to the god usually concerned the course of the future, a prophet functioned as the seer who foresaw and elusively described its course. The god would inspire the oracle, which the prophet would tender to the pilgrim questioner.[18]

For Hebrew, "prophet" translates both *ro'e* (seer) and *nav'i* (speaker). The Hebrew prophets were God's spokesmen. Growing up as an institution together with the monarchy, prophets not only foretold the future; they also commented tellingly on the present. In particular, they criticized Israel, both kings and commoners, for wandering from the covenant—worshiping images, paying cult to other gods, compromising the exclusive relationship between Israel and its god. Sometimes, the perceived breach might be what we would consider ethical, not cultic (such as defrauding the poor or not providing for the vulnerable, e.g., Isa 4.14–15, 10.1–2); but these two domains—distinct in our categories, not theirs—were both conditions of keeping the covenant.

Prophetic literature, no less than the other genres of literature encompassed within the vast collection that is the Hebrew Bible, presents to the modern scholarly view a stratigraphic record of traditions: writings about or attributed to these prophets actually span lifetimes of accumulated sayings, legends, warnings, curses, oracles, affirmations, consolations, visions and revisions, and experiences to either side of the events that they (whether notionally or actually) presage. Given the fluidity of oral tradition and of manuscript culture in antiquity, prophecies could be continuously sharpened, modified, or updated, the better to speak to current circumstances. And *the* circumstance, the event that more than any other left its mark on ancient Jewish prophecy and history, was the experience of the Exile under Nebuchadnezzar.

Many essential elements of biblical tradition, of course, substantially predate 586–538 B.C.E., the years of the Babylonian captivity. That particular experience was defining, however, because of its traumatic clarity.

Exile challenged Israelite identity in fundamental ways, undermining the constitutive ideas of covenant and promise, of peoplehood and Land; denying the clustered concepts of Jerusalem, temple, and messiah/Davidic dynast; calling into question the power, the loyalty, and the constancy of Israel's god. With the threat of the loss of the Northern Kingdom and, once that was realized, the threat to and loss of Judea in the south, the covenant could have seemed canceled, its agreements annulled.

Prophetic traditions urged otherwise. There was no question, they insisted, of Israel's god having been defeated by foreign gods; rather, Israel's god was using the nations for his own purposes, to discipline and to punish his own people. God's wrath was indeed dreadful, admonished the prophets; his patience with waywardness expired, his afflictions extreme. Speaking for God, the prophets heaped harrowing curses upon errant Israel: "I will dash [the residents of Jerusalem] one against the other, fathers and sons together, says the Lord. I will not pity or spare or have compassion. . . . I will make you serve your enemies in a land that you do not know, for in my anger a fire is kindled which shall burn forever" (Jer 13.14, 15.14). Enumerating the terrible sufferings that would devour Jerusalem, Ezekiel voiced the Lord's rage: "Because you . . . have not walked in my statutes or kept my ordinances, but have acted according to the ordinances of the nations round about you . . . I will do what I have never yet done, and the like of which I will never do again. Fathers shall eat their sons in the midst of you, and sons shall eat their fathers; and I will execute judgments on you, and any of you who survives I will scatter to all the winds" (Ezek 5.7–10). And the experience of Exile cast a giant shadow "backward," into the period of Israel's foundational history, because of post-Exilic traditions redacted into the earlier text. Thus Moses himself "spoke" of the Exile: if the people are not true to the terms of the covenant, he warned, God would "take delight in bringing ruin upon you and in destroying you; and you shall be plucked off the Land" (Deut 28.63).

These dire admonitions (and retrospective descriptions) framed prophetic discourse. But they did not exhaust it. Against history's disconfirmations of the covenant, the prophets also juxtaposed incandescent affirmations of the eternity of God's bond with Israel, the constancy of his love, the surety of his promise.

Comfort, comfort my people, says your god.
Speak tenderly to Jerusalem, and cry to her
That her time of service is ended, that her
    iniquity is pardoned,
That she received from the Lord's hand
    double for all her sins. (Isa 40.1–2)

But now thus says the Lord, he who created you, O Jacob,
He who formed you, O Israel:
Fear not, for I have redeemed you;
I have called you by name, you are mine.
When you pass through the waters I will be with you,
And through the rivers, they will not overwhelm you;
When you walk through fire you shall not be burned,
And the flame shall not consume you.
For I am the Lord your god,
The Holy One of Israel, your savior. . . .
Fear not, for I am with you; I will bring your offspring from the east,
And from the west I will gather you.
I will say to the north, Give up,
And to the south, Do not withhold.
Bring my sons from afar, and my daughters from the end of the earth,
Every one who is called by my name,
Whom I created for my glory, whom I formed and made. (Isa 43.1–7)

For this is like the days of Noah to me:
As I swore that the waters of Noah
Should no more go over the earth
So I have sworn that I will not be angry with you. . . .
For the mountains may depart, and the hills be removed,
But my steadfast love shall not depart from you,
And my covenant of peace shall not be removed,
Says the Lord, who has compassion on you. (Isa 54.9–10)

Suffering was not rejection, insisted the prophets. Rather, it was punishment; and punishment was itself a token of election: "Only you [Israel] have I chosen from among all the nations," warned the prophet Amos, "and *therefore* I will punish you for your sins" (Amos 3.2). By configuring Israel's suffering as punishment, in other words, the prophets reaffirmed God's and Israel's ongoing relationship. Punishment was redemptive: it had as its goal Israel's (re)turn to God. "You have rejected me," said Jeremiah, speaking for God to Jerusalem, "so I have stretched out my hand against you and destroyed you. . . . *If* you turn, I will restore you, and you shall stand before me" (Jer 15.6, 19).

In these ways, the historical experience of Exile and Return came in prophetic idiom to express as well a moral dialectic of sin/punishment and of repentance/forgiveness. Repentance/returning to God would lead to redemption/return to the Land. "When all these things come upon you," Moses again "prophesied" in Deuteronomy, ". . . and you call them to mind among all the nations where the Lord your god has driven you, and you return to the Lord your god, you and your children, and obey his voice in all that I command you this day . . . then the Lord your god will restore your fortunes, and have compassion on you, and he will gather you again from all the peoples where the Lord your god has scattered you . . . and will bring you into the Land which your fathers possessed, that you may possess it" (Deut 30.1–5).

As these traditions develop, the meanings of homecoming deepen. To this end, the same (post-Exilic) passage in Deuteronomy cited above also mobilizes the fundamental sign of the covenant between God and Abraham—that is, circumcision—to serve as a moral metaphor, the "circumcision of the heart": "And the Lord your god will circumcise your heart and the heart of your offspring, so that you will love the Lord your god with all your heart and with all your soul, that you may live" (Deut 30.6). Jeremiah speaks of this deepening commitment as having God's *torah* written upon the heart. When God effects his covenant with Israel in this way, "I shall be their god, and they shall be my people . . . and I will remember their sins no more" (Jer 31.31–32). "Harken to me, you who know righteousness, the people in whose heart is my *torah*," Isaiah calls out. "Fear not the reproach of men, be not dismayed by their revilings. . . . [M]y deliverance will be forever, and my salvation for all generations" (Isa 51.7–8).

Hopes for the restoration of David's house, as for God's house, likewise swell in these prophecies of consolation. "The days are surely coming," says the Lord through Jeremiah, when "I will cause a righteous branch to spring up for David; and he shall execute righteousness and justice in the Land. . . . David will never lack a man to sit on the throne of the house of Israel, and the Levitical priests shall never lack a man in my presence to offer burnt offerings and . . . to make sacrifices forever" (Jer 33.14–18; cf. 23.5). The covenants with David's house and with the temple and its priesthood are as steady and certain as are God's covenants with day and night, with heaven and earth—as sure, in other words, as God's bond with creation itself (Jer 33.19–26).

Isaiah thinks even bigger. "A shoot will come forth from the stump of Jesse," David's father, he proclaims (Isa 11.10; cf. Rom 15.12). He will be a righteous king, slaying the wicked and judging justly. Even the animal kingdoms—wolf and lamb, leopard and kid, calf and lion—will live in peace with one another (11.2–8). In those days, "the earth shall be full of the knowledge of the Lord" (11.9). Scattered Israel—even those who in the distant past, in the days of Moses, stayed in Egypt; even those tribes lost centuries earlier, in Assyria—will reassemble. But even more is envisaged: the *goyim* too, the other nations, will also seek out this Davidic king (11.10–16; cf. 27.12–13, 2.2–4). "I am coming to gather all nations and tongues, and they will come and see my glory," Isaiah prophesies (66.18; "all nations and tongues" echoes the Table of Nations tradition in Gen 10). Assembling on "this mountain," the mountain of the Lord's house in Jerusalem, all of these peoples, both Israel and the nations, will feast together on a meal made by God himself (25.6). God will wipe away every tear (25.8). He will "swallow up death for ever" (25.7). He will raise the dead (26.19).

New themes thus begin to sound as prophecy develops. The idea of redemption itself enlarges, growing in dimension from a spatial or locative image to also a moral and an eschatological one: redemption from slavery (the Egyptian paradigm) or from Exile (the Babylonian paradigm); redemption from sin and/or from its effects (divine anger not least); redemption, finally, from want, from war, from death itself. And the scope of this redemption enlarges. What had begun as an affirmation within normal history of Israel's particular relationship with their god—the patriarchal promises, the Law and the covenants, the messiah/David's dynasty, the temple and its cult (unique privileges still praised by Paul centuries later, Rom 9.4–5)—now expands to assertions of absolute divine prerogative. Not only does the remnant of Israel return to the Land; so do all twelve tribes, miraculously reassembled. Not only do all twelve tribes of Israel gather in Jerusalem; so too do all seventy nations. Not only do the living assemble, but also the dead who rise ("Thus says the Lord: Behold, I will open your graves, and I will raise you from your graves, O my people; and I will bring you home into the Land of Israel," Ezek 37.12). All humanity, both Israel and the nations, acknowledge Israel's god: "All flesh shall come to worship before me" (Isa 66.23).

In short, these later prophecies project Israel's experience under Babylon, the Exile and Return, onto the entire universe: Israel's future redemption will redeem as well all of the nations. The horizon line of normal history dissolves into huge visions of a posthistorical, idealized future, when earthly kingdoms will cede — *soon* — to the Kingdom of God. We are entering the world of apocalyptic eschatology.

THE EXPECTATION OF REDEMPTION

Paul's letters, like the traditions from and about Jesus of Nazareth eventually collected in the gospels, represent points along this arc of apocalyptic hope, an arc that stretches from the later passages of the classical prophets—Isaiah, Jeremiah, Ezekiel—through the aftermath of Bar Kokhba's revolt against Rome (132–135 C.E.). Apocalyptic prophecy in this period insists with mounting urgency that the good and all-powerful god of the Bible is indeed in command of history, the seeming counterevidence of current circumstances notwithstanding. If things were bad, it could only be because God was about to intervene to put them right.

But what was "bad"? That depended on the eye of the beholder. Certainly once Alexander the Great (d. 323 B.C.E.) conquered Persia, Jews in historically Jewish territories faced a new challenge, "Hellenization." Greek gods, Greek urban structures, Greek culture, Greek language: all these swept over and settled variously into the lands affected by Alexander's victories, including the Galilee, Samaria, and Judea. Changed and charged political realities developed as the successor dynasties of two of Alexander's generals, the Ptolemies in Egypt and the Seleucids in Syria, faced off with each other, polarizing relationships and affecting politics within Jerusalem's priestly ruling class. One result of these new circumstances was the

Hellenization of Jerusalem, and the effort of the Seleucid Antiochus Epiphanes to Hellenize the temple cult.[19] Another was the successful Maccabean rebellion, and the subsequent installation of the priestly Hasmonean family as Israel's new rulers (167–37 B.C.E.). And yet a third— in many ways the varied prophetic responses to this roiled political atmosphere—was the efflorescence of apocalyptic writings: Daniel, the Dead Sea Scrolls, various pseudepigrapha.[20] The production of such texts, and the missions of various charismatic figures who left no writings—John the Baptizer, Jesus of Nazareth, Theudas, the Egyptian, and those men whom Josephus refers to collectively as the "signs prophets"—continued as Israel was caught up in Rome's bumpy transition from republic to empire, in the uncertainties of Roman hegemony (especially following Herod's rule, 37–4 B.C.E.), and ultimately in two devastating wars against Rome (68–73 C.E. and 132–35 C.E., Bar Kokhba's revolt).

We can distill from this mass of writings a general pattern of End-time events, themselves amplifications of themes shaping the older prophetic paradigm of Exile and Return. Before the End comes, the righteous will suffer persecution at the hands of the wicked. Suddenly, though, things will begin to reverse.[21] The Day of the Lord will arrive, when the world will be convulsed by celestial and terrestrial catastrophes: earthquakes, plagues, darkness at noon, falling stars. A final battle will rage between the forces of Good and Evil: the Good will be led by God himself, or by a commanding angel, or by an anointed Davidic king. The wicked—foreign kings, evil nations, apostate Jews (especially those whose views differ from those of the writer)—will be defeated and destroyed. With the resurrection of the dead, the judgment of the wicked, and the vindication of the righteous, Israel will reassemble, all twelve tribes, and return to the Land. God's spirit will pour out onto "all flesh" (Joel 2.28). The redeemed will gather in Jerusalem, at a rebuilt or renewed temple. Peace unalterably established, the entire world, human and divine, will acknowledge and worship the god of Israel.[22]

Nothing in these scenarios, except the pattern of travail/bliss, is fixed. Some writings speak of a general resurrection and a final judgment, others only of a resurrection of the saints. For some, the approach of the End-time will be signaled by the temple's pollution (by a foreign idol, Dan

11.31; by priestly impurity, CD col. iii–v); for others, by the sight of foreign armies ringed round Jerusalem. Some apocalypses feature Elijah coming to anoint the messiah; others speak of two messiahs, one priestly and one military (thus Davidic); others lack a messianic figure entirely. And still others look forward to a final redeemer figure to come as the "Son of Man."[23] A breadth of speculation, in short, characterizes late Second Temple apocalyptic literatures. What unites them is not the details of their individual visions, but their sounding urgency and the conviction that marks their message: God's kingdom is *at hand.*

What place, if any, do non-Jews have in such a kingdom?

We can cluster these materials around two poles. At the negative extreme, the nations are destroyed, defeated, or in some way made subject to Israel. Foreign monarchs lick the dust at Israel's feet (Isa 49.23; Mic 7.16); gentile cities are devastated, or repopulated by Israel (Isa 54.3; Zeph 2.1–3.8); God destroys the nations and their idols (Mic 5.9, 15). "Rouse your [God's] anger and pour out your wrath; destroy the adversary and wipe out the enemy!" (Sirach 36.1–10). "All which is with the heathen shall be surrendered; the towers shall be inflamed with fire and be removed from the whole earth. They shall be thrown into the judgment of fire, and perish in wrath" (1 Enoch 91.9). "Your enemy has overtaken you, but you will soon see their destruction and will tread upon their necks. . . . Wretched will be those who afflicted you" (Baruch 4.25, 31). "The Lord's servants . . . will drive out their enemies . . . and they will see all of their judgments and all of their curses among their enemies" (Jub 23.30). The messiah "will have gentile nations serving under his yoke" (Pss Sol 7.30). "Rejoice, all you cities of Judah; keep your gates ever open, that the hosts of the nations may be brought in. Their kings shall serve you; all your oppressors shall bow down before you" (1 QM 12.10–13).

At the positive extreme, the nations are partners in Israel's redemption. The nations will stream to Jerusalem and worship the god of Jacob together with Israel (Isa 2.2–4; Mic 4.1ff.). As the Jews leave the lands of their dispersion, gentiles will accompany them: "In those days ten men from the nations of every tongue shall take hold of the robe of a Jew, saying, 'Let us go with you, for we have heard that God is with you'" (Zech 8.23, "the nations of every tongue" echoes the Table of Nations in Gen

10). Or the nations will carry the exiles back to Jerusalem themselves (Isa 49.22–23; Pss Sol 7.31–41). Burying their idols, "all people shall direct their sight to the path of uprightness" (1 Enoch 91.14). "Jerusalem will be rebuilt . . . and then the nations of the whole world will turn and worship God in truth, and they will all abandon their idols" (Tobit 14.5–6). Some gentiles, says Isaiah, will even serve in the eschatological temple as priests and as Levites (Isa 66.21)—a truly striking claim, since the status of these two clans within Israel was purely hereditary (that is, no ritual act could turn an Israelite into a priest [*cohen*] or a Levite).[24]

Apocalyptic traditions are not "doctrine," an authoritative, internally consistent, and coordinated body of teachings. Rather, they represent various and multivocal speculations, keyed to biblical themes. Nowhere are speculations more varied than on the issue of the role of gentiles at the End. Some texts, as we have seen, speak of the nations' total rejection, others speak of their full inclusion, and still others—such as Isaiah, or indeed Paul's letters—express both extremes, anticipating divine wrath falling upon idolators as well as their reform, rehabilitation, and ultimate redemption. No single paradigm controls the genre.

Jesus of Nazareth, intriguingly, and despite his commitment to the impending proximity of God's Kingdom, seems not to have engaged these ethnically inclusivist apocalyptic traditions: at least, none figures in the material that has come down to us. Nor, on the evidence, were many of his hearers pagans. The New Testament gospels present him as confining his mission for the most part to fellow Jews. Matthew's Jesus, indeed, restricts even his disciples' activity exclusively to "the lost sheep of the house of Israel" (Mt 10.5; cf. 15.24). Gentiles must wait until after his resurrection to be named by Matthew's Christ as a goal of the gospel message ("Go and make disciples of all nations," Mt 28.19–20). In Lucan narrative, heaven has to prod Peter to baptize a pagan centurion in Joppa (Acts 10.1–48). Luke foreshadows the gospel's spreading beyond Israel (Lk 2.32, when Simeon, holding the infant Jesus, praises God's "salvation which you have prepared in the presence of all peoples, a light for revelation to the nations"; cf. Lk 24.47, also Acts 9.15, on Paul's future role). Deliberate outreach to pagans as such, however, gets under way only in chapter 11 of Acts, once the mission had spread out from Jerusalem to Antioch in the Diaspora.

Yet within only a few years of Jesus's execution, on the evidence of
Paul's letter to the Galatians, the gospel had already reached as far as
Damascus (Gal 1.15–17). The mission there seems already to have involved
pagans; and indeed within twenty-odd years of Jesus's death, multiple
and competing gentile missions in Christ's name seem to be well established. Not only Paul but (much to his fury) other Jewish Christ-followers
also strive to bring the good news of the coming Kingdom to non-Jews
(Gal passim; 2 Cor 11.22–23; cf. Phil 3.2–6). And as Paul's anger and
arguments in Galatians especially evince, the very success of this messianic message among diaspora gentiles threatened to fracture the new
movement. Evidently no one, confronted with the unexpected and surprising success of this very Jewish message among non-Jews, knew quite
what to do.

The confusions and conflicts of this first generation allow us to infer
two things about the historical Jesus of Nazareth. First, Jesus himself
seems to have left no instructions on the integration of gentiles, nor did he
in his own mission model such "outreach" for his disciples. Perhaps he
assumed—along with the ancient scriptural paradigm—that gentiles
would enter into God's Kingdom as a divinely initiated final event. In any
case, gentiles as such seem not to have been his concern.[25] Yet, second,
Jesus himself nonetheless must have at some point alluded to the nations'
anticipated turning to the god of Israel at the End, because after his death
his followers, faced with active gentile interest and commitment, readily
(though variously) incorporated them into the movement. The inclusion
of gentiles as ex-pagan pagans, in other words, seems to have occurred as
a natural extension of the gospel message itself.

Jewish apocalyptic traditions focus on the redemption of Israel, thus
on the integrity of the biblical god's moral character and, by extension, on
the surety of his promises. (Paul's letter to the Romans, especially chapters
9 through 11 and 15.1–13, is paradigmatic in this regard.) Gentile participation in Israel's redemption, as we have seen, was simply one item among
many in the various prophecies and descriptions of events anticipated at
the End. Yet for what would eventually become Christianity, that gentile
participation looms large: by the mid-second century, for some gentile
Christians, the turning of the nations to Israel's god through the preaching

of the gospel served as paramount proof that Jesus was indeed the messiah of a new, non-Jewish Israel.[26]

What accounts for this shift of accent and emphasis? Why, in this story of Israel's redemption, do the nations ultimately come to assume such a high profile? To understand the answer, we have to turn our gaze from Hebrew-language biblical traditions, and from events (such as Jesus's mission) specific to Jews in the Land of Israel, and look out toward the reaches of Alexander's empire, to the Greek-speaking Jews of the western Diaspora.

2

FATHERLAND AND MOTHER CITY

The Jewish communities resident in Babylon had been the product of forced exile, the price of Jerusalem's defeat in its war against Nebuchadnezzar. No such exile stood behind the western Diaspora. Jews there had resettled for the most part voluntarily, pulled by the Macedonian diaspora occasioned by the victories of Alexander the Great. In the wake of Alexander's conquests, veterans, merchants, and colonists had established new cities and refounded older ones. Other populations, Jews among them, migrated in their turn.[1]

The new political order entailed a new cultural order as well. Through the medium of his exported *poleis*, Alexander transplanted Greek cult and culture. The organs of city life—the agora, the temple, the gymnasium, the theater—brought a Greek architectural and social vernacular abroad, where it recombined with indigenous styles to produce local variations of a hybrid Hellenism. A linguistic vernacular also spread: Greek became the English of antiquity, serving the West as a great trans-local linguistic medium.[2]

The newer and broader horizons of the Hellenistic world profoundly affected Jewish culture. By about 200 B.C.E., Jews had settled so thoroughly into their new landscapes and new language that their ancestral scriptures followed: these also shifted from Hebrew and/or Aramaic into Greek. These translations, often termed collectively the "Septuagint," in turn, after centuries, would profoundly affect ancient culture both around the Mediterranean and well beyond. It was through the Septuagint that the god of Israel would conquer the West.[3]

In Paul's lifetime, Jews lived throughout the cities of the eastern Mediterranean and Asia Minor (modern Turkey); they could be found in Egypt and in Syria, in Italy (especially Rome), and along the northern coast of Africa (cf. 1 Macc 15.22–23). "This people has made its way into every city," Josephus quotes the pagan geographer Strabo as saying, "and it is not easy to find any place in the habitable world which has not received [them]" (*AJ* 14.115). "So populous are the Jews," wrote Philo of Alexandria, Paul's elder contemporary, "that

> [n]o one country can hold them, and therefore they settle in very many of the most prosperous countries in Europe and in Asia. . . . And while they hold the Holy City [Jerusalem], where stands the sacred temple of the most high god, to be their mother city [*metropolis*, that is, *mater-polis*], yet those cities that they obtained from their fathers and grandfathers, and from ancestors even further back to dwell in, are . . . accounted by them to be their fatherland [*patris*], in which they were born and reared. (*In Flaccum* 46)

These diaspora cities—here claimed as Jewish "patrimonies" by Philo—again thanks to Alexander, often ran along the lines of the Greek *polis*. Citizens (the local male elite) ruled through a council (Greek *boulē*; Latin *curia*), while their adolescent sons, as ephebes, trained in the *gymnasium* for future civic leadership. Social and commercial life centered on the open public space of the city's *agora*, while various other public municipal sites hosted competitive events in music, in rhetoric, or in athletics. All of these venues and various institutions also held altars to and images of deities. This was because, as organs of civic life, all of these places were responsible for facilitating the regular, vital, and necessary transactions between the city's two premier populations: its citizens and its god(s).

These gods thickly inhabited the ancient city, structuring human time, space, and social relations. Dedicated festivals, celebrating seasons and days sacred to divine patrons both celestial and (in the Roman period) imperial, punctuated the civic year. The venues of these celebrations— the theater or amphitheater, the stadium or hippodrome, the museum or library or odeon, as well as the sacred precincts themselves—were all sites of cult. Household calendars and domestic space replicated civic structures in miniature, where celebrations of the clan or of the family—marriages, the *genius* of the family father (a transgenerational divine aspect of the father's status and power), a child's passage to adulthood—invoked and honored presiding deities and numinous ancestors. The gods were everywhere, not only in the public and private buildings of ancient municipalities, but also on insignia of office, on military standards, in solemn oaths and contracts, in vernacular benedictions and exclamations, and all throughout the curriculum of the educated. It was impossible to live in a Greco-Roman city without living with its gods.[4]

Gods and humans clustered in this way in Mediterranean cities because, in antiquity, relations between heaven and earth were inherited. Ancient peoples were born into their relationships with their gods. Cult was an aspect and a statement of a people's family connection, of their peoplehood, of their ethnicity. And the reverse also held true: ethnicity was an expression of cult.[5]

Our vocabulary, which draws on biblical sources, fights against our seeing this clearly. Modern English uses two different words, *gentiles* and *pagans*, whereas the biblical Greek on which both words rest has only one, *ta ethnē*, "the nations" (cf. Hebrew *goyim*). And the two different English words have different connotations. *Gentile* refers to ethnicity, but seems religiously neutral: the person so designated is not a Jew. *Pagan* refers specifically to religion: the person is neither a Jew nor a Christian.

But this distinction between ethnicity and religion is not native to Mediterranean antiquity, where gods and humans formed family groups. In Paul's period, there was no such thing as a religiously "neutral" ethnicity. For this reason—namely, that ancient people(s) were intrinsically in relation with their gods—I will often use the (religion-specific) ethnic term "pagan" rather than the (religion-neutral) ethnic term "gentile" when speaking of first-century *ethnē*, that is, of non-Jews. My phrase "ex-pagan pagans"—by which I mean to describe those non-Jewish members of the first generation of the messianic movement around Jesus—is thus deliberately oxymoronic. The term's inelegance highlights the extreme anomaly, socially and therefore religiously, that this first generation represented: they were non-Jews who, *as* non-Jews, committed themselves to the exclusive worship, in some specifically Jewish ways, of the Jewish god.

The chief point to remember, and the one that this grating terminology seeks to underscore, is that connections between heaven and earth (and especially between heaven and city) ran precisely along ethnic or "family" lines. That is, particular gods were the particular concern of a particular *ethnos* ("people"), *genos* ("race," "family," "clan," "descent group"), or *gens* (Latin for "people" or "family"), a transtemporal, intergenerational kinship unit constructed by notions of shared "blood."[6]

We see a classic statement of this cluster of ideas—gods, family, culture, cult—in a famous passage of the Greek historian Herodotus (fifth century B.C.E.). There, Herodotus defined "Greekness," *to hellēnikon*, in terms of shared blood (*homaimon*), language (*homoglōssa*), sancturaries and sacrifices (*theōn hidrumata koina kai thusiai*), and customs (*ethea homotropa*; *Histories* 8.144.2–3). Half a millennium later, in his letter to the Romans, Paul will define "Jewishness" by appeal to much the same categories. Israelites are his *syngeneis*, "kinsmen" (a "shared blood" term). To them, Paul says, belong the "glory" (*doxa*), the covenants (*diathēkai*), the giving of the Law (that is, the Torah, *nomothesia*), and the "worship" (*latreia*, Rom 9.4–5). The English of the Revised Standard Version obscures two of Paul's key identifiers here, *doxa* and *latreia*. Behind Paul's Greek word for "glory" stands the Hebrew *kavod*, which refers specifically to God's glorious presence, thus to the location of that presence, namely his temple in Jerusalem. And *latreia* ("worship" or "offerings") points to the Hebrew *avodah*: Paul here names the sacrificial cult, revealed in scripture and enacted around Jerusalem's altar, as a defining privilege of Israel. Paul's two words, *doxa* and *latreia*, in brief, correspond exactly to Herodotus's "sanctuaries and sacrifices." Despite the six centuries standing between them, both of these Greek thinkers, pagan and Jew, define cult via ethnicity, and ethnicity via cult.[7]

Being born into relationship with their gods, humans were also and accordingly born into protocols for maintaining and safeguarding their gods' good will. *Mos maiorum*; *hai patrikai paradoseis* (this is Paul's phrase, Gal 1.15); *paradoseis tōn paterōn*; *ta patria ethē*; *ta patria*; *ta patria nomima*; *hoi patrioi nomoi*: all of these terms, which function roughly as we conceive "religion," translate "ancestral custom." These inherited rules described and prescribed what humans had to do to demonstrate respect for and loyalty to their gods. "Belief" as moderns view it, the sincerity or authenticity or intensity of some inner disposition or psychological state of an individual believer, is not native to this world view. Ancients focused rather on acts of deference, on offerings, or on what we might designate "cult," which enacted affection and esteem. A person's *pietas* (Latin) or *eusebeia* (Greek), which come into English as "piety," indexed a person's attentive attitude toward and fastidious execution of his or her inherited protocols. (Gods cared about such honors, and were usually quick to let their displeasure be known were some offering somehow unacceptable. For good reason, a synonym for *eusebeia* was *phobos*, "fear.") *Fides* (Latin) or *pistis* (Greek) in antiquity meant not "belief" (another frequent modern translation) so much as something akin to "steadfastness" or "fidelity toward" or "conviction that" (cf. the Hebrew *emunah*). To have *pistis* in one's *patria ethē* does not mean "to believe in ancestral customs" so much as to have confidence in them (namely, that these customs did indeed please the god), to trust in them, and to execute them "faithfully," that is, with care and with respect.[8]

These inherited bonds between heaven and earth were sometimes constructed as actual lines of descent, whereby the human rulers of a *genos* or of an *ethnos* were seen as children of the god. Greek gods (Zeus in particular) and divine heroes (such as the widely wandering Heracles) famously had sexual relations with human partners: the prestige of ruling houses might partly rest upon retracing distinguished lineages back from contemporary, historical time to the time of myth and epic, when gods and mortals mingled. (The Ptolemaic dynasty descended from Heracles, the Seleucids from Apollo; the Julii, Caesar's family, via Aeneas, enjoyed a connection to Venus.) More metaphorically, as we have seen, the kings of David's line could also be presented as God's "sons," "begotten" as such on the day of their anointing into office (Ps 2.7).[9]

But divine descent was not the monopoly of royal houses: the populations of cities, too, could descend from a god, their citizens construed as the god's *genos*. So realistically were such civic lineages imagined that they served to create, articulate, and reinforce political alliances. Hellenistic and later Roman diplomats, conjuring distant unions between humans and gods, appealed to the *syngeneia*, "kinship," consequently shared by two lineages of descendants in different cities, the better to stabilize current agreements between them. Thus gods, like their cults, ran in the blood, both for individuals and for wider citizen groups. In this way, not only did the Julii descend from Aeneas: so too did some of Rome's citizens, the "Aeneadae."[10]

The Jewish god took no human sexual partner; accordingly, he did not leave behind human offspring in the ways that Greek gods did. In consequence, Hellenistic Jews had to scramble to avail themselves of this pan-Mediterranean system of diplomatic "kinship." A granddaughter of Abraham's, said to have married Heracles, was pressed into service. The putative offspring of their union helped to establish *syngeneia*, "kinship," between Sparta and Jerusalem in the second century B.C.E.—a politically useful connection for the new Hasmonean dynasty in the wake of the Maccabean revolt.[11]

And Israelite divine sonship, as we have seen, might also extend to the whole people (e.g., Exod 4.22, "Israel is my first-born son"; cf. Jer 3.19, 31.9, 31.20; Hos 11.1–4; and frequently). Paul himself repeats this idea in the passage in Romans 9.4 cited just above. There he lists among Israel's God-given privileges their *huiothesia*, the RSV's "sonship." The Greek term actually translates "adoption," being "made" a son as opposed to being "born" one—a distinction with a difference, when compared with the Greco-Roman conceptualizations of this same idea of divine-human lineage. But Paul, as we will see, will stretch this idea in new ways, arguing that, through Christ, sonship through adoption was also being offered to "the nations." His proclamation came linked to a substantial proviso, however: these pagans, in order to be adopted as God's sons, could worship only Israel's god (Gal 4.5; Rom 8.15).

We will explore this Pauline idea of the Jewish god's adoption of pagans at greater length below. The point for now is that, even in this last, very unusual, indeed unprecedented instance of integrating pagans into a dawning Jewish apocalyptic movement, the relationship between peoples and god(s)—in this case, between pagan peoples and Israel's god—still depended upon the idea, the language, the structure, and the authority of the patriarchal Mediterranean family.

JEWS IN PAGAN PLACES

Seen from this vantage of divine-human relationships, the cities of
Roman antiquity can be viewed as family-based religious institutions.
"Family"—blood-kinship—ran vertically, between heaven and earth,
uniting peoples with their gods. And "family" also ran horizontally, binding the citizens together in one *genos*. At the "micro" level of the individual *oikos* or *domus*, these divine-human continuities also held sway. A
new bride, entering her husband's household, assumed responsibility for
what were for her new ancestors and new gods. "It is becoming for a wife
to worship and to know only those gods whom her husband esteems"
(Plutarch, *Moralia* 140D). So too an adopted son would incur obligations
to the ancestors and gods of his new paternal family. And at the "macro"
level, "family" bound together the whole empire: Augustus, positioning
himself as the empire's *pater*, ensured the public and private worship of
his numinous aspect or *genius*. The emperor thereby turned his new
political unit into a single, vast "household."[12]

Jews living in the cities of the western Diaspora fit themselves into this
civic webbing of divine-human relationships. But how? They were aided
in part by the shift in the gods' ethnicity. Jewish scriptures heaped scorn
and abuse on Semitic pantheons, the "other gods" of the Canaanites and
the Philistines. Biblical writers reviled such deities, worshiped through
their images, for encouraging sexual excess and perversion, murder, even
infanticide. Some Hellenistic Jewish writers—such as the author of
Wisdom of Solomon (second century B.C.E.), and also the apostle Paul—
will similarly accuse Greek gods, generating vice-lists itemizing the moral
failings of idolators. (See, for lush examples, Gal 5.19–21; 1 Cor 6.9–10;
and esp. Rom 1.18–32.)

But in the Roman-period avatars of the *polis*, these Hellenic gods
structured civic and cultural life. Through the works shaping the literary
canon—Homer first of all; the classical playwrights; the work of Hellenistic
grammarians and rhetoricians—these gods mediated *paideia*, higher education, thus culture. For both science and philosophy, they structured
and organized the physical universe. (Our planets still answer to the
names of these deities.) "Do not revile the gods," counseled Moses in
Greek (Exod 22.28 LXX). Commenting on this verse, Philo noted that

such courtesy promoted peace, since "reviling each other's gods always causes war." And Philo went on to add that Moses thereby also enjoined respect for (pagan) rulers, who "according to the poets are of the same seed as the gods" (*Questions and Answers in Exodus* 2.5). Some Hellenistic Jews, in brief, advised and even advocated that Jews show a certain respect for their neighbors' pantheons.[13]

Western Jewish culture was itself a refraction of Hellenism, a fact literally embodied in the Septuagint translations. Greek theological, philosophical, and political vocabulary intimately shaped the new literary presentation of the Jewish god. When YHWH identified himself to Moses, for example, the Hebrew *ehyeh* ("I am") became the Greek *ho ōn*, "the Being" (Exod 3.14 LXX). God's creative *davar*, "word," became the philosophically laden *logos* (Ps 33.6 LXX).[14]

More subtly, and pervasively, the LXX acquired ways to distinguish between degrees of divinity, speaking of multiple gods *as* gods while making clear the supreme divinity of the Jewish god. This distinction was not native to Hebrew, where, as we have seen, the plural form *elohim* could indicate either the Jewish god himself or a multiplicity of other deities. Indeed, the translators of Exod 22.28 LXX took advantage precisely of the Hebrew word's ambiguity when they rendered the older text's "Do not revile God [*elohim*]" as "Do not revile the gods [*tous theous*]."

Finally, and extremely usefully, the LXX acquired Greek *daimonia*, "demons." These beings could serve to articulate an order of divinity along a cosmic gradient. *Daimon* in Greek originally had no negative connotation in the way that the English "demon" now does: the word simply indicated "a lower god." "Lower" within Greek philosophical-scientific discourse meant literally, spatially "lower": not only did such a divinity have lesser power and status than did those "above" it; a *daimon* (or its diminutive, *daimonion*) was also located "lower" in the cosmos, closer to earth, which stood in the center of antiquity's map of the universe.[15]

Within this originally pagan cosmological system, "up" was "good" and "down" was "bad" (or at least less good). Materiality and motion indexed inferiority: the changeable earth stood at the center of the universe "where the heaviest matter has sunk." The truly "real," what was metaphysically and morally superior, lay above the earth, beyond the sublunar realm. For ancients who thought with this map of the universe, the sphere of the moon demarcated that lower cosmic region where chance, change, and fate ruled life on earth. Above the moon, in ranks of ascending perfection and goodness, came the spheres of the sun and of the five planets known to antiquity. More perfect and more "good" still was the outermost visible cosmic sphere, the realm of the fixed stars and the cosmic wheel of the Zodiac, their astral luminosity and their very fixity, thus stability, indicating their moral and material superiority. And beyond this sphere, particularly for those of Platonic persuasion, lay the realm of immateriality, the realm of invisible "spirit," and thus the realm of the high god.[16]

This Greek idea of a gradient of divine power cohered with and facilitated Hellenistic Jewish theology. "The *elohim* of the *goyim* are idols," the Psalmist had sung in Hebrew (Ps 96.5). "The *theoi* of the *ethnē* are *daimonia*," however, is the way that his words were sounded in Greek: "the [lower] gods of the nations are demons" (Ps 95.5 LXX; cf. 1 Cor 10.20). This translation (or reinterpretation) of "idols" as "demons" had theological significance. Idols (as Jewish texts tirelessly taught) were man-made representations of powers: "they have eyes that cannot see; they have ears that cannot hear" (Ps 115.5–6, 135.16–17). An idol is a dumb image. A demon, however, is not an image of a supernatural power, but the power itself, a lower divinity. Any human can destroy an idol; no human can destroy a god. This Jewish translation of Psalm 95 (96), then, at once elevated and demoted the Greek gods, granting that they were more than mere idols while placing them, *qua* daimonia, in positions subordinate to the Jewish god on Hellenism's own cosmic map.

Not only were these gods "lower," thus lesser, in terms of place and power; they also expressed other characteristics of daimonia. They were associated with particular peoples and places (whereas the high god, in both his pagan and his Jewish iterations, was universal). They were visible, associated with stars and planets, thus having material bodies. They were subordinate to and perhaps even dependent upon *ho theos*, the superior high god. Philo deftly captures this nexus of ideas in his commentary on Genesis. The firmament, Philo said there, is "the most holy dwelling place of the manifest and visible gods" (*theōn emphanōn te kai aisthētōn*,

De opif. 7.27): manifest and visible gods are "lower" than, thus subordinate to, the highest god, who was invisible.[17]

For pagans (and for some later gentile Christians), the Jewish god was of course susceptible to this same demonic description. He too was "ethnic," associated with a particular people (the *Ioudaioi*) and a particular place (Jerusalem in Judea). He had changeably manifested himself in time and to humans in biblical narrative, just as the Homeric gods had done in the stories of the *Iliad* and the *Odyssey*. He clearly was invested in blood sacrifices, a concern typical of "lower" gods. And after 70 C.E., with the Roman destruction of his city and his temple, his political and military fortunes implied that he was lesser in power than were the gods of Rome.[18]

Jewish theology by and large resisted these associations and implications, however. Both before 70 and, indeed, forever after, Jews insisted on their own god's supremacy. Two very ancient idiosyncrasies of Jewish ancestral tradition reinforced this insistence, and indeed facilitated YHWH's Hellenistic makeover into the Jewish version of *paideia*'s supreme deity. The first was Jewish tradition's long-standing aniconism. The second was a consequence of its resolute focus on the temple in Jerusalem.

To cultic aniconism first. Jewish tradition had long forbidden visual representations of Israel's god. "No images" had been part and parcel of the Sinai revelation, distinguishing Israel's worship from that of the nations (Exod 20.4–5). In the visual vernacular of the western Mediterranean, however, where gods were frequently represented as and worshiped before statues of aesthetically beautiful humans, this Jewish iconic reticence was noted by pagans. Indeed, in the Holy of Holies, the inner sanctum of Jerusalem's temple, where a Greco-Roman sanctuary would house the statue of the god, the Jews were known to have "nothing whatever." This absence of a cult statue was an odd fact liturgically, but it was extremely (re)interpretable philosophically. Such principled aniconism facilitated some pagans' identification of the Jewish god with the acorporeal, radically nonphysical high god of paideia.[19]

The Jews' second peculiarity was their cultic focus on Jerusalem. Though prayer could be offered anywhere, and though Jewish scriptures seem to have been read (or, perhaps, recited) in community one day in every seven throughout the Diaspora, sacrifice itself was in principle restricted to the temple in the city of David. The existence of at least one other temple, at Leontopolis in Egypt—a manifestation of the internal turmoil that had divided priestly families between Ptolemies and Seleucids in the days preceding the Maccabean revolt—did not abridge this fact. Jerusalem unquestionably held the priority, enshrined as it was in scripture and in tradition. Further, under Herod the Great, who gloriously refurbished the temple precincts, Jerusalem grew to be a renowned destination both for international Jewish pilgrimage and for pagan religious tourism. And the temple tax—a voluntary donation meant to defray the daily costs of the temple's latreia—was widely collected abroad to be sent back specifically to Jerusalem. These monies, their purpose and destination, were respected by Roman authorities, and regarded as a premier obligation by many in the wide-flung Jewish nation. In brief, Jewish sacrificial cult was concentrated in Jerusalem.[20]

The practical result of this liturgical focus was that Jews did *not* offer sacrifices to their own god in their foreign cities of residence. Though diaspora Jews seem to have organized into communities and even gathered at local sites (the "prayer house," *proseuchē*, or "synagogue"), these community centers were not sites of sacrifice; nor did they hold cult statues. This practice—or, more accurately, this absence of an all-but-universal practice, namely making offerings before images—taken together with their general avoidance of public pagan cult, meant that diaspora Jews were the only conspicuously nonsacrificing population in the first-century empire. As a result, pagan observers sometimes accused Jews of *asebeia*, "impiety" against pagan gods. Yet by the same token, even so unsympathetic an outsider as Tacitus could be persuaded: by worshiping *mente sola*, with the "mind alone," with neither offerings nor images, Jews, he said, paid homage to the highest god.[21]

Textually, then, and philosophically (thus, theologically), educated Jews could fit themselves and their ancestral traditions within the god-congested world of the Greco-Roman city. But what about socially? What evidence do we have for Jews not only intellectually but also behaviorally accommodating themselves to their larger Greco-Roman environment?

For this question, papyri and inscriptions, as well as literary works, provide glimmers of answers. On the negative side—denials that Jews participated in wider society—we have a wealth of comments from irritated pagan writers. These authors remarked acidly on the Jews' *asebeia* ("impiety," meaning refusal to honor the gods of the majority), on their *amixia* ("separateness") and *misoxenia* ("hatred of strangers," i.e., of non-Jews), and their *misanthropia*. The Jews' refraining from normal activities one day out of every seven, observers complained, marked them out as "lazy"; their refusal to eat pork as at least odd. Jewish aniconism led pagans to surmise that Jews worshiped only the sky, or perhaps the clouds. And about male circumcision, outside opinion was joined: a disgusting self-mutilation, such a custom was fit only for derision.[22]

How are we to evaluate these outsiders' views? On the one hand, they seem to have some descriptive force. Sabbath observance for instance, howsoever variously interpreted and enacted by different Jews, was widespread enough that ethnographers both Greek and Roman, from different centuries and sites around the Mediterranean, comment on it. In ancient urban societies where time was not measured in seven-day increments, such regular caesurae in normal activity would have stood out. So committed to keeping the Sabbath were Rome's Jews that Augustus ruled that they could retrieve their corn dole on a different day of the week, if the regular distribution otherwise interfered. Diverse Jewish populations in the cities of Asia Minor negotiated understandings that allowed them to conduct business or to appear in court on days that would not abridge their ancestral custom. And when outsiders both pagan and, eventually, Christian criticized members of their own respective communities who "Judaized"—that is, who voluntarily adopted and adapted some Jewish practices—assumption of the Sabbath features prominently on their lists of complaints.[23]

Male circumcision, though also practiced by other ancient peoples, was particularly associated with Jews, to the point where the name *Apella* (*a pella*, "without [fore]skin") offered the opportunity for a sort of Jewish joke. The condition, however, would ironically be evident precisely when Jewish males were participating most actively in the larger culture, whether as ephebes in the gymnasium or as athletes in competitions (which were themselves activities dedicated to the gods; see 1 Macc 1.14–15). For example, a papyrus fragment from first-century B.C.E. Egypt alludes to an athlete's "Jewish load" (that is, circumcision): this man's Jewish identity would have been publicly emphasized precisely as his prowess in foot racing would have expressed his commitment to things Greek. Circumcision thus indeed functioned as an ethnic "identifier," but at the same time its visibility in our ancient evidence tells precisely against Jewish *amixia*.[24]

How then should we regard these remarks about Jews in our ancient sources? We need to remember, first, that simple *difference* was a fact of life, universally acknowledged as such. In a multiethnic empire, where different gods and their humans bumped up against each other routinely, and in a culture within which all gods were assumed to exist, variety in ethnic practices—food ways, rituals, calendars, protocols for managing relations between heaven and earth—was just the way things were. "Different nations have different customs," remarked Athenagoras, "and no one is hindered by law or by fear of punishment from following his ancestral customs, no matter how ridiculous these may be" (*Legatio* 1). Jews "observe a worship which may be very peculiar," observed the second-century pagan intellectual Celsus, "but it is at least traditional. In this respect they behave like the rest of mankind, because every *ethnos* honors the traditions of its fathers" (*c. Cel.* 5.25). In Mediterranean culture, for all groups, antiquity and ethnicity were the twin measure of respectability and of identity. In terms of these criteria of respectability, then, if not in their avoidance of public cult, Jews were like everybody else.

Here, also, on the question of Jewish difference and sameness, two other considerations need to be weighed: the nature of "learned" classical ethnographies, and the social indices unobtrusively preserved in inscriptions and on papyri.

The habits, customs, and behaviors of outsiders rarely inspired expressions of admiration from Greek and, later, Roman writers; and it is important to see what these authors say about other "exotic others" in order to take the measure of their remarks about Jews. Egyptians and Celts; Persians, Parthians, and Germans; Phoenicians and Syrians; Gauls and even (in the view of later Latin writers) Greeks: all came in for their share of ethnic insults, cross-cultural condescension, and invidious insinuation. Greeks considered themselves virile and virtuous, their Persian enemies "soft," effeminate, and servile; when later empire shifted west, "hard" Romans attributed these "soft" characteristics to the Greeks. Various exotic others, said these authors—like the Phoenicians, or the Jews, or the Germans—sacrificed humans and occasionally ate them. Egyptians, like Jews, were endlessly fussy about food; they were treacherous, cowardly, yet nonetheless arrogant; like Phoenicians, they were greedy; like Greeks (to later Romans), they were debauched. (And Egyptian zoolatry unnerved just about everybody.) Gauls were greedy; Phoenicians dishonest and duplicitous; Germans physically strong but intellectually weak. And so on (and on).[25]

Antisocial behaviors—sexual profligacy and cannibalism being two perennial favorites—were particularly attributed to outsiders: Greco-Roman authors idealized civilized sociability in their own cultures, and they brought this ideal into sharper focus by flamboyantly denying it to others. (Eventually, in the course of the second century C.E., pagans will accuse gentile Christians of such behaviors; and competing gentile churches will so accuse each other.) We should regard the accusations of extreme antisocial behavior leveled at ancient Jews, then, with a healthy skepticism. These seem to offer not reliable social description but, rather, the inverse measure of what learned pagan authors valued most in their own social world. Much more of the ethnographic insult remains for Jews than for other groups because of the accidents of history: the anti-Jewish material was preserved and reused, for different polemical ends, by later gentile Christians. But the insults themselves were common cultural coin. In the world of ancient ethnic stereotyping, as one historian has aptly observed, even the stereotypes were stereotyped.[26]

The evidence of inscriptions, further, runs counter to these accusations of Jewish self-segregation—and of some modern historians' imagining a pristine Jewish avoidance of pagan deities. Moschos, son of Moschion, for example, prompted in a dream by two local gods to manumit his slave, left an inscription attesting to his obedience in the gods' temple. Was this act "a defection to paganism or syncretism"? In the inscription, Moschos considers himself and identifies himself simply as *Ioudaios*, a "Jew." Again, in antiquity, worshiping "one god" or "the highest god" or only "our god" did not mean that one doubted the existence of other gods, only that one construed one's obligations to other gods differently. Showing respect to a god by way of obeying a direct command unquestionably demonstrated common sense: any god is more powerful than any human. But did Moschos, in obeying these gods, worship them in the same way that he did his own ancestral god? Why would we think so?[27]

Other inscriptions likewise preserve a random record of Jewish cultural embeddedness. Surprisingly, inscriptions by Jews thanking their own god have turned up in Egypt in a sanctuary to the god Pan. What are they (both the people and the inscriptions) doing there? Jesus, son of Antiphilos, and Eleazar, son of Eleazar, appear in a first-century list from Cyrene's ephebate. As ephebes, thus as citizens-in-training, they would have been present at civic activities honoring the gods who presided over their city. And the stele that records their names was itself dedicated to Heracles and Hermes, the gods of the gymnasium. How did Jesus and Eleazar manage? We cannot know. The only thing that we do and can know is what our inscription tells us: these two young men trained to be active participants in the life of their city, which was itself a (pagan) religious institution. Only the ethnic specificity of Jesus's and Eleazar's names, further, allows us to make this identification: Jews with entirely Greek names are invisible in our evidence. For all we know—the point being that we cannot know—this ephebate included the sons of other Jewish citizens as well.[28]

Still, citizenship could be a fraught issue for Jews, precisely because of its normal connection with urban gods and civic worship. "If the Jews wish to be citizens of Alexandria," complained Apion during the turmoil there in 39 c.e., "why don't they honor the Alexandrian gods?" We do not know, again, how individual Jews, as citizens and even as town councilors, would have squared their civic obligations with their ancestral ones; we can only note, on the evidence of various inscriptions and literary sources, that they managed to do so. (Acts of the Apostles, probably an early second-century text, without apology presents Paul as a citizen both of Tarsus, 21.39, and of Rome, 22.22–29.) Practice, and who knows what improvisations, doubtless varied between different individuals in different cities, or even—to think briefly of the case of Philo and his nephew, Tiberius Julius Alexander—between different individuals within the same family and the same city. Eventually, the general principle of Jewish exemption from public cult seems to have been acknowledged (or perhaps established) by imperial law around the year 200 C.E., when Severus and Caracalla permitted Jews to hold public office without performing duties that would "offend against their *superstitio*" (*Digest* 50.2.3.3).[29]

Pagan formulas and sacred calendars that appear in Jewish inscriptions also support this impression of a wide cultural comfort zone. "D.M."—*dis manibus*, "to the infernal gods"—a common funerary epigraphic convention, appears on Jewish grave finds, too. Zeus (the sky), Helios (the sun), and Gaia (the earth), major deities in the Greek pantheon, were commonly called to witness oaths; and so they appear as well in inscriptions suggesting a Jewish context. Pagan deities figure in the mosaic floors of Jewish houses and even of synagogues. "To God Most High, the Almighty and Blessed," begins the inscription of Pothos, son of Strabo, in the mid-first century C.E. Pothos records the manumission of his "house-bred female slave Chrysa," dedicating her "in the *proseuchē*" ("prayer house," a common term for a Jewish community gathering place); and he summons the three witnessing gods (Zeus, Helios, and Gē) in the inscription's final line. Another inscription, attesting to an endowment established by one Glykon, mentions the Jewish holidays of "Unleavened Bread" and "Pentecost" (that is, Shavuot), together with the "Kalends of the fourth month," that is, the sacred celebration of the Roman new year, January 1.[30]

Both in epigraphy and in literary sources, further, Jews turn up in theaters, hippodromes, and odeons, all sites of cultic as well as—or, rather, at the same time as—cultural activity. (Paul's references to athletic events in his letters imply not only his presumption of his congregations' familiarity with such activities, but his own familiarity, whether rhetorical or actual, too.) Jews watched performances and acted in them. And martial prowess was not limited to men with military careers: we also have evidence of Jewish gladiators, whose professional activities would have been particularly allied with the Roman cult of the emperor.[31]

Finally, the enormous wealth of Hellenistic Jewish literary production itself imposes on any reconstruction of the Jews' place within larger pagan society. Much of this literature is preserved in the works of later church fathers, who appealed to it in order to make their case that Judaism (and, thus, their own sects of Christianity) was superior to pagan cults in all the ways that mattered, especially in terms of antiquity. In a culture where older was better, Jewish traditions (urged educated Jews and, later, some gentile Christians) held the priority. Thus, the Egyptian Jew Artapanus argued, Jewish heroes were the true sources of majority culture: Joseph established Egyptian temples; Moses taught music to Orpheus and zoolatry to Egypt. Learned Jewish forgeries presented "pagan" sibyls' hymning Jewish superiority to pagan cult in Homeric hexameters. Historical fictions recounted pagan kings in quest of Jewish wisdom. The literary lions of the classical curriculum—Aeschylus, Sophocles, Euripides— "produced" Jewish verses, in effect attributing fundamental aspects of pagan *paideia* to the Jews or to their god. In short, the Jewish control of and commitment to these classical authors and traditions, and to the values and the authorities of gymnasium education, restate in a literary key what we know as well from inscriptions, archaeology, and historical writings: Jews lived, and lived thoroughly, in their cities of residence throughout the Diaspora.[32]

This last observation brings us back, by another path, to the quotation from Philo with which we began this chapter. By speaking of diaspora cities of residence as "fatherland" and of Jerusalem as the "mother city," Philo was not witnessing to an ancient version of the modern issue of "dual loyalties." His language echoed, rather, the vocabulary of his Greek biblical text, which in turn sounded the sensibility and civic rootedness of its third- and second-century B.C.E. Hellenistic Jewish translators.

In Hebrew, when referring to the sequelae of Nebuchadnezzar's conquest of Jerusalem, the Bible had spoken in terms of "exile," meaning expulsion or forced separation from the Land of Israel. One correlating Greek term is *diaspora*, "dispersion"; and this word, of course, in both noun and verb forms ("to disperse") occurs in the LXX also (e.g., Gen 49.6; Lev 26.33; Deut 28.25; Jer 41.17; Joel 3.2). But Philo, writing of Alexandria as his *patris*, was availing himself of a different idea, that of *voluntary* population movement from the homeland. This draws on the model of Greek colonization. In the next sentence of this passage, Philo continues: "Into some of these [cities] they came at the very moment of their foundation, sending an *apoikia* to do a favor for the founders" (*In Flaccum* 46). Here the key word is *apoikia*, "colony."

Apoikiai appear frequently in the historical books of the LXX to mean (Jewish) "communities abroad." As Greek colonies set out from a crowded mother-city, said Philo, so too did *Ioudaioi* set out from Jerusalem. In other words, Philo—and, well before him, the translators of the LXX— conceived of the western Jewish "dispersion" as *voluntary emigration.* Propelled by fecundity—that is, by sheer numbers of population and thus, in a sense, by well-being—Jews had established "colonies" outside the Land of Israel. In so doing, Philo claimed, Jews had remained loyal to the god and to the temple of their metropolis, Jerusalem; so, similarly, had those colonists from the cities of the Peloponnese who settled in new areas in Sicily. The Hebrew vocabulary of the older biblical text, in other words, had preserved the ideas of displacement and of alienation conjured by "exile." But as the vocabulary of the Bible's newer Greek versions attests, western Hellenistic Jewish populations enjoyed a very different experience: comfortably rooted, well settled in their *patris*, everywhere at home.[33]

PAGANS IN JEWISH PLACES

Interpenetration goes two ways. Jews in antiquity were visibly, actively present in pagan places, mingling with neighbors both human and divine. Can the same be said of pagans? Were they visibly present in Jewish places, interacting with Jews and thus, to some degree or other, with the Jewish god?

The Temple

Before 66 C.E., pagans came to Jerusalem. Its temple, under Herod the Great (king from 37 to 4 B.C.E.), had grown into one of the architectural marvels of the Roman world. Herod expanded the area of the old sacred precincts by some thirty-five acres, enclosing it with a magnificent wall, still visible today, running around its perimeter for nine-tenths of a mile. At the heart of this expanse, within the sanctuary itself, stood the Holy of Holies, "unapproachable, inviolable, invisible to all" (Josephus, *BJ* 5.219), the earthly abode of Israel's god (cf. Mt 23.19). Wrapped around this sanctuary, ranked in nested courtyards of graduated size, lay the areas dedicated for use by the priests (where the actual sacrificing and butchering took place), then for male Israelites, then for females. But encircling these three specifically Jewish zones spread the largest open space of the whole temple complex, the Court of the Nations (*c. Ap.* 2.103).[34]

In the period of the first temple, non-Jews evidently could bring and make their own offerings: see, for example, Numbers 15.14–16. The Hebrew word for non-Jew there, *ger*, came into Greek as *prosēlytos*. Eventually, "proselyte" will mean an outsider who voluntarily and fully assumes Jewish ancestral customs, in our terms a "convert." Originally, however, this word, like its Hebrew correlate *ger*, indicated a resident alien or stranger, that is, a non-native living in a land not his own. (Hebrews were *gerim* in Egypt, Lev 19.34; Num 15 refers to the *ger ha-gar*, a non-Jew living in the Land of Israel.) With the second temple, however, already in the Hellenistic period (late third/early second century B.C.E.), access to the altar seems to have grown more restricted until, by the time Herod undertook his construction project, the calibrations of proximity to the altar by *genos* or *ethnos* were well in place, and enforced. A balustrade demarcated the interior edge of the gentiles' court, posted with inscriptions warning the "foreigner" (*allogenēs*, literally, someone of "another people") to proceed no further (cf. *BJ* 5.194, *allophylos*, and *AJ* 15.417, *alloethnē*). Non-Jews could bring gifts, and could have offerings made on their own behalf—no less a personage than Augustus made such arrangements—but pagans visiting the temple's outermost court did not perform sacrifices themselves.[35]

These social calibrations—who stood where within the sacred precincts—expressed ritual ones. The temple's dedicated courtyards spatially articulated current interpretations of biblical purity laws. Outsiders stood furthest from the area of active offerings, beyond the sacred zones; next, Jewish women; next, Jewish men, whose own court terminated with a low balustrade marking off the priests' area. Between that point and the sanctuary, the area where the altar stood and the active sacrificing took place, was the space dedicated solely for the priests. When framing his beautification project, Herod had even gone so far as to train priests to be masons: even if busy with stone rather than sacrifice, priests alone would have access to the temple's interior courts (*AJ* 15.390).[36]

All purity rules in antiquity, whether pagan or Jewish, prescribed ritual procedures that prepared and enabled the worshiper to approach the divine. The zone of divine/human interaction, often but not always, was around altars, and thus had to do with sacrifices. (Not all offerings involved animals: wine, wheat, and oil, *inter alia*, could be brought, too. But blood sacrifices tended to develop the most elaborate cultic etiquettes.) Water rituals, abstention from sex and/or from certain foods, fasting, observing a certain liminal period of time, wearing or not wearing certain articles of clothing: this range of behaviors expressed ancient, and universal, techniques of purification.[37]

Specifically Jewish protocols of purity cluster in the books of Leviticus (chaps. 11–15) and Numbers (chap. 19). They governed access to God's altar through two binary distinctions. One was the distinction between "pure/impure" or "clean/unclean" (*tahor/tameh* in Hebrew; *katharos/akatharos* in Greek). The other was the distinction between holy/profane or (in plainer English) between "special" or "separated out" and "common" or "profane" (*kadosh* versus *chol* in Hebrew; *hagios* versus *bebēlos* [for the LXX] or, later, *koinos* in Greek). Only what was both pure and holy (meaning "special," that is, set aside specifically for this purpose) could be offered; and the person bringing the offering also had to be in a state of purity.[38]

This biblical pure/impure binary refers first of all to what scholars term "ritual" impurity, a highly contagious condition arising from certain normal (and involuntary) bodily processes (seminal ejaculation, for example; or menses; or childbirth); or from contact with certain polluting substances or objects (such as a corpse). Such a state was virtually unavoidable, all but universal, and, finally, temporary. *It implied no moral condition:* an impure person (say, someone who had just buried a corpse) was not on that account a sinful person. (On the contrary, burying the dead was an important obligation.) Most people had this sort of impurity most of the time: purity/impurity, in other words, were states that one moved into and out of. The main consequence of most of these forms of impurity was that they limited access to the temple. Purification—a system of wash-and-wait, plus occasionally some particular offering—cleansed this sort of impurity.

So too with the second set of biblical binaries, holy/profane or separated/common. Something "holy," intended to be used for worship, could be rendered "common" or "profane" (*pro-*, before; *fanes*, altar). An iron tool cutting the stone of the altar, for example, would render the altar unfit for use (Exod 20.22); so too if a perfect animal, intended as an offering, developed a blemish. And something ordinary could be made "holy," meaning separated out from the common, and dedicated to God. When presenting a perfect animal for an offering, for example, the worshiper would pronounce the animal *kadosh* ("holy, separate"; cf. Mk 7.11).[39]

How do these scriptural purity rules help to explain the physical placement of actual pagans within the precincts of the first-century Jerusalem temple? Were they restricted to an outermost court because pagans *as such* were "impure"?

Some scholars say no, others yes. Those in the first group point out, first, that ritual impurity in fact seems an irrelevant category: both the Bible and later rabbinic interpretations of it hold Israel alone as subject to this legislation. In other words, only Jews could have these types of specifically Jewish impurities. Within the Jewish system, pagans could neither contract Levitical impurities nor convey them. (Thus, for example, while the corpse of a Jew conveyed a very high level of impurity to and for another Jew, a pagan risked no such contagion; nor, according to the later rabbis, would a pagan corpse defile a Jew.) This view suggests that, unlike Jews, pagans did not have to undertake biblically prescribed acts of ritual purification in order to ascend the temple mount: such actions, for them, would have been moot. Since these rules of purity were part and parcel of Torah legislation, and since the Torah was the privilege and the responsibility uniquely of Israel (see Paul again, Rom 9.4–5), pagans did not share in its obligations, nor were they organized according to its categories.[40]

Why, then, were pagans kept so far from the altar? Was their placement in the Court of the Nations due to some other sort of contagion, one

specific to pagans? Again, academic opinion is divided. Biblical legislation is directed solely to Israel; but at certain points in the narrative God
had warned Moses that Israel was not to behave as did those other nations
whom God was displacing from the Land. "Do not defile yourself with
any of these things"—incest, adultery, ritual infanticide—"for by all these
things the nations that I cast out before you defiled themselves, and the
Land became defiled . . . and the Land vomited them out" (Lev 18.24).
"Impurity" here, contracted by non-Jews ("the nations that I cast out
before you"), seems to function as a moral metaphor for "sin." Unlike
Levitical impurity, *this* sort of defilement, moral impurity, was voluntary,
not involuntary (the sinner chooses to act in these forbidden ways) and
was avoidable (again, unlike most Levitical impurities).[41]

But can moral impurity be contagious, thus *ritually* polluting? And is
moral impurity, allied as it was to idolatry in the Jewish world view, in this
sense specific to pagans? Some later Hellenistic Jewish writers seemed to
think so. They generated "sin lists" ascribing precisely these condemned
Canaanite behaviors to their Greco-Roman contemporaries. Paul himself
offers a premier example of this sort of antipagan ethnic stereotyping.
"Now the works of the flesh are plain," Paul lectures his (gentile) communities in Galatia. "*Porneia, akatharsia* . . . *idōlolatria:* fornication,
uncleanness [otherwise unspecified], idol-worship" (Gal 5.19). "Do not
associate with fornicators," he warns his people in Corinth, "or with idolators, or a robber or a drunkard" (1 Cor 5.10–11). Idolators, fornicators, adulterers, other sexual malefactors: none of these "will inherit the Kingdom
of God; and such were some of you" (6.9–11). Those who worship idols
are filled with every kind of wickedness, Paul recounts to the "ex-pagan"
pagans in Rome (and he goes on to detail precisely what this wickedness
entails: murder, fornication, "unnatural" sex acts, and so on, Rom 1.18–
31). Perhaps, then, because of pagan traditions of idol-worship, Jews (or at
least some Jews, like Paul) considered pagans as somehow intrinsically
"impure."[42]

Here the architecture of Herod's temple complex complicates this
question in interesting ways. Patterns of foot traffic seem to argue against
a widespread view of gentile impurity. Precisely when Jews had to be
most concerned with their own purity—that is, when they went to the

temple—they were free to walk through the Court of the Nations on their way to their own areas without fear of defilement. Levitical impurities were contagious: a Jew could contract a secondary form of impurity by brushing up against a fellow Jew who was him- or herself impure. Were there such a general category as "gentile impurity," then, it was clearly *not* contagious, contractible through contact: it would thus be significantly less virulent than was the Jewish kind. More to the point: noncontagious *akatharsia* would be *of no practical consequence to the temple's operation*. Why, then, these spatial degrees of separation?

A theory of generalized "gentile impurity" does not seem to offer any clear answer to the question why, in the days of the late second temple, the pagan presence at the temple precincts was both permitted *and* circumscribed. We will return to this question later, however, because an answer to this question does seem available—remarkably enough, in the letters of Paul. Remember, then, this important architectural feature of Herod's temple, the vast and beautiful Court of the Nations. It will provide us with a way, as we will see, to understand a key element of Paul's gospel.

The Synagogue

Pagans of course did not have to journey to Jerusalem to encounter the Jewish god. Jews lived throughout the empire; and pagans, living with Jews, could involve themselves variously in these communities.

The most extreme level of engagement would have occurred when and if a pagan chose to "become" a *Ioudaios*, to undergo what moderns call "conversion." Such a decision, given ancient divinity's ethnic embeddedness, scarcely made sense: it went against a commonsense construal of "blood," of peoplehood (thus of social identity), and of ancestral custom (thus of piety). Showing respect to gods not one's own was a normal aspect of ancient Mediterranean life, for Jews (as we have seen) as well as for pagans. Forging an *exclusive* commitment to a foreign god, however—an act unique to Judaism in the pre-Christian period—was tantamount to changing ethnicity. A pagan's "becoming" a Jew in effect altered his past, reconfigured his ancestry, and cut his ties with his own patrimony, both human and divine. We will consider this category of committed former outsiders—*proselytoi,* "Jews" of a special sort—further on, when we look specifically at the life and work of the apostle Paul. For now we will simply note that there were such people, and that they did make up some part of diaspora synagogue communities.[43]

Jews referred to their communities by various names: *hieron, proseuchē, politeuma, collegium, synodos, koinon, thiasos, ekklēsia, synagōgē.* Such assemblies served as social centers and as "ethnic reading houses," places where Jews could gather at least one day out of every seven to hear instruction in their ancestral traditions. In the words of a first-century Greek inscription from Jerusalem, the synagogue provided a place "for the reading of the Law and for the teaching of the commandments." "From early generations Moses has had in every city those proclaiming him," says James in the Acts of the Apostles, "for he is read every Sabbath in the synagogues" (Acts 15.21).[44]

Synagogues also performed many other practical functions. They served as collecting-stations for the temple tax to be sent on to Jerusalem, and as a treasury for other monies. They housed sacred scrolls and community records, and kept calendars marking feasts, fasts, and celebrations. They sponsored local projects, sheltered Jewish travelers, and, like pagan temples, provided sites where members could erect votive tablets and memorial steles, and enact and record the manumission of slaves. And they honored conspicuous philanthropy with public inscriptions.[45]

These donor inscriptions provide us with glimpses of another population involved with Jewish communities: some of these synagogue benefactors were pagans. From Acmonia in Phrygia we learn about a contemporary of Paul's, Julia Severa. A Roman aristocrat as well as a priestess of the imperial cult, Julia built the *oikos* ("house," meaning synagogue) for Acmonia's Jews. Two centuries later, another wealthy Roman lady, Capitolina, epigraphically identified as a *theosebēs* ("god-fearer"), refurbished a synagogue interior in Tralles in Caria. Like Julia, she too came from a distinguished pagan family: Capitolina's father was the proconsul of Asia, her husband a Roman senator and a priest for life of Zeus Larasios. In nearby Aphrodisias, a Jewish inscription currently dated to the fourth or fifth century indexed benefactors by affiliation: some donors are born Jews, with Jewish names (Theodotos, Judas, Jesus); some are listed as "voluntary" Jews, that is, as "converts" (e.g., Samuel *prosēlytos*); and still others—fifty people, among whom are nine members of the city council—are given as "god-fearers" (*theosebeis*).[46]

"Fear," as we noted earlier, was a synonym for "piety." (Given the tenor of divine temperament in antiquity, the instinct was prudent.) And as with its modern usage ("She's a God-fearing woman"), so too with its ancient ones: sometimes god-fearer/*theosebēs* might simply mean "pious," without implying the sort of interethnic activity evinced by the inscriptions honoring Julia or Capitolina or the donors in Aphrodisias. In other places where *theosebeis* occurs—in funerary and votive memorials, in manumission inscriptions, in theater epigraphy—the ethnicity of the "god-fearers" mentioned can seem ambiguous or arguable; and scholars rightly worry about misidentifications. Epigraphical "god-fearers," in other words, may relate straightforwardly to "pious" pagans or Jews or (eventually) to Christians, rather than to the actively "cross-ethnic" pagans whom we meet here: gentiles who, as pagans, were involved (variously) with the Jewish community and thus with Jewish ancestral customs ("religion").[47]

When can we as historians know which kind of "god-fearer"—a pious person full stop, or a pagan who does (some) Jewish things—our ancient evidence bespeaks? As usual, we have to consider critically each case, without expecting complete agreement among our different interpretive arguments. Sometimes the ethnicity—thus, also, the "religious" orientation—of an inscription or (especially) of an incantation will elude us, thus reinforcing a larger and no less important point: different peoples regularly mixed with and borrowed from each other. And sometimes (as is the case, for example, with Julia Severa) the inscription will describe pagan involvement in Jewish projects without using the term "god-fearer" at all.[48]

In light of the epigraphical ambiguity, what should we call such pagans? On this point of vocabulary, the literary evidence seems less difficult. In a well-known poem, the Roman satirist Juvenal ridiculed a pagan for assuming some Jewish practices: this *metuens sabbata pater*, a "Sabbath-fearing father," stopped eating pork and "gave up every seventh day to idleness" (*Sat.* 14.96–106). Josephus characterizes Poppaea Sabina,

Nero's consort, as *theosebēs* ("god-fearer") because, though a pagan, she sympathized with Jewish causes (*AJ* 20.195). The Acts of the Apostles (early second century) famously features diaspora synagogues that teem on the Sabbath with *sebomenoi* and *phoboumenoi ton theon*, "those who fear God": the text usually distinguishes this population from *Ioudaioi* ("Jews") and from *prosēlytoi* ("proselytes," that is, "converts"). Describing the great wealth of Jerusalem's temple, Josephus mentions contributions from *sebomenoi* ("fearers") in Asia Minor and in Europe (*AJ* 14.110). And several centuries later, this same phenomenon—pagans who, as pagans, voluntarily involve themselves with Jews and with Jewish customs—is still named "god-fearing," both in rabbinic sources (*yirei shamayim*, "heaven-fearers") and in patristic ones (*theosebeis*). In literature if not in inscriptions, then, "[god-]fearing," not always but often, indeed seems to point primarily to pagans who to some degree or other engage with Jews, with Jewishness, and, thus, with the Jewish god.[49]

Another term that appears in ancient literature to indicate such activity—that is, a non-Jew's doing something that usually a Jew would do—is "Judaizing." Josephus uses this word also. *Ioudaiozantas* ("Judaizers") can be found in every city in Syria (*BJ* 2.463): these are non-Jews who evidently have adopted (some) Jewish customs. Elsewhere, he speaks of similar behaviors—the pagan adaptation of Jewish custom(s)—without using this particular verb. Most of the (gentile) wives in Damascus had "gone over to the Jewish *thrēskeia*" ("religious practice," *BJ* 2.560). In Antioch, Jews always drew to their *thrēskeia* a great multitude of Greeks "whom they made in some way a part of themselves" (*BJ* 7.45). Perhaps, then, we should use "Judaizing" rather than "god-fearing" to indicate those pagans who behave in (some) Jewish ways?

What is at stake in our choice of indicator? Part of the terminological difficulty stems less from the ambiguities of our ancient evidence than from the connotations of our modern terms. "Fearing" implies a "religious" reason, namely piety, for the voluntary pagan attachment to Jewish customs. "Judaizing," the other term for the same thing, draws attention back to ethnicity: the term hints at motivations or activities that might seem less "religious" than political, perhaps, or cultural or social. But Paul, in an ostensibly "religious" context—his report of his argument with

Peter on a point of principle within the ekklesia in Antioch—employs the language of ethnicity, not of piety. Jews can act "paganly" (ἐθνικῶς) and pagans can act "Jewishly" (Ἰουδαϊκῶς). And Christ-following ex-pagan pagans, Paul insists, should not be required "to Judaize" (Ἰουδαΐζειν, Gal 2.14). The immediate problem in Antioch seems to be about food, and/or about eating; the immediate problem framing Paul's account, whether ex-pagan pagans in Galatia should receive circumcision and thus "convert" as Christ-followers to Judaism (cf. Gal 5.3). Is Paul talking here about "religion," about "social practice," or about "ethnicity"?

Posing the question puts the answer: Paul at one and the same time speaks to all of these categories. And this is so because these categories, in his period, intimately correspond. In other words, the distinctions that we as Western twenty-first-century people draw between "religion," "ethnicity," and "traditional behaviors" (foodways, social gatherings, life-cycle celebrations, for example) measure the difference and distance between Paul's day and our own, a difference compounded by the complexities of translation. Our Western, post-Enlightenment culture defines "religion" as something personal, private, and largely propositional—we "believe in" or "believe that," which are mental operations. This obscures the ancient correspondence of heaven and earth, when peoples and their gods came bundled together, and when *doing* (as opposed to [primarily] "thinking") articulated this earth–heaven connection.

Ancient involvements with a *genos* or an *ethnos* different from one's own could thus imply involvement, to some degree or other, with the god(s) of that *genos* as well. Such cross-ethnic activity generated a particular linguistic form, taking the name of an ethnic group and "verbing" it, adding the infinitive ending (-ίζειν) to an "ethnic" noun. We saw above that Paul does this in Galatians 2.14 when, challenging Peter, he asks, "How can you require gentiles *to* Judaize?" *Only* an outsider can assume (some of the) behaviors characteristic of a foreign group. Jews could not "Judaize"; only non-Jews could. Only a non-Greek could "Hellenize," meaning to assume (some) Greek behaviors, which would entail socializing or interacting with Greeks both human and divine. (Jesus and Eleazar trained in the gymnasium under the numinous tutelage of Heracles and Hermes; centuries later, by using a Roman bath, Rabban

Gamaliel had to rationalize the presence of Aphrodite.) "To Persianize" (Μηδίζειν) meant a foreigner's enacting behaviors that we might parse variously as social, or as religious, or as political, or as cultural, but which would seem to another Hellene as, simply, "Persian."[50]

Thus, when pagans involved themselves in the synagogue activities of their Jewish neighbors, they involved themselves as well, in varying degrees, with the Jewish god. Their motivations doubtless varied as widely as did the range of behaviors that our evidence suggests. Professional healers and magical adepts listened to scriptures read aloud in the vernacular: these stories conveyed information important for conjuring a powerful deity. Other pagans co-celebrated Jewish feasts and fasts. Still others, such as the father in Juvenal's satire, personally adopted some Jewish observances: the sources speak most frequently of Sabbath rest and avoidance of pork. And still others—Julia Severa, or Luke's centurion Cornelius in Acts 10, or Capitolina, or the nine god-fearing town councilors of Aphrodisias—honored local Jewish communities, and thus the Jewish god, with conspicuous patronage. And all of these people continued their involvements with their native cults as well.

The motivations of all of these different people matter less, for the purposes of historical identification, than do their actions. Put otherwise: the inscriptional and literary evidence might identify such people as "Judaizers" (like the Syrian pagans mentioned by Josephus), or as "god-fearers" (like the town councilors of Aphrodisias), or simply as (cross-ethnically) involved pagans (like Julia Severa). We as historians may use whichever term we choose, as long as we have attestation for the interethnic activity that warrants the naming. In other words, "Judaizing" and "god-fearing" work functionally as synonyms. Put a third way: Julia Severa was no less a "god-fearer" than was Capitolina, even though only the latter's inscription actually uses the term itself; and both, by actively supporting Jewish communities, may be described as "Judaizing"—doing "Jewish" things (like building or refurbishing synagogue structures) while remaining, at the same time, pagans, that is, actively and publicly involved in the worship of non-Jewish deities. Their Jewish involvement was voluntary and ad hoc; and since pagans were *not* Jews, their observance of (some) Jewish traditions was regulated by no Jewish law.[51]

In their own view as much as in the view of their Jewish neighbors, these interested pagans were free to frequent Jewish gatherings, and to assume, should they so choose, whatever Jewish practices, traditions, and customs they wished, while continuing unimpeded in their own cults as well. Majority culture was religiously commodious. Jews, meanwhile, would have every reason to want to encourage the active admiration and patronage of proximate outsiders for their own local community. And finally, Jews themselves, as we have seen, participated to varying degrees in pagan activities, especially if they themselves were athletes, actors, and/or citizens. In all these ways, then, the Western synagogue joined the ranks of the gymnasium, the theater, the hippodrome, the odeon, and the baths as another institution of Greco-Roman urban culture.[52]

3

PAUL: MISSION AND PERSECUTION

WHO WAS PAUL, AND HOW DO WE KNOW?

Paul's textual homeland was the Jewish scriptures in Greek. Paul's social homeland (and eventual apostolic ambit) was the multiethnic, thus multireligious, Greco-Roman city. When he frequented a diaspora synagogue, interested pagans, perhaps also some proselytes, may very well have numbered among those present. When he watched footraces, Jews as well as pagans may have made up not only the spectators but also the contestants. And whether gazing up at the night sky, across a city street, or down at one of his own beloved sacred texts, Paul would have encountered the gods of the nations. Both before his call to be an apostle and, manifestly, after, Paul's activities triangulated between these three populations: fellow Jews, proximate pagans, and pagan gods.

The one great exception to this normal urban mix of gods and humans would have been Jerusalem, whose residential population was overwhelmingly Jewish and whose public architecture eschewed depictions of foreign gods. Paul visited there, we know (Gal 1.18 and 2.1); but did he ever live there? Did he study there under the Jewish sage Gamaliel? The Acts of the Apostles claims so (22.3; cf. 7.58 and 8.1). If true, though, then it is difficult to account for Paul's silences: he says nothing about Stephen when he speaks of his past as a persecutor, nothing about Gamaliel when he boasts of his Jewish credentials (1 Cor 15.9; Gal 1.13; Phil 3.6). Paul says specifically that he did *not* go to Jerusalem after receiving his call to be an

apostle (Gal 1.17), and that he was *not* known "by face" to the Christ
assemblies in Judea for some time afterward (1.22). Acts, by contrast, has
Paul (back) in Jerusalem and involved with the original apostles very
shortly after his experience of the risen Christ (Acts 9.26–29).

Only Luke, further, mentions Paul's Hebrew name ("Saul"), his home
city (Tarsus), his Roman citizenship, and his missionary practice of
preaching in synagogues: there is nothing of this in Paul's own letters.
And finally, Acts contradicts Paul's own descriptions of the character of his
initial encounter with the risen Christ: Acts foregrounds an auditory
epiphany to a blinded Saul (Acts 9.3–8; cf. 22.6–11, 26.9–18); Paul emphasizes, precisely, seeing (1 Cor 15.8; cf. 9.1). We might wonder, then, how
much historical material (including any of Paul's letters) Luke had to
work with, and how much of Acts' story is Luke's own invention or that
derived from other evolving traditions. I will appeal to some aspects of
Acts' presentation as historically reliable for reconstructing Paul further
on in our investigation. In our quest for the historical apostle, however,
Paul's own letters must have priority, and it is on these—1 Thessalonians,
1 and 2 Corinthians, Philippians, Philemon, Galatians, and Romans—
that our project will chiefly depend.[1]

Paul's letters are genuine letters; they are ancient letters; and they
are Greco-Roman letters. Each of these three aspects needs to be borne
in mind.

Paul did not leave behind orderly theological treatises or narrative histories. He left behind real letters (very few of which have come down to
us), communications addressed to particular communities (or, in the case
of Philemon, to an individual) with particular issues and problems, occasioned by specific incidents within a mutually familiar context. Much of
that context is now lost to us, and we have only the letters themselves as a
means to reconstruct it. Where Paul seems to be responding to questions
posed by his communities—the Thessalonians' concern about the deaths
of fellow believers in advance of Christ's return (1 Thes 4.13); the
Corinthians' uncertainty about correct sexual relations (1 Cor 7), or about
the status of meat sacrificed to idols (1 Cor 8 and 10)—we are on reasonably sure footing. Where Paul blasts unnamed opponents, arguing heatedly with his people against other apostles of Christ whose teachings

undermine his own, we have to use more care: distilling a coherent and sympathetic impression of these various competitors from Paul's over-heated rhetoric is a challenge.[2] And finally, since these texts are real let-ters, they presuppose ongoing contacts between Paul and his communities. All we have is a small slice of their communications, and within that slice only Paul's half of their ongoing dialogue. Consequently, we hear only Paul's side.

The antiquity of Paul's letters also affects their material status. Paul would have dictated them to a scribe sometime in the middle decades of the first century. We have no manuscript copies that go back to Paul's lifetime. Originally, Paul's Greek would have been written with no breaks between words and no punctuation: those are both conventions from later orthography. Simply reading Paul's sentences now, how we break up his clauses and connect his ideas, already depends upon many interpreta-tive decisions before we can even deal with the problem of how we trans-late him. Compounding this problem was how widely his letters were copied and circulated: changes both accidental and occasionally deliber-ate were introduced during the long centuries of manuscript transmis-sion, every time a scribe did his job. The result was numerous variants and, accordingly, some uncertainty about how Paul originally said what he said. Last, the transmission of the letters themselves seems to have occasionally gotten garbled: most scholars see at least two letters edited together in our current text of Philippians; and the redaction of 2 Corinthians—two letters? three?—remains problematic.[3] In sum, the let-ters as we now have them reflect only imperfectly what Paul's scribe, almost nineteen centuries ago, would have written.

Finally, Paul's letters are instances of Greco-Roman rhetoric. The conventions of ancient epistolary style and the rhetorical tropes that Paul employs to instruct and to persuade his hearers need to be taken into account when we try to interpret his letters. Of these, we must attend particularly to Paul's use of *diatribe* (illustrative argument) and of *prosopo-peia* ("speech in character," the rhetorical introduction of another "voice" or persona to sharpen the speaker's arguments) when interpreting him. More globally, we need to be aware of the adversarial conventions of Greco-Roman rhetorical culture in general when weighing aspects of

Paul's teaching, especially with respect to his complaints about his apostolic competition. The goal of ancient rhetoric and its primary purpose was persuasion, *not* accurate description of an opposing side's position. It taught speakers how to win oral arguments. If that was accomplished through artful overstatement, well and good: that is exactly what students of rhetoric were trained to do.[4]

Paul had a good education, he was passionate in his convictions, and he was a fierce (and trained) word-warrior. As we attempt to reconstruct the views of his communities and especially of his opponents, we must keep all of this in mind.

JEWS, BORN AND MADE

"Spirit" and "flesh" represent two of Paul's favorite and frequent verbal pairings. "Spirit" codes for something positive (such as his gospel, or the benefits of being "in Christ," or for his own position on some contested matter); "flesh," often but *not* always, for something negative (such as the views of his competitors, or for idolatry and the sins associated with it; sometimes, and more generally, for a negative moral force).

This contrast between flesh and spirit structures Philippians 3. Shifting abruptly from his preceding remarks on rejoicing in the Lord, Paul suddenly warns his community against "dogs" and "mutilators of the flesh" (presumably, other messengers of Christ whose gospel urged circumcision on these gentiles). "We are the circumcision," he urges his assembly, "the ones who worship God by spirit and who boast in Christ Jesus and who do not trust in flesh"—and then he catches himself:

> [E]ven though I have confidence in flesh also. If any man thinks he trusts in the flesh, I do so more: circumcised on the eighth day, of the people [*genos*] of Israel, of the tribe of Benjamin, a Hebrew born to Hebrew parents; according to the Law, a Pharisee; according to zeal, persecuting the ekklesia; according to righteousness with respect to the Law, blameless. (Phil 3.2–6)

In Galatia, circumcising apostles called forth a similar report from Paul about his past, where he again combines "zeal" with "persecution": "You have heard of my former behavior in *Ioudaïsmos,* how I persecuted the assembly of God to the utmost [*kath' huperbolēn*; cf. the RSV's "violently"] and assaulted it; and I progressed in *Ioudaïsmos* beyond many of my contemporaries among my own people [*genos*], because I was so zealous for my ancestral traditions" (Gal 1.13–14; cf. 1 Cor 15.9).[5] Toward the end of the same letter, Paul couples "circumcision" with "persecution": "Brothers, if I still proclaimed circumcision, why would I still be persecuted?" (Gal 5.11). And finally, against his circumcising apostolic competition, he brings up persecution again: "It is those who want to make a good showing in the flesh who try to compel you to be circumcised, so that they may not be persecuted for the cross of Christ" (6.12).

What can we derive from these slight passages? Why would gentiles-in-Christ seek to be circumcised? What would motivate a Jew—Paul's Christ-following competitors and evidently at one time, whether pre- or post-Christ, Paul himself—to urge circumcision on non-Jews? And what does Paul mean by "persecution," both giving and getting?

Sometimes, pagan outsiders wanted to be more than interested visitors: sometimes they sought to connect more strongly to the covenant community of Israel and to its god, to shift their status from outsiders to insiders. The modern term for such a transition, "conversion," fits poorly in Paul's period, when one's kinship group, the *genos* or *ethnos*, anchored and articulated piety. Given the essentialism of ethnicity in antiquity (as, for example, when Paul claims that he and Peter are both Jews *physei*, "by nature," Gal 2.15), how did a pagan "become" a Jew?

For some Jews, the answer was: impossible. A pagan cannot become a Jew.[6] This position privileged antiquity's normative connection of family and cult, and its realist construction of genealogy and "blood." Within Jewish tradition, it also represented an innovative extension of priestly standards to the entire nation, a view expressed in the post-Exilic biblical book of Ezra (fifth century B.C.E.). Just as the clan status of priest (*cohen*) or of Levite was inherited—no ritual act could turn a nonpriest (that is, a lay Israelite) into a priest—so also, according to this view, no act could turn a non-Jew into a Jew. Ezra extends this line of reasoning to an argument against exogamy: the "holy" or "separate" seed of Israel should stay within Israel, and not mix with "profane" or "common" foreign seed (Ezra 9.1–2).

In Paul's period, the Qumran community extended this argument further still to include marriages *within* Israel: priests should not marry lay Israelites, nor should Israelites marry *gerim*, foreigners who had attached themselves to Israel. The same word, *ger*, will function for the rabbis as the term for *prosēlytos*/"convert," who for the later rabbis became "an Israelite in all ways" (b Yeb. 47b).[7] In this sectarian view, however, the *ger* remains forever an outsider ("presumably in both senses—[notional] access to the sanctuary and intermarriage into the community").[8] Jubilees, a retelling of Genesis important to this community, further emphasized that any circumcision performed later than the eighth day of life could not effect entry into the covenant (Jub 15.25–26; cf. Gen 17.12–14). Gentiles, by divine design led astray by errant spirits, could never join Israel (15.30f.).[9]

This stringent sectarian position was not the dominant one in the late Second Temple period, when foreigners both male and female joined the nation. For pagan women—all but invisible in our Greco-Roman evidence—the normal way to enter into the people of Israel seems to have been through marriage. This was also the biblical paradigm, showcased in the story of Ruth the Moabite, the great-grandmother of no less a personage than King David. In Roman antiquity, a woman's "marrying in" to Jewishness by taking a Jewish husband would simply follow larger social convention: wives assumed the gods of their husbands' households. The child of such a union—in distinction to his or her status according to the later rabbinic view—would assume the social identity of the father (as, again, in the dominant biblical paradigm). The child of a Jewish father and a gentile mother would be a Jew, just as the child of a gentile father and a Jewish mother would be a non-Jew. (For this reason, the story in Acts 16.1–3 that Paul circumcised Timothy, whose father was a gentile, has confounded commentators.) But in fact, for the first century, we do not know how, outside of marriage, pagan women "became" Jews, other than by assuming Jewish practices.[10]

Pagan men are another story. Hellenistic and, later, Roman writers whether Jewish, pagan, or Christian all singled out circumcision as the premier mark both of the male Jew and of the ex-pagan new Jew. Tacitus comments that both native Jews and voluntary Jews are so marked (*circumcidere genitalia, Hist.* V.5.1, 2). Juvenal makes the same point differently: if the father observes the Sabbath (*metuens sabbata*), worships the sky, and avoids pork, the sons eventually circumcise and revere "the law that Moses handed over in his arcane scroll." That is, Juvenal complains, the sons of a Judaizing father will eventually "convert" through circumcision (*Sat.* 14.96–102; note again, however, that Juvenal has no word for "conversion," instead using the language of deserting the *romanas leges* for foreign laws, the *ius* of Moses, ll. 100–102). Josephus, in his account of the royal house of Adiabene, makes the same point yet a third way. Circumcision would render King Izates a "Jew" in the eyes of his (pagan) subjects, a devotee "of foreign customs" (*xenōn ethōn*). Consequently, both Izates' mother, Helene, and the Jewish merchant Ananias advise him against it (*AJ* 20.38–41; cf. 47). Circumcision, entailing as it did a commitment to the Jews' *ius* or *ethē*, is precisely what distinguished the male convert from the sympathizer.[11]

Paul himself seems to suggest the same when he warns his Galatian communities, "Whoever receives circumcision is bound to keep the whole Law" (Gal 5.3). Still: what did "keeping the whole Law" mean? According to whose interpretation? The evidence of vigorous Jewish variety of practice in the late Second Temple period should give us pause. Philo, for example, famously complained about a mysterious community of Jewish allegorizers in Alexandria. These people understood that physical circumcision was a sign pointing to a truer, higher meaning: sexual self-discipline. Why enact a mere fleshly protocol, then, if one grasped, and could live according to, the spiritual truth of which it was merely a symbol?

Philo endorsed the allegorizers' interpretation of circumcision's higher meaning, but he rejected their behavioral inference: the true philosopher, he urged, *does* the commandment as well as understands it. "If we keep and observe these" practices, Philo writes, "we shall gain a clearer idea of those things of which these are symbols" (*On the Migration of Abraham* 16.89–93). Jewishness—in Philo's view, the *true* philosophy—is for Philo a way of living, not just a way of thinking. Still, the objects of his disapprobation signal the possibility that some pious Jews, in the name of a more spiritual understanding of their ancestral laws and customs, may have ceased to practice circumcision. Perhaps then, if some Jews did not circumcise their own sons, other Jews saw no reason to circumcise pagan proselytes.[12]

Whatever latitude there may have been on this issue of proselyte circumcision internal to individual Jewish communities, it was a male pagan's circumcision *together with* his making an exclusive commitment to the god of Israel that was most obvious to pagan observers, and that occasioned their most hostile comments. A proselyte, offended patriotic pagans complained, turned his back on family, on ancestral custom, and on the gods. Tacitus bullets precisely these complaints: the earliest lesson that proselytes receive "is to despise the gods, to disown their own country (*patria*), and to regard their parents, children, and brothers as of little account" (*Hist.* V.5.1, 2). The problem with Juda*izing*, in the eyes of the pagan critics, was not (merely) that it was Jewish (therefore foreign), but that it could lead to Juda*ism*. And the problem with (voluntary) Judaism, unlike god-fearing, was that proselytes followed foreign laws *to the exclusion* of honoring their own inherited obligations.[13]

Such a radical degree of affiliation, because of Jewish cultic exclusivism, alienated not only the proselyte's human family but also his "superhuman" one as well, the gods who were his by birth and blood. Lack of cult made gods angry, and angry gods had a way of making their displeasure known. Earthquake, flood, and famine; shipwreck, storm, disease: these were the normal repertoire of divine anger. (Proper cult, for antiquity, would in modern categories fall under a city's defense budget.[14]) Pagan men nonetheless did occasionally decide to become circumcised and, thus, to make an exclusive commitment to Israel's god; and, with varying degrees of hostility, their decision seems to have been tolerated by most pagans most of the time.[15] But alienating the gods—as Paul himself, as we shall see, knew full well—carried real risks.

Even by Jews themselves, however, this cultic exclusivism was enacted variously. As our inscriptions especially attest, some Jews in the western Diaspora were comfortable showing respect (if not full, public cult) to alien divinities while at the same time asserting their own identities as *Ioudaioi*, evidently without any sense of conflict.[16] Accustomed as we are to drawing sharp lines between "monotheism" and "polytheism," we may be guilty of imposing modern distinctions on ancient actors, for whom divinity existed on a gradient, and for whom showing some degree of respect to foreign gods did not compromise their primary allegiance to their own god.

In other words, while active participation in sacrificial public cult, for proselytes as for born Jews, seems to have been out of the question—hostile pagan comments say as much—presence at cultic activities and flexibility on the question of meat sacrificed to these gods may well have been the norm. Paul himself allows a notable degree of latitude. In 1 Corinthians 8, writing to gentile Christ-followers about sacrifices to idols, Paul speaks of the ways that former idol-worshipers might still feel anxious around such sanctified foodstuffs: if they partake, their conscience might be defiled, presumably by feeling as if they were in some sort of genuine exchange with the god (1 Cor 8.7–8). Don't eat in a temple, Paul advises his community, if such a "weaker brother" might "stumble" in this regard (perhaps meaning that such a "brother" would thereby think that the divinity represented by the idol is really a god, as opposed to merely a *daimonion*, 8.9–13). And do not participate in public cult at all (10.14–22). If at a private dinner, eat freely unless someone else from the community is present and feels apprehensive about the status of the food. In that case—for his sake, not for one's own—do not eat (10.27–30). Paul sums up this teaching in Romans 14.20–21: "Do not, for the sake of food, destroy the work of God. . . . It is right not to eat meat or drink wine or do anything that makes your brother stumble." *For all we know*, Paul's own flexibility on this point when advising Christ-following gentiles in Corinth and in Rome reflected a *standing diaspora Jewish practice*: go ahead and eat, unless it alienates someone else within the community. Jews in the Diaspora would have had to deal with this issue of pagan foodstuffs long before Christ-following pagans would have done.[17]

CIRCUMCISING MISSIONS?

Some scholars, pointing to the well-attested fact of pagans "becoming" Jews, have argued that Jews actively sponsored *missions* to gentiles: late Second Temple Judaism, they contend, was a missionary religion.

Sometimes, such missions have been conjured to explain a supposed surge in antiquity's Jewish population: so vast was the increase, runs this argument, that only aggressive proselytizing can account for the numbers. Others see Jewish missions as providing a context for Hellenistic Jewish literature: the abundance of Jewish literature in Greek attests to Jewish efforts to attract pagans. Still others see in Jewish missions the explanation for later Christian rhetoric and theology *contra Iudaeos:* the bitterness of this Christian invective indexes the intensity of the supposed missionary competition between the two communities. And, finally, Jewish missions can provide a social context for interpreting two sentences in the New Testament, Matthew 23.15 (Pharisees crossing land and sea to make a single convert) and Galatians 5.11 (Paul's quondam preaching of circumcision).[18]

The first argument in favor of the existence of Jewish missions to turn pagans into Jews rested on speculation that the total numbers of Jews in the half-millennium between 586 B.C.E. (the destruction of the first temple) and 50 C.E. surged from 150,000 persons to roughly "four to eight million." These putative figures were distilled from scattered remarks in Philo, Josephus, and Bar Hebraeus (a thirteenth-century chronographer relating the number of Jews during the reign of the emperor Claudius). One problem with the argument is the hazard of staking *any* reconstruction on so-called population numbers: we do not and cannot know enough about ancient demography, whether for Jews or for any other ethnic group in antiquity, to make the case. Further, we do not know and cannot know how many pagans in antiquity would have fully assumed Jewish ancestral practices ("converted"): it is the *absence* of data that has led some scholars to postulate these huge numbers. And as we will see when we look at the social consequences of the mission of the early Jesus movement in the Diaspora, the likelihood of enormous numbers of converts to Judaism seems low.[19]

The second argument rests on assumptions about audience. Did non-Jews—enough to make the marketing effort effective—really savor reading tales of Jewish greatness in Greek? Perhaps some did. But the greatest consumers of this sort of apologetic literature would most likely have been other Greek-speaking Jews. Hellenistic Jewish writings, in other words—rewritten biblical stories, assertions of Jewish excellence, resounding affirmations of pagan admiration for the greater antiquity of Jewish scriptures, the priority of Jewish learning and the superiority of Jewish brains—first of all express Hellenistic Jews' pride in their own identity. We need not regard these writings as the literary residuum of an organized effort to turn pagans into Jews. The more probable (and causative) social context was these Hellenistic Jewish populations themselves.[20]

What about the ferocity and ubiquity of later Christian invective *adversus Iudaeos*? Does that not presuppose a fierce and sustained competition for a limited pagan market? While many tributaries combined to create and sustain this toxic tradition, later gentile Christianity's dependence upon Hellenistic Jewish sources—the LXX first of all, but also Paul's letters and later gospels—especially and significantly contributed. In these Jewish writings, complaints about Jews abound. Moses bemoaned Israel's stiff necks and stony hearts, the prophets denounced wayward Jewish practices, Jesus wrangled constantly with his compatriots (Pharisees, Sadducees, priests, and unspecified others), and Paul vigorously attacked fellow apostles who, like him, were Jews. ("Are they Hebrews? So am I. Are they Israelites? So am I. Are they the seed of Abraham? So am I. Are they apostles of Christ? I am a better one!" 2 Cor 11.22–23.)

Of course, these complaints were originally between Jews about Jews. Once in the second-century gentile context, however, these intra-Jewish critiques became *anti*-Jewish critiques, spurred in part by real rivalry not for potential pagan converts so much as for recognized "ownership" of Jewish scriptures and title to the name "Israel." Gentile Christians indeed trained this ammunition against Jewish contemporaries: Justin's *Dialogue with Trypho* is a parade example of this reuse of scriptural invective. But from the second and especially from the fourth century onward, gentile Christians directed it as well against gentile Christian rivals (as indeed, in his dialogue, did Justin).[21] In this intragentile war of words, the prime *casus belli* was Christian diversity ("heresy"), its main targets other gentile Christians. But the rhetorical ammunition of choice was anti-Judaism. By drawing on the negative stereotypes of Jews and Judaism available in Jewish writings (those that were eventually collected in the New Testament, and those in the Jewish scriptures themselves), these churchmen directed their most vicious anti-Jewish rhetoric against fellow gentile Christians of different doctrinal bent: their rivals were "just like the Jews," "as bad as the Jews," or "worse than the Jews."[22]

Availing themselves of (originally) intra-Jewish polemical rhetoric in this way, these later gentile Christians used biblical texts to authorize their own views, to backlight their own arguments, and to frame their own fights. And by labeling their own (gentile Christian) enemies "Pharisees" or "Judases," they rhetorically positioned themselves as Paul or as Jesus. In brief, and curiously, it was later intra-*Christian* diversity that seems to have occasioned the hyperdevelopment of Christianity's rhetorical "Jews" (the "Jew" as perennial Christian antitype). In light of these conflicts, a theory of the competitive marketing of rival Jewish/Christian missions is not only implausible but actually unnecessary to explain this long-lived vituperation *contra Iudaeos*.[23]

We are left, then, with the need to account for two sentences, one in Matthew, one in Paul. Must we rely on the Jewish missionary position to explain them? For Matthew, historians have speculated otherwise. Perhaps Matthew meant intra-Jewish "missions," efforts by one sect (the Pharisees) to persuade fellow Jews to join? *Prosēlytos*, however, in every other context known to us, indicates a non-native joiner. Perhaps, then, local Pharisees—much to Matthew's disapproval—began their own mission as an ad hoc response to missionizing by Matthew's group? Again, we can't know. But this last, more modest proposal of a spontaneous and local response to another Jewish group's evangelizing seems more plausible than postulating a standing policy of empire-wide, organized missions.[24]

What, then, of Paul's remark in Galatians 5.11, "If I still [*eti*] proclaimed circumcision, why am I still [*eti*] persecuted?" The audience for Paul's past proclamation would only be pagan: Jews, one assumes, would not need circumcision "proclaimed" to them (it already was, in their scriptures).[25] "Proclaiming circumcision" in a mixed-ethnic context implies the active solicitation of outsiders to come in. Some scholars have accordingly postulated that Paul was such a missionary—perhaps specifically a Pharisaic missionary (cf. Mt 23, 15).[26] We seem on this issue to be lapped by a hermeneutical circle, wherein Paul's remark can only be explained by Jewish missions, and Jewish missions must be surmised to account for Paul's statement.

There is a way out, but it comes by attending to the second part of Paul's remark in this context: persecution. What is this "persecution," who are its agents, and how does advocating or not advocating proselyte circumcision call it forth? We will attend to these broader questions shortly.

To sum up: did (any? some? most?) Jewish communities, especially those in the Diaspora, receive "converts"? Unquestionably. But receiving *prosēlytoi* is one thing; actively soliciting them is another.[27] On the Jewish side, we have no internal evidence for such missions, neither the name of a single Jewish missionary, nor a reckoning of any missionary procedures.[28] We might expect, at least from the rabbis—those Jews of antiquity most concerned about categories, boundary formation and maintenance, and halakhic precision—prescriptions for and legal discussion of correct missionary practice: in fact, we find nothing.[29] If such radical affiliation to Judaism were the result of actual and organized Jewish missions, we should have a better sense of how they would have proceeded. Rather, pagan interest in Judaism seems to have been the result of freelance, amateur, non-institutionally based efforts by individuals (such as Ananias and Eleazar with the royal house of Adiabene, as related by Josephus) or the side-effect of unstructured contact through diaspora synagogue communities.[30] And finally, on the evidence of Paul's letters, especially Galatians—a case that we will look at in some detail—no one, when faced with a (Christ-following) *mission* to turn pagans into Jews through circumcision, knew quite what to do.

ESCHATOLOGICAL GENTILES

Two last considerations, one historical, one historiographical, might shed a little more light on this question of Paul, pagan circumcision, and missions. The first relates to Jewish speculations about the ultimate fate of gentiles at the End of the Age, a theme arising within and read back into scriptural texts and apocalyptic or messianic traditions. As we have seen, such themes appear in very various literatures ranging broadly in period, provenance, and genre; and all are oriented around the idea that the god of Israel would end time with an assertion of his absolute sovereignty. Such scriptural attestations of this apocalyptic hope, however, do not provide us with any information on whether or to what degree such speculations had the slightest impact on the day-to-day life of ancient Jews and their various gentile associates.[31] We cannot, for example, extrapolate from prophetic statements about Israel as a light to the nations or about Israel's god as the god of the whole universe to a social reality of Hellenistic Jews engaging in missionary efforts. Quite the contrary: these traditions may attest to what apocalyptically minded Jews, Paul included, thought it would take to get most pagans to stop worshiping idols—nothing less than the definitive self-revelation of God at the End of the Age.

These inclusive eschatological traditions about receiving gentiles into God's Kingdom, finally, might seem little different from the inclusive quotidian Jewish practice of receiving pagans into diaspora synagogues. But there was a crucial difference, one that throws the diaspora Jesus movement into sharper relief. The synagogue's *prosēlytoi* were no longer pagans: they were Jews "of a peculiar sort."[32] The synagogue's god-fearers or Judaizers or sympathizers, however, seem to have been *active* pagans: they added the god of Israel to their native pantheons while continuing to worship their own gods as well. *But the Kingdom's pagans were a special and a purely theoretical category:* they were ex-pagan pagans, or (to use the wiggle-room afforded by our two English words) ex-pagan gentiles. *Like* god-fearers, these eschatological pagans would retain their native ethnicities; *unlike* god-fearers, these pagans would no longer worship their native gods. *Like* proselytes, these pagans would worship exclusively the god of Israel; *unlike* proselytes, these pagans would preserve their own ethnicities and—another way of saying the same thing—they would not assume the bulk of Jewish ancestral custom (such as, for males, circumcision).[33]

This last point bears repeating. The anticipated destruction of their idols did not imply, at the End, that scripture's eschatological pagans "converted" to Judaism, thereby "becoming" Jews. Such a transmutation of loyalties in the quotidian, as we have seen, entailed an ample assumption of Jewish ancestral practices and especially (for men) circumcision. Apocalyptic texts fall well short of making such a claim. Rather, at the

End, say these visionary texts, eschatological pagans *join with* Israel; but they do not "join" Israel. So, too, Paul in his closing catena of scriptural citations in Romans 15.9–12: the ἔθνη glorify God for his mercy; the ἔθνη rejoice *with* God's people, that is, Israel; the ἔθνη praise God; the ἔθνη are ruled by the coming "root of Jesse," that is, by the Davidic messiah, Christ (cf. 1.3); the ἔθνη hope in him. In this construction, *ta ethnē*, "the nations," even at the eschatological End-time, remain distinct from Israel. Put differently: gentiles are indeed included in Israel's redemption; but they are included *as* gentiles. Put yet a third way: *inclusion is not "conversion."*

Standard translations can obscure this point. When God redeems Israel, these texts proclaim, the nations will *turn from* the lesser gods whose images they worship and *turn to* the god of Israel—*epistrephō* in these Greek texts. *"Turn* to me!" cries God to the nations (Isa 45.22 LXX: *epistrephate*). "All the nations *will turn* in fear to the Lord God . . . and bury their idols" (Tobit 14.6: *epistrepsousin*). "You *turned* [*epistrepsate*] to God from idols," Paul tells his pagan community in Thessalonica, "to worship the true and living god, and to wait for his son from heaven" (1 Thes 1.9). But *epistrephō* came into Latin as *converto*, and *converto* came into English as "convert." Thus, incorrectly, the RSV translates this word at Acts 15.3: "The *conversion* of the gentiles" should read "the *turning* of the gentiles." (Cf., correctly, Acts 15.19 RSV: "the gentiles who *turn* to God.") And the RSV's notes for, e.g., Zephaniah 3.8–13, Zechariah 8.20–23, and Tobit 14.6 all claim—wrongly—that these texts speak of eschatological "conversion" rather than eschatological inclusion.

Isaiah 56.3–7 is sometimes adduced, wrongly, in support of a supposed tradition that Jews expected an End-time "conversion" of gentiles. But this passage of Isaiah speaks of the eschatological fate of *current* in-comers, former pagans who have "become" Jews at some indeterminate point before the End. The prophet assures such people that they will be brought together with native Israel at the eschatological in-gathering. "The foreigner who *has joined* himself to the Lord . . . the eunuchs who *keep my Sabbaths and hold fast my covenant* . . . I *will* give them an everlasting name. . . . The foreigners who join . . . these I *will* bring to my holy mountain." "Converts," these prophetic verses proclaim, foreigners who before the End "became" Jews, will be gathered in together with the native-born.[34]

In this passage of Isaiah, in other words, the prophet attests that current "voluntary" Jews "count" already as part of Israel. The nations, on the other hand, remain the nations right up to and even after the End. Once Israel—all twelve tribes—is gathered in from Exile, the nations (all seventy or seventy-two of them, by biblical count) will *at that point*—and not before—abandon idolatry. Gentiles are saved *as gentiles*. They do *not*, eschatologically, "become" Jews.[35] At the End of the Age pagans will "turn," this tradition anticipated, but they will not "convert." In short: "turning" is *not* "conversion."

My point in reviewing these visionary texts is to decouple them from the modern argument that ancient Jews embarked on missions to turn pagans into Jews. The only firm evidence we have for such a mission is that of Paul's apostolic opponents, mid-first century, in Galatia. In that singular instance, the motives for that mission stemmed from dynamics internal to the Jesus movement itself: the mission does not reflect a standard and widespread Jewish behavior. We will look more closely at these dynamics in the following chapter.

More generally, commitment to the idea that the god of Israel represented the ultimate religious destiny of all humanity—for those Jews who troubled to think in terms of an End-time, and who thus problematized pagan practices—would not in itself have stimulated or sustained some general policy of "missions" because, as these texts themselves declare, gentiles remain gentiles even in the eschatological age. God himself would address the "gentile problem," and even then only at the End. What reason or point, then, to address the "gentile problem"—*or even to think that it was a problem*—in the quotidian?[36]

Gentiles *qua* pagans, in other words, were *not* an urgent "problem" or a "question" *except* within forms of apocalyptic Judaism. On a day-to-day basis, a people's having the god(s) peculiar to it was just the way things were. Refracted through a scriptural prism, the nations' worship of "lesser" deities and *daimonia* was the inverse manifestation of biblical notions of revelation, election, and covenant: the nations had their gods, Israel their (bigger and better) god. At the End of the Age, it was God who would turn these pagans—and perhaps even their gods (cf. Ps 97.7; Phil 2.10; Rom 8.21, 38–39)—to himself. And even then, God would turn the nations to himself *qua ethnē*. Apocalyptic demography, in other words, would reflect quotidian demography: Jews and Gentiles, Israel *and* the nations.

These historical points about (or against) the idea of Jewish missions to pagans reinforce a historiographical one: the way that the very idea of missions confuses and obscures antiquity's normal and normative association of gods and peoples, kinship and cult. People were born into their obligations to their gods and, *outside of a Jewish apocalyptic context*, no evident urgency attached to this standing situation. In antiquity, most Jews did not spend most of their time pondering what God was going to do with "all these pagans," who were, after all, the vast majority of humankind. It was precisely and only the conviction that the End-time *loomed* that radically problematized paganism. Absent that conviction, the nations had their own gods, and Israel had theirs.[37]

Even in the socially blurred case of the god-fearers, no pressure, evidently, was brought to bear upon sympathizing pagans to commit exclusively to the god of Israel. (Later Christian observers will chide Jews precisely on this point.[38]) Finally, what we call "conversion" was so anomalous in antiquity that ancients in Paul's period had no word for it; hence their conceptualizing such a transition as confederation to a foreign law, and as disloyalty to one's own ancestral *ethē*.[39] And if "conversion" itself was an odd thought to think, then the idea of mass-marketing conversion through missions would have been that much odder.

WITNESS, RESISTANCE, AND "PERSECUTION"

How then, absent any developed concept of "mission," are we to explain the spread of this new movement to Jews out in the Diaspora—and thence in short order to pagan hearers as well—in the years immediately following the death of Jesus?

An intense expectation that the Kingdom was about to arrive had motivated Jesus's own teaching. His disciples had shared his conviction. Their confidence in his good news would have been radically challenged by the crushing disappointment of his crucifixion; just as radically, the postresurrection appearances would have reconfirmed it. Two of the prime promises of the messianic age—the resurrection of the dead and the vindication of the righteous—had been realized, they held, in the person of their executed leader. The Christophanies continued, and multiplied (1 Cor 15.4–7; Mt 28; Lk 24.13–51; Jn 20.15–21.19; Acts 1.1–11). Regrouping in Jerusalem, Jesus's disciples gathered their community, and waited.

For what? The materials that we have to draw on were all written decades after these events, and have doubtless been reshaped under the pressure of the passage of time. Already in our two earliest documents, Paul's letters and the gospel of Mark, we see the intense expectation of the Kingdom's definitive arrival coupled to anticipation of Jesus's triumphant *return*. Leading angelic armies to the sounding of the heavenly trumpet, Jesus returns as a victorious warrior to defeat the forces of evil, to raise the dead, to gather his elect—he returns, in other words, as a conquering messiah.[40]

But what was taking so long? Midcentury, Paul explained the Kingdom's delay in terms of turning pagans to the gospel: only once their "full number" came in would "the Redeemer come from Zion" and the final events unwind (Rom 11.25–32). Mark, sometime after 70 C.E., explained the Kingdom's evident delay by constructing a two-generation timeframe. The sinful and adulterous generation of Jesus's contemporaries were not to receive the sign of the Kingdom's coming (Mk 8.38). It was only the righteous generation—Mark's generation—that would be given the sign, namely, the Roman destruction of the temple in Jerusalem (Mk 13.1–4, 26). The apocalyptic significance of the temple's fall, the evangelist reassured his community, was that it indicated the nearness of Jesus's second coming as the triumphant Son of Man, thus the approach of the End and, thus, of redemption.[41]

Can we trace a trajectory backwards, from Mark c. 75 to Paul c. 50 to Jerusalem c. 30? Some two-plus decades before Paul wrote Romans, the original disciples would have had to explain to themselves and to their community why the Kingdom continued not to arrive *despite* the ongoing appearances of the risen Christ. (See Acts 1.6: "So when they had come together, they [the disciples] asked him, 'Lord, will you at this time restore the Kingdom to Israel?'") We can extrapolate from these sources what these early Jesus-followers, regrouped and regathered in Jerusalem, were waiting for: the definitive, final Christophany as the advent of the Kingdom. They would have been sustained in their hope by the empowerment of spirit: healing, prophesying, working exorcisms.[42] Their numbers would have increased, as would the pitch of their expectation (see Acts 2.41–47, set during and after the pilgrimage festival following Jesus's execution, that is, Shavuot/Pentecost).

And still nothing happened. What was wrong?

These disciples came up with an answer, based on their own experience of Jesus's mission. To prepare Israel for the coming Kingdom, Jesus had taken the good news to the Jewish villages of the Galilee and of Judea, and to Jerusalem itself. To continue his work, his committed followers reasoned, they must have to take the gospel out of the Galilee and Judea, to the Israel of the dispersion. Only when the greater part of Israel was prepared could the final events unwind.

It was at this point that the original community burst into energetic activity, spreading the good news to fellow Jews beyond their original ambit. ("The Kingdom is at hand: repent!") Traveling down from Jerusalem into the coastal plain, to Lydda, to Joppa, to Caesarea, these apostles would have moved through the network of Jewish communities ringed round the Mediterranean, continuing Jesus's work of preparing Israel for impending redemption, now coupled to his imminent messianic return. And as they moved into mixed cities, such as Joppa and Caesarea, and into diaspora cities, such as Antioch and Damascus, these Galilean and Jerusalemite apostles would have encountered within these synagogues—unexpectedly—a pagan presence as well.

Into Paul's synagogue community in Damascus, then, a few years at most after the crucifixion, came apostles enthusiastically proclaiming this message of the imminent arrival of God's Kingdom, now to be effected by the soon-to-return messiah. If we can generalize from the later picture in Paul's letters and in Acts, these apostles would have found opportunities within the synagogue context to announce their message, to interpret scripture, to debate with listeners, and to demonstrate their authority with charismatic healings and exorcisms.

Also present in this diaspora synagogue setting would have been pagans voluntarily associated there as god-fearers. This pagan presence

introduced a new factor in the spread of the gospel—one, I assume, that
as a practical matter would have initially caught these apostles by surprise.
Pagans would have been thin on the ground in rural Galilee and Judea.
Jesus had taught primarily in Jewish villages. Jerusalem, where he also
taught, would have held two significant pagan groups, especially during
the pilgrimage holidays: the Roman prefect with his 3,000 troops, and
pagan visitors to the temple. But pagans as such were not a population
that either Jesus or his disciples would have focused on or much interacted with. Now, however, the wider geographical world that the gospel
moved into brought with it a wider social world too.[43]

What happened next? Some of these pagan sympathizers would have
responded positively to the good news that the Kingdom approached. But
it was unthinkable to the apostles that active idolators be members of the
gospel assembly. These pagans, then, would have enacted their reception
of and commitment to the gospel message by abandoning cult to their
own gods, pledging themselves instead to Israel's god alone. Their unan-
ticipated response would in turn have only confirmed the apostles in their
conviction that the Kingdom truly was at hand: the nations, just as Isaiah
had long ago foretold, were turning from idols to "the true and living god"
(1 Thes 1.9). A small assembly of the convinced (the *ekklēsia*)—a mixed
group of apostles from the original community in Jerusalem, local Jews,
and local Judaizing gentiles—would have formed, initially within the
larger synagogue community itself. Assembling in the synagogue weekly
with the larger Jewish community for prayer and for hearing scripture,
assembling separately in their own smaller groups for prayer, prophecy,
interpreting scripture, and sharing meals, they proclaimed with increasing conviction that the Kingdom was at hand. Their charismata and the
intimate bond of their assembly reinforced their sense of the times.[44]

*Why would Paul and other local synagogue authorities in Damascus
"persecute" such a group?* And what do we mean by "persecution"? For
our answer we turn, again, to Paul's letter to the Galatians. Galatians
offers us glimpses of four discrete moments in the gospel's spread: (1)
the negative, hostile response on the part of Paul and (presumably) of
the Damascus synagogue authorities to this new group forming in its
midst (c. 33 C.E.? Gal 1.12–16); (2) a major decision affirmed in Jerusalem

concerning the obligations of gentiles involved in the movement (c. 49
C.E.? Gal 2.1–10); (3) the confusions occasioned by the close interaction of
Palestinian Jews, diaspora Jews, and Antiochene gentiles within Antioch's
ekklesia (early 50s C.E.? Gal 2.11–15); and (4) a current challenge to Paul's
authority in Galatia coming from other apostles who advocated circumcision of Christ-following gentiles, the immediate situation igniting this
letter (mid-50s C.E.?).

The crisis of the mid-50s was posed by other apostles who, preaching
a gospel different from Paul's, urged proselyte circumcision on Paul's
male gentiles, in effect thus "making" them Jews (Gal 1.6 and passim; cf.
5.2–4). Paul reports the three earlier episodes named above in service to
his current argument, in which he seeks to discredit the circumcisers'
challenge. The result is that he shapes his letter so that circumcision —
and his principled opposition to it — seems to be the central issue as
well in Damascus, in Jerusalem, and in Antioch.[45] That way, Paul can
position himself to claim that, from the moment he received his divine
revelation (1.12, 16), he had *always* opposed the position of his Galatian
challengers.

We know nothing about these challengers outside of Paul's hostile
characterizations of them. Were they radical Judaizers, gentile Christ-
followers committed to circumcision? Or were they "conservative" Jewish
apostles representing the Jerusalem church of James (see Gal 2.12)? Or,
perhaps, they were the "Hellenists," Greek-speaking Jewish members of
the new movement who sought to regularize gentile membership in the
ekklesia by "converting" pagan affiliates to Judaism. All sorts of identifications have been ventured.[46] Given Paul's strident opening emphasis on his
"zeal for the traditions of my fathers," his conjuring his own past persecutions of the ekklesia, and his insistence on his own excellence in
Ioudaïsmos, I suspect that these opponents, like the ones mentioned in
Philippians 3.2 and in 2 Corinthians 11, were virtually clones of himself:
Jewish apostles of the Christ movement who were taking the gospel of the
crucified and returning messiah to pagans. Paul emphasizes his own zeal
for Jewish ancestral practices (Gal 1.14; Phil 3.5) to claim the high ground
against his opponents. They think that *they* are zealous for Jewish traditions? Their zeal is nothing compared to Paul's! The "zeal" Paul trumpets

here, in other words, does not speak primarily to his past motivations for "persecuting." It speaks, rather, to the current challenge of his "zealous" competitors.[47]

But what in any case did Paul mean by *diōgmos*, "persecution"? For the Paul of Acts, "persecution" meant execution: Saul consents to Stephen's death, and he departs for Damascus "breathing threats and murder" (Acts 8.1, 9.1). In his lists of woes endured as an apostle in 2 Corinthians, however, Paul himself points the way to a different picture. Raging (once again) against other Jewish apostles ("such men are false apostles, deceitful workmen disguising themselves as apostles of Christ," 2 Cor 11.13), Paul reviews his own credentials both as a Jew and as an apostle (11.22–23), while relating the sufferings that his calling entailed:

> Five times I have received at the hands of the Jews forty lashes less one. Three times I have been beaten with rods; once I was stoned. Three times I have been shipwrecked, a night and a day I have been adrift at sea; on frequent journeys, in danger from rivers, danger from robbers, danger from my own people and danger from pagans, danger in the city, in the wilderness, and at sea; danger from false brethren, in toil and hardship. . . . (2 Cor 11.24–27)

Further:

> For the sake of Christ, I am content with weaknesses, insults, hardships, persecutions, and calamities. (2 Cor 12.10)

Paul's mention of thirty-nine lashes here might provide us with a clue for interpreting his prior activities as a Jew against other Jews who were members of the Damascus synagogue's ekklesia. "Thirty-nine lashes" was specifically an *intra-Jewish* disciplinary practice. If Paul as an apostle received this punishment "five times" in his apostolic sojourns, then perhaps in Damascus, presumably as some sort of authority figure within his synagogue community, this was the Jewish punishment that he gave. It bears emphasizing that those members of the ekklesia so disciplined by Paul could *only* have been fellow Jews: "Punishment implies inclusion" (the thirty-nine lashes were derived from a statute framed specifically for Israel, Deut 25.1–3); and in any case no synagogue would have had a jurisdictional authority over local gentiles.[48]

This understanding of Paul's both giving and getting thirty-nine blows might also give us more purchase on how we translate *kath' huperbolēn* at Galatians 1.13. The RSV renders this phrase as "violently," perhaps influenced by Luke's lurid mise-en-scène in Acts. Better would be "to the maximum" or "to the utmost," that is, the full number of thirty-nine lashes. In other words, Paul either oversaw or perhaps even personally administered this punishment of the maximum number of blows allowed, the same number that he as an apostle on five different occasions would later receive.[49]

But for what reason? What situation would speak both to the synagogue community in Damascus within a few years of Jesus's crucifixion and also, decades later, to these other diaspora synagogue communities that (for reasons unknown) also administered this penalty to Paul?

(1) Some scholars have conjectured that the core message of the new movement—the proclamation of a *crucified* messiah—would have deeply offended any and all Jews. In Galatians 3.13, Paul cites Deuteronomy 21.23: "Cursed be everyone who hangs on a tree." Jews in antiquity took "hanging on a tree" to mean crucifixion (so too, e.g., 11 Q Temple 64.6–13). On this scholarly construction, the early kerygma was an affront to pious Jews anywhere and everywhere, since a messiah known to have been crucified like a criminal would be viewed as dying a death "cursed by the Law": for this reason, Jews would be scandalized by the message of a crucified messiah (cf. 1 Cor 1.23). How could the messiah be "cursed of God"?

This is one of those tropes of New Testament scholarship that refuses to go away, despite all its problems as historical reconstruction. The mode of hanging referred to in Deuteronomy, first, speaks not to a method of capital execution (death by hanging), but to a post-mortem display of the executed criminal's body, a sort of publication of the offender's death. By the first century, "hanging on a tree" indeed could indicate "crucifixion" (as in 11 Q Temple, cited above). But no belief that crucifixion *eo ipso* meant a "cursed" death is *anywhere* attested outside of this interpretation of Paul's snarled passage in Galatians 3. Other Jewish texts actually provide counterevidence. The bodies of King Saul and of his son Jonathan, for example, were hanged, but nowhere is this taken to mean that they had died under a special curse (2 Sam 21.12). Closer to our period, Josephus relates that 800 Pharisees were crucified under Alexander Janneus (*AJ* 13.380); that the sons of Judah the Galilean were crucified by Rome (*AJ* 20.102); that the Roman legate Varus crucified 2,000 Jews in Judea during the troubles after Herod's death (*BJ* 2.75; *AJ* 17.295); and that Titus's troops crucified thousands of refugees fleeing from besieged Jerusalem (*BJ* 5.449–51). Yet he nowhere claims that other Jews regarded these people as therefore having died under a divine curse. The disposition of the deceased's body, in other words, provides no register of divine intent. And finally, while a pagan Roman might indeed regard a crucified Jew as a criminal, *hominem noxium et crucem eius*, to other first-century Jews he would probably look more like a victim, if not a fallen hero.[50]

In short: nothing in first-century Judaism (or thereafter) seems to require that a crucified man *ipso facto* be seen as "cursed of God," and we have no evidence of Jews ever actually having done so. The source of this interpretation of "crucifixion" as "curse," and its originary context, is not late second temple Judaism, but Paul's letter itself and the rhetorical chiasma of "blessing" and "curse" that he weaves in Galatians 3.10–14. The brief and novel exegetical association that he makes in this passage of his letter—Abraham/blessing, Law/curse, Christ/Law, curse/blessing— should not and cannot be generalized into a standing Jewish view of crucifixion *tout court*.[51] The idea that Jews would be (actively and aggressively) scandalized by the message of a crucified messiah because of his manner of death should be retired from New Testament scholarship.

(2) Why else might Paul have participated in having the Damascene *ekklesia*'s Jews subjected to lashing, c. 33 C.E.? And how would this shed light on why he, later, received the same punishment? Legal offense, other scholars propose: these itinerant apostles (often associated with the "Hellenists" of Acts), according to this argument already lax in their own Law observance, would have offended their host synagogue as "sinners." Worse—in fact, indicative of their level of observance—these apostles socialized with "impure" gentiles, eating together and praying together without first requiring that these gentiles be circumcised, that is, "become" Jews. And this same reconstruction serves to explain why Paul, later, was himself "persecuted": Paul's social practice of associating with gentiles

"shatters the ethnic mould" of synagogue Judaism; the new social entity of the ekklesia "transgresses the boundaries of the diaspora synagogue"; "Paul's assimilating practices and his lax (or at least inconsistent) observance of the Law earned him suspicion, opposition, and even punishment in the synagogue."[52]

This last reconstruction requires that the earliest gospel message be somehow in principle irreconcilable with Jewish practice. The ekklesia's ready inclusion of gentiles without requiring that they be circumcised is held up as prime proof of this while, again, weaving a causal web between Galatia in the mid-50s and Damascus c. 33. But as we have already seen, pagans were welcomed into the largest court of the temple complex itself. Pagans participated in diaspora synagogue life well before the introduction of the Jesus movement, and would do so—together with gentile Christians—for centuries thereafter. Diaspora synagogues, like the larger city of which they were a part, served as sites of Jews and gentiles mixing well into the post-Constantinian period. The mixed population within the tiny new ekklesia, then, with its uncircumcised gentiles, *cannot* in and of itself have moved Paul to "persecute," or have moved other Jews to "persecute" him. Such gentiles were already present in the synagogue: why worry, then, if they took a role in the (much smaller) ekklesia as well?[53]

(3) "Lax or at least inconsistent observance of the Law" as a reason for Paul's persecuting and for Paul's being persecuted, finally, relies upon an idea of consistency and of translocal standards of Jewish practice that sits oddly within the early Roman context, whether in the Land of Israel itself or, certainly, in the Diaspora, where local variety and variability characterize Jewish modes of life. "The problem for the historian of Judaism grappling with the persecution of early [Jewish] Christians is the abundant evidence of [Jewish] pluralism in this period." In Judea alone, Sadducees had major disagreements with Pharisees, who also had significant disagreements over the interpretation of the Law between each other; while the community by the Dead Sea wished a pox on both their houses. The level of practice among the *amme ha-aretz* occasioned arch comment from the more learned. These very significant differences and theological as well as practical disputes led neither to violent opposition nor to judicial punishment.[54]

Jewish behavior in the Diaspora likewise varied widely, as we have seen. Our inscriptions, the pagan and later gentile Christian comments and observations about Jews, Hellenistic Jewish literary sources—taken together, all these data bespeak a broad range of Jewish observance and practice. The simple *fact* of difference, in short, was not "actionable," nor could it ever have been. Jews in the Diaspora belonged to their communities voluntarily. If local religious authorities sought to flog synagogue members for perceived offenses of religious practice, the offender could always just walk away.[55] And if there was diversity in the homeland, there could only have been that much more diversity in the Diaspora.

Finally, this last conjecture about "persecution" for legal offense rests on a long-standing gentile Christian theological position, namely, that "observing the Law"—that is, living according to Jewish ancestral practices—is *intrinsically* incompatible with Christian "belief." Paul's so-called Law-free gospel preached to non-Jews thus sets the standard of behavior for this founding generation's Jews-in-Christ as well. The present study argues against both these suppositions. Paul's polarizing rhetoric should not be confused with historical description. First of all, even *his* gospel to *his* gentiles involved their assuming two fundamental and exclusively Jewish practices, namely, fidelity to the god of Israel alone and avoidance of pagan cult: both ancients and moderns commonly designate such behaviors as "Judaizing." And while his letters are addressed often (I think, only) to Christ-following gentiles, we have no statement from Paul to Jews about their no longer preserving Jewish tradition—and, as we will see, many statements from him about the Law as a privilege and a value, as a distinguishing divine gift to Israel, and even as a pathway to recognition of Jesus as the messiah (e.g., Rom 3.1, 7.12, 9.5, 10.4). Well into the second century, Christ-following Jews continued to live by their ancestral customs (Justin, *Trypho* 47). Why *assume* that the first Jewish generation, Paul included, would live any differently?

Toward the end of Galatians, Paul suggests that his *not* preaching circumcision—to gentiles, I assume, not to Jews—has something to do with the reason why he is persecuted. "If I still preach circumcision, why am I still persecuted?" (Gal 5.11). Note that he does not say by whom. And he suggests that his apostolic competition in Galatia advocates circumcising

Christ-following gentiles so that they themselves might avoid being persecuted. "Those who would . . . compel you to be circumcised . . . [do so]
only in order that they may not be persecuted for the cross of Christ" (Gal
6.12). *Note, again, that the agents of such persecution are not named.*

As long as we restrict the "persecution" endured by Paul to intra-
Jewish disciplinary lashing, and as long as we restrict the reasons for these
contentions primarily to the practice of Jewish ancestral customs, we
restrict both the identity of Paul's persecutors *to* Jews and the reasons for
his persecution (both giving and getting) to issues internal to Jewish communities. But Paul lists more than synagogue harassment in the woes of 2
Corinthians 11. He is also "persecuted" by Roman government officials:
three times beaten with rods (v. 25). He is once stoned, presumably by a
crowd action. Contrary winds, weather, and water—the domain of the
lower gods—impede his mission (vv. 25–26). Paul was "in danger from my
own people and *in danger from gentiles*" (pagans who are not Romans?),
as well as in danger from "false brethren" (v. 26; cf. Gal passim).

Who are all these other "persecutors"? What do they have in common
with Paul's synagogue persecutors? Why was everybody ganging up on
Paul? And why do these different persecutors pursue all those who do *not*
preach circumcision?

The answer to all of these questions emerges only once we consider
Paul's *entire* social world, not only its Jews but also its pagans and thus,
also, the pagans' gods. The moment that the early Jesus movement first
ventured out into the Diaspora, it encountered these gods as it encountered their peoples. The diaspora synagogue's long-standing and socially
stable practice gave pagans scope *qua* sympathizers to engage with
Israel's god while continuing in their native cults: god-fearing pagans, in
other words, risked offense neither to their human families nor to their
divine ones.

With gentile involvement in the ekklesia, however, things were otherwise. First, and significantly, apostles seem to have set the bar much
higher than did the local synagogue. (Male) pagans joining the ekklesia
could no longer sacrifice to their own gods.[56] "Indeed there are many
gods and many lords," Paul says to his gentile community in Corinth,
"but *for us* there is one god, the Father, . . . and one Lord, Jesus Christ"

(1 Cor 8.5–6). If a "brother"—that is, a baptized Christ-following gentile—continued to worship idols, he was to be shunned (5.11). "Formerly,
when you did not know God, you were in bondage to beings that by
nature are no gods" (Gal 4.8). "Beloved"—this again to the Corinthians—
"shun the worship of idols" (1 Cor 10.14). "You turned to God from idols,"
Paul tells his gentiles in Thessalonica, "to worship the true and living
god" (1 Thes 1.9).

This image of the nations "turning"—a good prophetic locution—
appears both in Paul and in Acts 15. It derives, as we have seen, from
Jewish apocalyptic traditions, preserved variously in prophetic texts and in
intertestamental writings. At the End of time, so say these passages, the
nations will *turn from* their native gods, destroying their images, and they
will *turn to* the god of Israel. In other words, Jewish apocalyptic traditions
provide the textual location of pagans who eschew their idols, who turn to
make an exclusive commitment to the god of Israel, and who do *not*
assume (other) Jewish ancestral practices, a.k.a. "the Law" (circumcision,
food laws, Sabbath, and so on). Such "eschatological gentiles" had long
been an imaginative construct, their exclusive commitment to the god of
Israel one of any number of anticipated End-time events. Once the Jesus
movement established itself in the Diaspora, they began to become a
social reality.

This apocalyptic tradition, inclusive of the nations, is what informs
the first apostles' improvised "gentile policy" from the beginning, as soon
as the movement encountered pagan god-fearers. James, Peter, and John
confirmed this "policy" for Paul when he went up to Jerusalem (Gal 2.1–
10). It was operative even in those gentile ekklesiai founded independently of Paul, such as the ones in Damascus and, later, in Rome.
Knowing what hour it was on God's clock, racing in the (for all they
knew) brief caesura between Christ's resurrection and his second coming
(1 Cor 15), seeing in the pneumatic behavior of their new gentile members confirmation of their own eschatological convictions, these Jewish
apostles welcomed gentiles who committed fully to the god of Israel into
their messianic assemblies. These ex-pagan pagans were a resounding
affirmation and validation of the gospel message: the Kingdom *must* truly
be at hand.

But the gods struck back. These lower deities, the *archontes tou aiōnes toutou*, the cosmic "rulers of this age," had crucified the son of Paul's god (1 Cor 2.8); now they persecuted and afflicted Paul and Paul's Christ-following gentiles, all of whom thereby shared in the sufferings of Christ. The *theos tou aiōnes toutou*, "the god of this age," blinded the minds of those who refused Paul's message (2 Cor 4.4). Paul acknowledges these gods' hostility but also holds them in contempt: their power, after all, was already broken and would soon be overwhelmed by the returning Christ, to whom they would submit (Phil 2.10). Those beings formerly worshiped by his congregations, he says, were not "gods by nature" but only cosmic lightweights, *stoicheia* unworthy of fear or worship (Gal 4.8–9). Such gods in fact are mere *daimonia*, subordinate deities, "demons" (1 Cor 10.20–21, nodding to Ps 95.5 LXX). Soon, however, Paul teaches, these cosmic powers—every *archē* and every *exousia* and every *dynamis*—will themselves acknowledge the god of Israel. The returning Christ will defeat them and establish the Kingdom of his father (1 Cor 15.24–27). In the End, at the Parousia, these superhuman beings, wherever they are—above the earth or upon the earth or below the earth—will "confess that Jesus is Lord, to the glory of God the Father" (Phil 2.10). Christ's return, Paul absolutely believed, besides raising the dead and transforming the living (1 Cor 15.23, 51–54), would bring about the *Götterdämmerung* of antiquity's cosmos.[57] In the ever-shortening meanwhile before the Kingdom came (Rom 13.11), those "in Christ" had only to endure this divine anger, and to wait.

The Jewish Jesus movement's nonnegotiable proviso to interested pagans—their absolute cessation of traditional worship—well explains the anger of their gods. And this divine anger in turn explains why Paul initially persecuted the movement, and why, later, he was persecuted—by Jews, by pagans whether Greek or Roman, and by lower cosmic gods—after joining the movement. We see this more clearly if we glance ahead to the second and third centuries, to a seemingly unrelated phenomenon: the pagan persecutions of ex-pagan Christians.

The fact that ancient gods ran in the blood meant that people were born into their obligations to particular deities—family gods, civic gods, and (a special case) imperial gods. If these pagans became Christ-followers, ceasing to honor their gods with cult, they risked alienating heaven and thereby endangered their city. This is why so many of the pre-Constantinian martyr stories turn upon the magistrates' efforts to encourage deferential compliance. At issue was not "belief"—everyone knew that these superhuman powers existed—but the public display of respect. "Hilarianus said: 'Offer the sacrifice for the welfare of the emperors.' 'I will not'" (*Perpetua* 6.3). "'Will you offer sacrifice?' the proconsul asked. 'No.' 'Offer sacrifice,' said the proconsul. 'I will not.' 'Do you attend to the air? Then offer sacrifice to the air!' 'No'" (*Pionius* 19). "'Swear by the genius of our lord the emperor.' 'I do not recognize the empire of this world'" (*Scillitan Martyrs* 5–6).[58]

Because these nonsacrificing pagans of the Christian movement refused to honor their gods, the Tiber might overflow or the Nile might not, the earth might move or the sky might not (Tertullian, *Apology* 40.2,2). "No rain, because of the Christians!" (Augustine, *City of God* 2.3). Divine wrath risked havoc. Gods struck with flood or famine, with drought and disease; they could level cities with earthquakes or allow foreign armies to invade. For this reason, uncoordinated local initiatives pre-250, and occasional imperial ones during the "crisis of the third century," attempted to coerce gentile Christians' cultic conformity. Whatever their new religious practices and preferences, these people in the eyes of their own family members, neighbors, and civic authorities were still obligated to the gods of the city and of the empire. It was as *deviant pagans* that these gentile Christians were coerced. These unprecedented persecutions were motivated, quite simply, by traditional piety—that is, by fear of the gods.[59]

A pagan's "becoming" a Jew—which in principle had the same effect in terms of sacrificing to the gods as becoming a Christ-follower did—was tolerated, if resented, because Judaism itself was a familiar point on the urban landscape. It was also widely recognized as both ancient and ancestral, the two criteria of respectable cult. No large-scale Jewish missions sought to turn gentiles into Jews, nor were significant numbers choosing to make such a transition, especially in light of the broad comfort zone afforded by "god-fearing." Those relatively few pagan men who would have effected this extreme degree of affiliation were by and large free to do so: majority culture—with whatever degree of resentment—had long tolerated such transitions, for which receiving circumcision was well known to be part of the process.

This fact, I think, provides the context for Paul's remarks in Galatians that "preaching circumcision" entailed no persecution: he meant, no persecution *by Roman authorities or by other pagans,* those other agents of his sorrows whom he lists in 2 Corinthians 11.[60] Acts offers a vivid and plausible picture of the sort of hostility that Paul in 2 Corinthians alludes to: as often as itinerant apostles were repudiated by their host synagogues, they were run out of town by irate pagans and occasionally punished by Roman magistrates who attempted to keep the peace.[61] In the eyes of majority culture, the ekklesia's "preaching circumcision" to fellow pagans would simply have produced Jewish proselytes. *Not* preaching circumcision but demanding cessation of traditional worship, by contrast, produced deviant pagans. And deviant pagans risked disrupting the *entente cordiale* between heaven and earth, the stability and security of the *pax deorum.*[62]

Their deviance was socially disruptive not only for the city, but also for the Christ-following pagans themselves. By these same criteria of respectability, antiquity and ancestry—and especially early on, in the middle decades of the first century—the gospel movement *for pagans* was, precisely, nothing.[63] (For other Jews, of course, the ekklesia was simply an internal—that is, a sectarian—option.) Not requiring complete, or ethnic, affiliation with Judaism via circumcision, insisting that native cults nonetheless be completely renounced, the early apostles walked these Christ-fearing pagans into a social and religious no-man's land. The apostles themselves as well as their gentiles may not have been too worried: after all, Christ was on the verge of returning, of gloriously summing up the ages, and of submitting the cosmos and everything in it to his divine father. But the pagan majority in these diaspora cities *was* worried. Divine anger could shatter the commonweal. Ancestral obligation, not particular beliefs—what people did, not what they thought—was what mattered.

In the early decades of the new movement, therefore, Jewish apostles in the Diaspora were targeted by anxious authorities—hence Paul's being beaten with rods three times, a Roman punishment (2 Cor 11.25)—precisely because they were raising pagan anxieties by drawing pagans away from their ancestral practices, *something that the synagogues with their god-fearers had never done.* For this same reason—the early movement's surprised and surprising success at turning pagans to the exclusive worship of the god of Israel—local diaspora synagogues subjected itinerant Jewish apostles to disciplinary flogging. Such a destabilizing and inflammatory message, radiating from the synagogue, could make the Jewish urban community itself the target of local anxieties and resentments. Alienating the gods put the city at risk;[64] alienating the pagan majority put the diaspora synagogue at risk—especially when the behavior occasioning that risk, an exclusive commitment to the god of Israel, was so universally and uniquely associated with Jews themselves.[65]

"The security of Jewish communities in diaspora cities depended above all on Jews not interfering in the civic life, not least the religious civic life, of the gentile majority."[66] And as Paul's list of woes suggests, any such perceived interference concerned Roman magistrates no less than local citizens (2 Cor 11.25–26). Consider, for the moment, a related though different consequence of Roman and local pagan anti-Jewish hostility: the casualty figures for mixed cities as a result of the outbreak of the First Revolt. In Caesarea, 20,000 Jews were killed; in Ptolemais, 2,000—the entire community; in Paul's home community, Damascus, variously 10,000 or 18,000 Jews were slain. Alexandria's convulsions in 38–41, and Antioch's in 40 and again in 66 and in 70, likewise attest to the vulnerability of resident Jewish communities to the violent hostility of local populations, especially if Roman authorities were estranged as well.[67] Alienating Rome and pagan neighbors, no less than alienating heaven, could entail severe consequences for Jews.

Until and unless we keep in view *all* of the social agents in Paul's world—not only its humans, but also its gods—we will misconstrue his reports of "persecution," both those he gave and those he got. Divine agents figure vividly in Paul's mission. They were a daily and an active (even aggressive) reality, dogging his work among their people. They were a practical consideration and a growing concern for those pagans, whether Romans or Greeks, whose families and cities were roiled—and, in their view, endangered—by the spread of the gospel. And they were key actors in the final apocalyptic battle, when their ultimate defeat and subjection to the god of Israel would be accomplished by the returning, triumphant Christ (1 Cor 15.24–26; Rom 8.18–30; Phil 2.10).

But as the years mounted between this proclamation and the Parousia, so too did the social complications between this movement's humans. How were the Jews and the gentiles of Christ's mixed assemblies to relate to each other as time, inextricably, continued to continue? By what means should and could ex-pagan pagans be integrated with greater social stability within these messianic ekklesiai? And how—especially in light of the increasing gentile presence—could the mission to Israel press forward?

By midcentury, these questions loomed large, for Paul as for others. For answers, he turned to "the pillars," to those who were apostles before him. Quitting his circuit in the Diaspora, he decided to seek the counsel of the founding *ekklēsia*. Paul left his mission and journeyed to the city of "the house," God's house. Paul went up to Jerusalem.

4

PAUL AND THE LAW

THE GOSPEL AND GENTILE CIRCUMCISION

From its inception, the gospel's mission to Israel in the Diaspora had absorbed sympathetic pagans without demanding that they receive circumcision. When they first began to join, these pagans had most likely seemed ancillary: the goal of the earliest mission, after all, had been to bring the good news to Israel. And the positive pagan response to the movement's apocalyptic message had most likely caught the early apostles off-guard: no plan for such a contingency was in place.[1] Accepting these gentiles *qua* gentiles into the ekklesia, however, would have cohered with local practice (*mutatis mutandis*), the host diaspora synagogue's quotidian custom of making a place for Judaizing pagans within the Jewish community. It also cohered with the general absence of any missionary program on the part of these diaspora communities. And finally, it cohered with the new movement's scripturally shaped apocalyptic commitments: pagans, once freed of their false gods, would enter into God's Kingdom as "eschatological gentiles," ex-pagan pagans, their inclusion now linked to Christ's return and to the impending redemption of Israel.

Neither quotidian practice nor prophetic tradition, then, can help us to account for the situation that Paul describes in Galatians 2. Some fourteen years after his first visit to Jerusalem, some seventeen years after receiving his call to join the Christ movement, Paul was prompted "by a revelation" to return (Gal 1.11–18, 2.1–2, thus c. 49 C.E.?). He wanted to place before "those of repute"—presumably, Peter/"Cephas," James, and John (cf. 2.9)—his gospel to the nations, "lest somehow I should be running or had run in vain" (2.2). In Galatians up to this point (2.3), Paul gives no further detail, whether about what he had been saying or why he now questioned it. Instead, and curiously, Paul reports that the Jerusalem leaders did not require his companion Titus to be circumcised "even though he was a Greek," that is, a gentile (2.3). *But why did the issue even arise?*

All we know about Titus from Paul's narration to this point in his letter is that he had come up from Antioch with Paul and Barnabas, that he was not Jewish, and perhaps that he too functioned as an apostle (Gal 2.1–3; Paul's references to him elsewhere reveal that Titus played a major role in organizing the collection for Jerusalem[2]). The "reputed pillars" before whom Paul testified were all Galilean Jews. They were thus presumably not accustomed to the mixed demography of synagogues in the Diaspora; and they were all three committed especially to the mission to other Jews (2.7–9). Perhaps, then, a gentile in a prominent leadership role within the movement made them uneasy. Perhaps it struck them as a potential liability vis-à-vis the movement's appeal to Israel. Perhaps for this reason, then, they suggested that Titus "become" a Jew. Whatever their motivation— Galatians is completely silent on this question—Paul insists, again without explanation, that the idea was dropped (v. 3).

Other Christ-following Jews ("false brothers" Paul calls them, Gal 2.4), just after this point, then intervened. Paul's furious review of their position implies that they urged circumcision, though whether for Titus in particular or as a criterion for gentile participation in the ekklesia more generally is unclear. Paul says only that they tried "to bring us into bondage" (Gal 2.4). (Paul himself, as "a Hebrew born to Hebrew parents," had been circumcised long ago, on his eighth day of life, Phil 3.5; his use of the first-person plural pronoun here registers his rhetorical identification with his current gentile addressees.) Why these other members of the movement came up with such a proposal—and even what their proposal actually was—Paul also passes over in silence.

But the "pillars" in any case once again rejected their idea (Gal 2.6–10). Instead, Paul relates, they acknowledged that Paul had been "entrusted with the gospel to the foreskins" (that is, to the gentiles), just as "Peter had been entrusted with the gospel of the circumcision" (that is, to the Jews; vv. 7–8). Paul, Barnabas, and the pillars all agree to this division of labor—that is, Paul and Barnabas to the nations (*ta ethnē*), they to the circumcision (v. 9)—with the request that the diaspora gentile mission contribute to the material support of the Jesus community in Jerusalem ("which indeed I was eager to do," 2.10). The question of Titus's receiving proselyte circumcision seemed definitively resolved.

Paul's letter then shifts to an account of a later sojourn of Peter's in Antioch. Initially eating in the mixed company of the Antiochene ekklesia,[3] Peter later withdrew once "certain men," whom Paul identifies as *tous ek peritomēs* (2.11–12), came from James. The RSV translates this phrase as "the circumcision party," implying that proselyte circumcision represented for these men some kind of "gentile policy." The text itself, however, states simply "the ones of [or from] circumcision," that is, "the Jews"—just as the phrase had been used twice, immediately preceding; and as the sentence continues about "the rest of the Jews" immediately following (*hoi loipoi Ioudaioi*, v. 13). And in any case, the issue at hand clearly concerned community eating—"before certain men came from James, he [Peter] *ate with* gentiles" (v. 12)—not circumcision as such.[4]

At this point, Paul states, he accused Peter of hypocrisy. Until the men from James arrived, Peter had been living "paganly" (*ethnikōs*) and not "Jewishly" (*Ioudaïkōs*); thereafter, says Paul, Peter sought to "compel" pagan Christ-followers "to Judaize" (*Ioudaïzein*, v. 14).

What was the problem? Was it eating with gentiles, that is, the uncircumcised? Though this episode is often read in this way, "uncircumcision" seems unlikely as the problem, for two reasons. First, the movement had long ago already embraced gentiles, providing that these people foreswore cult to their traditional gods; and, second, James, Peter, and John had already agreed back in Jerusalem to the principles of a gentile mission (2.7–10). Those scholars who speculate that these Jerusalem apostles had a problem with some putative gentile "impurity," further, should consider this fact: *if the source of such an impurity were idol-worship, these Christ-following gentiles, having foresworn their own gods, were no longer "carriers."* We will return to this question of "gentile impurity" at greater length in the following chapter. Readers should recall, however, that even gentiles who were *actively* pagan were welcomed both into the temple precincts in Jerusalem and into many diverse synagogue communities in the Diaspora. Proximity to gentiles as such—especially to these gentiles who had repudiated native deities—could hardly have been the problem.[5]

Many scholars nonetheless see the issue here as James's men insisting on circumcision: since these Antiochene Christ-following gentiles were not circumcised, so goes the argument, James's men would not eat with them, and neither would Peter and, eventually, Barnabas and the other (presumably native Antiochene) Jews. Such a situation would mean that James had essentially reneged on the agreement in Jerusalem (vv. 7–10)—a claim that Paul nowhere even hints at. Further, Paul continues throughout his missions to sponsor the "collection" for Jerusalem (v. 10; cf. 1 Cor 16.1–4; 2 Cor 8–9; Rom 15.25–29), which implies that he and James continued to have a positive working relationship. Finally, had Paul had a controversy with James specifically over the issue of gentile circumcision, we would expect some evidence of it, whether in Galatians or elsewhere; again, Paul says nothing of the sort. In brief, James's or his men's insisting on circumcision would have resulted in a real breach between Jerusalem and Paul. Evidence of such a breach is lacking—especially and most significantly in the epistle to the Galatians itself.

What then was the situation in Antioch that triggered the negative response of James's men, and on account of which Peter and "the rest of the Jews" withdrew? If the problem was not *who* ate together (the mix of Jewish and gentile Christ-followers), we are left with two other possibilities: *what* was eaten and *where* it was eaten—or perhaps a combination of both of these latter factors. Presumably, a problematic venue of consumption would be a gentile member's house. The Jerusalem apostles' withdrawal from Christ-following gentiles' households registered their discomfort with meeting in places that held images of foreign gods—a likelihood especially if the (female) gentile host was "married to an unbeliever" (1 Cor 7.12–13).[6] If the issue was what was consumed, the problem would have come from the food or, more likely, the wine. (Meat was extremely expensive and rarely on offer outside of major urban festivals and the banquets of the wealthy; wine, by contrast, was ubiquitous.[7]) James's men were uncomfortable with the ekklesia's meeting in gentile households. And it was Peter's support of James's men that prompted Paul to accuse him of "Judaizing."

In other words, the "Judaizing" in Antioch, as reported in Galatians 2, had nothing to do with urging circumcision on gentile members—despite Paul's deliberate rhetorical framing of the incident—and probably everything to do with avoiding pagan wine by/or avoiding pagan households. Recalling Paul's sangfroid about food offered to idols, we might speculate that that was the problem for the "men from James" here. Peter had originally followed a diaspora Jewish convention of eating and drinking in a private (though gentile) domestic setting as long as it did not scandalize another member of the community present (cf. 1 Cor 8 and 10, and Rom 14). But James's men, once they came, *were* scandalized. They declined to participate at such meals, and Peter himself withdrew. Why?

Again, Peter's concentration on the mission to Jews, combined with these Jerusalem apostles' discomfort in the diaspora setting, explains their actions clearly enough: in the view of James's men, consuming food and wine (which may have been offered to idols) *within a pagan household that itself would hold images of gods* was a further concession to gentile participation than they were prepared to make. Also, and naturally, they felt that such behavior would compromise the Jewish mission. (On the evidence, they were incorrect in their assessment: many Jews, as Paul himself and, initially, Peter reveal, were not put off by such contingencies.) Appealing to Peter's responsibility as apostle to the circumcised, James's men persuaded him to cease this practice too.[8]

Paul's anger surged not because James's men and Peter did not partake—that was, after all, Paul's own advice to believers in the Corinthian and Roman assemblies—but because Peter *withdrew* and *separated himself* (Gal 2.12). At issue was not the social company—Christ-following gentiles could eat with Christ-following Jews—but the *location* of these meals and, by extension, the status of what was consumed. Worse, from Paul's point of view, the combined authority of the visitors from Jerusalem and of Peter himself undermined Paul's own authority with the other, local Jewish members of Antioch's ekklesia, even Barnabas (2.13): from now on, members of this mixed community, when eating together, would meet only within Jewish households. This principled relocation of all community meals to Jewish households explains what Paul meant when he angrily accused Peter of having lived "paganly" before: Peter had previously participated at meals in gentile households. As for Peter's "compelling" Antiochene gentile members "to Judaize," Paul's word choice gives the measure of his rhetorical exaggerations: at worst, Peter was passive-aggressive, "compelling" these gentiles by "withdrawing."

As Paul's tirade continues in Galatians 2.13–21, the heat of his rhetoric obscures the point at which the frame of his address shifts from the past, when he challenged Peter, to the present, when he begins again to speak to his Galatian gentiles about the current crisis initiating this epistle. Other apostles, "preaching another gospel," have made inroads into Paul's communities (Gal 1.6–9). How does their message differ from Paul's? He states their differences clearly only toward the letter's end: evidently, his rivals advocate proselyte circumcision (5.2–3; cf. 6.12).

But long before he actually names this distinction between their respective gospels, Paul berates his congregations ("O foolish Galatians! Who has bewitched you?" 3.1). Pulsing binaries shape his invective: Law/faithfulness (2.15–17); spirit/flesh (3.3); blessing/curse (3.10–14); Law/promise (3.21–22); slaves/sons and, thus, heirs (4.3–7); slavery/freedom (4.21–31, 5.1).[9] The positive terms describe Paul's gospel: faithfulness, spirit, blessing, promise, sons, inheritance, freedom. Allegorically, this gospel is represented in Jewish scripture by Abraham's wife (Sarah), the mother of Isaac, whose status, like that of those Galatians who stay true to Paul's gospel, is as the son who inherits, the child of God's promise (4.26–28). The negative terms—slavery, flesh, works, curse, and, finally, circumcision—code for the gospel of Paul's competitors (allegorically represented by Hagar, 4.22–25). Their message, Paul asserts, undermines even salvation in Christ ("Now I, Paul, say to you that if you receive circumcision, Christ will be of no advantage to you," 5.2). Whoever they are—gentile proselytes themselves? Jewish Christ-followers, whether from the Diaspora or from Jerusalem?[10]—these other apostles, like the "false brethren" reviled in Galatians 2.4 and like the "dogs and mutilators of the flesh" abused in Philippians 3.2, think that gentiles committed to this messianic movement should "become" Jews. In other words, Paul aims his allegorizing polemic in Galatians against another form of Christ-mission, and not against

Judaism as such (which is the way that it has been read since the second century, and continues to be read to this day).[11]

In the nineteenth century, F. C. Baur argued that all of these various circumcising initiatives belonged to a single anti-Pauline movement coordinated from Jerusalem. This interpretive position, the so-called Tübingen school, has few defenders now.[12] In fact, we do not know the identities of these various other apostles, who could very well represent uncoordinated, disparate missions. All that we do know for certain is that Paul regarded them as direct threats to his own mission. (They may not have seen themselves as "opponents" at all.) For our purposes, however, their particular identities matter less than the position that they all seem to advocate. That provides our question here: why does the Jesus movement in the Diaspora produce our *only* clear evidence for Jewish circumcising missions to gentiles? What motivated them? Why, *midcentury*, do they suddenly and unambiguously appear?

Many commentators have seen in the circumcisers some sort of (supposedly) traditional Jewish view that gentiles in order to be saved—that is, to be included in God's Kingdom—must observe Torah.[13] These scholars are aided in this interpretation by misreading the prophets' vision of pagans "turning" to the god of Israel at the End of the Age as the pagans' "converting." In light of our review both of these Jewish traditions regarding eschatological gentiles, and of the diaspora synagogues' practice of welcoming sympathetic pagans rather than running missions to convert them, we know the opposite to be the case. Before midcentury, on the evidence of Paul's letters—that is to say, for the nearly twenty years of postresurrection missions—these messianic assemblies do not seem to have *ever* demanded proselyte circumcision as an entry requirement for (male) gentiles. Far from being traditionalists, then, the circumcisers were enacting a startling *novelty*, both within this young, Jewish messianic sect and *a fortiori* within Judaism.[14]

If we want to understand their motivations (which could have been various), we must set our speculations within the broader historical context of circumstances peculiar to the midcentury Jesus movement. What had changed between c. 30, the year of Jesus's death, and c. 49, the year of Paul's second meeting in Jerusalem (Gal 2.1)? Why in Jerusalem had "those of repute" even initially contemplated having Titus circumcised (2.3)? Why had the "false brethren" weighed in on the discussion (2.4)? Why, at some time several years later, had some other apostles started preaching circumcision to Paul's gentile assemblies in Galatia? What prompted circumcisers to reach out to the assembly of Christ in Philippi (Phil 3.2–9)?

Embedded in the chronology of these initiatives lies the answer to our question. By the time that a revelation prompted Paul to lay his gentile gospel before the pillars in Jerusalem (c. 49 C.E.? Gal 1.18, 2.1–2), he had been a member of a movement that had been preaching the imminent End of the Age *for almost a generation.* Among the community in Jerusalem, perhaps even among the "false" brethren, were those who had followed Jesus of Nazareth during his lifetime, and who accordingly had lived with this conviction for even longer. If Jesus's execution had crushed this hope, their experience of his resurrection had revived it. And as the Kingdom continued to tarry, some of them became apostles, taking this message out to Israel beyond Jerusalem, now linking the Kingdom's arrival to their expectation of Jesus's glorious, messianic return.[15]

Once in the mixed communities in coastal cities (Joppa, Caesarea) and in the Diaspora, these apostles received yet another confirmation of Jesus's prophetic timetable: pagans attached to synagogue communities now abandoned their idols to embrace the gospel, just as Isaiah had foretold they would. They welcomed these outliers in, providing they continued in their commitment to worship exclusively the god of Israel. Yet despite this unexpected confirmation of the nearness of the End-time, still the Kingdom did not come.

Time drags when you expect it to end. Put otherwise: all apocalyptic prophecies tend, of necessity, to have a short half-life. As the designated date fails, as the elusive End-time recedes, the prophecy itself can be undermined. If not reinterpreted, it runs the risk of being discredited altogether. Times are recalculated. Without ever arriving, fulfillment continues to loom. But in the ever-expanding meanwhile, those committed to the message have to find a way to carry on, to live their lives, to achieve a kind of day-to-day stability while retaining their commitment to a great and imminent change.[16]

Imagine the serial set points, still visible in our ancient evidence, that the mid-first-century assemblies of Christ had already lived through. If the Kingdom did not arrive in Jerusalem around Passover in the year 30, when Jesus and his followers went up for the holiday, then surely it would arrive soon thereafter, following Jesus's resurrection.[17] If not at that Passover, then surely by the following Pentecost/Shavuot (the story implicit in Acts 1–2). No? Then soon, especially once the message moved out into the Diaspora (c. 33?). Still not yet? Then at any time—"like a thief in the night" (1 Thes 5.2)—now that pagans too, through the gospel, were turning in numbers to Israel's god (c. 33–49?). No? When? Perhaps once the "full number" of the pagan nations was brought into Christ's assemblies (c. 56?; this is Paul's view, Rom 11.25–29). Or perhaps only once the ten tribes "lost" in the Diaspora were reunited with Israel-according-to-the-flesh (the view, perhaps, of Paul's circumcising competition).

"Where is the promise of his coming?" cried some weary insiders finally, in the early years of the second century. "For ever since the fathers fell asleep, all things have continued as they were from the beginning of creation" (2 Pet 3.4). Their impatience masked a silver lining, this Christian writer reassured his listeners. These very doubts, insisted "Peter," were themselves proof that "the last days" had arrived (3.3).

By the middle decade of the first century—the period of the factious meeting in Jerusalem, of the circumcising missions to Galatia, and of Paul's letters more generally—all of these early Christ-followers must have realized that their initial expectations had not been met. Jesus had not returned. The dead had not been raised. The evil powers of the age had not been defeated. Israel was not gathered in. The world still worshiped idols. The Kingdom had not come. Worse, the traditional prophetic scenario—from which the kerygma, in proclaiming a messiah crucified, raised, and returning, had already deviated—had gone awry. Though some pagans, disavowing their own gods, continued to join the movement in numbers, the mission to Jewish communities seems to have foundered (Rom 9 passim). What sense could be made of this unforeseen situation? How could the scattered communities of Christ, faced with these facts, continue to hope in the *euangelion*, to hold to their conviction that Jesus truly was the messiah, and to trust that his resurrection had indeed signaled the beginning of the turning of the age, the first fruits of the general resurrection, the proximity of his victorious return, the defeat of lower gods, the nearness of the End?

We see in Paul's terse review of his second trip to Jerusalem a variety of responses to the double disappointment of the Kingdom's continuing delay and the increasing indifference or (perhaps) hostility of diaspora Israel. One group of Jewish Christ-followers in Jerusalem—"false brethren" in Paul's estimate—had begun to insist that gentiles in the movement formally affiliate to Israel by receiving circumcision (Gal 2.4). Having only Paul's view of things, we must speculate on their rationale. Perhaps they adduced a causal connection between the Kingdom's delay and the worsening unreadiness of Israel. Perhaps—not unreasonably—they saw the increasing prominence of gentiles in the movement as a factor in Israel's resistance to the gospel. Perhaps they had in mind the circumcision not of all Christ-following gentiles, but only of those, like Titus, who held visible positions of leadership within diaspora communities. If Jews had to be reached, better the gospel's spokesmen were Jews; were Titus circumcised, he would be a Jew. For their conviction that Israel should be the movement's priority, these Christ-followers had no further to look than the teaching and the mission of Jesus himself and, behind him, to the tropes of prophetic eschatology in sacred scripture. Whatever their rationale, their motivation and their goal were, doubtless, to ensure the spread of the gospel.

But their proposal was denied. Jews other than Paul also objected to the idea of a mission to gentiles to turn them into Jews. We know the names of some: James, Peter, John, Barnabas (Gal 2.7–9). Did they deem such a mission too novel? Too unlikely in general to succeed? Impractical, in light of the nearness of the End? Nonsensical, given the ethnic embeddedness of cult? Again, we cannot know their reasons, because Paul does not say. What we do know is the effect of this decision: despite the stress points in the gospel message caused by the Kingdom's delay, the ancient, inclusive vision of Jewish apocalyptic traditions held. Pagans would be admitted into the Kingdom—and for the (as far as all of these apostles knew, brief) time remaining, into the ekklesia—with only the requirement (difficult enough) of "turning" to Israel's god. This meant no idols. But it also meant no circumcision: gentiles-in-Christ were to remain gentiles, up to and through the End (see Rom 15.9–12, 16.26–27).

Nevertheless, not even the prestige and the authority of the Jerusalem community's "pillars" were enough to discourage some diaspora Christ-followers from coupling the gospel message with a call to circumcision. By midcentury, as we see from Paul's letters, multiple diaspora missions were fracturing the movement over precisely this issue. What were these other apostles thinking?

Paul's enflamed hostility in Galatians makes the position of his perceived opponents difficult to reconstruct. They only want to make a good showing in the flesh, Paul tells his communities; these apostles are just trying to avoid being "persecuted" for the cross of Christ (Gal 6.12). If Paul's accusations bear any resemblance to reality, perhaps indeed the "persecution" that these other apostles sought to avoid was that pressure visited upon themselves by synagogue communities on account of their socially anomalous Christ-following pagans. Or perhaps they sought to spare these ex-pagan pagans, whose foreswearing of public cult to their own gods destabilized relations between heaven and earth, thus putting everyone—these apostles, their pagans, the synagogue, the larger city—at risk (see above, p. 89 ff.). Full assumption of a Jewish social identity— meaning, for males, circumcision—was a known, and thus a comparatively familiar, phenomenon. Were these Christ-following pagans to "become" Jews, they would at least gain a safe place to stand within the larger religious ecosystem of the Greco-Roman city. And they would be moved more directly under the protection of Israel's god. Circumcision, in other words, whatever social resentments it could trigger, might deflect the anger of pagans whether human or divine.

Or perhaps some of these apostles, prioritizing Israel's response to the gospel as the key event leading to the Kingdom, sought "Israel" among the nations quite literally. While the whole of the Jewish people could be designated "Israel," the term in scripture particularly designates the ten tribes of the north, those conquered—and scattered—by Assyria in 722 B.C.E. Thereafter, the Babylonian captivity notwithstanding, representatives of only three tribes—Judah, Benjamin, and Levi—remained in the south, in what would be called "Judea." As for the north, according to the prophet Hosea, it had "been mixed among the peoples" (*sunanamignumi*, Hos 7.8 LXX). "Israel"—that is, those in the north—"is swallowed up; they are now in the nations" (*ta ethnē*, Hos 8.8 LXX). Perhaps, then, in calling for (gentile) circumcision as a condition for entry into the ekklesia, these apostles were in their own minds achieving the reconstitution of the plenum of Israel. With all Israel regathered through the message of the messiah, the Kingdom could, finally, come (cf. Rom 11.26).[18]

Paul gives us so little to work with in terms of reconstructing these other apostles' principles and commitments that we can only speculate. The elaborate attention that he pays to Abraham in Galatians, however, suggests that Paul argues against these particular competitors' interpretation of the same figure. Abraham in Genesis was the primal patriarch of Israel. Scripture itself gave no reason for God's calling Abraham, but by Paul's period, late Second Temple biblical interpretation had filled in a backstory. Abraham's family had worshiped, and had even made, idols. Abraham, realizing that such worship was false, prayed instead to the true god, the Creator (Jub 11.17), who subsequently called upon Abraham to "leave your family and your country and your people and go to a land that I will show you" (Gen 12.1; cf. Jub 12.23). Abraham did not start out as a worshiper of God; he *became* one. Abraham, in short, was the model of the true "convert."[19]

Abraham and God begin their relationship in Genesis 12, with God's call, his vow of the Land, and his promise that, through Abraham, "all the nations will be blessed" (12.1–3). In Genesis 15, God promises that Abraham will have numberless descendants: "Look toward heaven and count the stars. . . . So shall be your *sperma*" ("seed," 15.5). And in Genesis 17, finally, promising that Abraham will be the father of many nations (*ethnē*), God requires circumcision of Abraham and of all the males of his family "throughout your generations" (17.12). It is only after Abraham's circumcision that his promised heir, Isaac, is conceived and born; and Isaac is himself sealed in the covenant when eight days old (21.1–4; Gen 17.12 had specified circumcision on the eighth day).

Did the gospel of these other apostles in Galatia lift up the example of Abraham's faithful obedience in Genesis 17, and so urge circumcision on

Paul's gentiles? They could make the case fairly. The story of Abraham's evolution had only begun with his renouncing idol-worship (Jub 11)—the same stage in which Paul's Christ-following gentiles remained. But the full arc of the story of the covenant between Abraham and God spanned from Genesis 12 to Genesis 17, and God's commanding circumcision. By following Abraham's example, these apostles perhaps urged, Paul's gentiles too would enter into the covenant, thus the redemption promised to Abraham's *sperma*, his descendants. By turning these many nations/*ethnē* into Jews, the gospel would sweep them into the redemption of Abraham's descendants vouchsafed by the returning Christ.

Some such argument would certainly help to explain Paul's own contravening emphases when retelling these same biblical stories to his Galatian communities. Paul focused instead on Genesis 15, and Abraham's *pistis*, his "fidelity to" or "confidence in" God's promise. It was through this *pistis* that Abraham was "righteoused" (Gal 3.6, citing Hab 2.4; I will explain this phrasing shortly), not through his circumcision. Paul's Galatians, too, insists Paul, had through Paul's work *already* been "righteoused," that is, pneumatically enabled to act righteously: in evidence, he points out that they had *already* received spirit. For what, then, did they need the "works of the Law" (3.2–4)?[20]

Besides, Paul continues, the *sperma* that God promised to Abraham were not Abraham's many descendants (the usual understanding of this singular collective noun, "seed"), but Christ himself (Gal 3.16). Hundreds of years before Sinai, Paul thus urged, gentile inclusion in Israel's redemption had already been promised to Abraham *through Christ* (3.17). And it is through Christ, not through circumcision, Paul continued, that gentiles are made not only into Abraham's sons; by their own *pistis*—steadfast confidence—in the divine promise, they become sons of God as well (3.26–29, sons and so heirs, that is, to God's Kingdom; cf. 4.5–7, the gentiles are adopted as sons). The gentiles, then, are, like Isaac, children of the promise and not—like those who receive his competitor's gospel—sons of Hagar the slave.[21]

Why is Paul so opposed to gentile circumcision—especially if, as he says here, he had once taught the same message himself (Gal 5.11)? What was so terrible about gentile circumcision that it even undid the benefit of

Christ (5.2)? Paul's intemperate language and agitated arguments are difficult to follow, and for this reason Galatians bathes the whole question in more heat than light. To grasp his thinking on the issue of gentile circumcision, we would perhaps do better to turn to Paul in a calmer moment.

One such moment occurred when he addressed his community in Corinth. Some of the men in Corinth's Christ-community had been circumcised at some point prior to Paul's visit there. Were they Jews by birth or by choice? Our interpretation depends on how we read what Paul says about circumcision there:

> Was someone called [that is, to the gospel] who was already circumcised? He should not seek to surgically remove his circumcision. Was someone called who was not circumcised [literally, "in foreskin"]? Let him not be circumcised. Circumcision is nothing and foreskin is nothing: what matters is keeping God's commandments. Everyone should remain as he was when called. (1 Cor 7.18–20)

Paul certainly knows that circumcision was indeed commanded of Israel. Elsewhere, he names the covenants with and promises to Abraham, Isaac, and Jacob, together with the giving of the Law, as among the abiding, defining, and divinely granted privileges of his own people (Rom 3.1–2, Jewish circumcision is of great value; 9.4–5, fleshly Israel's privileges; cf. 11.29, God's gifts and call to Israel are "irrevocable"). Indeed, these promises to "the fathers" form the foundation upon which salvation in Christ rests (Rom 15.8). Further, Paul boasts of his having been circumcised as an eight-day-old himself (Phil 3.5). *Jewish* circumcision, therefore, mattered very much to Paul, and (he believed) to Israel and to Israel's god: otherwise, Romans 3, 9–11, and 15 are inexplicable.[22]

In this passage in 1 Corinthians, then, Paul *cannot* be talking about God's commandments to Israel. Circumcision or foreskin does not matter, he must mean, specifically and only for *not*-Israel, that is, for gentiles. (In fact, this whole section of Paul's letter, 1 Cor 7, treats exclusively intra-*gentile* issues.) Thus, those who received Paul's gospel when "already circumcised" must be gentile proselytes, not born Jews. Yet Paul confusingly ties his statement that circumcision does *not* matter to these Christ-following gentiles' nonetheless "keeping God's commandments." God's commandments comprise Jewish law. So are gentiles to keep Jewish

Law—that is, God's Law—or not? Is the Law for gentiles a "curse" (Gal 3.13) or an obligation (Gal 5.14; 1 Cor 7.19; cf. Rom 13.8–10)? What, *with reference to gentiles*, does Paul mean by "Law"?

THE "LAW-FREE" MISSION AND THE "LAW-FREE" APOSTLE?

The Law's rhetorical valence varies wildly in Paul's epistles. Sometimes Law seems purely and powerfully negative: it is a curse (Gal 3.10), a form of enslavement (Gal 4 passim), a medium of sin, flesh, and death (Rom 7). Yet Law is also sometimes strongly positive. It is one of the abiding and God-given privileges of Israel (Rom 9.4); the measure for gentile Christ-followers of community love and the standard of decent community life (Rom 13.8–9; 1 Cor 7.19); a pathway to Christ (Rom 10.4). Faithfulness or steadfastness (*pistis*) upholds the Law (Rom 3.31). "The Law is holy, and the commandment is holy and just and good" (Rom 7.12). At one point Paul says that no one is made righteous (*dikaioutai*) before God by the Law (Gal 3.11); at another point he says that he himself was blameless with respect to just such righteousness (*dikaiosynē en nomōi*, "righteousness in the Law," Phil 3.6).

How can we read such seemingly inconsistent passages to make coherent sense of them? At least since the second century, gentile forms of Christianity have achieved theological coherence by minimizing Paul's positive statements about the Law and emphasizing his negative ones. The target of his invective against other apostles who urged proselyte circumcision on gentile Christ-followers thus shifted to Jews—and to Judaism—in general. From this reading Paul emerges as the champion of universalist ("spiritual") Christianity over particularist ("fleshly") Judaism. Paul the zealous Pharisee renounces the Law in coming over to Christ, becoming the preacher of grace and of justification by faith against the deadening works-righteousness of his old commitments. No longer Law-observant himself, Paul emerges as history's most famous convert, a sort of honorary gentile Christian *avant la lettre* and, at the same time and thereby, an ex- or anti-Jew. Indeed, some scholars still argue, Paul stands as history's first Christian theologian, urging a new faith that supersedes or subsumes the narrow *Ioudaïsmos* of his former allegiances.[23]

Imperial orthodoxy—that branch of the church that, after 312, was patronized by Constantine and that, after 395, was proactively enforced by Theodosian emperors—constructed its self-definition in part through opposition to the practice of Jewish ancestral customs. Christian Judaizing was criminalized, as were conversions to Judaism.[24] Jews themselves, increasingly marginalized in late Roman society, were subject to out-bursts of local violence fanned and directed by urban bishops, and villainized routinely in the toxic rhetoric of patristic theology *adversus Iudaeos*.[25] It was in these circumstances that the image of Paul the anti-Jew was set in cement.[26] Enhanced and rhetorically regirded during the Protestant Reformation (when "Jews" and especially "Pharisees" encoded the Roman Catholic enemies of the new reformed movements), the slo-gan "justification by faith" (as opposed to by Catholic, sacramental "works") became hard-wired in the biblical scholarship of Renaissance Protestant churchmen. This Paul—anti-Jewish, antiritual, anti-Torah—continues to flourish in academic publications, not least of all because he is so usable theologically. Indeed, this theological usability (hardly an accident, given the intellectual and social genealogy of Western Christendom) is sometimes even held up as a criterion of successful his-torical reconstruction.[27]

What if we place Paul, and his message to pagans, back into their mid-first-century apocalyptic Jewish context? How can we imagine Paul's per-sonal engagement with his own ancestral traditions *after* he joined the new Christ movement? And what does he advise his gentile Christ-following communities to do in terms of their own behavior vis-à-vis Jewish law?

+++

"Law-free" is a phrase habitually used to describe Paul's personal repu-diation of traditional Jewish practices, as well as Paul's core message to his gentiles. The phrase seems historically useful because it serves to signal, economically, *the* identifying characteristics of Paul's gentile mission: no to circumcision; no to "the works of the Law" (Sabbath, foodways, and especially circumcision); no to Torah; no to "Jewish ethnic pride." For Paul and for his communities, as one scholar has phrased it, the criterion of revelation and thus of salvation was "grace, not race."[28] And not only did Paul promote this message, so goes this interpretation; he himself embodied it. After the revelation of the risen Christ, Paul himself was "Law-free," dead to the Law (Gal 2.19).

This view of Paul's personal rejection of Jewish ancestral custom has proved remarkably enduring, stretching from earliest patristic theologies through to current modern and postmodern ones, uniting those scholars of the New Perspective with those of the "Two-Covenant" Perspective. No matter how various their interpretive frameworks, all of these scholars hold that Paul himself, in pursuit of his gentile mission, ceased to observe the "traditions of the fathers."[29]

Finally, this identification of "Christianity" with "Law-freeness"—an idea framed and mandated by Roman imperial law beginning in the late fourth century—is retrojected into the first century to explain the history of the earliest postresurrection movement itself. Why the split between the Hellenists and the Hebrews, as told in Acts? Hellenists (especially as represented by Stephen) were supposedly looser on the issue of Torah observance. Why did Paul persecute the ekklesia in Damascus (Gal 1.13)? Because its Jewish members mingled too closely with uncircumcised gentiles, an index of their own lax attitude toward the Law. And why eventually did Paul get as well as give synagogue punishment—"five times forty lashes less one" (2 Cor 11.24)? Because his own Law-freeness offended or enraged synagogue communities in the Diaspora, just as, pre-"conversion," such laxness had offended and enraged him. Paul the apostle was Paul the apostate.[30]

All of this supposed *Jewish* Law-freeness (of the Hellenists, or of the objects of Paul's "persecutions" in Damascus, or of Paul himself) rests on inferences drawn from *gentile* Christ-followers' "Law-freeness." Involvement in gentile ekklesiai implies, to many scholars, that these Jewish heralds of the gospel would themselves have ceased to observe Torah.

But this inference is wrong on two counts: that of Jewish Law-freeness in mixed Jewish institutions, and that of gentile Law-freeness in mixed Christ-following institutions.

To the inferred Jewish "Law-freeness" first. We encounter gentiles in many Jewish institutions: in the temple in Jerusalem, in numerous synagogues in the Diaspora, and as well in mixed ekklesiai, for example, in Antioch and in Damascus. But the pagan presence in the temple precincts tells us nothing about levels of Torah observance among the Jews also gathered there. And the pagan presence in diaspora synagogues tells us nothing about the level of Torah observance among synagogue Jews. (For that matter, the reverse social circumstance, Jews present in pagan institutions — the gymnasium, the odeon, the theater, the town council — also tells us nothing about Jewish levels of traditional observance.) So also, the pagan presence within the early ekklesiai tells us nothing about the level of Torah observance among the Jewish apostles and other Jewish Christ-followers also present.[31] And finally, then as now, there never was a single universal standard of Jewish practice against which to measure all the various other enactments and interpretations of Jewish tradition.[32]

In fact, a rather different question looms: If larger diaspora synagogue communities so often accommodated interested pagans, whence then their supposed offence at a small Jewish subgroup's doing exactly the same thing, *especially* given that the ekklesia's pagans, with respect to the Law, were *more* "kosher"?

More "kosher" how? What exactly *was* being demanded of Christ-following pagans? According to Paul, three things: (1) first and foremost, no more λατρεία to other, lower gods (*daimonia; stoicheia;* "the god of this age," 2 Cor 4.4). These pagans were to abandon the gods native to them, and to worship exclusively Paul's god, the god of Israel — a much more radical form of Judaizing than diaspora synagogues ever requested, much less required. (2) No "switching" ethnicities — that is, not "becoming" Jews (for males, by receiving circumcision). These *ethnē* had to remain exactly that, *ethnē*, albeit *ethnē* with a difference. This was because (3) since they had received holy spirit, these gentiles were to live as *hagioi*, "holy" or "sanctified" or "separated-out" *ethnē*, according to standards of community behavior described precisely in "the Law" (Gal 5.14; 1 Cor 7.19; Rom 2.13, 25–27 on doing the Law; 13.8–10, specifically referencing the Ten Commandments; 15.16 on gentile sanctification) — another radical form of Judaizing never demanded by the Temple or by the synagogue. Let us consider each of these criteria of gentile membership in turn.

Gods and the One God

Paul's polarizing rhetoric in Galatians masks the degree to which his, too, is a Judaizing gospel, *one that would have been readily recognized as such by his own contemporaries.*[33] "To Judaize" normally indicated an outsider's assumption of (some) Jewish customs. (It was an elastic term, and Paul for rhetorical purposes stretched it considerably in Galatians. When Paul accused the reclusive Peter of "forcing" gentile members of the local ekklesia "to Judaize," he evidently had in mind Peter's withdrawal as pressuring them to attend community meals solely in Jewish households, 2.14; above, p. 98.)

On a sliding scale of behaviors, Judaizing might range from a pagan's adding Israel's god to his native pantheon up to his fully committing to Jewish traditions as far as circumcision. Paul explicitly condemns both of these latter options: Continuing to worship *daimonia* was absolutely unacceptable ("Do not associate with anyone who calls himself a 'brother' if he . . . worships idols," 1 Cor 5.11; cf. 10.14–22). And proselyte circumcision, for him, was no less so (those who are circumcised are thereby "severed from Christ," Gal 5.4).

Yet Paul's core message to his gentiles about their behavior was not "Do not circumcise!" It was "No more *latreia* to lower gods!" His pagans were to worship strictly and only the *Jewish* god. They were to conform their new religious behavior precisely to the mandates of *Jewish* worship, the first table of the Jewish Law, the first two of Sinai's Ten Commandments: no other gods, and no idols (Exod 20.1; Deut 5.6). In this regard—withholding public acts of deference to powerful local deities—his gentiles were to act "as if" they were Jews without, for males, receiving circumcision. By radically, exclusively affiliating to Israel's god, Paul's *ethnē* were to assume that public behavior universally identified, by pagans and Jews alike, as uniquely Jewish. That is to say, Paul's gentiles—by the normal and contemporary definition of the term—Judaized.[34]

Ethnic Distinctions

New Testament scholars often see Paul's position on circumcision as a bold spiritualizing and universalizing of the gospel message. Peter, James, and the circumcising apostles are, in this view, "exclusivist," "too Jewish," stuck in an "old" paradigm, thinking small, lacking Paul's scope. Paul, by teaching against circumcision, thought expansively, supposedly erasing the markers of "ethnic difference."

But Paul nowhere in his letters says anything about (much less against) Jews circumcising their own sons, and he explicitly preaches against epispasm (the surgical "making a foreskin" derided in 1 Macc 1.15; cf. 1 Cor 7.18, *mē epispasthō*).[35] He opposed circumcision *for gentiles*, not for Jews.[36] Paul expressed no view on Jewish circumcision, most likely because he assumed one: Jews who honored their ancestral customs circumcised their sons into the covenant on the eighth day (cf. Phil 3.5). If Israel is to remain Israel—rejoicing with the gentiles (Rom 15.10)—then why would Israel cease enacting their covenant with the god of their redemption? Paul's acutely foreshortened timeframe, further, afforded him very little reason to think in terms of a next generation: outside of a brief mention in 1 Corinthians 7.14, on the status of families where only one pagan parent was a Christ-follower, Paul nowhere discusses children at all.[37] And, finally, the fact that all of his extant letters are addressed solely to gentile assemblies gives us no opportunity to hear him discourse on Jewish practice by Jews.

Flip the question: why would the Jewish observance of Jewish ancestral practices by Christ-following Jews *not* have continued within the ekklesia, by Paul no less than by others? What we with historical retrospect see as "earliest Christianity" was in its own generation—which Christ-followers were convinced was history's last generation—a sect of Judaism. As Christ-followers, these Jews—again, Paul emphatically included—continued to worship the Jewish god, to draw on Jewish scriptures, and to proclaim the Jewish message that the god of Israel's anointed son was coming to establish that god's Kingdom. And that Kingdom was to contain not only gentiles, but also Israel, defined as that people set apart by God by his Laws (e.g., Lev 20.22–24). Why then think that these

Christ-following Jews would cease living according to their own ancestral traditions, circumcision included, while they awaited the triumphant return of their messiah?[38]

Further: Paul's emphatic insistence that pagan Christ-followers *not* be circumcised in fact *reinscribes* this distinction *kata sarka* between "Israel" and "the nations." Israel alone (whether within the movement or without) shared a covenant relationship with their god, represented and instantiated by flesh-circumcision; and this flesh-circumcision was to express, inspire, and reinforce heart-circumcision (e.g., Lev 12.4, 26.41; Deut 10.16, 30.6). Pagans in general had neither covenantal flesh- nor heart-circumcision (though we will need to explore this observation more carefully when we consider Romans 2). Christ-following pagans, finally, may have "heart-circumcision," but they still do not (or, according to Paul, they should not) have flesh-circumcision. In short: Jews and Greeks, men and women, the enslaved and the free might all be "one in Christ Jesus" (Gal 3.28), that is, *kata pneuma*, "in spirit" (an idea that we'll explore shortly); but *kata sarka* they all remained distinct, both socially and ethnically. Or, to quote Paul, Jews are distinct from gentiles "by nature" (*physei*, Gal 2.15).

Thus we see that Paul maintains, and nowhere erases, the distinction between Israel and the nations; nor does he redefine "Israel" so that it means (and means only) the followers of Christ.[39] What his rhetoric does do, intriguingly, is erase the distinctions between and among "the nations" themselves. The *goyim/ethnē* of the Jewish scriptures had been manifold and individuated: Egyptians, Philistines, and Canaanites; Ammonites, Moabites, Edomites (e.g., Deut 23.4–8). The *ethnē* of Pauline discourse, by contrast, do not break down this way, that is, as ethnically specific kinship groups (though once Paul does distinguish between "Greeks" and "barbarians," meaning "all gentiles," Rom 1.14). Rather, Paul's *ethnē* function as a mass of undifferentiated "foreskinned" idol-worshipers (if outside the movement) or of "foreskinned" ex-idol-worshipers (if within).

For Paul, all humanity except for Israel are *ethnē*. This sharply dichotomized couplet, Israel/*ethnē*, marks out a developmental stage within Jewish ethnic discourse between scripture's many different "nations" and the individualized *goy* (a non-Jewish male) of the later rabbis.[40] Whence

Paul's dichotomizing rhetoric of ethnicity? From the prophetic traditions of apocalyptic eschatology that serve as his sources. We might discern this more clearly by focusing on that other corresponding and defining dimension of ethnicity in the ancient world: the ethnicity not of humans, but of gods.

Peoples, lands, languages, gods: we have seen how this collection of ethnic identifiers shaped ancient discourse, whether Jewish or pagan, about peoplehood (p. 35 above). In Jewish scriptures, these organizing principles appear framed in the primordial past, when Genesis 10 narrates the descent and distribution of the families sprung from Noah, according to "their lands, according to their tongues, after their families, in their nations" (Gen 10.5, 20, 31–32). "Gods" (or at least superhuman powers) join this mix in Deuteronomy 32.8, which refers to this primordial moment in human social time: "When God apportioned the nations, when he divided humanity, he fixed the boundaries of the peoples according to the number of gods."[41]

Israel's god, in Jewish tradition, stands at the apex of divinity. The other *elohim* bow down to him; he alone is supreme. But his universality is ethnically inflected: this god chooses Israel from among all the other nations, setting them apart by giving them his *torah*, "teaching." He speaks to Israel's patriarchs and prophets in Hebrew. He is the "father" of Israel, and of Israel's Davidic kings. He, too, keeps the Sabbath, accompanied by two orders of circumcised angels. His earthly dwelling-place is in Jerusalem, at the temple; and it is in Jerusalem, around his temple, that his Kingdom will come. This god is the source of Israel's election and the divine partner in their covenant. In brief, according to Jewish traditions, Israel's god is himself "Jewish."[42]

This divine ethnicity, refracted through the lens of prophetic eschatology, reveals and highlights three interconnected ideas: first, that Israel alone has "known" God; second, that the other nations have not known God; third, that at the End, these nations, too, will know God. Despite its insistence on God's ethnicity, in other words, Jewish scripture also presses this larger claim peculiar to its religious culture: Israel's god is *also* the god of other ethnic groups, "the god of the *ethnē* also," as Paul says in Romans 3.29. *But the nations by and large will know this only at the End.*

Seen in this light, the establishment of the Kingdom is quite literally the Jewish god's ultimate act of cross-ethnic outreach.

This foretold divine cross-ethnic outreach was already (and awkwardly) beginning to occur, various apostles were convinced, in the intense interregnum between Jesus's resurrection and his return. The irruption of eschatology into the quotidian complicated questions of the other nations' relation to the (ethnically specific) Law(s) of Israel's god. We will examine this issue momentarily. The point to bear in mind here is that, whether for Isaiah or for Paul, *the more intense the pitch of apocalyptic expectation, the greater the contrast between Israel and the nations.* Why? Because the *narrative* function of the nations in these traditions is precisely to represent *not*-Israel, all those other peoples who have not known God and who do not know God. Eschatological redemption emphasizes and intensifies this high contrast between Israel (knowing God) and everyone else (not knowing God until the End). The sharp us–them distinction, to phrase this slightly differently, is drawn on *theological* lines and, therefore, articulates ethnic lines as well. Consider the echo of the Table of Nations (Gen 10) in Isaiah 66.18–20:

> . . . I am coming to gather all the nations and tongues, and they will come and see my glory. . . . From them I will send survivors to the nations . . . to the distant islands that have neither heard my fame nor seen my glory. And they shall declare my glory among the nations. And they shall bring all your brothers from all the nations as an offering to the Lord . . . to my holy mountain, Jerusalem, says YHWH.

The ethnic-theological difference between Israel and the nations, the nations' ignorance of the true god, is what binds all of these other *ethnē* together into one undifferentiated mass of lumpen idolators. In the End, for Isaiah as for Paul, this sharp dichotomy is resolved *theologically,* but *not ethnically*: Israel remains Israel, the nations remain the nations (cf. Isa 11.10; Rom 15.10). Paul, convinced that he lived in the very last days, and convinced no less of the importance of his own role in bringing the *ethnē* to the worship of the god of Israel, emphasizes and dichotomizes this ethnic difference even more than does Isaiah.

But Paul's circumstances are also different from those of his scriptural sources. His mission (and those of others, such as whoever first

established the community at Rome) had *already* generated "eschatological gentiles" in advance of the apocalyptic End. Paul's discourse of ethnic
dichotomizing accordingly left him with a conundrum: he—like us—has
no good term for the ekklesia's non-Jewish ex-idol-worshipers. They are
not "converts"/*prosēlytoi*: the only thing for these pagans to "convert" to in
the mid-first century was Judaism, an idea that Paul heatedly rejects. And
yet they are not "god-fearers"—at least, fumes Paul, they had better not
be!—affiliated with Jewish communities and yet still involved with their
own gods as well. Nor are they "Christians"—a term, and arguably a concept, that had yet to be invented.[43] So what word appropriately names
these people? Paul stumbles around: they are ex-pagans/ex-gentiles
("When you were *ethnē*," 1 Cor 12.2), and yet they are still pagans/still
gentiles ("Now I am speaking to you *ethnē*," Rom 11.13). Sometimes he
calls them *hagioi*, "holy" or "separated-out" ones; at other times *adelphoi*,
brothers.[44] But if we take the last chapters of Romans as in some sense
Paul's final word, *ethnē* remains his term of choice (15.8–12, 16–18, 27;
16.4, the *ekklesiai tōn ethnōn*; 16.26).[45]

Again, the normal and normative ethnic embeddedness of divinity in
the ancient Mediterranean, where gods and peoples form family groups,
meant that Paul affirmed a paradox: the nations who in Christ turn from
their own gods are to worship Israel's god in Jewish ways (no other gods;
no images); but they are nonetheless still *not*-Israel. They are thus not
responsible to and for Jewish Law. And yet, Paul also insists, they are.

The Law, the Ethnē, and "Justification by Faith"

Paul's *ethnē*-in-Christ are not only enjoined to Judaize to the extent
that they commit to the worship of Israel's god alone and eschew idol-
worship. They also, according to Paul, must behave toward each other in
such a way that they fulfill the Law.

Paul states as much obliquely, when he exhorts his communities to
live according to ethics idealized by Jews about Jews (many of the standards of which were also shared by the pagan ethicists). Monogamous
marriages, sexual self-discipline within marriage, love of community,
community self-governance, support for the poor (said especially with

reference to the collection for Jerusalem)—Paul's exhortations sound all
these notes. Elsewhere, Paul cites from Torah explicitly to drive home
social and ethical instruction: Israel's experience of the Golden Calf was
a warning to the Corinthians about the dangers of idol-worship and *porneia* (1 Cor 10.6–14); Moses's instructions about not harnessing oxen
threshing grain encoded a message about community support for itinerant apostles (1 Cor 9.8–11); God's instruction in Leviticus to love the
neighbor helps the *ethnē* to fulfill "the whole Law" (Gal 5.14; cf. Rom
13.10); women in community are to keep silent and be subordinate "even
as the Law says" (1 Cor 14.34). And finally, Paul forthrightly and pointedly
urges Christ-followers to honor the commandments of the Law's second
table: no adultery, no murder, no theft, no coveting; loving the neighbor
fulfills the Law (Rom 13.8, 10; cf. Gal 5.14; 1 Cor 7.19).

Paul's invocation of the Law's second table connects him, as we have
seen, with the message of John the Baptizer and of Jesus. These two had
called Jews to repent and return to the Torah in preparation for the imminent End of Days; and the Ten Commandments, according both to
Josephus and to the gospels, had featured prominently in their missions.[46]
In these Greek traditions about John and Jesus, the two words "piety"
(εὐσέβεια, behavior toward God) and "justice" or "righteousness"
(δικαιοσύνη, behavior toward people) had encoded Sinai's ten "Laws."

Eusebeia/Piety toward God	*Dikaiosynē*/Justice toward Others
1. No other gods	6. No murder
2. No graven images (idols)	7. No adultery
3. No abuse of God's name	8. No theft
4. Keep the Sabbath	9. No lying
5. Honor parents	10. No coveting

Speaking to Christ-following gentiles, Paul draws instruction from the
first and second Laws of the first table, and he specifically invokes Laws
6, 7, 8, and 10 from the second, though in Romans 13.9, where this list
occurs, he also invokes all the rest of Torah—"any other commandment"—
as well. And, as we have seen, he elsewhere quotes Leviticus 19.18 on
loving the neighbor as "fulfilling the whole Law." Note too that Paul's
Torah-based instruction does not break down along a supposed divide

between "ethical law" and "ritual law." While the laws of the second table do indeed concern social justice, "worship"—and specifically making or not making offerings before images—is what moderns would designate *ritual* behavior.[47] Paul urges both—or, perhaps better, for Paul the way that one worships and what god one worships stand on an immediate continuum with how one behaves, a point that he makes explicitly in his condemnation of idolatry in Romans 1.18–32, and the ways that the worship of idols leads to "all manner of wickedness" (v. 29).

This simple exercise of attending to his positive remarks on Torah reveals the inadequacy of characterizing Paul's mission as "Law-free." But more than this, Paul's positive stance toward gentile Torah observance also gives us some purchase in interpreting a key word-package in his language *about* the Law: *dikaiosynē*, "justice/righteousness," and its relation to *pistis*, too often translated as "faith" or "belief." We do best to situate these words, and the concept cluster that they evoke, back into the circumstances of Paul's mission.

When Paul called his pagans from the worship of their own gods to an exclusive commitment to the god of Israel, these people were not *return*ing to their native god and their native ancestral laws (the Jewish meaning of μετάνοια, "repentance"), but *turning to* him for the first time (ἐπιστρέφω in various forms, e.g., 1 Thes 1.9: "You turned [*epestrépsate*] to God from idols to serve a living and true god"). "Indeed there are many gods and many lords," Paul writes to his community in Corinth, "yet *for us* there is one god, the Father . . . and one lord, Jesus Christ" (1 Cor 8.5–6).

Of course Paul, and Paul's pagan assemblies, had then to cope with the anger of these lower gods, who lashed back. But they were fortified by holy πνεῦμα, "spirit," communicated to them through immersion into Christ's death and resurrection (Rom 8.9–17). These committed pagans, like Paul himself, were accordingly enabled by that spirit to utter prophecies, to speak in tongues, to heal, and to discern between spirits (1 Cor 12.1–11), validated in their apocalyptic convictions by these very charismata. With πίστις ("confidence" or "steadfastness") they awaited Christ's imminent return, his defeat of these hostile powers, the transformation of the quick and the dead, and the redemption of creation (including, perhaps, of their former gods; Phil 2.10–11; Rom 8.22). Scripture had foreseen that God would δικαιοῖ τὰ ἔθνη ἐκ πίστεως (Gal 3.8 RSV: "justify the gentiles by faith"), and now, through Christ, he had. In the brief time remaining, these pagans ἐν Χριστῷ were enabled by and through their πίστις in Christ, and through God's (or Christ's) πνεῦμα infused in them, to fulfill the Law and to conduct community life in accordance with it (e.g., Gal 5.13–25). Though not "under the Law" (Gal 5.18), these inspirited gentiles can now fulfill the Law. They were δικαιωθέντες ἐκ πίστεως (Rom 5:1). What does Paul mean by this phrase?

The connotations of our modern English words impede translation of our ancient Greek texts, which depend on nuanced construals of *pistis* and *dikaiosynē*, both in their nominal forms (as here) and especially in their verbal forms. "Faith" as a translation of *pistis*, for example, cannot help but be refracted through the prism of a long Christian cultural history that runs at least from Tertullian (*credo quia absurdum*) to Kierkegaard. It has come to imply all sorts of psychological inner states concerning authenticity or sincerity or intensity of "belief." As we have noted, however, πίστις, and its Latin equivalent *fides*, in antiquity connoted "steadfastness" or "conviction" or "loyalty." Thus, in Romans 1.5, Paul couples *pistis* with "obedience": Paul's apostleship is meant to bring pagans to the "obedience of 'commitment'" to the gospel. (Compare the different nuance of "obedience of faith"—and certainly not "of 'the' faith," as given in the RSV: the Greek has no article.) "Salvation is now nearer to us," he tells these Christ-following pagans in Rome, "than when we ἐπιστεύσαμεν" (Rom 13.11). Standard English versions give for this sentence "than when we first believed." A rendering closer to Paul's tone and meaning would be: "Salvation is nearer to us now than it was when we first *became convinced*" (cf. Rom 13.11 RSV).[48]

Dikaiosynē and its related verbal forms present even more daunting challenges to English, which lacks much-needed precision.[49] English words for the term often wander between "justification"/"being justified" and "righteousness"/"being made righteous." These translations too often conjure the forensic theologizing of late medieval (and especially Lutheran) piety, wherein God as a gift—that is, through grace—renders the sinner "righteous" despite his sin (the Lutheran *simul iustus et peccator*, "at once just and a sinner"). In this interpretation, he is "justified"/"made righteous" by and through his "faith" in Christ, or by his faith in the gospel, achieving salvation *through* "faith" *as opposed to* by "works." This reading invariably places its emphasis on the individual and his transition from condemnation/sin to salvation/grace. In this way, "Torah" comes to serve as the antipode to "Christ," "Law" to "grace," "Judaism" to "Christianity."[50]

These oppositions, conjured by the West's long cultural and theological habit of looking at Judaism as somehow Christianity's opposite, dissolve once we place our key terms back into their mid-first-century context. *Dikaiosynē* has a community nexus for Paul: it resonates with the second table of the Law and thus with ideas about the individual's behavior within a divinely mandated and established community context of *social justice*. We best capture the meaning of Paul's usages of "justification"/ "being righteoused" and of "faith," then, by translating and interpreting while holding in mind the Ten Commandments, most specifically the Law's second table.

When Paul's pagans adhered steadfastly to the good news brought by his message (the RSV's "believed in the gospel"), they ceased worshiping their own gods and committed themselves to the god of Israel through his son (the cluster of ideas around πιστεύω, "to be steadfast"). Made right by God toward God, they were likewise pneumatically enabled to make right toward each other by acting rightly toward each other — "not like the ἔθνη who do not know God" (1 Thes 4.5; cf. Rom 1.18–32 and 13.13–14, for "typically pagan" bad behaviors). Their πίστις in the gospel (confidence that Christ had died, been raised, and was soon coming back) righteoused these ex-pagan pagans "as a gift" (χάριτι, "by grace"), that is, by eschatological fiat of God through Christ. Accordingly, they could now "fulfill the Law," most specifically the Law's second table, δικαιοσύνη, "justice/ rightness toward others."

Thus in the same place where Paul reviews the sins of the flesh that Christ-following pagans have left behind (Rom 13.13–14), and where he speaks urgently of the impending End (13.11–12), he also lists the commandments of the second table (13.9–10). "Righteoused" pagans, spirit-filled, accordingly "have peace with God" (5.1), being "reconciled" with him, thus delivered from his coming "wrath" (5.9–11; cf. 1 Thes 1.4–5,

9–10; 2 Cor 5.18–21). Enabled by their steadfast commitment to and trust in Christ and, through him, to and in the good news of God's coming Kingdom, these inspirited ex-pagan gentiles can now act "rightly" toward their fellows in community. *This* is what Paul meant by δικαιωθέντες ἐκ πίστεως, the RSV's "justified by faith."

THE LAW'S CURSE

Paul praises the Law, glories in its mandates, rejoices in its privilege, and urges its standards of behavior both toward God and toward fellow Christ-followers on his gentile communities. Neither Paul himself, nor his mission, nor his ekklesiai, accordingly, can be simply described as "Law-free." But if this is the case, what then are we to make of all his negative statements about the Law?

Posing the question means wading into another hermeneutical quagmire. Paul's negative statements about the Law have long been read as condemnations of Judaism *tout court*, whether because the Jewish understanding of Law itself was (or is) supposedly spiritually deadening (the antilegalist interpretation), or because the Jews' keeping Jewish Law led to "pride" and ethnic separatism (the anti-ethnicity interpretation, associated with the so-called New Perspective on Paul).[51]

Some scholars, focusing on this issue of ethnicity, have rotated it, attending not to Paul's own identity (and, thus, taking his negative statements about Jewish Law as condemnation of Jewish traditions), but rather to that of his addressees. *All* of the assemblies to which Paul writes are comprised primarily if not exclusively of Christ-following ex-pagan pagans: in Thessalonica (a group who just turned to God from idols, 1 Thes 1.9), in Corinth (much concerned with close relations between Christ-following pagans and pagans outside of the ekklesia), in Galatia (whose members "formerly did not know God," 4.8; also, only non-Jews could be candidates for adult circumcision), in Philippi (a similar issue, Phil 3.2), and finally—a group he did not found and had not yet visited— in Rome (addressed specifically as *ethnē*, 1.6, 13 and 11.13). Perhaps, then, when Paul in his letters speaks negatively about the Law he speaks *specifically with respect to gentiles*, not with respect to Jews.[52]

For any of these readings, Romans 7.7–25 represents a particularly fraught passage. In this part of his letter, addressing a community that he does not yet know, Paul frames the Law with a rhetorical roster featuring flesh, death, and enslavement to sin. The "I" of this passage—a Jewish sinner, pre-Christ? a pagan sinner, pre-Christ? Paul himself, whether before his call to be an apostle or perhaps even after?—laments his inability to keep the commandment, and to escape the power of sin. The speaker on the one hand defends the goodness of the Law: "The Law is holy, and the commandment is holy and just and good" (7.12); "The Law is spiritual, but I am fleshly, sold under sin" (7.14); "If I do what I do not want, I agree that the Law is good" (7.16). But at the same time, the speaker seems to assert that the Law is part of the problem—enslavement to sin—not part of the solution ("Apart from the Law, sin lies dead," 7.8). Or is he talking about two different "laws," one the Law of God, which he serves with his mind, and the other "the law of sin," which he serves with his flesh (7.25)?

The persona that we ascribe to the "I" of this passage immediately affects how we read the rest. Is Paul speaking for himself? If we are tempted to think so, we must also consider the high marks that Paul gives himself elsewhere in terms of his own performance of and commitment to Jewish tradition: circumcised on the eighth day (to his parents' credit, not his own!), Pharisaic in terms of orientation toward the interpretation of scripture, "blameless" with respect to *dikaiosynēn tēn en nomōi*, "right behavior in the Law" (Phil 3.4–5), exceptionally advanced and "extremely zealous for the ancestral traditions" (Gal 1.14). This is the voice of a robust conscience, not of someone languishing, morally paralyzed, "under the Law."[53]

Who then is Paul's "I"? In view of the ascribed readers of Romans, the *ethnē* of 1.6 (Paul's apostleship is to "all the pagans/gentiles/nations, including you") and of 11.13 ("Now, I am speaking to you pagans/gentiles"), Paul's first-person pronoun here in chapter 7 may be directed at gentiles, too. Such a device, *prosopopoeia*, or "speech in character," was in antiquity a common rhetorical device by which the speaker presented the thought of a fictive character, the better to strengthen or to illustrate the speaker's own point(s).[54] In other words, Paul's "I" in this passage functions rhetorically to impersonate such an individual as representative of Paul's addressed audience: the non-Jew who struggles to live according to Jewish ancestral customs.

Reading Romans 7 in light of this ancient and well-known mode of dramatized instruction transforms the chapter. Rather than serving as a psychologizing portrait of an individual's inner turmoil (Paul's, or anyone else's, supposed torment) before the impossible demands of Jewish law, or as a summary statement of a universal human condition (moral paralysis resolved only through grace, that is, belief in Christ), Romans 7 speaks directly and specifically to *gentile* moral struggles, particularly with problems of self-mastery or self-control.[55] Paul's point in this snarled passage, then, would not be to lament some general impossibility of living according to the precepts of Jewish Law (especially since, by his own lights, he himself had succeeded amply in this effort, Phil 3.6), but rather to lament the futility of a non-Christ-following gentile's efforts to do so. Gentiles *can* fulfill (some) Jewish law, Paul urges, and they *should*. But, as he emphasizes here and elsewhere, gentiles are enabled to do so *solely through Christ* (Rom 7.25), or through the spirit of God or of Christ (8.1–11).

But why would Paul think that gentiles apart from Christ were so morally hamstrung? Here we need to step back and look at the two other topics that attract Paul's most negative comments: pagan behavior generally, and Jewish law *with reference to* pagan behavior.

For Paul as for the greater number of biblical and postbiblical traditions that he draws on, pagans are "sinners" (Ἡμεῖς φύσει Ἰουδαῖοι καὶ οὐκ ἐξ ἐθνῶν ἁμαρτωλοίν, Gal 2.15; this can be read as implying that gentiles are sinners "by nature" as well). Jewish antipagan rhetoric lavishes lurid details on its descriptions of pagan behaviors. Pagans notoriously indulge in the "works of the flesh": fornication, impurity, licentiousness, idol-worship, sorcery, enmity, strife, jealousy, anger, rivalries, divisiveness, envy, drunken carousing (Gal 5.19–21). Corinth, prior to receiving Paul's message, had teemed with "fornicators, idol-worshipers, adulterers, sexual exploiters and effeminates, thieves, greedy ones, drunkards, revilers, robbers" ("And such were some of you!" 1 Cor 6.9–10).[56] Pagan "works of darkness" include drunkenness, debauchery, licentiousness, quarreling, and jealousy (Rom 13.12–13). Left to their own devices, pagans degrade themselves with passions and with demeaning sexual acts; their minds are debased, their ways malicious, their societies violent, their families distempered (Rom 1.18–32). All of these social and sexual sins are the varied expression of a deeper, graver error: rather than worship the Creator—that is, the Jewish god—pagans adore stars, planets, and, finally, man-made images. "Since they did not see fit to acknowledge God, God gave them up to a base mind and to indecent conduct" (Rom 1.28). The fundamental pagan sin was idolatry. From that, all the rest followed.[57]

But surely there could be such a thing as a morally good gentile? A broad range of ancient Jewish thinkers from the Hellenistic period on through to the later rabbis thought there could be. Within these discussions, a gentile's moral goodness might manifest itself as his acknowledgment that the Jewish god is the highest god; or he might adapt and adopt some Jewish ancestral practices; or he might admire Jewish learning and, thus, Jewish moral and philosophical excellence; or he might simply act in ways that accord with Jewish Law (as Paul states in Rom 2.26–29). In other words, the Jewish idea of a "good gentile" correlates positively in these discussions with what we might otherwise term "Judaizing."[58]

It is on this point—namely, that the only good gentile is a Judaizing gentile—that Paul *in a very specific way* stands out. For Paul, as we have just seen, the gentile-in-Christ *should* Judaize, even radically Judaize. That is, he should worship the Jewish god alone; he should cease attending to other, lower gods; he should in various ways within the ekklesia "fulfill the Law." But a Judaizing gentile *without* Christ, says Paul in Romans 7, *cannot* successfully Judaize—that is, *he is not able to Judaize*, try as he might. For such a gentile, the Law only points out how much and in what ways he sins. He *cannot* act as he wants to, as he knows that he should. The Law points the way, but he cannot follow. The conflicted "I" of Romans 7 is the pagan who attempts to Judaize, that is, to fulfill the Law, *without* Christ.[59] He *can* overcome his difficulties, but only *in* Christ, through his *pistis*, his confidence in or fidelity toward Christ. (We will see how and why this is so in the final chapter.) "Wretched man that I am! Who will deliver me from this body of death?" laments the rhetorical Judaizing pagan of Romans 7. "Thanks be to God, through Jesus Christ our Lord!" (Rom 7.24–25).

Taking this as our point of reference—that the lament in Romans 7 enacts the experience of the gentile who, without Christ, attempts unsuccessfully to Judaize and so languishes under the Law—we can begin to make sense of Paul's negative statements without ignoring, dismissing, or devaluing all of his other, ringingly positive statements about the Law. Paul *wants* gentiles to Judaize, that is, to act in (some) Jewish ways. He *urges* his gentiles-in-Christ to act Jewishly, specifically with respect to cultic and ethical behaviors. *But the gentile who tries to Judaize without Christ, he warns, will only and inevitably sin.* Paul's negative remarks about the Law are meant to discourage gentiles from attempting to live according to its precepts in any way other than how *Paul* defines as "in Christ."

Whom does Paul address? What audience of pagans might have been tempted to Judaize in ways other than the way that Paul approved? Where in the ancient world would Paul have found pagans who had been exposed to the precepts of Jewish tradition, who perhaps had even begun living according to some of them, while continuing actively to worship their own gods as well? Where could Paul have found pagans of sufficient "biblical literacy" to understand his own references to Jewish ideas, starting with "christos," the messiah; to the deity represented as *ho theos, the* god, meaning the god of Israel; to God's Kingdom, David's son, bodily resurrection, the scriptures, the covenants; to Abraham, Moses, the Law, and the prophets; to Jerusalem, its temple, and its sacrificial cult?

The answer, of course, is "in the diaspora synagogue." Paul drew his pagans from that penumbra of already-interested outsiders, the "god-fearers."[60] As a population, they fit both criteria: formerly active "idol-worshipers" familiar enough with biblical ideas and imagery that Paul could be reasonably sure, when he preached to them and wrote to them, that he was not talking to himself.[61] And as a population, they would also represent those pagans more likely to give a sympathetic hearing to arguments propounding circumcision, whether from teachers within the synagogue (as perhaps Paul himself in Damascus had once been, Gal 5.11), or from itinerant apostles preaching the imminent return of the messiah and the coming Kingdom of the Jewish god (such as Paul as well as those whom Paul considered his opponents). And Paul's pursuit of such synagogue-affiliated pagans also accounts for his repeatedly receiving disciplinary lashing from (worried?) Jewish authorities (2 Cor 11.24).

Paul's negative remarks about the Law to his communities midcentury are meant to dissuade Christ-following pagans from Judaizing *in any way other than in Paul's way*. His biggest challengers—and therefore the targets of his most corrosive polemic—were Jewish apostles like himself, preaching specifically to gentiles about the coming Kingdom, to be inaugurated by God's returning messiah.[62] Some of them (like the "false brothers" of Gal 2.4–5) thought perhaps that all apostles (like Titus) should themselves be Jews, whether by birth or by conversion: Paul dismissed this as "slavery." Some of them (like the men whom James sent to Antioch) thought perhaps that Christ-following assemblies should meet only in Jewish households, the better to avoid eating or drinking what may have been offered to idols, or doing so where idols might be present; Paul disagreed, objecting to this as "forced Judaizing" (Gal 2.12–14). And some apostles-in-Christ preached circumcision.

It was this advocacy of adult proselyte circumcision that drew Paul's fiercest ire. Why? Most theological commentators, whether "old perspective" or "new," have argued that Paul objected to "works" over "grace" (essentially, to "Judaism" over "Christianity"), or to ethnic specificity (that is, Jewishness) over a new, inclusive, universal humanity. In this view, circumcision stands *pars pro toto* as (the supreme example of) the "works of the Law," or as a source of "Jewish ethnic pride."[63] *Sonderweg* scholars, more recently, have urged that Paul was committed to two discrete paths to salvation, Torah for Jews and Christ for gentiles. The significance of Jesus as *Israel's* messiah accordingly shrinks: Jews did not need Christ, because they already had Torah. Paul objected to circumcision, in this view, because gentiles did not need it: they (and only they) were saved in Christ.[64]

Whatever their various theological and historical complications, many of these explanations for Paul's strong position against gentile circumcision draw substantially upon the modern idea of "religion" as a system of beliefs motivated primarily by a concern with "salvation." What

Christianity only eventually became, in other words, sets the terms for understanding its own originary social matrix.[65]

Sensitive to these problems of method, other scholars have tried to articulate Paul's commitments in the terms native to his own time, place, and writings. Antiquity configured "family"—that is, kinship or ethnic groups—both vertically (between heaven and earth) and horizontally (between humans and across generations). Framed in this way, Paul's concern with lineages and genealogies leaps to the fore.[66] And framed with the issue of genealogy, Paul's problem specifically with circumcision can be—and recently has been—radically reconfigured. Paul objected to proselyte circumcision not because he thought that pagans *should not* become Jews, say these scholars, but rather because he thought that pagans *could not* become Jews.[67]

No ritual act can change flesh and blood. This is the realist genealogical thinking that informs Jewish texts such as Ezra, Jubilees, and some of the Dead Sea Scrolls (e.g., 4QFl i.3–4 and 4QMMT).[68] Paul speaks negatively about Jewish law to gentiles in the effort to turn them away from the attractions of apostles advocating circumcision, on this interpretation, because he views its effectiveness as null. Paul frames his dissuasion by mobilizing Hellenistic categories that contrast divine to human law. Divine law, in this rhetoric, was unwritten, universal, rational, and unchanging. Human law, by contrast, was written, particular (that is, to a given city or people), and contingent (changing across time). By ascribing to Torah the characteristics of human law *as opposed to* those of divine law, so runs this argument, Paul deliberately, and for these strategic reasons, devalued Jewish law to his gentile audience:

> Paul had to find a way to preserve the exclusive character of the Mosaic Law as a law for the genealogical seed of Isaac alone, and to do so without causing offense, because he believed that the inclusion of Gentiles was a condition of the coming kingdom. . . . Paul distanced the Mosaic Law from classical conceptions of divine law and applied to it classical discourses associated with human . . . law. He asserted that like human . . . law, the particular Mosaic Law is counter to nature; it is lifeless, bringing slavery, sin, and death; it does not guarantee virtue. . . . The conclusion toward which his rhetoric points is that the Mosaic Law is the written law for a particular, genealogically

defined people. . . . It is because Paul must both affirm and denigrate the Law to his Gentile audience, it is because he wants Gentiles to *join with* Israel without *joining* Israel, that he adopts, and is so well served by, a rhetoric informed by Greco-Roman discourses of ambivalence.[69]

Or perhaps Paul was committed to the idea that covenantal circumcision of necessity could occur only on the eighth day of the male child's life (see Phil 3.5), a position that would limit it specifically to Jews. He would have had on his side the Greek text of Genesis 17.14: "And the uncircumcised male, who shall not be circumcised in the flesh of his foreskin *on the eighth day*, that soul shall be cut off from his people, for he has broken my covenant" (LXX; cf. Jub 15.25–26). Lacking this phrase "on the eighth day," the Masoretic text of this verse opens up the possibility of circumcision at other times and, thus, of circumcision as a rite of entry of an adult non-Jew into Israel.[70] In the Hellenistic and Roman periods, in the Diaspora (the LXX's language notwithstanding), and in the Land of Israel, the inclusive force of this view of circumcision as a rite of entry is the one that prevailed.

Allied to the more stringent, genealogically restrictive view—and, it must be said, to a minority view—Paul according to this construction holds that circumcision was of no value *for the adult male gentile*, whether Christ-following or not. Proselyte circumcision would not bring him into Israel's covenant—just, indeed, as Ishmael's circumcision at age thirteen did not bring him into Israel's covenant (Gal 4.21–31; Rom 9.7). "Circumcision benefits, *if* you keep the Law. But if you are a transgressor of the Law, your circumcision has become foreskin" (Rom 2.25). When Paul speaks this way in Romans, he speaks to a Judaizing gentile, and he has *the law of eighth-day circumcision* specifically in mind. The Judaizing gentile—clearly older than eight days—who subjects himself to circumcision accordingly transgresses the "law of circumcision" even as he tries to honor it, precisely because he is more than eight days old: for him, then, circumcision counts as uncircumcision.[71] His circumcision notwithstanding, the pagan is still a pagan, still outside the covenant of Abraham, Isaac, and Jacob; still trapped, accordingly, in his servitude to the flesh, to sin, and to death (Rom 7); still enslaved to the *stoicheia* of the universe (Gal 4.9–10).[72] The only way *for the gentile* to share in the blessing promised to

Abraham, Paul urges, is through Christ, thus through spirit; not through flesh, thus not through circumcision.

✦✦✦

Paul speaks both positively and negatively about the Law. We have tried to sort through the various subjects on which he sounds approbation and enthusiasm (such as gentiles' keeping the Law's commandments) and those that draw his angry disapproval, even condemnation (the gentile reception of circumcision). As a point of orientation for any interpretation, though, the audience of Paul's remarks must always be kept in mind. All of his extant letters are addressed to gentiles. This means that, whatever Paul says about the Law, he says it first of all with reference to gentiles. And this in turn means that the Law is not a curse for all people (in fact, it is a God-given privilege of Israel's, Rom 9.4), but it is a curse for gentiles who, *without Christ,* cannot live according to its demands (because they need Christ's *pneuma* to enable them). Therefore, when Paul speaks against Law observance, he speaks against non-Pauline construals of gentile Judaizing, not against Jewish Torah observance; and when he speaks against circumcision, he speaks against the circumcision of gentiles, not of Jews. In short, and in this specific way, Paul rejects (some forms of) Juda*izing*, not (all forms of) Juda*ism.*

But, as we have seen as well, Paul also speaks positively of the Law with respect to gentiles-in-Christ. Enabled by spirit, through Christ, gentiles *can* do what the Law requires, and Paul urges them to live by its precepts. "Being righteoused through faithfulness" enables this fulfillment. *"Law" and "faithfulness" in this sense are complementary and synergistic, not contesting and contrary.* Both modalities of expression, in sum, the positive no less than the negative, are sounded in Paul's letters.

But these two modalities do not exhaust his range. Paul also, and everywhere, speaks with great urgency. *Now,* he proclaims; *soon.* It is to this question, finally—the drive wheel of this study—that we now turn. Whence Paul's urgency? Why, on its account, does he focus his attention so acutely on gentiles? And what do gentiles have to do with the redemption of "all Israel" (Rom 11.26)?

5

CHRIST AND THE KINGDOM

For this we declare to you by the word of the Lord, that *we who are alive, who are left until the Parousia* of the Lord, will not precede those who have "fallen asleep." For the Lord himself will descend from heaven with a cry of command, with the archangel's voice, and the sound of the trumpet of God. And the dead in Christ will rise first, and then *we the living who remain* will be snatched up together with them in the clouds, meeting the Lord in the air, so that we shall always be with the Lord. Comfort each other with these words.

1 Thessalonians 4.15–18

The Lord is *near.*

Philippians 4.5

The time has been shortened ... the form of *this world is passing away.*

1 Corinthians 7.29

These things were written down for *us, upon whom the ends of the ages have come.*

1 Corinthians 10.11

Lo! I tell you a mystery. We shall not all "sleep," but we shall all be changed. .... For the trumpet will sound, the dead will rise imperishable, *and we shall all be changed.*

1 Corinthians 15.51–52

> *Now* is the acceptable time; behold, *now* is the day of salvation.
>
>   2 Corinthians 6.2

> You know what the hour is, how it is full time now for you to
> awake. . . . For *salvation is even nearer to us* than when we first
> became convinced. The night is far gone; *the day is at hand.*
>
>   Romans 13.11–12

From first (that is, from his earliest letter, 1 Thessalonians) to last (his
letter to the Romans), Paul remained convinced that Christ was about to
return, to redeem history, to raise the dead, and to establish the Kingdom
of his father.[1] *We* who are left alive, *we* shall all be changed, salvation is
nearer to *us*: Paul himself expects to live to see Christ's triumphant return
and the coming of the Kingdom. It was Christ's resurrection, communicated to Paul by his own vision, that convinced him of the nearness of the
End (1 Cor 15.8, 12). Christ risen could *only* mean that the general resurrection was at hand (cf. Rom 1.4): Christ was the "first fruits" of the resurrection of all the dead (1 Cor 15.20). The intrinsic significance of this
singular event was that it immediately entailed the final, communal one
(vv. 12–15). Indeed, by Paul's reckoning, Christ's resurrection is precisely
not a "singular" event at all, but rather the first in a series of eschatological
events, to end in the establishment of God's Kingdom.

This theme of the nearness of the End shapes the substance of Paul's
pastoral advice. Some members of the Thessalonian *ekklesia* had died in
advance of Christ's return, surprising survivors—and giving us an index of
their (and of Paul's) timeframe. Paul writes to console them while they
"wait for [God's] son from heaven, whom he raised from the dead, Jesus
who delivers us from the coming wrath" (1 Thes 1.10), and to describe for
them how the final events will unwind (4.15–18, quoted above). But he
also writes to reassert how close these events are, for the recipients of this
letter will be alive, too, at the second coming. "May your spirit and soul
and body be kept sound and blameless at the coming of our Lord Jesus
Christ" (1 Thes 5.23; cf. 1 Cor 11.30: such deaths before the Parousia may
be punitive, therefore exceptional). So close is the End that Paul can
reasonably instruct his gentiles in Corinth to foreswear sexual activity, if

they are able. The unmarried should stay unmarried; the married should if possible live as if they were not married, while not seeking to divorce (1 Cor 7.1–38). "It is upon *us*," he tells his assembly there, "that the *ends of the ages have come*"—and therefore they should not worship demons (10.11; cf. vv. 6–22 for the full context against idolatry). "*Soon* the god of peace," he tells the Romans, "will crush Satan under your feet" (*en taxei*, in the Greek final emphatic position; 16.20).

Jesus is the messiah; he has been raised and *therefore* he will soon return; with his return, the dead too will be raised and God's Kingdom established. Paul had been taking this message (mainly) to pagans for some twenty years by the time he dictates the letters that we have in the New Testament. What had sustained him during all this time? And how do these eschatological convictions account for his gentile mission?

CHRIST, THE SON OF DAVID, PART 1: THE *ESCHATON*

In Paul's opening salvo against the circumcisers in Galatia, he proclaims that his gospel had no human source (οὐκ ἔστιν κατὰ ἄνθρωπον, Gal 1.11), but that it came to him by a revelation of Jesus Christ (v. 12; I take this as an objective genitive: Jesus was revealed to Paul; cf. v. 16: God revealed his son to Paul).[2] God effected this revelation, Paul continues, so that Paul would "preach him [Christ] among the nations" (v. 16). Yet in 1 Corinthians 15.3–11, Paul states unambiguously that he received the core of the gospel—"Christ died for our sins . . . was raised on the third day . . . and appeared"—from those who were apostles before him: "I delivered to you [Corinthians] as of first importance what I also received" (1 Cor 15.3–5).

The two statements are complementary, not contradictory. Paul could only have received the core content of the kerygma from others who were already within the movement—initially, then, those Jewish apostles whom he encountered (and confronted) in his own synagogue in Damascus, within a few years of Jesus's crucifixion (cf. Gal 1.17, "I again returned to Damascus"). And this message of Jesus's crucifixion, death, resurrection, and impending return would have come together with a further affirmation, namely, that Jesus was ὁ χριστὸς, the messiah. It was an identification that Paul took to heart: in his seven undisputed letters, he repeats the term 269 times.

How a wandering charismatic exorcist and prophet came to be regarded as "messiah" is one of the most perennially confounding questions of New Testament scholarship. Multiple messianic paradigms proliferated in the late Second Temple period—the Qumran library alone presents an eschatological Davidic warrior, a perfect priest, a final prophet, and an enthroned heavenly redeemer—but Jesus himself fits none of them. Historians infer, on the basis of Jesus's crucifixion as "King of the Jews," that his identification as messiah must have preceded his death, though perhaps not by much. According to the evangelists, the only moment when Jesus was so publicly acclaimed—or at least publicly associated with messianic themes—came in the week before his crucifixion, when he together with other pilgrims entered Jerusalem for Pesach. "Hosanna to the Son of David! Blessed is the one who comes in the name of the Lord!"(Mt 21.9). "Blessed is the coming kingdom of our father David!" (Mk 11.10). "Blessed is the king who comes in the name of the Lord!" (Lk 19.38). "Blessed is the one who comes in the name of the Lord, the King of Israel!" (Jn 12.13). Does a historical event echo through these verses? Such popular acclaim would not endear any indigenous figure to Rome.[3]

This diversity of messianic paradigms should not obscure the prime importance of the royal messiah, the son of David, who remains the most widely attested figure. "See, Lord, and raise up for them their king, the son of David," the author of the pseudonymous Psalms of Solomon prayed, sometime in the first century B.C.E., "at the time that you have knowledge of [that is, the End-time]; and gird him with strength, so that he may smash those who rule without justice. . . . Their king shall be the lord messiah" (*christos kurios*, 17.21–32). This eschatological prince would recapitulate the valor and virtues of his distant ancestor, David the king. Where he appears in apocalyptic texts, he defeats God's enemies and routs foreign armies; he executes judgment, reigns over a restored Israel, and builds up Jerusalem; he rules over gentile nations who likewise worship at God's temple, and he establishes unending peace.

Paul addressed his letters to communities that had already been instructed in the gospel. "Both the apostle and his churches are already convinced of the messiahship of Jesus; other things are at issue in the letters."[4] In those letters, Paul typically refers to Jesus, in various ways, as "Christ." Very occasionally the use is titular (*ho Christos*, "the Christ," e.g., Rom 9.5); most often the word appears without the article, or in combination with "Jesus." So frequent is this appellation, and so routinely unexplained, that for a long time scholars argued that the word *Christos* functioned in Paul's letters simply as a proper name, without "messianic" content. That view has been retired by more recent work, which holds that "Christ" in Paul serves as an honorific. "An honorific was taken or bestowed on its bearer, usually in connection with military exploits or accession to power." *Christos* fits this onomastic category.[5]

Paul, as others before him, refers this honorific *Christos* to Jesus. In texts roughly contemporary with his letters, *Christos* most commonly stands for an End-time Davidic warrior and ruler. Traditions visible both in Paul's letters and in the later gospels also present Jesus as such a redemptive End-time figure: returning with angels, coming on clouds of glory to gather his elect, bringing in the Kingdom with power.[6]

We can (only) speculate on the sequence of events that initiated this identification of Jesus with the final, Davidic messiah. During his mission to Jews in the Galilee and in Judea, Jesus had spoken of a coming Kingdom, and he presented himself as an authoritative prophet of that Kingdom. Before his final Pesach in Jerusalem, crowds (whether already-involved followers or pilgrims swept up in his message) hailed the "Kingdom of our father David that is coming" and identified Jesus as its harbinger. Soon thereafter, arrested by Pilate, Jesus died on a cross as "King of the Jews"—a title with obviously royal, thus Davidic, resonance. And shortly later, by increasing numbers of apostles and followers, Jesus "was seen" again, raised from the dead (1 Cor 15.3–7).

The resurrection experiences would not have been a reason in themselves to identify Jesus as the messiah. No such tradition of a dying, rising, and returning *Christos* existed before this new movement created it. But the resurrection appearances evidently did confirm Jesus's prophecy for his followers: the Kingdom must indeed be at hand. This unexpected disruption of the more traditional scenario—first the triumphant messiah, then the other End-time events, such as communal resurrection—occasioned

Jesus's disciples' original reinterpretation. The Kingdom was indeed on its way, they held; but it would come with the risen Jesus in its vanguard, functioning at his second coming as the final messiah.[7]

In other words, the initial attribution of messianic status to Jesus must have occurred before his death, because that alone accounts for his crucifixion as "King of the Jews." For those followers who subsequently received the vision of him risen from the dead, that messianic attribution necessarily required a two-stage confirmation. Stage 1 was the appearance of the resurrected Jesus to select insiders (among whom, Paul insists, is Paul, 1 Cor 15.5–8). Stage 2 would be his public manifestation in power, his Parousia, together with God's Kingdom.

By the mid-first century, this "insider's" attribution is firmly established. Paul everywhere speaks of Jesus as "Christ." But he designates him explicitly as the *Davidic* messiah only twice, both times in his letter to the Romans (1.3 and 15.12). These two places, at the letter's opening and toward its end, form a kind of messianic *inclusio*. Paul ties this Davidic identification, in both places, immediately to his own mission to the nations. "Paul . . . called to be an apostle . . . for the gospel concerning [God's] son, descended from David according to the flesh . . . to bring about obedience of faithfulness . . . among all the pagans/gentiles/nations, including yourselves": thus Paul's self-introduction, in Romans' opening sentence (Rom 1.1–6). And, toward the letter's end, he closes with a citation of Isaiah 11.10, "The root of Jesse will come, he who rises to rule the gentiles, in him shall the gentiles hope" (Rom 15.12; cf. 16.26: the mystery disclosed through prophetic writings that is now "made known to all the nations").[8]

Paul's most fundamental sense of himself was as "apostle to the nations": it was for this purpose, he claimed in Galatians, that God had set him apart from his mother's womb (Gal 1.15–16, deliberately echoing Jer 1.4–5; cf. Isa 49.1–6; Rom 1.1, 6). It is our good luck that, in Romans, we have a letter from him addressed to a community that he had not himself established: to introduce himself, he had to expand upon his gospel and his mission more fully than he had in the other correspondence that survives. As his messianic framing of Romans reveals, Paul linked his heavenly commission in the final days, his work in bringing gentiles to

the worship of the true god, immediately and intimately to his proclamation of Jesus as the scion of David's house. To understand the apostle,
then, we need to understand his Christology.

I use the word *Christology* advisedly. It is a term of formal theology,
whereas Paul's definitions of Christ and his view of Christ's role in the
imminent redemption of the cosmos rest on messianic, charismatic biblical exegesis,[9] not on systematic dogma or doctrine. Paul is not worried
about coordinating pneumatology, Incarnation, soteriology, theology, and
so on. Nor is he burdened with an obligation to later church councils,
especially Nicea (with its doctrine of Christ as "fully God") and Chalcedon
(with its concern about Christ's "two natures," human and divine). Paul is
a mid-first-century Jew, and a charismatic, apocalyptic visionary: it is
within that context that his definitions of messiah/*Christos* must stand.

Two particular places in Paul's letters, however, seem effortlessly to
support these later fourth- and fifth-century ecclesiastical Christologies.
The first, on Christ's "divine nature," is Philippians 2.6–11, the so-called
Christological Hymn.[10] The second, on Christ's "two natures," is Romans
1.3–4. We need to look closely at each of these passages.

To Philippians first. In English, it runs as follows:

> . . . Christ Jesus (6) who, though he was in the form of God, did not
> count equality with God a thing to be grasped, (7) but emptied him-
> self, taking the form of a slave, being born in human likeness. (8) And
> being found in human form, he humbled himself, becoming obedient
> to the point of death, even death on a cross; (9) on account of which,
> God highly exalted him and gave to him the name above every name,
> (10) so that at the name of Jesus every knee should bend, whether in
> heaven or on earth or below the earth, (11) and every tongue should
> acknowledge that Jesus Christ is Lord, to the glory of God the Father.

The above represents the Revised Standard Version's translation. With
the text rendered this way, and with the convention of capitalizing "God"
as the proper name of the highest biblical divinity, the reader may very
well wonder why it took until 325 C.E. for the church to produce the doctrine of the Council of Nicea. Here, Christ is in the same "form" as God
(whatever that may mean);[11] he prescinds from seizing "equality with God"
(which suggests that it was an option); and he is exalted by the biblical

deity's own title/name, that is, "Lord." These verses certainly seem to promote a vision of two almost equal or radically identified gods.[12] Paul, then,
might seem to speak here specifically as a "di-theist" Christian, not as a
"monotheist" Jew.

The Greek, however, does not quite correspond to the RSV's English.
In Philippians 2.6, Jesus is not "in the form of the [high] God," but in the
form of "[*a*] god." Jesus does not demur from equality with God the
Father, but from "god-status" or, closer to Paul's word choice, equality
with "[a] god." The god who exalts Jesus in verse 9, by contrast, *is* the high
god (*ho theos, the* god), referred to as "God the Father" in verse 11. The
conventions of English capitalization—"God" with the upper-case G in
all clauses—obscure Paul's Greek. Paul distinguishes between *degrees* of
divinity here. Jesus is not "God."[13]

I would translate what Paul says as follows:

Christ Jesus who, though existing in god-form, did not consider divine
status [or, "being the same as a god"] something to seize upon; but he
emptied himself, taking on a slave-form, being born in human likeness. And being found in human form, he humbled himself, becoming obedient to the point of death, even death on a cross. Because of
this, God highly exalted him and gave to him the name above every
name, so that at the name of Jesus every knee should bend—whether
of heavenly beings or of earthly beings or of subterranean beings—and
every tongue should acknowledge that Jesus Christ is Lord/Lord Jesus
is Christ, to the glory of God the Father.

Jesus had a divine status—which he declined to hold onto. God the
Father exalted him. No confusion between degrees of divinity. Note, too,
Paul's caution here: he does not say that Jesus was (also) a god, but that he
was "in the form" of one. Paul nowhere describes Jesus as *theos* ("god")
nor even as an *angelos* ("messenger" or, specifically in this connection, an
"angel"):[14] rather, as he will insist elsewhere, Jesus is *anthrōpos*, a human
being, albeit a human being *ex ouranou*, "from heaven" (1 Cor 15.48). I
will return to this ancient idea of celestial or divine human being shortly.

But what about the conferral of "Lord"/*kurios*—which in the LXX
often designates God—on Jesus?[15] Doesn't that let Nicea in by a back
door? *Kurios* in the Septuagint does usually refer to God. But in everyday

Greek, *kurios* was also the way that one referred to and deferred to *any* social superior, whether human or divine. This is why I have translated the final line as I did, in two iterations, both supported by Paul's phrasing: what is (or will be) universally recognized is the elevated status of the figure of Jesus as the eschatological, royal messiah (*Christos*, or perhaps "Lord Messiah").[16]

How did Paul think that this universal acknowledgment would occur? If Philippians were the only letter from him that we had, we could read this passage as implying the answer "at Christ's ascension," that point following his resurrection when Jesus was raised up/exalted (Phil 2.9; cf. Acts 1.9–11). And, indeed, many commentators do read these verses this way, taking Philippians as describing a two-phase cycle of descent/ascent.[17]

But we should note also the special status of all these "knees": they belong to heavenly and to subterranean entities as well as to surface-dwelling humans and demons. Paul lives in the geocentric Ptolemaic universe, and he speaks here about a *cosmic* acknowledgment of Jesus's messianic status, similar to the ways that he speaks elsewhere, in 1 Thessalonians 4, in 1 Corinthians 15, and in Romans 8. These letters, taken collectively, indicate how Paul envisaged the grand finale of Philippians 2.9. Cosmic acknowledgment of Christ's status as the eschatological—that is, the final—messiah occurs only at his Parousia, his second coming. Jesus might have been raised up at or through his own resurrection because of his obedient death on a cross, but his *cosmic* affirmation, to the glory of God the father, Paul says here, is contingent upon his triumphant return as Lord Messiah, the victorious eschatological Christ.

We see this especially clearly in 1 Corinthians 15.[18] Having just urged his assembly to understand that Christ's resurrection necessarily and immediately entails the general resurrection, Paul says:

> (20) But now Christ has been raised from the dead, first fruit of those who have fallen asleep. (21) For as by a man came death, so also by a man came resurrection of the dead. (22) For as in Adam all die, so also in Christ all will be made alive. (23) But each in his own order: Christ the first fruits; after, at his Parousia, those of Christ. (24) Then comes the End, when he delivers the Kingdom to God the Father, when he

abolishes every rule [*archē*] and every authority [*exousia*] and every power [*dynamis*]. (25) For he must reign until he has "put every enemy under his feet" [Ps 109.1 LXX]. (26) The last enemy to be abolished is death. (27) "For he has put all things in subjection under his feet" [Ps 8.7]. (1 Cor 15.20–27)

"Rule," "authority," and "power" sound like earthly governments. But in antiquity these words also indicated cosmic "governments" as well, the realm of hostile superhuman forces (cf. the "many gods and many lords" of 1 Cor 8.5–6, and "the god of this world," 2 Cor 4.4).[19] So too the *archontes tou aiones toutou* (1 Cor 2.8): "the rulers of this age" (if by this phrase Paul intends astral powers rather than Roman) have crucified the son of Paul's god. These are the superhuman entities whom the returning Christ will subjugate (cf. Rom 8.38, angels, principalities, and powers; also cf. Eph 6.12).[20] These entities are the supercelestial powers who ruled over gentile nations, and whom, in turn, these nations worshiped.[21] And these are the beings who provide the superhuman knees in Philippians that "will bend" when acknowledging Jesus as the eschatological Lord Messiah.

Until Christ returns, Paul himself and his congregations also struggle against these forces. But when Christ manifests in power, bringing about the resurrection of the dead, at the End, these forces will submit. Philippians 2 thus actually implies or even presupposes a *four*-stage cycle: descent (in "human form"); ascent/exaltation (following Jesus's own resurrection); descent again (presumably at the Parousia, to subject those above the earth and on the earth and below the earth); absolute acknowledgment (all bowing at the name of Jesus, acknowledging him as *Christos*, to the glory of God the Father).

Philippians 2 hymns the final universal acknowledgment of Jesus as the lord messiah, the eschatological redeemer, a theme that Paul reverts to in Philippians 3.20–21: Christ's power will enable him to "subject all things to himself" when he returns to transform the bodies of the redeemed. 1 Corinthians 15 specifically frames Christ's eschatological activity with two psalms of David, Psalm 109 LXX (a royal enthronement psalm) and Psalm 8.[22] And this language of martial subjugation resonates as well with Jesus's (re)appearance as a cosmic warrior in 1 Thessalonians 4, descending with a cry of command to the sound of the heavenly trumpet and the archangel's voice (cf. Dan 7.13–14, about one "like a son of man"). Jesus's death on the cross, at his first coming, may have unsettled more familiar Jewish messianic traditions (the message was "a stumbling block to Jews," 1 Cor 1.23); but when he returned to sum up the ages, Jesus would return in the way that a warrior-messiah—a messiah son of David—should return: conquering, triumphant, establishing the Kingdom, in power.

CHRIST, THE SON OF DAVID, PART 2: ROMANS

Standard readings (and translations) of Romans 1.3–4 work against the interpretation given above. This passage has long stood in support of "two-nature" Christologies, wherein Paul is seen to frame Jesus in terms both human and divine. In the opening lines of what is arguably his most renowned letter, Paul evidently correlates the "son of David" with weakness and mortality ("flesh"), and contrasts this Davidic sonship to divine sonship, in power.[23] Here is the text in the RSV:

> (1) Paul, a servant of Jesus Christ, called to be an apostle, set apart for the gospel of God, (2) which he promised beforehand through his prophets in the holy scriptures, (3) the gospel concerning his Son, who was descended from David according to the flesh, (4) and designated Son of God in power according to the spirit of holiness by his resurrection from the dead, Jesus Christ our Lord.

The contrast seems not only between flesh and spirit, but also between Son of David (the human Jesus?) and Son of God (the divine Son?). And this translation also puts the emphasis on Jesus's own, personal resurrection: *that* is how his divine sonship was "designated" or "appointed" or "declared."

I will return to the significance of Jesus's being declared "son of God" further on. Here I want to point out how the RSV mistranslates this passage, and therefore misplaces the point at which Jesus's identity as "son of God in power" is manifest. According to Paul, this did *not* happen—*pace* the RSV—at or by Jesus's own resurrection. *That* divine act was revealed only to a select few, a small band of "brothers" and apostles—including, Paul insists, Paul himself—sometime after the crucifixion (1 Cor 15.5–9).

Rather, according to Paul's Greek, here as elsewhere in his letters, Christ's manifestation *in power*—in public, to the cosmos—is tied to the *general* resurrection, thus to the coming of the Kingdom at the End.

Here is the text, more schematically, in English:

Paul the slave of Christ Jesus,
   called [to be an] apostle
   separated for the good news of God
[the good news] which he promised beforehand through his prophets
in the holy writings concerning his son
   the one born by the seed of David according to the flesh
   the one appointed son of God in power according to the spirit of
   holiness by the resurrection of the dead
Jesus Christ our lord.[24]

Laying this out more clearly to see the parallel structure, we have:

The good news concerning his son,
the one BORN *according to flesh* by the seed of David,
the one APPOINTED SON OF GOD IN POWER *according to spirit* by
resurrection of the dead.

In other words, *flesh* expresses Davidic genealogical descent (see Rom 9.5), *spirit* expresses appointment as the eschatological messiah by the End-time resurrection of the dead—a very public event, and one that Paul and others still awaited. Special insiders (such as those listed in 1 Cor 15.5–8) knew that the Kingdom, thus the general resurrection, was close, because they themselves had seen the risen Christ. But the point of Jesus's own resurrection appearances, according to Paul elsewhere, was not to assert his divine status, but to inform this select, elect community of ("Israelite"?) insiders—the "remnant" currently chosen by grace (Rom 11.5)—of what time it was on God's clock.

Taking Romans 1.4 as meaning "Jesus's own resurrection" has become hermeneutical boilerplate.[25] But that is not what Paul's Greek says. Like English, Greek depends on prepositions to establish the relation between words. Paul follows his term for resurrection, *anastasis*, with a noun in the genitive plural, *of the dead*. If he had wanted to say "resurrection *from* the dead"—as he does elsewhere say—he would have had to use the preposition "from," *ek*—as he does elsewhere do.

We see both usages cheek by jowl in another passage, 1 Corinthians 15.12–21:

> (12) Now if Christ is proclaimed as raised *from* the dead [ἐκ νεκρῶν], how can some of you say that there is no resurrection *of* the dead [ἀνάστασις νεκρῶν]. (13) If there is no resurrection *of* the dead [ἀνάστασις νεκρῶν], then neither has Christ been raised. . . . (20) But now Christ has been raised *from* the dead [ἐκ νεκρῶν], the first fruit of those who have fallen asleep. (21) For since through a human being [came] death, so also through a human being [came? will come?] resurrection *of* the dead [ἀνάστασις νεκρῶν]. (RSV, modified)

My interpretation of these verses in Romans was ventured seventeen centuries ago by Augustine of Hippo. In his Bible, the Latin of Romans 1.4 did indeed capture the Greek: for ἐξ ἀναστάσεως νεκρῶν, Augustine's text read *ex resurrectione mortuorum*, "by the resurrection of the dead." In his unfinished commentary on Paul's letter, *Epistulae ad Romanos inchoata expositio* (394/95 C.E.), Augustine accordingly argued against exactly the idea eventually represented by the RSV translation: "Moreover, Paul does *not* say that Christ was predestined by *his* resurrection *from* the dead [*ex resurrectione a̱ mortuis*], but by *the* resurrection *of* the dead [*ex resurrectione mortuorum*]. For [Christ's] own resurrection does not show how he is the Son of God . . . since others will also be raised from the dead. . . . But he was so designated by the resurrection of *all* the dead [*omnium mortuorum*]" (*Inch. Exp.* 5.11)—that is, by the End-time, general resurrection.[26]

These opening verses of Romans, in other words, should be read in light of the "heroic" messianic verses of 1 Thessalonians 4, of Philippians 2, of 1 Corinthians 15, and finally of Romans 8, which describe the return of the conquering messiah. It is the resurrection of *all* the dead—thus, Christ's royal, military, glorious second coming, his Parousia—that triggers the respectful submission of the entire cosmos (all those Philippian knees) and establishes God's Kingdom thanks to the victories of his son, the messiah—and who therefore, and at the same moment, is the eschatological scion of David's house.

If this is so, then perhaps it is time to consider afresh Paul's use of *son of God, son of David,* and *Lord.* Commitments to an early high

Christology—to Jesus's unique divinity, his "pre-existence"—have led some scholars to posit a stark contrast between the "incarnate" Christ (the "earthly" Jesus, David's son *kata sarka*; cf. Rom 9.5) and the eternal Christ (God's pre-existent son, whose own resurrection signaled or revealed his special status).[27] "Son of David" and "son of God," in the perspective of these formulations, stand for two different and incommensurate paternities. Paul's use of "Lord" is then read in support of this view. Since "Lord" in the Old Testament frequently indicates God, "Lord" in Paul's letters, used of Jesus, bespeaks a radical "binitarianism," Jesus's special status as God's uniquely divine son.[28]

Paul does indeed have a high Christology. His Jesus existed in a god-form before appearing in a human likeness (Phil 2.5); he is the cosmic agent "through whom are all things and through whom we are" (1 Cor 8.6). But even though his Jesus is "from heaven," Paul nevertheless and unambiguously identifies this heavenly Jesus as *anthrōpos*, "human" (1 Cor 15.48). Given the clear distinctions that moderns draw between the categories "humanity" and "divinity," Paul's flexibility on this point can seem confusing, contradictory, or virtually Chalcedonian. But Paul lived in a culture habituated to constructing divinity *on a gradient* that spanned heaven and earth; a culture where the paterfamilias—whether of the individual *gens* or of the whole empire—was worshiped for his *genius*, his numinous dimension; where stars and planets were regarded as divine embodied intelligences; where, long after Constantine, cult continued to be paid to the divine emperor. On the evidence, a divine human, whether in the first century or thereafter, for pagans and even for Jews and, later, for Christians, was not that hard a thought to think.[29]

But Paul thought that thought without all of its fourth- and fifth-century philosophical, thus theological, framing (*homoousia*, personae, and so on). He thinks biblically, apocalyptically, messianically. I want to urge, then, that we try to interpret both Paul and his Christology in innocence of the imperial church's later creedal formulas. If we do so, we can more easily see how Paul's three identifiers for Jesus, in his own time, function. *They are synonyms.* "Son of God" and "Son of David" and "Lord" indicate the same person in an eschatological messianic context—hence Paul's appeal to Isaiah 11.10 in his closing catena of scriptural citations in Romans 15.12. The final messiah *is* David's son, that is, a genealogical descendant from David's house (cf. 9.5); and as such, he is God's son, too. This is how and why the early traditions about Jesus come to appropriate so easily the kingship psalms of the Septuagint.[30] And likewise with *Kurios*, "Lord"—a reference, I think, to this final royal messiah also. "*Kurios* is to some extent an appropriate rendering of *Christos*, because it has a royal connotation that 'Christos' would not have had in Greek."[31] *Kurios*, in other words, also encodes this same figure of the final messiah, the scion of David's house.

Here, once again, we see the eschatological significance of Jesus's followers' visions. Their conviction that Jesus had been raised was not meaningful in and of itself, full stop. The risen Christ mattered because he confirmed Jesus's original *evangelion* that the Kingdom indeed was at hand (as Paul asserts in 1 Cor 15.3–20), to be established imminently at his triumphant—and classically martial, thus, Davidic—return.

Thus, too, Romans 10.9 and 13 is not a statement about the risen Christ's lordship and soteriological efficacy as such. It is a declaration of eschatological messianism. "If you confess with your mouth 'Jesus is lord,' and you trust in your heart that God raised him from the dead, you will be saved. . . . For 'everyone who calls upon the name of the Lord will be saved'" (Joel 2.32). "Lord" here means "final Davidic, royal messiah." Jesus's resurrection entails immediately the general resurrection, thus and necessarily Jesus's triumphant return, which is when that resurrection would occur. Those who call upon his name—"Come, Lord!"— would be "saved," that is, they would enter the (fast-approaching) Kingdom. The point is that *Kurios* here does not function primarily as a special title for a metaphysical divine entity ("Jesus as Lord," the "lordship of Jesus"), but as an indicator of Jesus's royal, Davidic, messianic role— thus, his status as God's eschatological champion.

INTERMEZZO: THE TURNING OF THE NATIONS

Meanwhile—what? The cosmic caesura between Christ's resurrection and his second coming went on and on, one day at a time, inexplicably continuing to continue. Those first followers of Jesus who had been granted a vision of him risen had regrouped, relocated permanently to Jerusalem, and awaited his triumphant return.[32] Eventually, they burst into sustained intra-Jewish missionary activity, spreading out from Jerusalem into synagogue communities in the Diaspora. From Paul's letters and from the later material in the gospels and in Acts, we can extrapolate how these early apostles would have broadcast and authorized their *evangelion:* proclaiming the nearness of the Kingdom (now tied to their witness of the risen Christ), performing charismatic acts (exorcisms, inspired prayer and prophecy, healings, "works of power"),[33] arguing with fellow Jews over passages of scripture. Along the way, and initially to their surprise, they began, too, to acquire interested gentiles— members drawn from these "mixed" synagogues' god-fearing pagans— along with local Jews (such as, eventually though not initially, Paul himself).

I have argued three points about this gentile involvement in the early Jesus movement. These points are interrelated, and together they form our framework for interpreting the mission and message of Paul.

(1) *Gentile Christ-followers were initially, in the first years of the movement, an accidental consequence of the gospel's postcrucifixion spread out to mixed pagan-Jewish cities*—thus, to mixed Jewish-pagan synagogue communities—at first within Judea (Joppa, Caesarea) and, shortly thereafter, in the Diaspora. Nothing in Jesus's own mission to Israel had prepared his apostles for this positive pagan response in advance of the Kingdom's arrival. This gentile response, and its social consequences, also provide an imprecise and impressionistic index of the numbers of pagan god-fearers attached in some way or other to these mixed synagogue communities.

(2) *These early apostles, drawing on the inclusive traditions of broader biblical and post-biblical apocalyptic prophecy, improvised a "gentile policy."* For the (brief) time remaining, these pagans would be admitted into the ekklesia *neither* as "converts" (thus, for men, with the requirement of proselyte circumcision) *nor* as god-fearers (thus, as pagans who worship Israel's god as a god among many). They were admitted, rather, as "eschatological gentiles": pagans who had renounced their own gods and made an exclusive commitment to Israel's god. Previously, such pagans had had

only a literary life, as an apocalyptic trope and an apocalyptic hope. Now, within the Jesus movement, they were becoming a social reality—and a social complication.[34] Still, and on balance, the net effect was beneficial to the new movement. This positive pagan response would only have confirmed these apostles in their apocalyptic convictions: if pagans renounced their own gods and worshiped only Israel's god, then the Kingdom truly must be at hand. *This improvised gentile policy—in the language of New Testament scholarship, "a Law-free mission to the gentiles"—thus preceded Paul's involvement with the movement.*[35]

(3) *On this account, however, anxious synagogue authorities, including initially Paul himself, subjected these apostles and their Jewish followers to disciplinary lashing.* (Paul says *kath' hyperbolēn,* "excessively" or "to the utmost," referring perhaps to the full number of thirty-nine blows, and/or perhaps to his own attitude when so prosecuting, Gal 1.13–17). This was because the gospel, by involving ex-pagan pagans on these "eschatological" terms, disrupted the relations between heaven and earth, thereby alienating both local gods and their humans, and so unsettling the synagogues' place within their cities (see above, p. 80 ff.).[36]

It was only after his hostile contacts with these apostles in Damascus that Paul had his own Christophany (Gal 1.13–14, 17; cf. 1 Cor 15.8). That vision confirmed for him the core content of the gospel message, which he repeats in 1 Corinthians 15: the risen Christ was about to return, the Kingdom was at hand. And this vision profoundly redirected him, focusing him exactly on the issue that had initially led to his own previous hostile activity, and that thenceforth dominated his own life and mission: Paul would preach God's son "to the nations" (Gal 1.16; cf. Rom 1.6, "among all the nations"; 16.26, "to all the nations").

Some two decades after this moment, as we know from Paul's letters, no single coordinated set of practices governed how these scattered messianic groups assimilated pagans into their small assemblies.[37] All of these ex-pagan pagans, *Paul's included,* "Judaized" to some degree: that is, they as non-Jews assumed some ancestral practices *of* Jews. The extent of what they assumed, however, varied. Everyone seems to have been required to commit to those twinned, most singularly Jewish behaviors, shunning public cult and worshiping Israel's god alone. Some Christ-following gentiles contributed to the collection for those back in Jerusalem. Others became scrupulous about wine or foodstuffs. And still others sought full identification with ethnic Israel through proselyte circumcision.

Paul rails against those other apostles whose "gentile policy" differs from his own. To the degree that he himself urged observance of "the commandments" on his own Christ-following gentiles, however, to that degree his gospel overlapped in some regards with those of his competitors. But if Paul insisted that "his" gentiles not formally join Israel through proselyte circumcision, how did he imagine their new and exclusive association in advance of the Kingdom, through Christ, with Israel's god?

Lineage/Huiothesia

Paul frequently addresses his hearers as *adelphoi*, "brothers." The New Revised Standard Version, sensitive to issues of gender-inclusion, occasionally translates this term by the more neutral "believers" or as "brothers and sisters." And indeed, as we see for example in 1 Corinthians 7 and 11, Paul does address both women and men in his communities. But where Paul argues using family kinship language, he has males particularly in mind. At issue is *inheritance*—in this case, inheriting the "promise" to Abraham, thus the Kingdom (see 1 Cor 6.9)—and the Roman "making" of sons through adoption, *huiothesia* (Gal 4.5; Rom 8.15).[38]

Paul's ideas on gentile "adoption" in (and into) Christ reveal his thought at one and the same time at its most *Roman*, at its most traditionally *Jewish*, and at its most *ancient*. Roman legal culture had long availed itself of this form of fictive kinship—sons not begotten but made—as a way to settle and to stabilize the next generation of "family" both for issues of property/inheritance and for issues of ancestry/continuation of patrilineal cult.[39] The new son was thereafter responsible to and for his "new" paternal ancestors and to and for the *genius* (inherited *numen*) of his new father and family (*gens*). In Paul's reuse of this idea of adoption, it is immersion and conferral of spirit (variously the spirit of God, or of Christ, or simply "holy spirit") that binds the Christ-following gentile into a new family, so that he, too, can inherit. (In Romans 8.23, the full adoption has to await the Parousia and the transformation of fleshly body; Galatians' adoption timetable seems more immediate, though the to-be-inherited Kingdom promised to Abraham and his *sperma*, Christ, still lies off in the future.)

Especially in Galatians 3–4, arguing against apostolic competitors who want male believers to be circumcised, Paul stresses that this sonship, *huiothesia*, comes through spirit (thus *pistis*, faithfulness to or confidence in the good news, Gal 3.2–5), not through flesh (the site of circumcision; thus, through the Law). Spirit binds the believer in and to Abraham's *sperma*, Christ, bringing the gentile into the same family as a son and, thus, as an heir (4.7; cf. 3.26, 29). The ex-pagan gentile thereby becomes a "son of Abraham" apart from the Law, apart from the flesh, and can inherit the promised redemption (3.6–9). The spirit of Christ, God's son, indeed, binds the entire community together (4.6), so that there is "neither Jew nor Greek, neither slave nor free, neither male nor female: you are all one in Christ Jesus" (3.28).

"All one," a single family, but exclusively according to "the spirit of his [God's] son" (Gal 4.6). *Kata sarka*, "according to flesh," these people still retain their ethnic and social differences, which Paul elsewhere emphatically asserts, and which the lack of circumcision, for males, evinces. Redeemed gentiles rejoice *with* Israel, but do not "join" Israel (Rom 15.7–12); runaway slaves return to their owners (thus the letter to Philemon);[40] the Corinthian women are to be subordinate to their husbands (1 Cor 11.3–16). United in and by spirit, Jewish and gentile Christ-followers together await Christ's return and the cascade of final events surveyed, we shall shortly see, in Romans 8–16. *Kata sarka*, however, they remain distinct, as indeed is the case with all human adoption.

Here Paul's allegiances to his *syngeneis*, Israelites *kata sarka*, are unambiguous and, therefore, transparent upon biblical paradigms (cf. Rom 9.4–5). Abraham in these final days may have become the father of "many nations" through the spirit of his *sperma*, the Christ; but Israelites themselves have many "fathers"—Abraham, Isaac, Jacob; the twelve patriarchs of the eponymous tribes. To them, God made many promises (15.8; cf. 9.4, 11.29).[41] It was precisely to fulfill those promises that Christ came as a servant to his own blood-kinsmen ("the circumcision," 15.8; cf. 9.6). The salvation of all Israel—ethnic, genealogical, fleshly Israel—is, indeed, the gospel's goal (Rom 11.25–26), "for the gifts and the promises of God are irrevocable" (v. 29).

These distinctions bear emphasizing, because so many readers often think that Paul speaks of an undifferentiated humankind united "in Christ." "Israel" in these interpretations changes from the real (or realistically imagined) historical kinship community that Paul describes in Romans 9.4–5 to a metaphor for the church, "spiritual" Israel, "the Israel of God" (Gal 6.16). Paul's much-touted proclamation of oneness in Christ, Galatians 3.28, trumps all those many other places where Paul speaks of a community striated by significant internal distinctions: apostles, prophets, interpreters, healers (1 Cor 12.7–26; Rom 12.4–8); male and female (1 Cor 11.5–16; cf. 14.34–36); Jew and Greek (Rom 2.9, 11); Israel and the nations, both redeemed (Rom 11.25–26, 15.9–12).

Paul's kinship language, however, does indeed put his different *gentiles* all on the same basis: they are siblings together with and through Christ, who is "the first born of many *adelphoi*" (Rom 8.29). But within this family unity, Paul nonetheless asserts his own people's singular, enduring identity. Ethnic Israelites, quite apart from Christ, already have *huiothesia* (Rom 9.4; cf. Exod 4.22, "Israel is my first-born son"); they are already in a family relationship with Christ (Rom 9.5, the Christ is from Israel *kata sarka*); and the *ethnē*—the redeemed nations—rejoice *with* God's people, his *laos*, Israel (Rom 11.1, 15.10; Deut 32.43).

In his reconfiguring gentile lineage via Abraham through *huiothesia*, adoption through spirit into Christ, Abraham's *sperma*, Paul is at his most innovatively Roman: gentiles-in-Christ now count as sons, thus heirs, and they are now responsible to the patrilineal cult of their new adoptive family. And in his adherence to the biblical paradigm, wherein God through the giving of his Law had separated Israel out for himself, wherein Israel remains Israel even (as in Isaiah) at the End, Paul is at his most traditionally, most recognizably Jewish. But in his eschatologically inspired "cross-ethnic" outreach, whereby some gentiles now—and, at the very End, their *plērōma* ("fullness" or "full number," Rom 11.25)—turn to worship Israel's god, Paul's adoption model ultimately coheres with the broader, ancient, pan-Mediterranean construction of divine–human relations: *gods and their humans form family groups.*

If the nations, through an eschatological miracle (*chariti*, "by grace") now worshiped Israel's god alone, then, Paul insists, they must be brought into that god's family—but not through flesh and the Law (that is, circumcision and "conversion"): adoption into and through Christ can never work by "flesh." Rather, gentiles become *adelphoi* through spirit, and through faithfulness to the good news of the returning Davidic messiah and of the coming Kingdom (*pistis* in the *evangelion*). Thus, despite their new Abrahamic lineage, the "father" who ultimately counts for these gentiles is not Abraham, but rather God (see Gal 3.26). It is *God*, not Abraham, whom these gentiles—like their older brother Jesus, and like ethnic Israel—can now call "Father" (Gal 4.7; Rom 8.15).[42] Note too the significance of this divine appellative, transliterated in Paul's Greek letters from Hebrew, the ancestral Jewish *glossa:* God's new sons call him Aββα, addressing Israel's god by his "Jewish" family name.

Separation/Hagiasmos

Paul's pagans received divine spirit through baptism, specifically baptism into Jesus's death and resurrection (Rom 6.3–4). The spirit also "sanctified" these pagans, which is why Paul will address them as *hagioi* (the RSV's "saints," Rom 1.7). This idea of "holiness" or "sanctification" correlates to others: ideas about separation, about acceptable sacrifice, and about proximity to divine presence; ideas, too, about Israel's genealogy. To understand them, and to grasp how and why Paul uses *hagioi* of his gentiles, we have to look to the rules of Leviticus, and to the operation of the temple in Jerusalem.[43]

Recall the two sets of biblical binaries that governed Israel's access to the altar. The first was the distinction between pure and impure (*tahor/ tameh* in Hebrew; *katharos/akatharos* in Greek). The second binary distinguished between holy and profane (*pro*, before or outside; *fanes*, altar) or—a different way of saying the same thing—between separated (*kadosh* in Hebrew) and common (*chol* in Hebrew; *bebēlos* in the LXX, *koinos* in later Jewish Greek). Only those *both* pure *and* holy (or dedicated, or separated: these are all synonyms) could be offered at the ultimate zone of holiness, the court of the priests that stood nearest the sanctuary.[44]

Recall now the layout of Herod's temple, with its series of nested courts: the largest, exterior one for pagans; within that, the court for Jewish women; within that, the court for Jewish men; within that, the priests' court. That innermost area held the altar and served as the zone of active sacrificing in front of the sanctuary itself, the dwelling place of God's glorious presence, his *doxa*, as Paul called it (Rom 9.4).

What, with regard to late Second Temple Jewish constructions of holiness, was at issue with pagans? Why were they kept at such a distance from the "zone of exchange," near the altar? Scholarly speculations about some sort of "gentile impurity" have spackled over the gaps in our knowledge, accounting for everything from the temple's architecture to Paul's persecution of the early ekklesia to why James's men would not eat with gentile Christ-followers in Antioch. But as we saw in chapter 2, ritual purity/impurity, a "real" physical state that implied no moral condition, seems largely irrelevant to gentiles: such legislation was incumbent *only* upon Israel. If pagans were kept furthest from the sacred zone around the altar, this had little to do with "purity"/"impurity" of this sort.

"Moral impurity" caused by certain defiling social and sexual acts— idolatry, incest, murder—was indeed imputed to pagans by some Jews (notably Paul).[45] Pagans, in this view, would be not intrinsically impure but functionally impure, made such by their enduring attachment to idols (not to mention by the various forms of *porneia* that invariably accompany idolatry in Jewish antipagan rhetoric). But moral defilement, even that contracted through the worship of idols, is not contagious, and the layout of Herod's temple underscores this fact: Jews walked through the gentiles' court to get to their own areas evidently unconcerned about contamination.[46]

This prompts the question: is "impurity" the key issue here at all? Paul's language of *hagiasmos*, "sanctification," with respect to his gentiles-in-Christ, and the way that his thought integrates gentiles with Jerusalem's temple, points us toward the second set of cultic binaries, holy/profane or separated/common (e.g., Lev 10.10). Though the first category of reference for this language is sacrifices—something brought to the altar had to be both pure and dedicated/separated—a second category of reference is ethnicity or genealogy.[47] Israel as a nation was that people God set apart for himself: in this sense, Israel was "separated," *hagios*, a "holy" nation (e.g., Exod 19.6). By contrast, other nations were not so distinguished: that is, the gentile nations were inherently *koinos*, "common," *not* distinguished one from another in the way that Israel, through descent and through God's *torah*, "teaching," was set apart from all of them.[48]

Some version of this thinking might explain the spatial architecture of Jerusalem's temple, and specifically the separation of pagans from the activity of sacrifice. The issue was not that a pagan was "impure" as such: that status was disputed. Rather, he was "profane" or "common," *koinos* relative to Israel, and for that reason kept at a distance. This would explain as well why no defilement was at issue for Jews traversing the gentiles' court on their way to their own: the *hagios/koinos* binary establishes no contagious condition.

Paul mobilizes this language of *hagiasmos* with respect to his pagans-in-Christ, while representing his own work as a priestly service, *hierour-gounta* ("sacrificing," or "offering" the gospel, Rom 15.16). The rituals and the ritual space of Jerusalem's temple serve him as a template. His Thessalonian pagans, for example, having turned from their idols to the living and true god, have attained *hagiasmos*: the RSV translates this as "sanctification," but we should equally understand "separation" or "dedication." These Christ-following pagans, Paul tells them, having received spirit and having changed their earlier ritual and sexual behavior, are separated or distinguished from the other pagans, the ones who do not know God (1 Thes 4.4–5). Those who *do* know God have been called "not to impurity"—the moral consequence of idolatry and *porneia*—but "in holiness" (v. 7). Elsewhere, Paul simply refers to these ex-pagan pagans as "holy ones" (*hagioi*, RSV "saints," Rom 1.7; 1 Cor 1.2). They have been made holy—or separated, or dedicated to God—by God, through spirit, in Christ (1 Cor 1.2).[49]

We should hear Paul's language of purity, separation, and sanctification in terms of these biblically based binary pairs *tahor/tameh* and *kadosh/chol* that govern access to the sanctuary in Jerusalem. Thanks to

God's spirit (or to Christ's spirit), these pagans have been separated out
from their fellows, adopted into God's family, cleansed to participate in
the eucharistic sacrifice of Christ: 1 Corinthians 10.14–22 elaborates this
whole set of ideas.[50] When speaking of God's spirit, Paul likens his pagans
to the Jerusalem temple: "Don't you know that you are God's temple, for
God's spirit dwells in you? . . . For God's temple is *hagios*, as you are"
(1 Cor 3.16). "Your body is a temple of holy spirit" (6.19). "We are the
temple of the living god" (2 Cor 6.16).

New Testament scholars often point to these verses by way of arguing
that, for Paul, Jerusalem's temple has been superseded by this new "temple" of the Christian community. I argue the opposite: Paul praises the
new community by likening it to something that he values supremely—
the sanctity, dignity, and probity of the temple cult. If he valued the temple less, he would not use it as his touchstone.[51] This is not an either/or
situation: for Paul, God's spirit dwells *both* in Jerusalem's temple *and* in
the "new temple" of the believer and of the community (Rom 9.4; cf. Mt
23.21).[52] These Christ-following pagans, having moved from wrong *latreia*
(the worship of idols and of lower gods) to right *latreia* (the worship of the
god of Israel; cf. Rom 12.1), have likewise been divinely separated out from
the nations who do not know God.

Paul's gentiles are thus *hagioi*, fit for intimate contact with the divine.
They proleptically experience this new closeness both through the in-
dwelling of divine spirit and through the "sacrifice" of the eucharist (1
Cor 10.14–18, explicitly likening community participation in the eucharist
to sacrifices in the Jerusalem temple).[53] In their support of Paul's mission,
they metaphorically stand by Israel's altar, making "a fragrant offering, a
sacrifice acceptable and pleasing to God" (Phil 4.18; cf. 2 Cor 2.15, the
community is itself the "sweet smell" of the sacrifice of Christ).

Through their adoption into Abrahamic lineage, then, and through
their separation/sanctification—the twin accomplishments, through
Christ, of their infusion with divine spirit—Paul's ex-pagan *ethnē* stood at
the edge of time, in the prophecy-confirming vanguard of the coming
Kingdom. So why, then, midcentury, were things still taking so long?
What was God waiting for? In his letter to the community at Rome, Paul
answered these questions.

THE CHORAL SYMPHONY: PAUL'S LETTER TO THE ROMANS

Where is the Kingdom? Why is it late? What else had to happen before Christ returned to raise the dead, to conquer the cosmic gods, to redeem humanity, to hand over the Kingdom to his father? These questions dominate the final movement of Paul's letter to the Romans, chapters 9 through 11, reprised in chapter 15. And, specific to this letter, the prophet Isaiah provides much of the scriptural material by which Paul shapes his answers.[54] Paul's deference to Isaianic traditions of eschatological pilgrimage to Jerusalem, combined with the pagan focus of his own mission, meant that he had to reflect on the significance of his gospel *tois ethnesin*, "to the pagans," to and for his own kinsmen, Israel *kata sarka*.[55] And in doing so, Paul built a bridge between the current gentile assemblies of Christ and God's ancient promises to the Jews.

Whatever the actual ethnic makeup of the ekklesia in Rome,[56] Paul addressed his letter solely and explicitly to its gentiles, while insisting on his own divinely granted authority to do so. "Paul . . . called to be apostle, set apart for the gospel of God . . . to bring about obedience of faithfulness . . . among all the *ethnē*, including yourselves" (1.1–6). Paul is coming to Rome "in order that I may reap some harvest among you as well as among the rest of the *ethnē* . . . both Greeks and barbarians, the wise and the foolish" (1.13–14). "Now I am speaking to you *ethnē*" (11.13). "On some points I have written to you very boldly . . . because of the grace given to me by God to be an altar-servant [*leitourgos*] to the *ethnē* . . . to win obedience from the *ethnē* by word and deed, by the power of signs and wonders, by the power of spirit" (15.16–19). Paul preaches according to "the revelation of the mystery which was kept secret for long ages but is now disclosed and through the prophetic writings is made known to all the *ethnē*, according to the command of the eternal God, to bring about the obedience of faithfulness" (16.25–26, the letter's finale).[57]

Paul's unambiguous address to Rome's Christ-following *ethnē* implies that the identity of the letter's "encoded" or "ideal" audience is also gentile, although (given the density of his biblical references) these are gentiles who are fairly well acquainted with Israel's scriptures (thus, gentiles "who know the Law," Rom 7.1). Taking this identification as our interpretive plumb line—Paul addressed his letter to gentiles and therefore (no matter the actual ethnic composition of the listening Roman community) Paul *encoded* a gentile reader (or hearer) for his letter[58]—in turn affects how we understand the fictive interlocutors that Paul deploys to move his discussion along. And this, in turn, affects how we read the entire letter.

Traditional Christian theologies (from the patristic period through to our own year of grace) have taken Paul's indictment of moral turpitude in Romans 1—despite its explicit focus on idolatry—to encompass all humanity, Jew and gentile alike.[59] Chapter 2 then serves to radically redefine "Jew" and "circumcision": both of these terms, so goes this argument, point to internal, spiritual (understand: Christian) realities, not to external, fleshly ones (understand: Jewish, 2.28–29).[60] The "I" of chapter 7 thus becomes a Jew (whether Paul or anyone else) tormented by his inability to live rightly under the Law: humanity can be justified only through faith in Christ (3.28–31). Only a remnant of Jewish Israel will be saved (9.27, 11.5); the "all Israel" to be redeemed will be a mixed eschatological Christian community of Jews and gentiles together (11.26). In this traditional view, Romans is Paul's timeless clarion call to Christ, a resounding declaration of the superiority of (Christian) grace and faith to (Jewish) works and law.

But if we take Paul at his word—that he is addressing his remarks explicitly to gentiles (Rom 1.6, 13; 11.13)—then this letter opens up quite differently. Romans 1 indicts pagan idolatry and idolators. Paul's fictive interlocutor in chapter 2, a pedagogical stand-in for his addressees, is also a gentile, though one "who calls himself a Jew" (2.17); that is, a Judaizing gentile, perhaps even a proselyte.[61] This rhetorical persona "represents or speaks for the letter's recipient(s)," and his gentile identity remains stable throughout all the letter's subsequent exchanges in later chapters (such as chapter 7).[62] The reading of Romans that I offer here, in short, assumes that Paul's letter speaks to gentiles; that he addresses gentile issues and problems; that he mobilizes a rhetorical gentile to make his points; and that he authorizes his case to these Christ-following Roman gentiles (whom he has never met, 15.22–23) by invoking his divine appointment as apostle to gentiles. Romans speaks most directly not to the justification of sinners in general, but to the justification specifically of gentiles-in-Christ.

Romans is Paul's resounding declaration of the gracious inclusion of the nations in the impending redemption of all Israel, Paul's "kinsmen according to the flesh" (9.4, 11.26).[63]

Romans 2–7: Problems with Gentile Judaizing

We have seen how Paul objects not to Judaizing per se—his own gospel demanded that gentiles-in-Christ assume Jewish practices and principles—but to Judaizing in any way other than in his way. In chapters 2 through 7 of Romans, Paul returns to this issue, tracing the problems, in his view, caused for gentiles who Judaize, who may even be circumcised, but who are not yet "in Christ." Prefacing his remarks with a full-throated condemnation of *pagan* gentiles (failing to acknowledge the Creator through his creation, they worship idols and fall into "all manner of wickedness," 1.29; the full panoply of perversions is detailed in 1.18–32), Paul then abruptly pivots around to accuse the *non*idolatrous gentile who judges his fellow gentiles for their behavior (2.1–5).

This judging gentile (2.1)—one "who calls [himself] a Jew" (2.17)—is inconsistent in his behavior (v. 3), saying one thing but doing another as he continues to sin in "typically gentile" ways (stealing, adultery, sacrilege, vv. 21–23),[64] boasting in the Law and yet breaking the Law (as this person will lament in 7.7–24). But even non-Judaizing pagans, ones who do not have the Law, may nonetheless act according to the Law, Paul insists. They have the Law "written on their hearts" (2.15). As actual "doers of the Law," then, such pagans "will be justified," deemed righteous, before God (2.13).

The judgmental pagan proselyte who considers himself a Jew, however, will himself be judged (2.5). His circumcision counts as "foreskin," whereas the "foreskinned" whose hearts are circumcised will be praised by God (2.25–29).[65] The circumcision that Paul devalues, then, is proselyte circumcision, though he here insists that *Jewish* circumcision is of great value ("much in every way," 3.2). To be sure, Jews too, like gentiles, have sinned (3.9–18, 22–23). The non-Jew's position, however, is worse vis-à-vis the Law, which can bring him only knowledge of sin (3.20). But God, putting Christ forward as a conciliation (*hilastērion*) between himself and the gentiles,[66] has displayed his own righteousness by offering righteousness *apart* from the Law, through faithfulness or loyalty to Jesus (vv. 21–26). And this faithfulness, Paul insists, does not overthrow the Law but upholds it (v. 31).

What exactly is so bad about the Law for gentiles? Paul had answered this question in a fury when writing to his communities in Galatia. Proselyte circumcision was like Ishmael's circumcision; it could not make the gentile into Abraham's heir. Only through Christ—through *pneuma*, spirit—could the non-Jew be adopted into the family as a son, thus an heir. In Romans, calmer, Paul addresses these same issues using the same biblical figure.[67] Before receiving circumcision, Abraham had trusted that God would fulfill his promise: Abraham thus was righteoused by his *pistis* (conviction, steadfastness) while still uncircumcised, in this way becoming the father of both gentiles-in-Christ and of Jews (chap. 4), who have themselves received holy spirit (5.5). Pneumatic infusion comes through immersion into Christ's death, so that the believer, too, "dies" to sin even though he still lives in sinful flesh (6.6).

"Death to sin" is not achieved *ex opere operato*: Paul exhorts baptized gentiles not to yield to the mortal body's passions (Rom 6.12–15, resonating with Paul's narration of these passions in 1.18–32 and again at 13.13–14).[68] But Christ's death and resurrection have enabled the gentile who trusts in this good news to cease being enslaved to sin, and instead to be a slave to righteousness, thus a slave of God (6.18). He thereby achieves *hagiasmos*, "sanctification," and its *telos* (goal), eternal life. "For the wages of sin is death, but the gift [*charisma*] of God is eternal life in Christ Jesus our lord" (6.22–23). The Law for a gentile without Christ (a Judaizing pagan? a proselyte? Paul's point remains the same) only makes his situation worse, articulating sins that he cannot help but commit as long as he is in "this body of death" (7.4–24). The Law itself is not at fault here: the Law is not sin ("God forbid!" 7.7); it is holy, as is the commandment (7.12). But for the gentile, the Law has been weakened by the flesh (8.3). Only through Christ, once infused with spirit, can he fulfill the just requirement of the Law (8.4).

Paul brings this first section of his letter to port by conjuring the eschatological transformation of the mortal body—something still awaited, to be achieved only at Christ's glorious return, when he subdues cosmic forces and raises the dead (Rom 8.38). Meanwhile, the gentile believer lives in his fleshly body though he is really "in spirit," since God's spirit or Christ's spirit lives "in" his body. Nonetheless, the gentile's complete *huiothesia*, his "adoption" as a son, will be finally and fully realized only at the End (8.23; cf. 14–17). Only then will all creation, which now also groans in travail, "be set free from its bondage to decay" (8.21–23).[69]

In his other letters, Paul had described this moment: both the living and the dead will be caught up in the air with the victorious Christ (1 Thes 4.14–17); mortal, fleshly bodies will be transformed into glorious bodies (Phil 3.20–21), bodies no longer of flesh and blood but rather of spirit (1 Cor 15.39–54; *pneumatikon sōma*, v. 44; cf. 2 Cor 5.1–9). All humanity will then stand before Christ the judge (2 Cor 5.10; cf. Rom 14.10–12, where God judges). But the ultimate verdict is not in doubt: gentile believers have been "called," "foreknown," "fore-ordained," "conformed" to Christ's image, "chosen" (Rom 8.28–33). Living now by hope—the word occurs six times in chapter 8—the gentile-in-Christ can rest assured that nothing "will be able to separate us from the love of God in Christ Jesus our lord" (8.39).

But what of Israel?

Romans 9–11: Israel and the Nations

In this distinct section of his letter, Paul continues to address Rome's gentile believers ("Now I am speaking to you *ethnē*," 11.13), but his focus emphatically shifts. Paul turns from his soaring evocation of the impending redemption in Christ to speak of his "great sorrow and unceasing anguish" on account of his blood brothers, ethnic Israel (9.2–3). Whence Paul's sorrow? Though the nations are turning to the gospel in numbers, to this point in time, "a remnant" of Israel has accepted the good news (9.27—note the RSV's "only," which is not in Paul's text—and 9.31, 11.7). Has God walked away from the covenant? Would history end with God breaking his promises to Israel (9.4; cf. 15.8)? *Mē genoito!* Paul responds. "Has God forsaken his people? God forbid!" (11.1). Then how can Paul—and his hearers—understand how things currently stand?

Ingeniously, tortuously, Paul integrates biblical prophecy and his commitments as a Jew to God's constancy and goodness with precisely this discouraging fact. And in so doing, he explains not only why the Kingdom had tarried, but also why he himself has "glorified" his own gentile mission (*doxazō*, Rom 11.14), and why he was *still* convinced that "salvation"—that is, God's Kingdom—was "now near," in fact, closer than ever (13.11).

The formative history of Israel (Genesis and Exodus) and the words of the prophets, Isaiah in particular, orient Paul and his hearers.[70] "It is not as though the word of God has failed," Paul urges (Rom 9.6): God has always exercised a sovereign control over history, shaping Israel not according to the flesh but by the promise (vv. 6–9, referring to Isaac and Ishmael), reversing expectations by "electing" or "calling" the younger (Jacob) to be served by the elder (Esau, vv. 10–13). God has mercy on, or hardens, whomever he will, according to his purpose (vv. 14–24; "so that my name may be proclaimed in all the earth," v. 18). The mission's current disproportion of gentiles to Jews had long ago been foreseen (9.25–26, Hosea on the calling of the gentiles; 9.27–29, on the remnant of Israel; cf. 10.20–21, 11.5). And this disproportion represents another of God's surprising reversals, since gentiles-in-Christ, who earlier as pagans had not pursued "righteousness" or "justice" (*dikaiosynē*), have now attained it, whereas Israel, who had pursued "a law of righteousness[,] did not arrive at Law" (cf. RSV "fulfill that Law," vv. 30–31), since the goal or end (*telos*) of the Law for righteousness is Christ (10.4).[71]

Paul insists that Israel's lack of conviction in the good news is an anomaly. They have heard the message (Rom 10.14–18) — it was witnessed in their own scriptures, after all (3.2, 20–21) — yet they remain "disobedient and contrary," while the gentiles have found the god they did not seek (10.18, 20–21). The only explanation is that God, once again, is controlling events. Currently he has chosen a remnant of Israel; the rest he has rendered insensible (RSV "hardened," 11.7). Paul's remnant language harkens back, again, to Isaiah: this elect portion of Israel points ahead to the future restoration of the entire nation.[72]

If the letter to the Romans is Paul's Ninth Symphony, Romans 11.11 begins its fourth movement, Paul's own "Ode to Joy." *Alle Menschen werden Brüder*, and the apostle, divining God's plan, knows how. Too many gentiles? No: more, in fact, will come in, because God will save their "fullness" or "full number" (*plērōma*, Rom 11.25, harkening to Gen 10). Too few Jews? No: God has rendered them insensible only temporarily and strategically, to allow more time for the gentile mission (cf. 11.30–31). For the time being, the native branches of the olive tree of Israel have been broken off, to allow place for "wild olive" branches to be grafted in *para physin*, "against nature" (11.24). But the native branches will also be grafted back in (11.24). How many? Their "fullness" (*plērōma*); "all Israel" (*pas Israēl*, 11.12, 26).

> (25) I do not want you to be ignorant, brothers, of this mystery, . . . that insensibility has come upon a part of Israel, until the *fullness of the nations* comes in, (26) and then *all Israel* will be saved, as it is written, "A Redeemer will come from Zion, he will banish impiety from Jacob." "And this will be my covenant with them, when I take away their sins." (Isa 59.20–21, 27.9)

The "fullness of the nations" and "all Israel" are not vague abstractions. They resonate with grand scriptural themes. The first phrase recalls the Table of Nations in Genesis 10, when Noah's three sons, Japhet, Shem, and Ham, repopulated the earth after the flood. The seventy nations that resulted were dispersed according to their languages, their lands, their kinship-groups, and their gods (Gen 10 LXX; Deut 32.8; p. 13–14 above). And these *ethnē* later defined the scope of End-time redemption: Isaiah's great vision echoed the Table of Nations. "I am coming," God proclaims, "to gather all the nations and languages" (*panta ta ethnē kai pas glōssas*, Isa 66.18 LXX).

When Paul in his turn speaks of End-time redemption, he too recalls this ancient lineage going back to Noah: the gentiles' *plērōma* means "all seventy nations." So too Paul's evocation of the *plērōma* of Israel, *pas Israēl*: his phrasing recalls the patriarchal narratives, the lineage of Abraham passing through Isaac to Jacob and thence to Jacob's twelve sons, the "fathers" of Israel's tribes. "All Israel" conjures the full restoration of these twelve tribes, another traditionally eschatological event. As in Deuteronomy 32.43, which Paul will quote at the end of this letter, so also here in Romans 11: the ingathering of Israel is linked immediately to the inclusion of the nations.[73]

But what of those objects of God's wrath, both human and divine, against whom the apostle had also thundered: unbelievers, sinners, the nations' gods? By the time Paul reaches his paean of praise in Romans 11, human sinners, whether pagans or Jews, seem excused: 11.25–26 speaks in terms of the salvation of all humanity (seventy gentile nations and the twelve tribes of Israel) once "the Redeemer appears from Zion." And the lower cosmic gods? In 1 Corinthians 15.24, Paul had predicted their destruction; but in Romans 8.19–22, they groan together with the rest of creation and await redemption. Here, as in Philippians 2.10, these superhuman beings seem eschatologically rehabilitated to join in the praise of God (cf. Gen 32.43; Ps 97.7).

Paul "magnifies" his mission to the gentiles, he says to Rome's assembly of *ethnē*, precisely to make his fellow Jews jealous "and thus save some of them" now (11.14; cf. 10.19, an astonishing reworking of Deut 32.23). But Israel is ultimately in God's hands, and God, Paul avers, will come through in the End. "In regard to the gospel, they are enemies;[74] but as regards election they are beloved, because of the forefathers, for the gifts and the call of God are irrevocable" (Rom 11.28–29). Gentiles have benefited from Israel's current disobedience (that is, to the gospel): in this respect, God has shown them mercy (v. 30). Israel will soon receive such mercy too, because "God has imprisoned all in disobedience, so that he may show mercy to all" (*tous pantas*, 11.31).

Moved by this vision of impending universal redemption, Paul again breaks out in praise:

> O the depth of the riches and wisdom and knowledge of God! How inscrutable his judgments, how unsearchable his paths! For who has known the mind of the Lord? Who has been his counselor? Who has given him a gift in order to receive a gift back from him? From him and through him and to him are all things. Glory to him forever! (Rom 11.33–36)

How much longer, then, before history reaches this happy climax? "You know the time," Paul tells the Roman community, "that it is now the hour for you to rise up from sleep. Salvation is nearer to us than when we first became convinced [RSV: "believed"]. The night is far gone; the day has drawn close" (Rom 13.11–12). Israel's ancient scriptures are transparent on current events: indeed, the present moment was the reason why they were written down, "so that we might have hope" (15.4). In a single sentence, Paul then sums up the vision of eschatological fulfillment that he had unrolled in chapters 9 through 11: "I tell you that Christ became a servant to the circumcision [Israel] on account of the truth of God, in order to confirm the promises made to the patriarchs; and so that the nations might glorify God for his mercy" (15.8).[75] Chanting a catena of biblical verses that celebrate the nations' turning to Israel's god, their worshiping together with Israel, and their subordination to the Davidic messiah, "Jesse's root"—and so closing the messianic inclusio begun in the opening line of his letter (1.3)—Paul winds up his coda of "hope":

> Therefore I will praise You among the *ethnē*, and sing to Your name. (Ps 18.49)
>
> Rejoice O *ethnē* with his people. (Deut 32.43)
>
> Praise the Lord, O you *ethnē*, and let all the peoples praise him. (Ps 117.1)
>
> And again Isaiah says: The root of Jesse will come, he who rises to rule the *ethnē*; in Him shall the *ethnē* hope. (Isa 11.10; Rom 15.9–12)

This movement of Romans opened with the temple and Jerusalem (site of God's "glory" and of his cult, Rom 9.4), and closes with the temple and Jerusalem. As Christ's minister to the nations, Paul like a priest "sacrifices" the gospel, "so that the offering of the nations might be acceptable, having been sanctified by holy spirit" (15.16; this "sanctified sacrifice" can be understood both as the collection from the gentile assemblies in support of Jerusalem's poor, vv. 25–27, and as the sanctified gentiles themselves). He sketches what he hopes will be his own future apostolic itinerary: first back to Jerusalem, then westward again to Rome, and then on to Spain (vv. 24–25, 28). The arc of this journey, from Jerusalem through Rome to Iberia, corresponds in Jewish geography to those territories given by God to Noah's son Japhet, primal ancestor of Greek peoples, and Paul's particular mission field.[76] Once he completes that circuit, Paul will have done his part to proclaim God's name, and that of his messiah, from Jerusalem to the ends of the earth (cf. 9.17). Does this give us his timeframe? I speculate again. But Romans 16 does close by once more invoking the nearness of the End (*en taxei*, "soon," 16.20; *nun*, the mystery "now" disclosed and made known to all the nations, v. 26).

✦✦✦

However he construed "soon," Paul remained convinced that he lived and worked in history's final hours, in the charismatic caesura between Christ's resurrection and his Parousia. He speaks in terms of past completed action: it is upon his gentile community that the ends of the ages *have come* (*katēntēken*, 1 Cor 10.11). And his reading of scripture, clearly, not only confirmed him in his convictions: it also articulated for him how he had to proceed. Heaven had commissioned Paul specifically to go to pagans, to turn them to Israel's god. Like the biblical prophets whose words he drew on, Paul expected God's kingdom to contain two human populations: Israel *and* the nations.

This meant that gentiles needed to remain gentiles.[77] And this necessity in turn accounts for Paul's principled resistance to proselyte circumcision. If he had once encouraged sympathetic pagans to join Israel fully through "conversion" (Gal 5.11),[78] after his experience of the risen Christ, Paul did so no longer. The particular arguments of the circumcisers in Galatia had driven Paul's creative (and heated) interpretation of the figure of Abraham and his original pronouncements about gentile *huiothesia*: spiritual sonship could not be achieved through fleshly circumcision. But behind that argument, indeed framing Paul's whole enterprise (as his letter to the Romans in particular shows us), was the eschatological vision of the prophets, especially of Isaiah: at the End of the Age, the nations, too, would worship Israel's god alone.[79]

Paul saw this happening before him, with his own eyes, through his own agency—and, he was convinced, through the agency of divine spirit. The teaching of the Lord had gone forth from Zion, and the word of the Lord from Jerusalem (Isa 2.4): the original disciples, spreading out from the community in Jerusalem, had proclaimed the coming Kingdom to the whole world, to the Jew first and also to the Greek (Rom 2.9–10).[80] Pagans renounced and defied their native deities, the lower *daimonia* of the cosmos, whose phased defeat itself indexed the approaching final triumph of David's son, the eschatological messiah. Gentiles baptized into the dying, rising, and returning Christ in turn received and embodied *charismata* and *pneumata*, as did Paul himself. Paul names these frequently: spirit and prophecy (1 Thes 5.19); power and holy spirit (1 Thes 1.5); spirit and working powerful deeds (Gal 3.5); signs, wonders, powerful deeds (2 Cor 12.11); speaking wisdom, knowledge and tongues, working cures and deeds of power, prophesying, distinguishing between spirits, interpreting tongues (1 Cor 12.8–11); signs and wonders and the power of spirit (Rom 15.19); prophecy, teaching, exhortation (Rom 12.6–7). Throughout the god-congested cities of Roman antiquity, these assemblies of Christ were establishing beachheads of the Kingdom.[81]

These ex-pagan pagans, in other words, provided Paul with an ongoing existential confirmation of his convictions, and a profound validation of his own work. Though clearly he witnessed to Jews as well as to gentiles—at the very least, the disciplinary lashings that he received presuppose synagogue settings (2 Cor 11.24)—Paul approached the two groups differently. "To the Jews I became as a Jew, in order to win Jews" (1 Cor 9.20): Paul the Pharisee, expert in his ancestral traditions, argued with his *syngeneis* on the basis of Jewish scriptures. But with god-fearing non-Jews he preached not only through appeals to biblical texts but also "in the demonstration of spirit and of power" (1 Cor 2.4; cf. 9.21). It was among gentiles that Paul most enacted his own charismatic authority; it was the gentiles who provided the strongest empirical evidence that the End-time had indeed dawned; and it was consequently on the gentile mission that Paul most focused his energies and efforts.[82]

But for this scriptural vision to be realized, not only must eschatological gentiles remain gentiles: so too Israel must remain Israel, that family group, God's "sons" and Paul's blood brothers, united by the covenants, the Law, the temple cult, the promises, the patriarchs, and—again the family, "flesh" connection—by the Christ, the son of David (Rom 9.4–5; cf. 1.3, 15.9). Why, then, should Paul, or any other apostle who was a member of this covenant community, have ceased to live according to the Law? The Law was a curse *for gentiles*. The Law only revealed sin *for gentiles*. The Law was a service of death *for gentiles*. But for Israel the Law, God-given, was a defining privilege.[83]

The vast majority of his kinsmen, Paul was nevertheless convinced, misunderstood the Law when they heard it. Its *telos* was the returning Christ (Rom 10.4), but most of Israel did not understand this: "for to this day, when they read the ancient covenant, that same veil remains unlifted because only through Christ is it taken away. Yes, to this day, whenever Moses is read a veil lies over their minds, but turning to the Lord takes away the veil" (2 Cor 3.14–15). Israel would so turn—that is, they would indeed recognize Jesus as the son of David, the eschatological Lord Messiah—only when God enabled them.[84] And God would do so soon, once "the fullness of the nations" was brought in (Rom 11.25). On this point we see how Paul linked his own gentile mission to Israel's divinely assured destiny. By working to turn pagans from their gods to his god, Paul worked as well, beneath a canopy of biblical promises, for the redemption of his own people.[85]

POSTSCRIPT

Paul's tireless and wide-ranging efforts at pagan recruitment; his insistence on maintaining ethnic distinctions between gentiles and Israel; his defiance of pagan gods; his empowerment by spirit: in all these ways, Paul lived his commitment to the good news of God's coming Kingdom. In the beginning, his vision of the risen Christ moved Paul from persecuting outsider to charismatic insider. But over the long decades following that event, it was the turning of the nations from pagan gods to Israel's god — "the strange success of the Gentile mission"[1] — that sustained and even affirmed Paul in his conviction that he knew the hour on God's clock. Paul awaited the Lord's Parousia, while working toward it, for the rest of his life.

This vivid apocalyptic expectation was the drive-wheel of the first generation of the movement — which firmly believed that it would be the *only* generation of the movement. This conviction unites the teaching of Jesus of Nazareth with the resurrection experiences of his early followers. It accounts for their decision to spread Jesus's message of the coming Kingdom outside of the homeland to Israel in the Diaspora. And it explains their (initially startled?) incorporation of pagan god-fearers *qua* "eschatological gentiles" into their new, charismatic assemblies.

The prominence of the biblical theme of gentile inclusion in Jewish End-time traditions, further, not only explains *why* the earliest movement, once it spread abroad, saw the inclusion of gentiles as a natural extension of its mission to other Jews. It also explains *what* the early apostles identified as the paramount condition for those gentiles who wanted to join: they had to make an exclusive commitment to the god of Israel and, thus, to renounce their own gods.

Disrupting relations between gods and their humans in this way meant disrupting as well ancient relations between heaven and earth. Such disruption risked divine wrath; and for this reason, both Roman magistrates and pagan populations actively resisted the apostles' activities. Diaspora synagogue communities—the initial source of the new movement's god-fearing pagans—likewise began to work to dissociate themselves from the disruptive gospel message.[2] It was the ekklesia's socially destabilizing practice of separating a city's pagans from their gods, and not some imagined infraction of Jewish practice, that explains Paul's both giving and, later, getting disciplinary flogging. All of this hostility (in Paul's view, "persecution")—from Roman governors, from irate pagans, from diaspora synagogues, and, Paul was convinced, from the nations' gods themselves—was the social consequence of this apocalyptic movement's production of "eschatological gentiles."

It was also through these gentiles that Paul connected the triumphant apocalyptic lord messiah to the figure of Jesus of Nazareth. By his resurrection, Paul taught, Jesus had already begun the defeat of the cosmic forces: Paul's charismatic gentile communities, themselves empowered with holy spirit, were living proof of the erosion of the power of these lower gods. Both for Paul and for those Jews who were apostles before him, then, their visions of the resurrected Jesus served as a powerful vindication of the message of the impending Kingdom. But it was the subsequent turning of the gentiles—a biblically prophesied but socially unprecedented phenomenon—that proved so successful, so widespread, and so long-lived. These ex-pagan pagans further and continuingly reinforced the apostles' convictions,[3] compelling some of them to press ahead with outreach to pagans, to make disciples of all nations. It was over these nations that the triumphant returning Christ would rule (Rom 15.10; Isa 11.10 LXX).

These ex-pagan pagans represented, indeed embodied, both the final Davidic messiah's staged victory over foreign gods *and* the confirmation of God's ancient promises to Israel. The longer the mission continued, the greater the number of gentiles who joined. On account of their surprising and ongoing response, Paul could state in Romans that the Kingdom was even closer than it had been decades earlier, back in Damascus, where and when he had first "become convinced" (Rom 13.11). Perhaps, indeed, it had been those quondam god-fearers of his original synagogue community, receiving the gospel with its unprecedented demand for them to leave their own gods, who had prompted the shift in Paul's convictions to begin with.

Yet time did not end. The Kingdom did not come. And the gospel movement—already fracturing in Paul's own lifetime—continued to thrive in vigorous variety.

Paul's legacy itself shifted and changed as later followers, writing in his name, updated his message for newer contexts. Thus the "Paul" of 2 Thessalonians explained the reasons for the Kingdom's evident delay, adding a punch-list of necessary further events before the final apocalyptic scenario could unwind (2 Thes 2.1–11). The author of Ephesians trumpeted a new universal humanity, undoing the distinction between Israel and the nations upon which the historical Paul had staked so much (Eph 2.11–16).[4] In Colossians, the cosmic "principalities and powers" are already disarmed (Col 2.15); the believer is already "raised with Christ" (Col 3.1; cf. Paul's careful deferral of this "resurrection," Rom 6.4–5). And the "Paul" of the Pastoral Epistles (1 and 2 Timothy and Titus) establishes church organizations, offices, and structures: this is a community settled within time, not one glowing with charismata on time's edge.[5]

Finally, in chapter 21 of the Acts of the Apostles, we glimpse a disavowed misrepresentation of Paul that would go on to have a long and defining future. In Luke's narrative, Paul and his entourage have just arrived in Jerusalem. James then warns Paul about a rumor circulating about him, "that you teach all the Jews who live among the gentiles to forsake Moses, telling them neither to circumcise their children nor to observe the ancestral customs" (Acts 21.21).

Luke repudiates this rumor, as does his hero, Paul (Acts 21.24, 28–29; 25.8).[6] Yet exactly this view of a de-Judaized Paul describes how many of his early "continuators" regarded him; and, indeed, this view continues to dominate New Testament scholarship to this day. Overlooking the explicit address, in all his letters, to ex-pagan pagans, these interpreters insist that

Paul directed his teachings against circumcision—and, by extension, against the gentile assumption of Jewish ancestral practices, "the works of the Law"—as well and as much to Jews. That Paul himself ceased to live according to Jewish custom. That Paul himself held that Christ had terminated Israel's law. That Paul himself viewed the Law as a curse.[7]

Paul's Jewish identity, Acts tells us, was already being called into question by the early second century. In that same century, Paul's god underwent a similar identity crisis. The ethnicity of the high god shifted: God the Father lost his Jewish identity too.

Though some pagans continued to identify the high god as the god of the Jews,[8] educated ex-pagan Christian theologians increasingly thought otherwise. In the work of Valentinus (fl. 130s), of Marcion (fl. 140s), and of Justin Martyr (fl. 150s), we can trace this process whereby God the father of Christ became no longer Jewish. The point of orientation shared by all three thinkers—a point fundamental to the theology of Middle Platonism—was that the highest god was radically transcendent and changeless, and that another, lower god, a *demiurgos*, organized the material cosmos. This demiurge, functioning as a metaphysical buffer, protected the high god's immutability, radical stability, and absolute perfection. It was he, not the high god, who arranged unstable matter into cosmos, "order." Any imperfections, ills, and evils, which particularly characterized life in the sublunar realm, could be referred to him, or rather to the poor material (itself eternally coexistent with the divine) that he had to work with.[9]

Middle Platonism supplied the criteria of coherent theology for these Christian thinkers. And like Paul, these second-century thinkers urged that Christ's father was indeed the highest god. But all three defined this paternal deity as the radically transcendent, ethnically featureless high god of philosophical *paideia*. "The nature of the Ungenerated Father of All is incorruption and self-existent," explained Valentinus's disciple Ptolemy to a catechumen, "simple, and homogeneous light" (*Ep. ad Floram*, *Panarion* 33.7,7). This god, insisted Marcion, the *summum bonum et optimus* (Tertullian, *adv. Marcionem* 1.24,7; 27,2; 2.11,3), was pure benignity (1.2,3), absolutely good (1.26,2)—and, before the revelation of Christ, utterly unknown. God "abides eternally above the heavens,

invisible, holding personal intercourse with none ... the Father of All,"
taught Justin (*Trypho* 56). Unbegotten and without passion, this god was
also without form, unchanging, unnamed (1 *Apol.* 9.1; 10.1; 13.4; 25.2).

Who, then, was the god of Jewish scripture? The busy and involved
god who organized the physical cosmos, who showed up in history, who
spoke to Abraham and to Moses and to David and to Israel's prophets?
Again, these three gentile Christians agreed: clearly this biblical god was
a lower divinity, inferior and subordinate to the high god. The Septuagintal
texts themselves proclaimed this. He appeared at the very beginning of
these books as a deity embroiled in time and with matter, with doing and
deciding and creating. This lower cosmic deity, the theologians further
concurred, was indeed the god who gave the Jews their Law; the god who
commanded circumcision, blood sacrifices, and Sabbath observance; the
god of Jewish history. For all these reasons, they urged, this god was *not* to
be confused with the high god, God the Father. ("It is evident that this
Law was not ordained by the perfect God and Father," wrote Ptolemy,
"because it is not only imperfect ... but it also contains commandments
which are not consonant with the [ethical] nature and disposition of a
perfect god," *Panarion* 33.3,4.) And if that were the case—if the high god
was *not* represented in Jewish scriptures—then what was this biblical
god's relation to the high god's son, the Christ?

On this question, our theologians parted company. According to
Valentinian Christians, the author of the Law, the god of the Jews, was a
"middling" deity, "neither the perfect God himself nor the Devil ... but
the demiurge ... the rewarder of the justice which conforms to him ...
inferior to the perfect god" (*Panarion* 33.7,1–6). Christ came to fulfill the
good laws of this lower god, and to destroy those laws "intertwined with
baseness and injustice ... [such as] that an eye should be cut out for an
eye" (33.5,1–4). Finally, Christ came to decode the "exemplary laws,"
meaning those ritual mandates whose fundamental meaning was sym-
bolic and spiritual, and whose truest referent was himself (33.5,8–14). By
revealing the Law's truer or higher or spiritual meanings, Christ pointed
the way back to his Father, the high god.[10]

Marcion's views are harder to reconstruct, for two reasons: first,
because all of his writings were lost, suppressed by the later rival church;

and second, because recently scholars have focused on Marcion, with the result that current reconstructions are contested.[11] And to complicate matters, the earliest and chief source of Marcion's teachings lies in their rhetorically charged refutation, the five books of Tertullian's *Adversus Marcionem*. Despite all this uncertainty, however, some points remain clear. Marcion evidently held Paul's letters — an early collection of which he made — in special esteem. He seems to have morally polarized the high god (all good, all-loving, and, until the advent of Christ, unknown) and the demiurge (the god of Jewish Law and of material creation; an opponent of the gospel, the "god of this world," 2 Cor 4.4).[12] The places in his letters where Paul spoke positively of Jewish texts and traditions, Marcion therefore assumed, were "Judaizing" manuscript corruptions: editing these out, Marcion in his own view actually "restored" the letters to their original condition. In a first-order way, for Marcion, Christian revelation was textually embodied not in the LXX, but in "the gospel" and in the letters of Paul.[13]

Justin, finally, while subscribing to the same high god/lower god principle of Middle Platonic theology as did Valentinus and Marcion, unpacked the identity of the biblical god in a more daring way. This demiurgic deity, said Justin, was indeed a *heteros theos*, "another god" (as distinct from the high god). And it was he who had spoken to Abraham as to other heroic figures of the Jewish scriptures (*Trypho* 56). But rather than cast the god of the Bible, the Jews' god, as some sort of contrary subordinate of God the Father, Justin insisted that the Jews' scriptures presented "the Son of God," that is, Christ himself, before his incarnation.

In short, for Justin, the god of the Jews *really* was the god of the Christians, the pre-incarnate Son. The heroes of Jewish scripture (Abraham, Moses, David, Isaiah) had known this, though their stiff-necked descendants did not. Jewish obduracy on this point drove Justin to distraction. "Even now, all Jews teach that the Unnamable God spoke to Moses. . . . [They] have always supposed that the Father of All spoke to Moses, when really it was the Son of God" (1 *Apol.* 63.1,14). The true source of Jewish Law, in brief, was none other than Christ himself. And since Christ gave the Jews their Law, then *all* of it, not (as per Valentinus) just some of it, pertained symbolically *to* Christ. The Jews utterly misconstrued their own traditions. These Laws, never meant to be enacted actually (*kata sarka*, in a "fleshly," unenlightened way) but rather to be understood spiritually, found their true meaning in (Justin's) Christ (cf. *Trypho* 59).

All of these varied configurations of second-century learned gentile theology came together on one exact point: the identity and characteristics of the transcendent high god. These interpreters thus radically de-ethnicized Paul's god; and, accordingly, they also reconceptualized his Kingdom. Redemption receded beyond history's horizon-line. For Valentinus as for Marcion, the Kingdom was the verbal cipher for a spiritual heaven, an upper- and otherworldly realm that awaited the individual soul after death (denounced as such by Justin, *Trypho* 80). For Justin, the Kingdom glowed as a distant hope of a tempered millenarianism, a thousand-year reign of the saints, raised in the flesh, when time, eventually, would end (80–81).[14]

Paul's agonistic rhetoric, with its contrasting binaries of Law and gospel, works and grace; his resolute opposition to proselyte circumcision; his anger with apostolic challengers; his absolute certainty that he knew what was about to happen—once time slipped away and the later gentile churches settled into history, these features of his letters took on the pattern of polarized opposites: Law *or* gospel; works *or* grace; and, as Paul's later theological champions would characterize his position, Judaism *or* Christianity.

Paul would not have recognized his message in these rigid polarities. He conceived of his mission to pagans as entirely consistent with God's promises to his own people, Israel. And he was utterly convinced—*pisteuō*, he wholeheartedly "believed"—that he and his assemblies would live to see the realization of those promises. In his undisputed letters, he never wavered in this conviction. Should his own death anticipate Christ's victorious second coming, Paul averred, he would nevertheless retain his confidence that history's happy ending would come soon (cf. Phil 1.23–26).

If we can move aside the veils of later ecclesiastical tradition, if we can see past their images of Paul the ex-Jew and of Paul the anti-Jew, if we can imagine ourselves back into the full-hearted eschatological conviction of this movement's founding generation—which thought that it was history's *final* generation—it is this other Paul whom we will more clearly see. Paul the dynamic, original, passionately committed late Second Temple visionary. Paul the apostle of the final Davidic messiah. Paul the brilliant student of Jewish law. Paul the expert interpreter of his people's ancient scriptures. Paul the charismatic worker of mighty deeds. Paul the messenger of the Kingdom. Paul, the pagans' apostle.

ACKNOWLEDGMENTS

———————————

First things first: my husband put up with this book, and with my writing it, for a lot longer than I had said that he would have to. Sorry, Alfred I. Tauber. The next one will take less time, I promise.

Next things next: Sandy Dijkstra—super literary agent; voice of sanity; coach and cheering section—could I have done this without you? Maybe; but I can't imagine it. Ben Frankel—writer of beautiful prose; survivor of many of my graduate seminars at the Hebrew University—could I have done this without you? Maybe; but then the bibliography would still not be finished. Heartfelt thanks to you both.

♦♦♦

Something is going on in Pauline studies. While the majoritarian Paul—Paul as the First Christian Theologian or as the Second Founder of Christianity—is still alive and well (and has been the subject, in the past ten years alone, of thousands upon thousands of pages of scholarship), another Paul has also clearly emerged. This is a Paul who fits within his Jewish, Greek, and Roman contexts by way of conformation rather than contrast. A Paul who had no idea that his life's work would eventuate— and only long years after his death, as a belated historical phase-change— in gentile Christianity. A Paul whose very success at turning pagans from their gods to his god, the god of Abraham, Isaac, and Jacob, confirmed him in his conviction that he stood at the edge of history's end. A Paul, in other words, who lived his life entirely within his native Judaism.

175

This is no longer a lonely position to take, as a flurry of recent and not-so-recent titles attests: Stanley Stowers' pathbreaking *Rereading of Romans* (1994); John Gager's *Reinventing Paul* (2000) and his *Jewish Lives of the Apostle Paul* (2015); Pam Eisenbaum's *Paul Was Not a Christian* (2009); Joshua Garroway's *Paul's Gentile-Jews* (2012); Bert Harrill's *Paul the Apostle: His Life and Legacy in their Roman Context* (2012); Mark Nanos and Magnus Zetterholm's anthology *Paul within Judaism* (2015); Gabrielle Boccaccini and Carlos Segovia's collection *Paul the Jew* (2016); Rafael Rodriguez and Matthew Thiessen's gathered essays for *The So-Called Jew in Paul's Letter to the Romans* (2016). *Paul: The Pagans' Apostle* is part of this developing conversation.

✦✦✦

As books grow, so do their authors' debts. Mine are many. I owe deepest thanks first of all to two colleagues and friends, Ishay Rosen-Zvi (Tel Aviv University) and Larry Hurtado (University of Edinburgh). They each read the entirety of my first draft of the book, commented copiously and critically, suggested titles for my own further reading, and saved me from errors large and small. Ishay, Larry: it was a privilege to learn from you in this way. Thank you.

Yale University Press could not have been more efficient, effective, and author-friendly; and I thank the many hands there who made work light, especially Harry Haskell, for close and careful copyediting, and Ann-Marie Imbornoni, for shepherding my text from typescript to print. Special thanks, too, to my always-responsive editor, Jennifer Banks. Guided by who knows what wonderful instinct, she also solicited comments from several readers. They replied with extraordinary intellectual generosity and insight. Their suggestions enriched the process of revision enormously. To these colleagues, whoever and wherever you are: many thanks, not only for your time and care but also for your example.

My warm thanks to Mark Nanos who, over decades of attending various New Testament conferences together with me, has provided endless supplies of encouragement and good ideas, as well as a model of patient perseverance. I thank Mark, together with Magnus and Karin Zetterholm, Anders Runesson, Pam Eisenbaum, and Kathy Ehrensperger, for the work that we have been able to do together in organizing the "Paul within Judaism" section of the Society of Biblical Literature. Emma Wasserman and Caroline Johnson Hodge, through their own publications and by their warm collegiality in organizing the Pauline Epistles section of the SBL, have stimulated my thinking in more ways than they can know; and Caroline's *If Sons, Then Heirs* (2007) remains my go-to source for reflecting upon issues of kinship and ethnicity in Paul. Emma, Caroline: thank you.

To the Theology Faculty at the University of Lund, and to the members of the seminar on "Reading Paul's Letters in Context" at the 2016 meeting of the Studiorum Novi Testamenti Societas, I was able to present earlier drafts of my final chapter, "Christ and the Kingdom." I benefited enormously from my colleagues' conversation, and especially from their criticisms. My thanks go to them, and to Magnus Zetterholm (Lund) and William Campbell (SNTS) for initiating these invitations.

For the past nine years, I have been privileged to be a member of the Humanities Faculty at the Hebrew University of Jerusalem. With its astounding concentration of archaeologists, Byzantinists, classicists, Talmudists, art historians, and historians of Jews, of Judaism (including Philo and the Dead Sea Scrolls), and of ancient comparative religions, Jerusalem has got to be one of the very best places in the world to study ancient Christianity. I offer my deepest thanks to President Menachem Ben Sassoon, for my appointment as Distinguished Visiting Professor; to Dean Dror Wahrman, for his support of and interest in my work; and to my friends, faculty colleagues, and especially to my fellow ancient-and-Late-Antique Christianists: Brouria Bitton-Ashkelony, Oded Irshai, Yoni Moss, Serge Ruzer, and David Satran.

Five books by younger scholars so enriched my research and thus, ultimately, my thinking, that I would be remiss not to name them here: *Christ among the Messiahs*, by Matthew Novenson (2012); *The Son of God in the Roman World*, by Michael Peppard (2011); *Contesting Conversion*, by Matthew Thiessen (2011); *Paul's Interlocutor in Romans 2*, by Runar Thorsteinsson (2003); and *Heralds of the Good News*, by Ross Wagner (2002). I thank these authors warmly, not only for their work but also for their patience while I electronically peppered them with questions and/or sought them out at various conferences.

E. P. Sanders's *Paul and Palestinian Judaism* (1977) revolutionized New Testament studies. That great book began the serious academic retrieval of Second Temple Judaism as the defining context, in positive ways, of Paul's life and work. Thank you, Ed, for your moral summons as well as for your enduring intellectual achievement.

One final—and for me, formative—academic debt, appropriately acknowledged here: to Krister Stendahl for his luminous essay "Paul and the Introspective Conscience of the West." I did not know at the time, when I as an undergraduate first read it, but this article of Krister's would set the parameters for my own future work. Inspired by his insights, I have always studied Paul within two contexts: that of the mid-first century, and that of the Latin West; the Paul of late Second Temple Judaism, and Augustine's Paul, the Christian theologian of grace (and, lest we forget, of predestination). In my *Augustine on Jews and Judaism* (Yale University Press, 2010), the historical Paul could play only a cameo role. *Paul, the Pagans' Apostle* more fully sketches the features of that compelling character whom Krister first introduced me to: self-confident ("as to righteousness under the Law, blameless!" Phil 3.6), urgent in his apocalyptic convictions, addressing his Jewish message—especially and explicitly in Romans—to the gentile nations. It seems only right, then, to dedicate this book to him. In peace your sleep, Krister, and may your memory be for a blessing.

♦♦♦

Paul: The Pagans' Apostle—as a glance at the bibliography of secondary sources under my name will suggest—has been a culminative effort: it mobilizes conclusions reached in work spanning from 1986 ("Paul and Augustine: Conversion Narratives, Orthodox Traditions, and the Retrospective Self") to 2017 ("How Jewish Is God? Divine Ethnicity in Paul's Theology"). For their permission to draw on these earlier essays and books, I thank my publishers: Alfred A. Knopf, Brepols, Brown University Press, Cambridge University Press, Fortress Press, Oxford University Press, Princeton University Press, Scholars Press, the Society of Biblical Literature, University of Notre Dame Press, and Yale University Press.

ABBREVIATIONS

adv. Marc.	Tertullian, *Against Marcion (Adversus Marcionem)*
ABD	*Anchor Bible Dictionary*
AJ	Josephus, *Antiquities of the Jews (Antiquitates Iudaicae)*
AJS	*Association of Jewish Studies*
Apol.	*Apology*
BAGD	*A Greek-English Lexicon of the New Testament*, 3rd ed., ed. W. Bauer, W. F. Arndt, F. W. Gingrich, and F. W. Danker
BJ	Josephus, *Jewish War (Bellum Iudaicum)*
c. Ap.	Josephus, *Against Apion (Contra Apionem)*
c. Cel.	Origen, *Against Celsus (Contra Celsum)*
c. Faust.	Augustine, *Against Faustus (Contra Faustum)*
CHJ	*Cambridge History of Judaism*
CIJ	J.-B. Frey, *Corpus Inscriptionum Iudaicarum*
Comm. Rom.	Origen, *Commentary on the Letter to the Romans*
CTh	*Codex Theodosianus* (Law-code of Emperor Theodosius)
De opif.	Philo, *On the Creation of the World (De opificio mundi)*
EH	Eusebius, *Ecclesiastical History*
GLAJJ	M. Stern, *Greek and Latin Authors on Jews and Judaism*
Hist.	*Histories*
HJP	Emil Schürer-Geza Vermes et al., *The History of the Jewish People in the Age of Jesus Christ*
HTR	*Harvard Theological Review*

IJO	W. Ameling, *Inscriptiones Judaicae Orientis* II: *Kleinasien*
Inch. Exp.	Augustine, *Unfinished Commentary on Romans (Epistulae ad Romanos Inchoata Expositio)*
JAAR	*Journal of the American Academy of Religion*
JBL	*Journal of Biblical Literature*
JECS	*Journal of Early Christian Studies*
JJMJS	*Journal of the Jesus Movement in Its Jewish Setting*
JJS	*Journal of Jewish Studies*
JQR	*Jewish Quarterly Review*
JR	*Journal of Religion*
JRS	*Journal of Roman Studies*
JSJ	*Journal for the Study of Judaism*
JSNT	*Journal for the Study of the New Testament*
JTS	*Journal of Theological Studies*
Jub	Jubilees
LXX	Septuagint
NovT	*Novum Testamentum*
NTh	*Novels of Theodosius II*
NTS	*New Testament Studies*
PGM	*Greek Magical Papyri (Papyri Graecae Magicae)*
PLJP	E. P. Sanders, *Paul, the Law, and the Jewish People*
PPJ	E. P. Sanders, *Paul and Palestinian Judaism*
Propp	Augustine, *Notes on Romans (Expositio 84 propositionum ex epistula ad Romanos)*
SC	Sources chrétiennes
SCI	*Scripta Classica Israelica*
SR	*Studies in Religion/Sciences Religieuses*
Trypho	Justin Martyr, *Dialogue with Trypho the Jew*
VC	*Vigiliae Christianae*

Standard abbreviations for the Dead Sea Scrolls cited in the present study may be found in Emmanuel Tov, *The Texts from the Judaean Desert: Indices and an Introduction to the Discoveries in the Judaean Desert* series (Oxford: Clarendon Press, 2002), and, by the same author, *Revised Lists of the Texts from the Judaean Desert* (Leiden: Brill, 2010).

NOTES

INTRODUCTION

1. Thus Jesus's itinerary according to the gospel of John. The three Synoptic gospels, by contrast, present a one-way, one-time progression from Jesus's mission in the Galilee to his proclamation—and death—in Jerusalem. For a defense of the Johannine itinerary, and its greater plausibility in comparison to that of the Synoptics, see Paula Fredriksen, *Jesus of Nazareth, King of the Jews: A Jewish Life and the Emergence of Christianity* (New York: A. A. Knopf, 1999), 220–59 and notes; and Fredriksen, "Gospel Chronologies, the Scene in the Temple, and the Crucifixion of Jesus," in *Redefining First-Century Jewish and Christian Identities: Essays in Honor of Ed Parish Sanders*, ed. Fabian E. Udoh et al. (Notre Dame, IN: University of Notre Dame Press, 2008), 246–82.

2. On John's role as Jesus's mentor, and the apocalyptic tenor of John's own mission, see esp. John P. Meier, *A Marginal Jew: Rethinking the Historical Jesus*, vol. 2: *Mentor, Message and Miracles* (New York: Doubleday, 1994), 19–233; see also Joan E. Taylor, *The Immerser: John the Baptist within Second Temple Judaism* (Grand Rapids, MI: Eerdmans, 1997).

3. Did Paul take his message of the risen Christ to Jews as well as to gentiles? His letters can be read this way, since he refers to circumcised members of the *ekklēsia* (e.g., 1 Cor 7.18, "Was anyone at the time of his call already circumcised?"); but such sentences could equally refer to those who were proselytes to Judaism, that is, non-native "Jews" of a special sort (see above, p. 107). Equally unclear is whether, before joining the Jesus movement, Paul was a Jewish missionary to pagans to turn them to some (Pharisaic?) form of Judaism: much depends on how one interprets *Ioudaïsmos* in Gal 1.13–14, and how one reads Gal 5.11 ("If I still preached circumcision, why am I still persecuted?"). For the view that Paul was also a pre-Christian missionary, and that Ioudaïsmos should be understood as attempting to get pagans to "Judaize," see most recently Matthew Thiessen, *Paul and the Gentile Problem* (Oxford: Oxford University Press, 2016),

37–41; against this position, and arguing for Ioudaïsmos as an intra-Jewish intensification as a type of political program, Matthew Novenson, "Paul's Former
Occupation in Ioudaismos," in *Galatians and Christian Theology: Justification,
the Gospel, and Ethics in Paul's Letters*, ed. Mark W. Elliott et al. (Grand Rapids,
MI: Baker Academic, 2014), 24–39. Both scholars draw on two preceding essays of
fundamental importance: Steve Mason, "Jews, Judaeans, Judaizing, Judaism:
Problems of Categorization in Ancient History," *JSJ* 38 (2007): 457–512, and,
before him, Shaye J. D. Cohen, *The Beginnings of Jewishness: Boundaries,
Varieties, Uncertainties* (Berkeley: University of California Press, 1999), 175–97.
We will consider these questions at length in chaps. 3 and 5 below.

4. On the ways that an intra-Jewish message of repentance indicates rededication to
Torah, see Paula Fredriksen, *Sin: The Early History of an Idea* (Princeton, NJ:
Princeton University Press, 2012), 6–22.

5. The Bible arranges these commandments variously: see Exod 201–17 and Deut
5.6–21. E. P. Sanders notes that "these two words [*eusebeia* and *dikaiosynē*] were
used very widely by Greek-speaking Jews to summarize their religion," *The
Historical Figure of Jesus* (London: Allen Lane, Penguin, 1993), 92. εὐσέβεια and
δικαιοσύνη also appear in Philo's summary of the Law's two chief principles or
κεφαλαία (*kephalaia*), *Spec.* 2.63; cf. *Decal.* 19, on "honoring parents" within the
Law's First Table. David Flusser surveys the variety of twofold summaries
of Torah (love of God and of neighbor; piety and justice) from Jubilees to
Lactantius in "The Ten Commandments and the New Testament," in *The Ten
Commandments in History and Tradition*, ed. Ben-Zion Segal, trans. Gershon
Levi (Jerusalem: Magnus Press, 1990), 219–46. Similarly, b. Mak. 24a runs the
numbers down from 613 commandments to two (Isa 56.1) to one (Hab 2.4, the
righteous man will live by his *emunah*, "strength" or "steadfastness"; cf. Paul's ἐκ
πίστεως ζήσεται [Gal 3.11]). On *emunah* not as "faith" but as "firmness, steadfast-
ness, fidelity," see Frances Brown, S. R. Driver, and Charles A. Briggs, eds., *A
Hebrew-English Lexicon of the Old Testament* (Oxford: Clarendon Press, 1939),
53. This same tendency to streamline moral teachings appears in the philosophical epitomes of contemporary Greco-Roman culture (Epicurus's *Kyriai Doxai*,
Epictetus's *Encheiridion*): see Hans Dieter Betz, *The Sermon on the Mount: A
Commentary of the Sermon on the Mount, including the Sermon on the Plain
(Matthew 5:3–7:27 and Luke 6:20–49)*, ed. Adela Yarbro Collins (Minneapolis,
MN: Fortress, 1995), 76–79, with notes to the key literature.

See Sanders's comments on this Matthean passage, the so-called
Matthean Antitheses (Mt 5.21-48), *Historical Figure*, 210–12; also Flusser, "Ten
Commandments," 234. Cf. Lk 11.42, another coded reference, where neglecting
"judgment" (τὴν κρίσιν) indicates neglecting justice. Emphasis on the Ten
Commandments in mid-first-century Palestinian Judaism is perhaps reflected
as well in tefillin from Qumran. The later tractate y. Ber. 9b comments that
while the Ten Commandments used to be recited every day in the Temple,
they no longer are "on account of the *minim* ('sectarians')," who hold that no
other commandments were given on Sinai: Ephraim E. Urbach, *The Sages, Their*

Concepts and Beliefs, trans. Israel Abrahams (Jerusalem: Magnes, 1975), 2: 844 n. 75.

6. A long academic tradition has held that "Christ" in Paul's letters had been so leached of traditional messianic content that the word functioned fundamentally and simply just as another name for Jesus. This position has been demonstrably and definitively put to rest by Matthew Novenson, *Christ among the Messiahs: Christ Language in Paul and Messiah Language in Ancient Judaism* (New York: Oxford University Press, 2012), who argues that *Christos* in Paul serves as an "honorific."

7. Mark ends abruptly with the empty tomb and the fearful silence of Mary of Magdala, Mary the mother of James, and one Salome (Mk 16.1–8). Matthew has two witnesses to the risen Christ, Mary Magdalene and "the other Mary" (Mt 28.1, 9–10), and a later Christophany to the (eleven) disciples on a mountain in the Galilee (28.16–20). Luke's resurrection stories are quite different: "the women who had followed him from Galilee" find the tomb empty (23.55; these are later identified as Mary Magdalene, Johanna, Mary the mother of James, "and the other women," 24.1–10); the risen Christ appears incognito to two disciples at Emmaus (24.13–31), to Peter (off stage, 24.34), and then to the assembled group back in Jerusalem (24.36; Acts 1.1–9 sketches forty days of postresurrection appearances, all in Jerusalem). John is different again: Mary Magdalene sees the risen Christ near the tomb (Jn 20.11–18); then Jesus appears to an assembled group in Jerusalem and later has his dialogue with the doubting Thomas (20.19–29), while chap. 21 continues with Christophanies in the Galilee.

8. Paul not only identifies the risen body as a *pneumatikon sōma* ("spiritual body," 1 Cor 15.44); he says specifically that "flesh and blood cannot inherit the Kingdom of God" (15.50). Once fleshly (as opposed to merely bodily) resurrection became an article of church doctrine (which is to say, by the fourth century), commentators had to work to square Paul's remarks with a commitment to saved flesh. For one ingenious ancient effort, see Augustine, *City of God*, who speaks of "spiritual body" as flesh oriented according to the moral and metaphysical agency of divine spirit (22.21). For a more recent effort to attribute some version of such thinking to Paul himself, see James Ware, "Paul's Understanding of the Resurrection in 1 Corinthians 15:36–54," *JBL* 133 (2014): 809–35. For the ways that ideas about "flesh," monastic and lay ascetic practices, and imperially sponsored episcopal politics collide in the fourth century, see Elizabeth A. Clark, *The Origenist Controversy* (Princeton, NJ: Princeton University Press, 1992).

9. Josephus narrates the movements that formed around these charismatic figures in *BJ*, book 2, and in *AJ*, book 20. See too the study by Rebecca Gray, *Prophetic Figures in Late Second Temple Jewish Palestine* (Oxford: Oxford University Press, 1993). On "messianism" more generally, *HJP* 2: 488–554.

10. The Synoptic gospels put Jesus's wonder working within the larger framework of his *evangelion*: his powers validate his authority to announce the coming Kingdom, e.g., Mt 11.2–24/Lk 7.18–35. For the argument on the ways that these traditions might illumine the mission of the historical Jesus, see Fredriksen, *Jesus*

of Nazareth, 110–17; Sanders, *Historical Figure*, 132–68; and the lengthy consideration in Meier, *Marginal Jew*, 2: 508–1,038.

11. For the most recent and comprehensive analysis of Jesus's own eschatological message, see Dale C. Allison, Jr., *Constructing Jesus: Memory, Imagination, and History* (Grand Rapids, MI: Baker Academic, 2010), esp. 31–219. Allison begins his consideration with the nice epigram drawn from Harris Lenowitz, *The Jewish Messiahs: From the Galilee to Crown Heights* (New York: Oxford University Press, 1998): "The time scheme, the calendar, for a messianic movement has but a single date: Now."

The academic genealogy of the apocalyptic Jesus traces back to Johannes Weiss (*Jesus' Proclamation of the Kingdom of God*; German original 1892) and Albert Schweitzer (*The Quest of the Historical Jesus*; German original 1906). Continuators of this stemma include E. P. Sanders, *Jesus and Judaism* (London: SCM, 1985); John P. Meier (*A Marginal Jew: Rethinking the Historical Jesus*, 5 vols., 1991–2016); Dale C. Allison, Jr., *Jesus of Nazareth: Millenarian Prophet* (Minneapolis, MN: Fortress, 1998); Bart D. Ehrman, *Jesus: Apocalyptic Prophet of the New Millennium* (Oxford: Oxford University Press, 1999); as well as Paula Fredriksen, *From Jesus to Christ: The Origins of the New Testament Images of Jesus*, 2nd ed. (New Haven, CT: Yale University Press, 2000), and *Jesus of Nazareth*. For a review of the work of scholars committed to a nonapocalyptic Jesus (Jesus as shaman, Cynic, Jewish Cynic, "Spirit-person," and post-Jewish anti-"nationalist"), see Paula Fredriksen, "What You See Is What You Get: Context and Content in Current Research on the Historical Jesus," *Theology Today* 52 (1995): 195–204, and the Introduction to the second edition of *From Jesus to Christ*, xiii–xxviii.

"Apocalypse" means "revelation." In an academic setting, the term means different things to different scholars: for a sampling and orientation of the literature, focused on the work of J. Louis Martyn, Martinus de Boer, Beverly Gaventa, and Douglas Campbell, see J. P. Davies, *Paul among the Apocalypses?* (London: Bloomsbury T. & T. Clark, 2016), esp. his concluding chapter, pp. 198–203. In this book, as I will repeatedly emphasize, I use "apocalypse"—often in combination with "eschatology"—to describe Paul's dramatically foreshortened time frame for expected or prophesied final events. The Kingdom comes (almost) *now*.

1. ISRAEL AND THE NATIONS

1. These texts are conveniently assembled in English translation as James H. Charlesworth, ed., *The Old Testament Pseudepigrapha*, 2 vols. (Garden City, NY: Doubleday, 1983–85). Apocrypha are available in the Oxford NRSV edition of the Bible. See too, for an exploration of this world of rewritten Jewish scriptures, Hindy Najman, "The Vitality of Scripture within and beyond the 'Canon,'" *JSJ* 43 (2012): 497–518. John J. Collins surveys this literature in "The 'Apocryphal' Old Testament," in *The New Cambridge History of the Bible*, vol. 1, *From the*

Beginnings to 600, ed. James Carleton Paget and Joachim Schaper (Cambridge: Cambridge University Press, 2013), 165–89.

2. On the text of the Hebrew Bible, and the Dead Sea Scrolls' place in that story, see Emanuel Tov, *Textual Criticism of the Hebrew Bible*, 2nd rev. ed. (Minneapolis, MN: Fortress, 2001); the figures on the Isaiah variants come from p. 161. See too Eugene Ulrich, "Isaiah, Book of," in *Encyclopedia of the Dead Sea Scrolls*, ed. Lawrence H. Schiffman and James C. VanderKam (Oxford: Oxford University Press, 2000), 386–87. Isaiah looms large in the scriptures preserved at Qumran: Timothy M. Law provides the statistical breakdown in *When God Spoke Greek: The Septuagint and the Making of the Christian Bible* (New York: Oxford University Press, 2013), 25, while half of Paul's scriptural citations in his letter to the Romans are from Isaiah: J. Ross Wagner, *Heralds of the Good News: Isaiah and Paul "in Concert" in the Letter to the Romans* (Leiden: Brill, 2002), 2. For the ways that the LXX sheds light on earlier Hebrew manuscript traditions, see Emanuel Tov, *The Text-Critical Use of the Septuagint in Biblical Research*, 2nd ed. (Jerusalem: Simor, 1997).

3. "Apocalypse" comes from the Greek word for "revelation." "Eschaton" means "the end" or "the last thing." "Apocalyptic eschatology" thus means "revelation of knowledge (*-logy*) about the End." *I use the terms here and throughout the book to convey the idea of "expecting the End soon."* "The End" in this genre of Jewish tradition meant a qualitative change in circumstances (such as the establishment of universal peace, abundance, and acknowledgment of Israel's god) and in time (especially given its linkage with hopes for the resurrection of the dead), but the venue of the Kingdom usually remains terrestrial: both Israel and the nations gather in a (renewed and glorious) Jerusalem, at the temple mount. Paul's message is an intriguing variation on this theme. Throughout this book, I emphasize (a) time (the cosmos is due to change *soon*) and (b) miracle (the dead will rise; eternal peace will be established). The day *after* the Kingdom comes, in short, would look different from the day before—which means that there would be no mistaking that the Kingdom had not yet arrived.

   That said, "apocalyptic" has been interpreted in all sorts of ways that efface its foreshortened timeframe: on this point, Wayne Meeks's observations about the term and its theological refractions are as apt now as they were in 1983, *The First Urban Christians: The Social World of the Apostle Paul* (New Haven, CT: Yale University Press, 1983), 171–72 and 240 n. 20. A monumental example of such interpretation is (at 1,218 pages) Douglas A. Campbell's *The Deliverance of God: An Apocalyptic Rereading of Justification in Paul* (Grand Rapids, MI: Eerdmans, 2009). For smaller samplings of these modern positions that stretch from Ernst Käsemann to N. T. Wright, see (some of) the essays collected in Ben C. Blackwell, John K. Goodrich, and Jason Maston, eds., *Paul and the Apocalyptic Imagination* (Minneapolis, MN: Fortress, 2016); also (concentrating on the work of Beker, Martyn, Campbell, and Gaventa), J. P. Davies, *Paul among the Apocalypses? An Evaluation of the "Apocalyptic Paul" in the Context of Jewish and Christian Apocalyptic Literature* (London: Bloomsbury T. & T. Clark, 2016). For a concise history of the variety of definitions surrounding this term, see John J. Collins, *The Apocalyptic Imagination: An Introduction to Jewish Apocalyptic Literature*, 2nd ed. (Grand Rapids, MI: Eerdmans, 1998), 1–42. Once again, the present book emphasizes the fast-approaching, impending future.

4. This narrative structure of eschatological thought shapes Paul's later scriptural references too: see Richard B. Hays, *Echoes of Scripture in the Letters of Paul* (New Haven, CT: Yale University Press, 1989), 157–58. On the ways that a messianic understanding of Greek Isaiah shapes Paul's sensibility, especially in his letter to Rome, see the beautiful study by Ross Wagner, *Heralds of the Good News*. On apocalyptic hope more generally, and the ways that it corresponded to and was stimulated by Second Temple Jewish experience, see Paula Fredriksen, *From Jesus to Christ: The Origins of the New Testament Images of Jesus*, 2nd ed. (New Haven, CT: Yale University Press, 2000), 77–93; E. P. Sanders, *Jesus and Judaism* (London: SCM, 1985), 61–122 and, with particular reference to gentiles, 212–21; also 335–40. On expressions of these expectations and hopes in various late Second Temple literatures, Collins, *Apocalyptic Imagination*, 43–233.

5. The "Let us" of Gen 1.26 presented an irresistible opportunity for later interpreters to posit various recipients of God's address. Jubilees fills in the gap by describing the divine creation on the first day of the orders of angels, who then assist with the rest of God's work (Jub 2.1–3). For a survey of late Second Temple to Roman period divine assistants to YHWH, see Larry W. Hurtado, *One God, One Lord: Early Christian Devotion and Ancient Jewish Monotheism*, 2nd ed. (London: T. & T. Clark, 1998), 41–50 (personified divine attributes), 51–69 (exalted patriarchs), and 71–92 (principal angels). On YHWH's divine assistants in the DSS, John J. Collins, "Powers in Heaven: God, Gods and Angels in the Dead Sea Scrolls," in *Religion in the Dead Sea Scrolls*, ed. John J. Collins and Robert A. Kugler (Grand Rapids, MI: Eerdmans, 2000), 9–28.

6. Cf. Jub 11.17–22, on God's Sabbath observance, shared with the two highest orders of (circumcised!) angels (15.27); lower angelic orders, meanwhile, keep the world running on the seventh day. See James Kugel, "4Q369 'Prayer of Enosh' and Ancient Biblical Interpretation," *Dead Sea Discoveries* 5 (1998): 119–48, at pp. 123–26.

7. Annette Y. Reed traces the long arc of this tradition, from Enoch to Justin Martyr, in "The Trickery of the Fallen Angels and the Demonic Mimesis of the Divine: Aetiology, Demonology, and Polemics in the Writings of Justin Martyr," *JECS* 12 (2004): 141–71; see too Reed, *Fallen Angels in the History of Judaism and Christianity: The Reception of Enochic Literature* (Cambridge: Cambridge University Press, 2005). Further on the genealogy of this idea, Dale B. Martin, "When Did Angels Become Demons?" *JBL* 129 (2010): 657–77.

8. In 1 Cor 8.4–5, Paul at once denies the existence of other gods while at the same time complaining about them and also denigrating them, in this regard echoing his great predecessor and inspiration, Second Isaiah (e.g., Isa 45.6). For a full consideration of the vocabulary and polemical logic of Jewish texts coping with categorizing these superhuman powers while concerned "to assert the

incomparable power of the high God" of Israel, see Emma Wasserman, "'An Idol Is Nothing in the World' (1 Cor 8.4): The Metaphysical Contradictions of 1 Corinthians 8:1–11:1 in the Context of Jewish Idolatry Polemics," in *Portraits of Jesus: Studies in Christology*, ed. Susan E. Meyers (Tübingen: Mohr Siebeck, 2012), 201–27; quotation from p. 227.

9. On this question of terminology, and the difficulties with using the word (thus, the concept) "monotheism" for antiquity, see Michael S. Heiser, "Monotheism, Polytheism, Monolatry, or Henotheism? Toward an Assessment of Divine Plurality in the Hebrew Bible," *Bulletin for Biblical Research* 18 (2008): 1–30; Paula Fredriksen, "Mandatory Retirement: Ideas in the Study of Christian Origins Whose Time Has Come to Go," *SR* 35 (2006): 231–46; Peter Hayman, "Monotheism—a Misused Word in Jewish Studies?" *JJS* 42 (1991): 1–15.

10. Pagan monotheism, both that of educated elites and that of patriotic city-dwellers ("Great is Artemis of the Ephesians!" Acts 19.28), has recently been explored in two excellent scholarly anthologies: *Pagan Monotheism in Late Antiquity*, ed. Polymnia Athanassiadi and Michael Frede (Oxford: Clarendon Press, 1999), and *One God: Pagan Monotheism in the Roman Empire*, ed. Stephen Mitchell and Peter van Nuffelen (Cambridge: Cambridge University Press, 2010). In the latter book see especially the essays by Christoph Markschies ("The Price of Monotheism: Some New Observations on a Current Debate about Late Antiquity," conceptualizing the issue vis-à-vis the study of ancient religions), Angelos Chaniotis ("Megatheism: The Search for the Almighty God and the Competition of Cults," on the ways that the claim *heis theos en ouranōi*, "one god in heaven," asserted superiority, not singularity), and Nicole Belayche ("*Deus deum ... summorum maximus* [Apuleius]: Ritual Expressions of Distinction in the Divine World in the Imperial Period," on divine hierarchy and plurality).

11. James M. Scott, *Paul and the Nations: The Old Testament and Jewish Background of Paul's Mission to the Nations with Special Reference to the Destination of Galatians*, WUNT 1, 84 (Tübingen: Mohr Siebeck, 1995), gives a clear and sweeping introduction to and analysis of this important scriptural idea. See especially his chart on p. 7.

12. The Song of Moses at Deut 32.8–9 LXX does allude to these ethnic-theological identity markers, when God hands over the governance of the *ethnē* to other superhuman powers (*angelōn theou*; cf. the *benei elohim*, "sons of God," in the Scrolls, 4QDeut^j), while governing Israel directly himself. By contrast, the Masoretic Hebrew text apportions the nations to the governance of the "sons of Israel." Richard Bauckham's allegiance to a modern definition of monotheism— only one god exists—makes this passage harder to interpret than it needs to be: *Jesus and the God of Israel: God Crucified and Other Studies on the New Testament's Christology of Divine Identity* (Grand Rapids, MI: Eerdmans, 2008), 111–14. See on this interesting scriptural passage the remarks of Wasserman, "'An Idol Is Nothing,'" 207–10; also and especially Scott, *Paul and the Nations*, 5–6 n. 2, for copious references to the scholarly literature.

13. 1 Chron 1.1–2.2; Ezek 38–39; Dan 11; Isa 66.18–20; Jub 8–9; from Qumran, 1Q *Genesis Apocryphon* and 1 QM 2.10–14 (the War Scroll); Sibylline Oracles, book 3; Josephus, *AJ* 1.120–147; Ps-Philo, *Biblical Antiquities* 4–5; in later rabbinic tradition, y Megilla 71b, b Yoma 10a; Genesis Rabbah 37.1–8; various targumim, which correlate the biblical names on this table with contemporary Roman provincial areas (Scott, *Paul and the Nations*, 53). For an incisive review of all of these sources, and an analysis of how the Table of Nations "provided a fundamental point of orientation for describing Israel's place among the nations of the world and the basis for envisioning world geography and ethnography both in the present and for the eschatological future," see Scott, *Paul and the Nations*, 8–56; quotation from p. 54.

14. The rabbis eventually articulate and emphasize difference, seeing "the nations" as Noah's descendants, whereas Israel descends particularly from Abraham (himself a descendant of Shem), Isaac, and Jacob, *Mekhilta* to Deut 12.30. On the evolution of the rabbinic concept of the "Noahide laws"—seven biblically derived rules to which the nations were notionally obligated—see most recently Christine E. Hayes, *What's Divine about Divine Law?* (Princeton, NJ: Princeton University Press, 2015), 350–70; for discussion of the earlier literature, Paula Fredriksen, "Judaism, the Circumcision of Gentiles, and Apocalyptic Hope: Another Look at Galatians 1 and 2," *JTS* 42 (1991): 535 and nn. 8–9.

15. Deuteronomy speaks of a divine *coup de foudre*: God falls in love. "It was not because you were more numerous than any other people that the Lord set his heart on you and chose you, for you were the fewest of all people. It was because the Lord loved you . . ." (Deut 7.7–8). "Although heaven and the heaven of heavens belong to the Lord your god, the earth with all that is in it, yet the Lord set his heart in love on your ancestors alone and chose you, their descendants, out of all the peoples, as it is today. Circumcise, therefore, the foreskin of your heart . . ." (10.14–16). I thank Ishay Rosen-Zvi for bringing to my attention this language of *heshek/agapē*. Jub 15 provides a backstory, later to enter rabbinic midrash: Abraham's family were makers of idols, but Abraham repudiated idolatry and, after destroying his father's idol-factory, was called by God: *Lech le-cha*, "Go out!" (Gen 12.1; Jub 12.1–8, 12–22).

16. See, for example, the range of the instructions given in Lev 19, which represents an explication and an expansion of the Ten Commandments, especially of the second table.

17. Jer 31, for example, expresses hope for their full restoration (see too 3.6–12, 16.14–16, 23.3–6, 30.3). On these traditions about the ten "lost" tribes, and the ways that Paul's letters and the gospels resonate with these traditions, see Jason A. Staples, "What Do the Gentiles Have to Do with 'All Israel'? A Fresh Look at Romans 11:25–27," *JBL* 130 (2011): 371–90, esp. pp. 374–78 for late Second Temple materials, including DSS.

18. For the Greek practice of prophecy, see Lisa Maurizio, "Delphic Oracles as Oral Performances: Authenticity and Historical Evidence," *Classical Antiquity* 16 (1997): 308–34; and Hugh Bowden, *Classical Athens and the Delphic*

Oracle: Divination and Democracy (Cambridge: Cambridge University Press, 2005).

19. Was this effort at Hellenization a "religious" persecution (as it seems to be presented in 1 and 2 Macc), or primarily a Greek mode of political federation? Can we even meaningfully distinguish these two categories, "religion" and "politics," in antiquity? The historiography, like the history, divides along these lines: John Ma, "Relire les *Institutions des Séleucides* de Bickerman," in *Rome, a City and Its Empire in Perspective: The Impact of the Roman World through Fergus Millar's Research* (Leiden: Brill, 2012), 59–84.

20. For a coherent historical orientation in this turbulent cultural terrain, see E. P. Sanders, *Judaism: Practice and Belief, 63 BCE–66 CE* (Philadelphia: Trinity Press International, 1992), 3–43; for discussion with copious bibliography, *HJP*, vols. 1–3.

21. "The last days" as an eschatological clarion of history's close sounds already in Gen 49.1 LXX; Num 24.14; Isa 2.2; Jer 23.20; Dan 10.14. It repeats in Paul as the "ends of the ages," 1 Cor 10.11; cf. "the fullness of time," Gal 4.4. Annette Steudel surveys the DSS on this theme, "אחרית הימים in the Texts from Qumran," *Revue de Qumrân* 16 (1993): 225–46.

22. On these themes in Jewish restoration eschatology, see Sanders, *Jesus and Judaism*, 77, 119, 222–41 (reconstructing Jesus's own views); *HJP* 2: 514–46, for a systematic review of these very *un*systematic traditions. The outpouring of divine spirit in the last days figures prominently in Paul's letters, as we shall see: cf. Isa 32.15, 34.16, 44.3–4, 61.1; Ezek 11.19, 36.25–27, 37.1–14, 39.29; Joel 2.28–29; Zech 12.10; 1 QS 4.21–22; Jub 1.23–25; 1 Enoch 49.3; Pss Sol 17.37. The list given above of eschatological events, however, should not be taken to imply a fixed sequence or some sort of canonical punch-list: different themes appear in different combinations in different texts.

23. John J. Collins, *The Scepter and the Star: Messianism in Light of the Dead Sea Scrolls* (New York: Doubleday, 1995) reviews the diversity of messianic figures; see too, more recently, Adela Yarbro Collins and John J. Collins, *King and Messiah as Son of God: Divine, Human, and Angelic Messianic Figures in Biblical and Related Literature* (Grand Rapids, MI: Eerdmans, 2008); also Jan Willem van Henten, "The Hasmonean Period," in *Redemption and Resistance: The Messianic Hopes of Jews and Christians in Antiquity*, ed. Markus Bockmuehl and James Carleton Paget (London: T. & T. Clark, 2009), 15–28, for particular attention to the eschatological messiahs of Aaron and of David attested in the DSS. Matthew V. Novenson points out the "manifest diversity" of these traditions even within the specific subcategory of "Davidic messiah": "Paul has a Davidic messiah who dies and rises from the dead (Rom 1.3–4). 4 Ezra 7.28–29 has a Davidic messiah who dies but does not rise from the dead. The Qumran *Community Rule* has a Davidic messiah who is an accessory to a priestly messiah (1 QS IX, 11). The epistle to the Hebrews has a Davidic messiah who is himself a priestly messiah (Heb 7.11–17). Bavli Sanhedrin even has a Davidic messiah who judges cases by a divinely inspired sense of smell (b. Sanh. 93b). All of these texts represent defensible ancient interpretations of certain biblical house of David texts, but they do not

remotely constitute a single model of the Davidic messiah," "The Messiah ben Abraham in Galatians: A Response to Joel Willitts," *Journal for the Study of Paul and His Letters* 2 (2012): 163–69, at p. 165.

24. Florilegia of these texts are gathered and analyzed in Joachim Jeremias, *Jesus' Promise to the Nations* (London: SCM, 1967), 46–75; Sanders, *Jesus and Judaism*, 214; and earlier, with analysis, E. P. Sanders, *Paul and Palestinian Judaism: A Comparison of Patterns of Religion* (Philadelphia: Fortress, 1977), 329–428; Fredriksen, "Circumcision of Gentiles," 544–48; Terence L. Donaldson, "The 'Curse of the Law' and the Inclusion of the Gentiles: Galatians 3:13–14," NTS 32 (1986): 110 nn. 43–50; and by the same author, more recently, *Judaism and the Gentiles: Jewish Patterns of Universalism (to 135 CE)* (Waco, TX: Baylor University Press, 2007), 499–505, with individual texts examined *infra*.

25. Albert Schweitzer's remarks on this distinction between Jesus's mission (to Jews only) and Paul's (to pagans) still repay reading, *The Mysticism of Paul the Apostle*, trans. William Montgomery, intro. by Jaroslav Pelikan (Baltimore, MD: Johns Hopkins University Press, 1998), 178–81.

26. Thus in his *Dialogue with Trypho*, Justin quotes Ps 72.17 LXX ("His name shall rise up forever above the sun; and in him shall all nations be blessed") as proof of Jesus's identity as the Christ: "If all the nations are blessed in Christ, and we from all the nations believe in him, then he is indeed the Christ. . . . To us [gentiles] therefore it has been granted to see, to hear, to understand, and to be saved by this Christ," *Trypho* 121.

2. FATHERLAND AND MOTHER CITY

1. *Aristeas* (12–27) and Josephus (*AJ* 12.11–33) mention that some Jews entered Egypt as slaves during the Ptolemaic period, while other Jews served the political and cultural interests of their new Hellenistic rulers (thus Josephus, *AJ* 12.147–53, on Antiochus the Great settling 2,000 Babylonian Jewish families in Asia Minor, and *c. Ap.* 2.44, a Ptolemaic king using Jewish subjects to garrison outposts of his territories).

2. The Mediterranean world had been crisscrossed by competing maritime traders for centuries by the time of Alexander (d. 323 B.C.E.). But Alexander's conquests of the eastern Mediterranean, and the subsequent Roman appreciation and appropriation of Greek culture (which then spread into territories reaching as far west as Britain), sponsored a new kind of cultural coherence. For a dramatic recounting of the backstory of the Punic role in spreading Greek culture to the western Mediterranean, see Richard Miles, *Carthage Must Be Destroyed: The Rise and Fall of an Ancient Civilization* (New York: Viking, 2011); for Alexander's cultural consequence, Frank W. Walbank, *The Hellenistic World* (Cambridge, MA: Harvard University Press, 1992); on the ways that the (political and architectural) structure of the city expressed and enabled this culture, A. H. M. Jones's great study, *The Greek City from Alexander to Justinian* (Oxford: Clarendon Press, 1940). My discussion of this western Jewish population owes much to the work of

John M. G. Barclay, *Jews in the Mediterranean Diaspora: From Alexander to Trajan (323 BCE–117 CE)* (Edinburgh: T. & T. Clark, 1996), and to Erich S. Gruen, *Heritage and Hellenism: The Reinvention of Jewish Tradition* (Berkeley: University of California Press, 1998) and *Diaspora: Jews amidst Greeks and Romans* (Cambridge, MA: Harvard University Press, 2002). For a very full survey of relevant primary material, *HJP's* three volumes.

3. Two recent introductions to the social and intellectual histories behind the Septuagint are Tessa Rajak's *Translation and Survival: The Greek Bible of the Ancient Jewish Diaspora* (Oxford: Oxford University Press, 2009) and Timothy Law, *When God Spoke Greek* (New York: Oxford University Press, 2013). Together with Alison G. Salvesen, Law is editing the forthcoming *Oxford Handbook of the Septuagint.* Still, the effect of the LXX on non-Jewish Greeks was a while in coming, as Arnaldo Momigliano long ago observed, *Alien Wisdom: The Limits of Hellenization* (Cambridge: Cambridge University Press, 1975), esp. 90–92: its broad dissemination is attributable to the rise of Christianity.

4. This paragraph draws especially on Tertullian's fulminations against the gods' omnipresence in *De spectaculis* and *De idololatria*. In the latter treatise he specifies private family festivities (16), insignia of civic office (18), military standards (19), education (10), oaths, contracts, and vernacular expressions (20–23). Contemporary rabbis in Palestine were no less aware of the civic throw-weight of these gods: Mishnah *Avodah Zarah* 1.3 names Kalends (a winter festival eight days after the solstice), the Saturnalia (eight days before the winter solstice), and the *kratasis* (days celebrating imperial accession to office), as well as imperial birthdays and death days, as "the festivals of the gentiles": see Fritz Graf, "Roman Festivals in Syria Palaestina," in *The Talmud Yerushalmi and Graeco-Roman Culture,* ed. Peter Schäfer (Tübingen: Mohr Siebeck, 2002), 435–51. Further on domestic cult, Jonathan Z. Smith, "Here, There, and Anywhere," in *Relating Religion: Essays in the Study of Religion* (Chicago: University of Chicago Press, 2004), 323–39; and the essays assembled by John Bodel and Saul M. Olyan in *Household and Family Religion in Antiquity* (Malden, MA: Blackwell, 2008). Specifically on the worship of the family father's *genius*, Michael Peppard, *The Son of God in the Roman World: Divine Sonship in Its Social and Political Context* (Oxford: Oxford University Press, 2011), 39, 43, 63–66, 113–15.

5. On "gods in the blood," see my earlier discussion in Paula Fredriksen, *Augustine and the Jews: A Christian Defense of Jews and Judaism* (New York: Doubleday, 2008), 6–15 and corresponding notes; on the general point, and its consequences for our understanding of ancient "religion," Brent Nongbri, *Before Religion: A History of a Modern Concept* (New Haven, CT: Yale University Press, 2013). Further on this correspondence between "ethnicity" and "religion"—allowing for the anachronism of both terms—the essays in Irad Malkin, ed., *Ancient Perceptions of Greek Ethnicity* (Washington, DC: Center for Hellenic Studies, Trustees for Harvard University, 2001). Many of the authors draw attention to the passage in Herodotus, *Histories* 8, quoted p. 35 above.

6. The word *pagan* is of course itself anachronistic for the first century, coming into use only in late antiquity as a coinage by gentile Christians to distinguish themselves from non-Christian and non-Jewish contemporaries, and to emphasize the non-Christian gentiles' enduring attachment to the "old" gods. Further on the term and the concept, see Christopher P. Jones, "The Fuzziness of 'Paganism,'" *Common Knowledge* 18 (2012): 249–54.

7. Linguistically, first-century Jews were broadly divided between Greek speakers and Aramaic or Hebrew speakers, hence Paul's inability to use "common language" as an identifier in the way that Herodotus did (though, as we will see in chap. 5, he does conceptualize Hebrew as "Jewish" language, shared between God and his human "sons"). These two passages, however, also resonate with the "Table of Nations" in Gen 10, where peoples are divided up according to their kin-groups, languages, and lands. That chapter, as noted above, quite strikingly does *not* include "gods" among its list of ethnic identifiers. When this idea of "the number of the nations" is reprised in Deut 32.8, however, "gods" are introduced: humanity divides into nations "according to the number of the sons of God," the beings in his heavenly court. (These become "God's messengers," *angeloi*, in the LXX.) Philo, too, Paul's elder contemporary, will associate ethnicity ("kinfolk by blood"), cult, territory, customs, and temples, *On the Virtues* 102; see Scott, *Paul and the Nations*, 95.

8. As the terms given above attest, cult itself was envisaged as a kind of family association. "In the Roman world, religion and ethnic loyalties were inseparable," Benjamin H. Isaac, *The Invention of Racism in Classical Antiquity* (Princeton, NJ: Princeton University Press, 2004), 500. Teresa Morgan, *Roman Faith and Christian Faith: Pistis and Fides in the Early Roman Empire and Early Churches* (Oxford: Oxford University Press, 2015), provides a thorough and fascinating discussion of Roman *fides* ("loyalty to" or "faithfulness toward"), and the way that the concept contrasts with later ideas of Christian "faith": pp. 1–26 (a discussion of the problems with the later usages of *pistis* and of *fides* in Jewish and Christian texts); 36–175 (the Roman context); 176–211 (the transmutations of the idea in and through the LXX). On Roman enactments of respect to the divine more generally, see John Scheid, *Quand faire, c'est croire: Les rites sacrificiels des Romains* (Paris: Aubier Flammarion, 2011).

9. On Octavian's status as "son of God," see Peppard, *Son of God*, 46–48.

10. On the civic construction of divine lineages, and the ways that diplomats mobilized these to secure and to stabilize inter-city agreements, see esp. the elegant study by Christopher P. Jones, *Kinship Diplomacy in the Ancient World* (Cambridge, MA: Harvard University Press, 1999). Jones comments on Romans as "Aeneadae" on p. 88; cf. Acts 18.24, which uses this civic/ethnic construction to introduce "the Jew Apollos . . . an Alexandrian by *genos*," which could indicate not birthplace, but Alexandrian citizenship.

11. "After reading a certain document," announces a Spartan king to the Jewish high priest, "we have found that Jews and Lacedaemonians [Spartans] are of one γένος, and share a connection with Abraham," *AJ* 12.226. This συγγένεια also

appears in 1 Macc 12.21 and 2 Macc 5.9; for Heracles' union with Abraham's granddaughter, *AJ* 1.240–41. (Note: the divine status of Heracles as founder of Spartan lineage is unremarked upon in all of these Hellenistic Jewish texts.) Analysis of the Abraham-Heracles tradition in Jones, *Kinship Diplomacy*, 72–80; Erich S. Gruen, "Jewish Perspectives on Greek Ethnicity," in *Ancient Perceptions of Greek Ethnicity*, ed. Irad Malkin (Washington, DC: Center for Hellenic Studies, 2001), 347–73, at pp. 361–64. Paul also will avail himself of this idea of Abraham as "the father of many nations," Rom 4.11–18; Gal 3.7–14; cf. Gen 17.5; see Stanley K. Stowers, *A Rereading of Romans: Justice, Jews, and Gentiles* (New Haven, CT: Yale University Press, 1994), 227–50.

12. See Peppard, *Son of God*, 60–70, for the ways that the emperor Augustus, in positioning himself as *pater familias* of the empire, constructed a family relationship between himself and others in the Roman world, thereby spreading abroad the worship of his *genius* and *numen* ("divine power," which Tertullian discounts as a *daemonium*, *Apol.* 32.2). For the changes in pantheon expected and enacted through adoption, see ibid., 50–60; on the ritual maintenance and creation of "descent," Caroline E. Johnson Hodge, *If Sons, Then Heirs: A Study of Kinship and Ethnicity in the Letters of Paul* (Oxford: Oxford University Press, 2007), 26–36. Johnson Hodge nicely defines both the *domus* (Roman household), and by extension the imperial state, as "a sacrificing kinship group headed by the paterfamilias" (27). Further on gods and families: Ann E. Hanson, "The Roman Family," in *Life, Death and Entertainment in the Roman Empire*, ed. D. S. Potter and D. J. Mattingly (Ann Arbor: University of Michigan Press, 1999), 19–66; on gods and cities, the essays in Richard Buxton, ed., *Oxford Readings in Greek Religion* (New York: Oxford University Press, 2000); on gods, rulers who become gods, and larger political units, Simon R. F. Price, *Rituals and Power: The Roman Imperial Cult in Asia Minor* (Cambridge: Cambridge University Press, 1984), and Ittai Gradel, *Emperor Worship and Roman Religion* (Oxford: Clarendon Press, 2002); on civic and imperial piety and the way that it combined especially with athletics and other dedicated competitions, David S. Potter, "Entertainers in the Roman Empire," in *Life, Death and Entertainment in the Roman Empire*, 256–325.

13. "How miserable are those, their hopes set on dead things, who give the name 'gods' to the work of human hands!" (Wis 13.10). Such people kill children in their initiation ceremonies and give themselves over to frenzied revels; they defile their own marriages with adultery, their societies with treachery and murder; they prophesy falsehoods and commit perjury; they lie, cheat and steal (14.23–28). Paul repeats this pervervid antipagan rhetoric in Rom 1.18–32. Accusations of sexual profligacy were a reliable trope in ancient slander, on which see esp. Jennifer W. Knust, *Abandoned to Lust: Sexual Slander and Ancient Christianity* (New York: Columbia University Press, 2006). Canaanite and later Punic peoples did indeed practice child sacrifice (Miles, *Carthage Must Be Destroyed*, 68–73); but the idea as a trope of derogation survives well into the Roman imperial period, combined with accusations of cannibalism and sexual misconduct (incest especially). Pagans will aim these charges against Christians, and Christians will aim them

against each other: see, p. 198 and n. 26. Justin will train this polemic against Jews, e.g., *Trypho* 20, 27, 29, 73, 133.

On the LXX rendering of Exod 22.28(27), and its "liberal" interpretation by Philo and Josephus, see Pieter W. van der Horst, "'Thou Shalt Not Revile the Gods': The LXX Translation of Ex. 22: 28 (27), Its Background and Influence," *Studia Philonica Annual* 5 (1993): 1–8. Further on the Jewish admiration for and appropriation of Greek culture, Erich S. Gruen, *Diaspora: Jews amidst Greeks and Romans* (Cambridge, MA: Harvard University Press, 2002), 213–31; Barclay, *Jews in the Mediterranean Diaspora*, 82–181.

14. For a classic essay on the ways that transition into Greek transformed biblical texts and key terms, see C. H. Dodd, *The Bible and the Greeks* (London: Hodder & Stoughton, 1935), esp. 3–95 ("God," "Law," "Righteousness, Mercy and Truth," "Sin," and "Atonement").

15. Pagan *daimones* could be either good or evil: see Henry Chadwick, "Oracles of the End in the Conflict of Paganism and Christianity in the Fourth Century," in *Mémorial André-Jean Festugière: Antiquité païenne et chrétienne*, ed. E. Lucchesi and H. D. Saffrey (Geneva: P. Cramer, 1984), 125–29, on Plutarch and Porphyry; J. B. Rives, "Human Sacrifice among Pagans and Christians," *JRS* 85 (1995): 68-83, at pp. 80–83; Maijastina Kahlos, *Debate and Dialogue: Christian and Pagan Cultures c. 360–430* (Aldershot, UK: Ashgate, 2007), 172–81. Origen, evidently annoyed by the pagan Celsus's conflation of lower gods, angels ("messengers"), and demons, enunciates clearly this difference between pagan and Septuagintal, thus Christian, views: "Celsus fails to notice that the name of daemons is not morally neutral like that of men, among whom some are good and some are bad; nor is it good like the name of gods, which is not to be applied to evil daemons. . . . The name of daemons is always applied to *evil* powers . . . they lead men astray and distract them, and drag them down," *c. Cel.* 5.5.

Some Hellenistic Jews, such as the author of Wisdom and, eventually, the apostle Paul, took *daimonia* as exclusively evil, bound up as they were with the cultic worship of images. We find this same view in later Christian writers, such as Justin: see Reed, "The Trickery of the Fallen Angels." On the particular link between (malevolent) demons (*qua* pagan gods) and blood sacrifices, Justin, *2 Apol.* 5; *Trypho* 19, 22, 43, and frequently (there aimed against Jewish sacrifice). The idea that high gods neither want nor need sacrifices, but that lower gods do, was originally pagan, hence Porphyry's reference to Theophrastus, *On Abstinence* 2.27,1–3. Further on Theophrastus, and on Greek philosophical theology more generally, Dale B. Martin, *Inventing Superstition: From the Hippocratics to the Christians* (Cambridge, MA: Harvard University Press, 2004), 21–78. The comment below on earth's representing the collecting-point for heaviest matter comes from Sallustius, *Concerning the Gods and the Universe*, VII. For the religious significance of this cosmic architecture, see the following two notes.

16. A. D. Nock, in his edition of Sallustius, *Concerning the Gods and the Universe* (Hildesheim: G. Olms, 1966), provides a tour through the metaphysics of this idea of cosmos and introduces some of its many intermediaries; see further E. R.

Dodds, *Pagan and Christian in an Age of Anxiety: Some Aspects of Religious Experience from Marcus Aurelius to Constantine* (Cambridge: Cambridge University Press, 1965), 6–14; Fredriksen, *Sin*, 51–58, esp. on the correspondences between this model of the cosmos and textual interpretation; also Alan Scott, *Origen and the Life of the Stars: A History of an Idea* (Oxford: Clarendon Press, 1991), 53–172. According to Plato, souls passing to and from the earth traversed the spheres of the planets, *Phaedrus* 248C–E, *Timaeus* 41D–42E. Matter altered, bodies became finer as they ascended this cosmic order, as Paul states in 1 Cor 15.39–42, on which see Dale B. Martin, *The Corinthian Body* (New Haven, CT: Yale University Press, 1995), esp. 104–36 on the astral transformation of the resurrected body; also Troels Engberg-Pedersen, *Cosmology and Self in the Apostle Paul* (Oxford: Oxford University Press, 2010), specifically on Stoic cosmology in Paul; Thiessen, *Gentile Problem*, 129–160, on Paul, *pneuma*, "seed," and star bodies.

17. This Jewish association of stars and planets, pagan gods, and idols finally fuses in the rabbinic word *akkum*, an abbreviation for "a worshiper of stars and planets" (*eved kohkavim v-mazzalot*), applied in Talmudic literature to idolators.

18. While it was obvious to many gentile Christians that the high god was the father of Jesus Christ, that still left in question the identity of the god represented in the LXX. Mid-second century, both Valentinian and Marcionite Christians identified the biblical deity as the "lower," ethnic god of the Jews, as such not immediately relevant to Christian revelation: see, for example, Ptolemy's *Epistle to Flora* 7.4; see too Augustine, *Against Faustus* 18.2, for a late fourth-century Latin iteration of the same idea of the Jewish god as an ethnic demon. Justin Martyr argued, on the basis of this god's appearances in the LXX's narratives, that he cannot be the high god, e.g., *Trypho* 60; 1 *Apol.* 63. The Postscript of the present study will survey these different Christian theological positions.

    That gods were defeated when their humans were was an extension of the normal identification of peoples and pantheons: we hear echoes of this idea in those Christian apologies that insist on the high status of Israel's god despite the Jews' defeat by Rome. Speaking in the voice of a skeptical pagan, Christian author Minucius Felix wrote, "The lonely and miserable nationality of the Jews worshiped one god, peculiar to itself; and he has so little force or power that he is enslaved, with his own special nation, to the Roman gods," *Octavius* 10.4; cf. Tertullian, *Apol.* 26.3; cf. 25.14–16 on other defeated, ethnic gods; Origen, *Against Celsus* 4.32; Faustus in Augustine, *Against Faustus* 15.1. Jews were themselves no less traumatized by the theological implications of military defeat: see Adiel Schremer, "'The Lord Has Forsaken the Land': Radical Explanations of the Military and Political Defeat of the Jews in Tannaitic Literature," *JJS* 59 (2008): 183–200.

19. Within "the innermost chamber [of Jerusalem's temple] . . . was nothing whatever. It was unapproachable, inviolable, and invisible to all," wrote Josephus, "and it was called the Holy of Holies" (*BJ* 5.219). Pagans were well aware of this singular aspect of Jewish cult. Varro (*apud* Augustine, *City of God* 4.31) contrasted Roman worship unfavorably with Jewish aniconism, while historians Livy

in the early first century C.E. and Cassius Dio one century later likewise com-
ment favorably on the Jews' aversion to visual representations of their god: see
GLAJJ 1.330, No. 133 (Livy), and 2.349–51, No. 406 (Cassius Dio). On the Second
Commandment's prohibition of worshiping God through images, Exod 20.4–6;
Deut 5.8–10. Such aniconism accorded well with the uniquely invisible, incorpo-
real, and uncreated nature of (the Jewish) God, said Philo, e.g., *Leg. All.* 3.36;
Decal. 64–67; and frequently elsewhere.

This pagan awareness of Jewish aniconism has immediate implications for
how we read Rom 1.18–32. Even a gentile Christ-following auditor, argues
Matthew Thiessen, would understand Paul's rhetorical targets to be pagans, not
"humanity in general," i.e., Jews as well: see *Paul and the Gentile Problem*, 47–52;
against, e.g., most recently John M. G. Barclay, *Paul and the Gift* (Grand Rapids,
MI: Eerdmans, 2015), 462–66 and passim, who sees this passage in Romans as a
universal indictment of humanity. We will see later how, in the second century,
attempting to make philosophical sense of the LXX, different gentile Christians
will shift the ethnicity of the high god once again.

20. On the weekly Sabbath gatherings for hearing the Law, see, e.g., Josephus, *c. Ap.*
2.175; Philo, *De somniis* 2.123, 127, and *Spec. Laws* 2.62; also Acts 15.21, cited above,
p. 55; on the ways that this synagogue setting in the western Diaspora promoted
Greek Jewish biblical interpretation that interacted with pagan Hellenistic learning, William Horbury, "Biblical Interpretation in Greek Jewish Writings," in *The
New Cambridge History of the Bible*, vol. 1: *From the Beginnings to 600*, ed. James
Carleton Paget and Joachim Schaper (Cambridge: Cambridge University Press,
2013), 289–320. "In view of the strict centralization of the Jewish cult," observes
Schürer-Vermes, "the Jewish temple at Leontopolis is a remarkable phenomenon," *HJP* 3: 145; cf. *BJ* 7.423–32 for Josephus's description of this temple in Egypt
and its origins in the political turmoil of the mid-second century B.C.E.; also *HJP*
3: 47–48, 145–47. For the Jerusalem temple, Herod's architectural program, and its
international draw, Sanders, *Practice and Belief*, 47–169. Sanders estimates (p. 127)
that the temple area could accommodate about 400,000 pilgrims; on the temple
tax, pp. 83–84; Lee I. Levine, *Jerusalem: Its Sanctity and Centrality to Judaism,
Christianity, and Islam* (New York: Continuum, 1999), 137ff.

21. "The Jews conceive of one god only," says Tacitus, "and that with the mind only;
and they regard as impious those who make from perishable materials representations of god as a type of human. That supreme and eternal being is to them inca-
pable of representation, and without end. Therefore they set up no statues in their
cities, still less in their temples," *History* V.5.5,4. By "temples" (*templa*), Tacitus
probably intends synagogues (*GLAJJ* 2.26, No. 281), and he goes on to note that
Jews accordingly do not show honor to Caesar. In the mid-third century, Origen
noted this same pagan acquiescence to Jewish theological claims: "The supreme
God is called 'the God of the Hebrews' even by people alien to our faith," *c. Cel.*
5.50. A century or so later, the emperor Julian—himself a convert from orthodox
Christianity to "classical" paganism—made the same identification. Informing
Jewish subjects that he wished to rebuild the temple in Jerusalem, Julian pledged

to "invest all my enthusiasm in restoring the temple of the Highest God [*hypsistou theou*]," *Ep. et leg.* No. 134 (Bidez/Cumont). The Postscript will return to this issue of the high god's ethnicity; see also Paula Fredriksen, "How Jewish Is God? Divine Ethnicity in Paul's Theology."

Celsus, the second-century pagan critic of Christianity, confuses Jewish aniconism with worshiping the sky and derides Jews for this inconsistency (that is, for worshiping heaven in general but denying divinity to heavenly bodies), *c. Cel.* 5.6. For the broader pagan perception of Jews as a nation of philosophers, see Peter Schäfer, *Judeophobia: Attitudes toward the Jews in the Ancient World* (Cambridge, MA: Harvard University Press, 1997); John G. Gager, *The Origins of Anti-Semitism: Attitudes toward Judaism in Pagan and Christian Antiquity* (New York: Oxford University Press, 1983); Louis H. Feldman, *Jew and Gentile in the Ancient World: Attitudes and Interactions from Alexander to Justinian* (Princeton, NJ: Princeton University Press, 1993), 201–32. The roll-call of such admiring pagans (Theophrastus, Megasthenes, Clearchus of Stoli, Hermippus of Smyrna, Ocellus of Lucanus) is sounded in all treatments of Hellenistic Judaism. Where there are fragments, they can be found in *GLAJJ*. The pagan Pythagorean Numenius of Apamea famously asked, "What is Plato, but Moses speaking Greek?" This saying nods to the perception, vigorously cultivated by Hellenistic Jews and thence much repeated by later church fathers, that what the Greeks got right (especially philosophy), they actually derived from Jewish learning: see *GLAJJ* on Numenius, 2.206–11, Nos. 363a–e; also Gruen, *Diaspora*, 213–31. For the flip side of this coin, namely that diaspora Jews by absenting themselves from cult were guilty of impiety, see the following note.

22. These insults are collected and categorized by Schäfer, *Judeophobia*, 66–81 (food ways), 82–92 (Sabbath, thus laziness), 93–105 (circumcision). Feldman, *Jew and Gentile*, breaks these down according to popular (pp. 107–22) and intellectual prejudice (pp. 123–76). On the gentile view of Jewish circumcision as a "mutilation" and a "shameful deformity," see Origen, *Commentary on Romans* 2.13, 27–29. Both the Jews and their god were seen as antisocial (*akoinōnētos*; Numenius again; *GLAJJ* 2.214, No. 367). For discussion of the ancient accusations of *amixia*, esp. Isaac, *Invention of Racism*, 450–54; on Jewish "atheism," 460 (with special reference to proselytes, on which more below). Josephus responds to accusations of Jewish impiety and misanthropy in *c. Ap.* 2.148; on cloud-worship, see Juvenal, *Sat.* 14.97; cf. *c. Cel.* 5.6 (heaven-worship).

23. "Of all the festivals celebrated by Diaspora Jews, the Sabbath was, in social terms, by far the most important, since its observance was so regular, so noticeable, and so socially problematic, affecting . . . not only personal but also financial, legal, and political relationships," Barclay, *Jews in the Mediterranean Diaspora*, 440. Philo mentions Augustus's leniency about the Roman Jews' corn dole, *Legatio* 158. Josephus discusses the various arrangements made by Asian Jews to safeguard Sabbath observance in *AJ*, book 14; cf. 16.27 and 45, on Jews in Ionia regarding temple monies. On pagan Sabbath observance, Josephus remarks, "there is not one city, Greek or barbarian, nor a single nation [*ethnos*], to which our custom of

abstaining from work on the seventh day has not spread," *c. Ap.* 2.282. For pagan complaints about pagans keeping Sabbath, e.g., Juvenal, *Sat.* 14.105; Plutarch, *De superstitione* 3 and 8, *GLAJJ* 1.549, Nos. 255 and 256. On later gentile Christians and the Sabbath, e.g., Origen, *In Lev. Hom.* 5.8; *Sel. in Exod.* 12.46; famously, Chrysostom's eight sermons preached in Antioch *contra Iudaeos* (actually, against Judaizing Christians); Augustine, *Ep.* 54.2, 3.

24. Circumcision, says Philo, is considered "ridiculous by the great majority" (*Spec. Laws* 1.1.1–2). On Roman humor and Jewish foreskins (or lack thereof), see Feldman, *Jew and Gentile,* 155–56, who mentions a comedy by Naevius (see discussion on p. 507 n. 75), and lines by Horace (*Satires* 1.9.70 and 1.5.100), by Persius (*Saturae* 5.184; *GLAJJ* 1.436, No. 190), and by Petronius (*Satyricon* 68.8; *GLAJJ* 1.442, No. 193). 1 Macc opens with Jews who exercise in the gymnasium seeking to "make foreskins," that is, to remove the mark of circumcision surgically (i.e., by epispasm; 1 Macc 1.11–15). On Jews as athletes (thus contestants in dedicated events), the papyrus discussed by Allen Kerkeslager, "'Maintaining Jewish Identity in the Greek Gymnasium: A Jewish Load' in *CPJ* 3.519 (= P. Schub. 37 = P. Berol. 13406)," *JSJ* 28 (1997): 12–33. Further on Jewish athletes in inscriptions, Paul R. Trebilco, "The Christian and Jewish Eumeneian Formula," in *Negotiating Diaspora: Jewish Strategies in the Roman Empire,* ed. John M. G. Barclay (London: T. & T. Clark, 2004), 80 n. 86; on Jewish athletes, gladiators, and spectators, Zeev Weiss, *Public Spectacles in Roman and Late Antique Palestine* (Cambridge, MA: Harvard University Press, 2014), 195–226; for inscriptional and literary evidence, Margaret H. Williams, *The Jews among the Greeks and Romans: A Diasporan Sourcebook* (Baltimore, MD: Johns Hopkins University Press, 1998), 114–17.

25. On this whole cluster of issues—ethnic difference, racial superiority and inferiority, genealogically fixed inherited moral characteristics, and so on—see the magisterial study by Isaac, *Invention of Racism.* Isaac breaks down this discourse by ethnic target: Greeks on Easterners (chap. 4); Romans on Easterners (chap. 5) and on Greeks (chap. 9); classical ethnographers on Phoenicians, Carthaginians, and Syrians (chap. 6), on Egyptians (chap. 7), on Parthians and Persians (chap. 8), on Gauls (chap. 11), on Germans (chap. 12), and on Jews (chap. 13). See also the following note.

26. Gideon Bohak's nice oberservation: see his essay, "The Ibis and the Jewish Question: Ancient 'Anti-Semitism' in Historical Context," in *Jews and Gentiles in the Holy Land in the Days of the Second Temple, the Mishnah and the Talmud: A Collection of Articles* (Jerusalem: Yad Ben-Zvi Press, 2003), 27–43; quotation from p. 43. On specifically anti-Jewish accusations of cannibalism, Pieter W. van der Horst, "The Myth of Jewish Cannibalism: A Chapter in the History of Antisemitism," in *Studies in Ancient Judaism and Early Christianity* (Leiden: Brill, 2014), 173–87. On pagan anti-Christian calumnies, especially cannibalism and incest, e.g., Tertullian, *Apol.* 8.1–5; cf. Pliny, *Ep.* 10.96, 2 and 7; Isaac, *Invention of Racism,* 485. Justin hints at the "nefarious and impious rites" of pagans and of other sects of gentile Christians, *Trypho* 35; two-plus centuries

later, Augustine will subtly suggest Manichean moral enormities, *c. Fortunatum* 2–3. On later Christians preserving and passing on originally pagan anti-Jewish ethnic stereotyping, Isaac, *Invention of Racism*, 441. Finally, on human sacrifice as the ultimate antisocial behavior, Rives, "Human Sacrifice," and van der Horst, "Jewish Cannibalism."

    Pagan accusations of Jewish separateness—now read 500 years after the forced segregation of Jews in European urban ghettos, and after the post-Holocaust self-segregation of various Jewish haredi sects in North America and in Israel—are sometimes taken at face value by modern historians, who then retroject modern constructions of Jewish "orthodoxy" or, conversely, of "assimilation" onto ancient Jewish populations. This is a historiographical problem. I hope that this quick survey of the comfortable diversity of our varied ancient evidence makes the case that, historically, there was no way to index "orthodoxy" (other than rhetorically: orthodoxy is *"my* doxy"); and that ethnic specificity (people-hood; narratives of the past; foodways; connection to specific lands; inherited protocols of worship; language) vitally coexisted with interethnic social (thus "religious") activities in the cities of the early empire. See too the apposite comments on this issue by Gidi Bohak, "Ethnic Continuity in the Jewish Diaspora in Antiquity," in *Jews in the Hellenistic and Roman Cities*, ed. John R. Bartlett (London: Routledge, 2002), 175–92, at pp. 183–85.

27. For the text of this inscription, *HJP* 3: 65; Fergus Millar gives the judgment of "defection to paganism or syncretism" on p. 138. Cf. Feldman on Artapanus and ancient "orthodox" Judaism, n. 32 below.

28. On these two Jewish inscriptions, giving thanks to the Jewish god, that were left in the temple of Pan, see Irina Levinskaya, *The Book of Acts in Its Diaspora Setting* (Grand Rapids, MI: Eerdmans, 1996), 94–95. *HJP* 3: 58 gives the text of these inscriptions, commenting that both thank "'the god' without mention of his name. Whether this was Pan or Yahweh seems not to have been of great importance to them." But each dedication specifies that its donor was a *Ioudaios* (and the article before the noun, *ho theos*, in my view denotes *the* god, that is, the high god), thereby signifying the ethnicity of their divinity as well as their own, as Levinskaya rightly points out, p. 95. Further on the ephebes Jesus and Eleazar, Barclay, *Jews in the Mediterranean Diaspora*, 234–31, who discusses other inscriptions that imply Jewish citizenship. See also the discussion on Jewish citizens in the communities of Asia Minor, and the ways in which such status would involve them with pagan gods, in Paul R. Trebilco, *Jewish Communities in Asia Minor* (Cambridge: Cambridge University Press, 1991), 172–85.

29. For Apion's complaint, see Josephus, *c. Ap.* 2.65; for similar complaints from cities in Asia Minor, e.g., *AJ* 12.125–26, where the pagan Ionians speak of citizens as *syngeneis*, "kinsmen" who worship the same gods. For an overview of the legal history that Josephus preserves, see Miriam Pucci Ben Zeev, *Jewish Rights in the Roman World: The Greek and Roman Documents Quoted by Josephus Flavius* (Tübingen: Mohr Siebeck, 1998). On Tiberius, Philo's nephew, *AJ* 20.100 (Tiberius did not adhere to his *patria ethē*); Barclay, *Jews in the Mediterranean*

Diaspora, 105f. Further on inscriptions about Jewish town councilors, Trebilco, "Eumeneian Formula," 79–80. The legal text from the Digest is given with translation and discussion in Amnon Linder, ed. and trans., *The Jews in Roman Imperial Legislation* (Detroit, MI: Wayne State University Press, 1987), No. 2, wherein *superstitio* should be understood as "foreign cult."

30. On Jews and the "D.M." inscriptions, see Ross S. Kraemer, "Jewish Tuna and Christian Fish: Identifying Religious Affiliation in Epigraphic Sources," *HTR* 84 (1991): 141–62; Leonard V. Rutgers, *"Dis Manibus* in Jewish Inscriptions from Rome," in *Jews in Late Ancient Rome: Evidence of Cultural Interaction in the Roman Diaspora* (Leiden: Brill, 1995), 269–72; Erwin R. Goodenough, *Jewish Symbols in the Greco-Roman Period*, 13 vols., Bollingen Series 37 (New York: Pantheon Books, 1953–1968), 2: 137–40. The manumission inscriptions from the Bosphorus are available in J.-B. Frey, *CIJ* 1, Nos. 683, 684, 690; comments and literature cited in Lee I. Levine, *The Ancient Synagogue: The First Thousand Years* (New Haven, CT: Yale University Press, 2000), 114 and notes. For Pothos's inscription in particular, Levinskaya, *Acts*, 111–16, with full text of the inscription on p. 239 (Pothos was a pagan sympathizer): cf. Levine, *Ancient Synagogue*, 113–23 (Pothos was a Jew, p. 114). Whatever the ethnicity of the inscription's author, its very interpretive ambiguity makes the larger and more important point: ethnic "boundaries" were not patrolled borders.

   Further on Jews as ephebes, town councilors, and officers in pagan armies, Williams, *Jews among the Greeks and Romans*, 107–31. On Jews' funding of pagan liturgies, *HJP* 3: 25 (Niketas, for Dionysis); on Herod's largesse to pagan activities, Josephus, *AJ* 16.136–49; discussion in Fredriksen, "Judaizing," 232–52, at p. 236f. On the endowment of Glykon, see Walter Ameling, *Inscriptiones Judaicae Orientis*, vol. 2: *Kleinasien*, ed. Martin Hengel and Peter Schäfer (Tübingen: Mohr Siebeck, 2004), No. 196, 414–22. Was Glykon a Jew or perhaps a pagan sympathetic to things Jewish? Either identification is plausible, ibid., 422. For a longer consideration of this issue of ambiguity, Philip A. Harland, "Acculturation and Identity in the Diaspora: A Jewish Family and 'Pagan' Guilds at Hierapolis," in *The Religious History of the Roman Empire: Pagans, Jews, and Christians*, ed. J. A. North and S. R. F. Price (Oxford: Oxford University Press, 2011), 385–418. The main point to bear in mind: complaints of classical ethnographers notwithstanding, diaspora Jews were neither unintegrated in society nor completely uninvolved with local gods.

31. On Jews in pagan recreational places (whether as spectators or as participants), see most recently Weiss, *Public Spectacles*, esp. 207 and notes, for primary references to inscriptions, and to literary evidence from Philo, from irritated church fathers, and from no less irritated rabbis. See too the older essay by Peder Borgen, "'Yes,' 'No,' 'How Far?': The Participation of Jews and Christians in Pagan Cults," in *Paul in His Hellenistic Context*, ed. Troels Engberg-Pedersen (Edinburgh: T. & T. Clark, 1994), 30–59. Tertullian, in *De spectaculis, De idololatria*, and *Apologeticus*, offers vivid descriptions of the cultic dimension of urban activities and festivals.

32. On Artapanus, whose writings are known through the excerpts preserved in Book 9 of Eusebius's *Praeparatio evangelica*, see Barclay, *Jews in the Mediterranean Diaspora*, 127–32. Feldman sees in Artapanus's claims that Joseph and Moses founded Egyptian and Greek (thus, pagan) cultures evidence that he cannot have been "an observant Jew" (*Jew and Gentile*, 208), whereas Barclay sees "a proud Egyptian and a self-conscious Jew" (p. 132; cf. too his remarks against anachronistic assignments of "orthodoxy" and "deviance," pp. 83–102). Noting how Artapanus refers interchangeably to God and to gods, Barclay comments, "even as a Jew he is both a monotheist and a polytheist" (p. 132); but the exact same thing, for the same reason, can be said also of Philo, of Paul, and of virtually any ancient monotheist whether pagan, Jewish, or, eventually, Christian. Aristobulus, a Hellenistic Jewish author thoroughly familiar with the Greek cultural canon, argues at length that Jewish thought is both prior and superior to that of the Greeks, who whether as philosophers or as poets derived all their truths from Moses. (Evidently, these cultural plagiarizers had had access to a Greek translation of the Pentateuch made well before the LXX, Eusebius, *Praep. Evang.* 12.1.; cf. *Aristeas*, 312–16.) For Hellenistic Jews under false colors, whether as Greek *littérateurs* or as pagan seers, see discussion and bibliography in *HJP* 3: 618–54 and 654–700; for an appreciation of their "brazen inventiveness," Gruen, *Diaspora*, 213–31. Further on the cultural and social embeddedness of diaspora Jewish communities, Pieter W. van der Horst, "The Jews of Ancient Phrygia" and "Judaism in Asia Minor," in *Studies in Ancient Judaism and Early Christianity* (Leiden: Brill, 2014), 134–60.

33. My description rests on the excellent essay by Sarah Pearce, "Jerusalem as 'Mother-City' in the Writings of Philo of Alexandria," in *Negotiating Diaspora: Jewish Strategies in the Roman Empire*, ed. John M. G. Barclay (London: T. & T. Clark, 2004), 19–36. On the LXX's use of *apoikia*, ibid., p. 33, drawing on the essay by Joseph M. Mélèze-Modrzejewski, "How to Be a Jew in Hellenistic Egypt?" in *Diasporas in Antiquity*, ed. Shaye J. D. Cohen and Ernest S. Frerichs (Atlanta, GA: Scholars Press, 1993), 65–91. On the complexities of citizenship vis-à-vis residence for Greek-speaking Jews, Bohak, "Ethnic Continuity." Bohak discusses this passage from Philo on p. 182. Cynthia Baker, using this same passage from Philo, rotates the framework by speaking of multiple Jewish "ethnicities," privileging place and language (in the multitudes of different Jewish cities of residence) over "blood" in these construals of group identities, "From Every Nation under Heaven."

34. Sanders gives the details of the temple's interior layout, *Practice and Belief*, 55–72; see Levine, *Jerusalem*, 219–60, for a broader picture.

35. The transition of *ger* to *prosēlytos*, and thence from "resident alien" to "convert," has been traced by Matthew Thiessen, "Revisiting the προσηλυτος in the LXX," *JBL* 132 (2013): 333–50; we will return to this issue below, when we consider "conversion" in antiquity. On the *soreg* (the demarcation of the pagan area of the temple courts), see Sanders, *Practice and Belief*, 61; Elias J. Bickerman, "The Warning Inscriptions of Herod's Temple," *JQR*, n.s. 37 (1947): 387–405; also Stephen R. Llewelyn and Dionysia van Beek, "Reading the Temple Warning as a

Greek Visitor," *JSJ* 42 (2011): 1–22. Such restrictions are known from other sanctuaries, as Bickerman notes. On Delos (another tourist draw), the founder's shrine
was forbidden to the non-Delian *xenos*. Christiane Sourvinou-Inwood explores
this us/them aspect of Mediterranean cult in "Further Aspects of *Polis* Religion,"
in *Oxford Readings in Greek Religion,* ed. Richard Buxton (New York: Oxford
University Press, 2000), 38–55; on Delos in particular, p. 50. Philo speaks of
Augustus's paying for daily burnt offerings at the temple, *Legatio* 157; Josephus, of
the hecatomb (100 oxen!) offered by Marcus Agrippa, *AJ* 16.14. For the whole
question of pagan participation in the Jerusalem cult, see *HJP* 2: 309–13.

36. Priests of course had more purity rules than anybody else, given their role in the
temple's operation. For broader discussion of the way that purity assumes a major
role in late Second Temple Judaism—and the ways that modern historians have
(mis)interpreted this—see esp. E. P. Sanders, *Jewish Law from Jesus to the
Mishnah: Five Studies* (London: SCM, 1990), 131–254; Jonathan Klawans,
Impurity and Sin in Ancient Judaism (Oxford: Oxford University Press, 2000); and
Klawans, *Purity, Sacrifice and the Temple: Symbolism and Supersessionism in the
Study of Ancient Judaism* (Oxford: Oxford University Press, 2006).

37. Gods had to be approached carefully, and purification (protocols for which were
often divinely revealed) was an important, even necessary way for worshipers to
prepare for the encounter. For the idea of purity rules and the ways that they
shape their cultures, see esp. anthropologist Mary Douglas, *Purity and Danger:
An Analysis of the Concept of Pollution and Taboo* (London: Routledge, 2002).
On Jewish purity in particular, J. Milgrom, *Leviticus 1–16: A New Translation
with Introduction and Commentary* (New York: Doubleday, 1991); and Jacob
Neusner, "The Idea of Purity in Ancient Judaism," *JAAR* 43 (1975): 15–26. Sanders
examines these regulations for the period around Paul's lifetime in *Jewish Law*,
29–41, 131–254 (Pharisees—of whom Paul was one), 258–71 (diaspora communi-
ties); see too his chart on biblical purification, p. 151; also *HJP* 2: 475–78 and
555–90 (Essenes, who especially developed and extended the application of these
codes). For pagan protocols, Robin Lane Fox, *Pagans and Christians* (New York:
Viking, 1987), 83, 347, 543; Robert Parker, *Miasma: Pollution and Purification in
Early Greek Religion* (Oxford: Clarendon Press, 1983); and the essays collected in
Petra Rösch and Udo Simon, eds., *How Purity Is Made* (Wiesbaden: Harrassowitz
Verlag, 2012). See further the essays—on pagan, Jewish, and Christian ideologies
of sacrifice—in Jennifer Wright Knust and Zsuzsanna Várhelyi, eds., *Ancient
Mediterranean Sacrifice* (New York: Oxford University Press, 2011).

38. "Pure" (*tahor/katharos*) and "holy" (*kadosh/hagios*) are two distinct concepts; but
the Greek *koinos*, "common," begins to function as an antonym for *katharos* in
some Hellenistic Jewish texts. Thus, e.g., 1 Macc 1.62, people refuse to eat
"unclean" or "impure" food; Rom 14.14; Mk 7.2, 5; Acts 10.14–15. See also chap. 5
below. On the ethical complexities posed by ancient concepts of purity (wherein
good/bad did not map directly onto pure/impure), and the consequent ethicizing
of pagan purity codes, see Angelos Chaniotis, "Greek Ritual Purity: From
Automatisms to Moral Distinctions," in *How Purity Is Made,* 123–39.

39. Similarly, a Jewish groom pronounces his bride *kadosh li*, "sanctified to me," set apart from all others for himself. For early rabbinic comments on the biblical protocols of sanctifying and offering, see *Sifra, parasha* B, 4.

40. See Sanders, *Practice and Belief*, 72–76, and also the literature cited in the following note.

41. For the articulation of sexual behaviors as sins, see, e.g., Lev 18.1–30; 20.10–21; ritual sins (idolatry, cultic infanticide, magic), Lev 20.1–5; Deut 7.25 and 12.29–31 (idol worship). On "impurity" as moral error or fault, esp. Adolf Büchler, "The Levitical Impurity of the Gentile in Palestine before the Year 70," *JQR* 17 (1926): 1–81; also, exhaustively, Jonathan Klawans, "Notions of Gentile Impurity in Ancient Judaism," *AJS Review* 20 (1995): 285–312; Christine E. Hayes, *Gentile Impurities and Jewish Identities: Intermarriage and Conversion from the Bible to the Talmud* (Oxford: Oxford University Press, 2002), esp. chap. 6.

   The Büchler-Klawans-Hayes line of interpretation on gentile impurities has been challenged in two carefully argued essays by Vered Noam, "Another Look at the Rabbinic Conception of Gentiles from the Perspective of Impurity Laws," in *Judaea-Palaestina, Babylon and Rome: Jews in Antiquity*, ed. Benjamin Isaac and Yuval Shahar (Tübingen: Mohr Siebeck, 2012), 89–110; and "'The Gentileness of the Gentiles': Two Approaches to the Impurity of Non-Jews," in *Halakhah in Light of Epigraphy*, ed. Albert I. Baumgarten et al. (Göttingen: Vandenhoeck & Ruprecht, 2011), 27–41; and by Saul M. Olyan, "Purity Ideology in Ezra-Nehemiah as a Tool to Reconstitute the Community," *JSJ* 35 (2004): 1–16.

   The texts are various, the arguments complicated—as is the relation of what later rabbis thought should have been the case to the actual functioning of the Herodian temple. The indisputable historical fact that pagans could gather in the surrounding temple plaza, however, inclines me to agree with the Büchler-Klawans-Hayes line of interpretation. If most Jews—or even if only Jerusalem's priests—had thought that pagans carried some sort of contagious impurity, Jews would not have been able to walk through the largest plaza of the temple compound, which they routinely did, to make their way to their own courts. Some late Second Temple Jews may indeed have held the views reconstructed by Noam and Olyan; but the temple itself evidently ran along different lines.

42. Paul certainly seems to be thinking in terms of pollution and of temple protocols when he inveighs against Corinthian Christ-followers' frequenting prostitutes, 1 Cor 6.13–19 (the body as temple of holy spirit [v. 19]—like the temple in Jerusalem—is not meant for *porneia*). Acts 10.28 (confusingly) presents Peter as hesitating to go to Cornelius because non-Jews are *akatharoi* and *koinoi* ("impure" and "common"): such association would be "unlawful" (*athemitos*) for Jews. On the basis of this sentence, untold numbers of college undergraduates and even, alas, a significant group of New Testament specialists hold that ancient Jews in principle avoided association with non-Jews because Jewish law forbade it: see, e.g., Philip F. Esler, *Conflict and Identity in Romans: The Social Setting of Paul's Letter* (Minneapolis, MN: Fortress, 2003), 101; N. T. Wright, *Paul and the Faithfulness of God* (Minneapolis, MN: Fortress, 2013), passim. Such a view not

only flies in the face of all the primary evidence, surveyed above, for Jews in pagan places; it also contradicts Luke's own narrative elsewhere in Acts (8.27–36, Philip has no problem sharing a chariot with an Ethiopian; and "god-fearers"— pagans who voluntarily assume some Jewish customs—are thick on the ground in Luke's diaspora synagogues: Acts 10.2, 22; 13.16, 26, 43, 50; 14.1; 16.14; 17.1–4; 18.7). For a refreshingly coherent interpretation of Peter's vision in Acts 10, see Matthew Thiessen, *Contesting Conversion: Genealogy, Circumcision, and Identity in Ancient Judaism and Christianity* (New York: Oxford University Press, 2011), 124–41; see too E. P. Sanders, "Jewish Association with Gentiles and Galatians 2:11–14," in *The Conversation Continues: Studies in Paul and John in Honor of J. Louis Martyn*, ed. Robert T. Fortna and Beverly R. Gaventa (Nashville, TN: Abingdon Press, 1990), 170–88. More on pagans in Jewish places below.

43. Any generalization about pagans "becoming" Jews breaks down around issues of gender. In antiquity, women were normally expected to follow the ancestral customs of their husbands: thus, I assume, when a pagan woman married a Jewish man, she would conform to his custom, and vice versa when a Jewish woman married a pagan man. On this point, see Cohen, *Beginnings of Jewishness*, 169–70. Pagan males who became proselytes had to deal with circumcision, an issue that was extremely fraught culturally.

44. See too the list of synagogue terms given in Anders Runesson, Donald D. Binder, and Birger Olsson, *The Ancient Synagogue from its Origins to 200 C.E.: A Source Book* (Leiden: Brill, 2008), 328.

> "Theodotos the son of Vettenus, priest and ruler of the synagogue, son of a ruler of the synagogue, son's son of a ruler of the synagogue, built the synagogue for the reading of the Law and for the teaching of the commandments, and also the guest chamber and the upper rooms and the waters to accommodate those needing them from abroad, which [synagogue] his fathers and the elders and Simonides founded." (*CIJ* 2, No. 1404; text and translation in Runesson et al., No. 26, 52–54)

> This first-century C.E. Greek inscription from Jerusalem commemorates the foundation of a synagogue, reasonably near the temple, by a third-generation priestly *archēsynagōgos* (synagogue officer). The building provided housing and a place for hearing Torah for Greek-speaking Jewish pilgrims. On the synagogue as "ethnic reading house," see Frances Young, *Biblical Exegesis and the Formation of Christian Culture* (Cambridge: Cambridge University Press, 1997), 13. On the ubiquity of such community organizations, Gruen, *Diaspora*, 105–32; Levine, *Ancient Synagogue*; specifically for these various designations, 121 ff.; *HJP* 2: 423–54, also 3.2: 996–97, for many entries in the index.

45. See Runesson et al. for the sources, literary and epigraphical; for synagogue functions and offices, Williams, *Jews among the Greeks and Romans*, 33–48. These community organizations in many ways resembled urban pagan associations, on which see Philip A. Harland, *Associations, Synagogues and Congregations: Claiming a Place in Ancient Mediterranean Society* (Minneapolis, MN: Fortress,

2003). Theodotos's inscription refers to its role as a sort of hostel. Fergus Millar points out that, at least in fourth-century Rome, the synagogue could also act as a lending library: see Jerome, *Ep.* 36.1, "The Jews of the Graeco-Roman Diaspora between Paganism and Christianity," in *The Jews among Pagans and Christians in the Roman Empire,* ed. Judith Lieu, John North, and Tessa Rajak (London: Routledge, 1992), 97–123, at p. 115. Funerary inscriptions mention penalties to be paid to "the holy association" or to the "most sacred treasury" if tombs are violated, e.g., *CIJ* 2, No. 791; for a collection of such inscriptions, Williams, *Jews among the Greeks and Romans,* 129–30 ("Tomb Protection").

46. See *IJO* 2: 348–55, No. 168 (Julia); 140–43, No. 27 (Capitolina); 71–112, No. 14 (Aphrodisias). The original editors of the Aphrodisias inscription, Joyce Reynolds and Robert Tannenbaum, dated it to the third century (*Jews and God-Fearers at Aphrodisias: Greek Inscriptions with Commentary* [Cambridge: Cambridge Philological Society, 1987]); for the fourth- or fifth-century dating, see Angelos Chaniotis, "The Jews of Aphrodisias: New Evidence and Old Problems," *Scripta Classica Israelica* 21 (2002): 209–42. This later dating raises the interesting possibility that some of the donors named may have been Christians. Also, by this point, conversion to Judaism was prohibited by imperial law, the violation of which the inscription publicly announces.

47. See, for example, the interpretive disputes surrounding the inscribed manumission of Elpias, *IJO* 1: 279–83, BS7. The editors of the *IJO* take *tēs synagōgēs tōn Ioudaiōn kai theon sebōn* as "the synagogue of the Jews and of the god-fearers"; Runesson et al. take it to mean "the synagogue of the Jews, and [Elpias] reveres God" (*Ancient Synagogue,* 159); Stephen Mitchell, "Further Thoughts on the Cult of Theos Hypsistos," *One God,* 193–94, takes up the *IJO* interpretation, "of the god-fearers." Mitchell's essay contains an excellent discussion of the whole issue of interpreting *theosebeis,* 167–208; see too Levinskaya, *Acts,* 51–116. In light of these problems, one fastidious response would be to abandon the term entirely, as Ross Kraemer urges, Ross S. Kraemer, "Giving Up the Godfearers," *JAJ* 5 (2014): 61–87; see esp. pp. 63–82, where she reviews and problematizes much of the epigraphic and literary evidence. For my dissent to this proposal, Paula Fredriksen, "If It Looks Like a Duck, and It Quacks Like a Duck . . .: On Not Giving Up the Godfearers," in *A Most Reliable Witness: Essays in Honor of Ross Shepard Kraemer,* ed. Susan Ashbrook Harvey et al. (Providence, RI: Brown Judaic Studies, 2015), 25–34.

48. "Magic" is a great opportunity for cross-ethnic/"religious" sharing, in part because its goals are so eminently practical. Origen notes that the names of the patriarchs are "so powerful when linked with the name of God that the formula 'the god of Abraham, the god of Isaac, the god of Jacob' is used not only by members of the Jewish nation . . . but also by almost all those who deal in magic and spells," *c. Cel.* 4.33. On the difficulty in discerning the "ethnicity" of spells, see further Joseph Emanuel Sanzo, "'For Our Lord Was Pursued by the Jew . . .': The (Ab)Use of the Motif of 'Jewish' Violence against Jesus on a Greek Amulet (P. Heid. 1101)," in *One in Christ Jesus: Essays on Early Christianity and "All That Jazz" in Honor*

of S. Scott Bartchy, ed. David Lertis Matson and K. C. Richardson (Eugene, OR: Pickwick Publications, 2014), 86–98. Recently, Mika Ahuvia has explored a fascinating case of a Jewish female adept who calls on Babylonian goddesses to mediate her spell: see Mika Ahuvia, "Israel among the Angels: A Study of Angels in Jewish Texts from the Fourth to Eighth Century CE" (Ph.D. diss., Princeton University, 2014), 171–78.

49. For an extensive discussion of Juvenal's "Sabbath-fearer," see *GLAJJ* 2: 102–7, No. 301; also *HJP* 3: 150–76. Acts in one instance mentions *sebomenoi prosēlytoi,* "pious proselytes" or "devout converts" (13.42, RSV); otherwise, the text distinguishes between Jews, proselytes, and "god-fearers," e.g., 10.2, 22; 13.16; 16.14, etc. Stern's note in *GLAJJ,* and Feldman, *Jew and Gentile,* 353–56, give rabbinic references for and discussion of *yirei shamayim.* Later patristic writers speak of (or complain about) this pagan behavior: Justin, in his dialogue, has Trypho distinguish between gentiles who, as Christians, do not keep Jewish custom, whereas all *phoboumenoi ton theon* do, *Trypho* 10.2. Some pagans keep the Sabbath and Passover, yet worship at traditional altars, Tertullian, *To the Nations* 1.13.3–4; men in Phoenicia and in Palestine who call themselves *theosebeis* inconsistently follow both Jewish and Greek (that is, pagan) customs, Cyril of Alexandria, *On Worship in Spirit and Truth* 3.92, 93; the "half-Jew" scrambles from synagogue to pagan shrine, when the Jews ought to tell him that it is wrong to worship the gods, Commodian, *Instructions* 1.24.11, 37.10.

50. See on this last point (about "ethnic verbs" and behaviors) Nongbri's remarks, *Before Religion,* 46–50; earlier, and specifically on "Judaizing," Cohen, *Beginnings of Jewishness,* 185–92; Steve Mason, "Jews, Judeans." On the famous anecdote in *Avodah Zara* 3,4 concerning the pagan Proklos's challenge to Rabban Gamaliel's using the Baths of Aphrodite in Akko/Ptolemais, Paula Fredriksen and Oded Irshai, "'Include Me Out': Tertullian, the Rabbis, and the Graeco-Roman City," in *Identité à travers l'éthique: Nouvelles perspectives sur la formation des identités collectives dans le monde gréco-romain,* ed. K. Berthelot, R. Naiweld, and D. Stoekl ben Ezra (Turnhout, Belgium: Brepols, 2015), 117–32, at pp. 126–27.

51. Philo of Alexandria in the first century spoke of "multitudes of others" who, together with Jews, commemorate the translation of the LXX (*Life of Moses* 2.41–42); some 400 years later, John Chrysostom famously complained of his gentile Christians feasting and fasting with Jewish neighbors, *Against the Judaizing Christians.* Further on this pagan/gentile population and its various involvements with Jewish communities throughout antiquity, see Bernd Wander, *Gottesfürchtige und Sympathisanten: Studien zum heidnischen Umfeld von Diasporasynagogen* (Tübingen: Mohr Siebeck, 1998); Feldman, *Jew and Gentile,* 483–501; Trebilco, *Jewish Communities,* 145–66; J. H. W. G. Liebeschuetz, "The Influence of Judaism among Non-Jews in the Imperial Period," *JJS* 52 (2001): 235–52, at pp. 240–41.

52. See, e.g., John Gager, *Jewish Lives of the Apostle Paul* (New York: Columbia University Press, 2015), 53–86 ("Let's Meet Downtown in the Synagogue").

3. PAUL: MISSION AND PERSECUTION

1. On the problems in using Acts to fill in gaps in our knowledge of Paul's life, the classic essay is John Knox, *Chapters in a Life of Paul* (New York: Abingdon-Cokesbury Press, 1950), esp. pp. 13–73. For my own thoughts, "Paul and Augustine: Conversion Narratives, Orthodox Traditions, and the Retrospective Self," *JTS* 37 (1986): 3–34, at pp. 5–20 and the literature cited at p. 4 n. 5. The present study argues that many of Paul's gentile hearers, familiar with the Jewish elements and message of his gospel, would have to have come from the penumbra of god-fearing pagans to be found around diaspora synagogue communities. This demographic inference, plus Paul's own report of receiving synagogue disciplinary lashing five times (2 Cor 11.24), now inclines me to trust the general impression that Luke gives of Paul's operating via the interurban networks of diaspora synagogues; see too Johannes Munck, *Paul and the Salvation of Mankind*, trans. Frank Clarke (Richmond, VA: John Knox Press, 1959), 78–81, 202 ("Acts may serve as a historical source where it does not contradict Paul's letters").

Against this view, and arguing that Paul's contacts with pagans would have been ad hoc, see Ronald F. Hock, *The Social Context of Paul's Ministry: Tentmaking and Apostleship* (Minneapolis, MN: Fortress, 1980), supported most recently in E. P. Sanders, *Paul: The Apostle's Life, Letters and Thought* (Minneapolis, MN: Fortress, 2015), 111–18 (though Sanders unfortunately confuses "god-fearing" with "renouncing idolatry" [p. 116], whereas god-fearers normally continued in traditional cults, adding the god of Israel to their native pantheons). Further, disputing Paul's communities' levels of scriptural comprehension, Christopher D. Stanley, *Arguing with Scripture: The Rhetoric of Quotations in the Letters of Paul* (New York: T. & T. Clark, 2004). Meeks, *First Urban Christians*, also held that Paul's *ekklēsiai* were largely independent of synagogue communities both socially and structurally (see, e.g., pp. 80–81). I will argue below that a separation between the two, while early, was only gradual, "accidental," and a function of (religious and thus political) relations between the larger Jewish and pagan urban populations: initially, however, diaspora synagogues served as the matrix for the spread of this messianic movement.

Two recent discussions of Pauline chronology and the redactional complications with Paul's letters are Gregory Tatum, *New Chapters in the Life of Paul: The Relative Chronology of his Career* (Washington, DC: Catholic Biblical Association of America, 2006); and J. Albert Harrill, *Paul the Apostle: His Life and Legacy in Their Roman Context* (Cambridge: Cambridge University Press, 2012), esp. 97–101 (on using Acts), and Appendix 2 (on textual problems with 2 Cor). I am not persuaded by the new chronology, which integrates 2 Thessalonians, Ephesians, and Colossians as genuinely Pauline, proposed by Douglas A. Campbell, *Framing Paul: An Epistolary Biography* (Grand Rapids, MI: Eerdmans, 2014). Questions of interpolations—as with the ending of Rom, esp. chap. 16; with 1 Cor 14.34; and with 1 Thes 2.13–16, on which I am still persuaded by Birger A. Pearson, "1 Thessalonians 2:13–16: A Deutero-Pauline Interpolation," *HTR* 64 (1971): 79–94—will be discussed in any commentary.

2. See esp. John M. G. Barclay's helpful animadversions, "Mirror-Reading a Polemical Letter: Galatians as a Test Case," *JSNT* 31 (1987): 73–93.

3. On which, see Margaret M. Mitchell, "Paul's Letter to Corinth: The Interpretive Intertwining of Literary and Historical Reconstruction," in *Urban Religion in Roman Corinth: Interdisciplinary Approaches*, ed. Daniel N. Showalter and Steven J. Friesen (Cambridge, MA: Harvard University Press, 2005), 307–38.

4. For a comprehensive introduction, see Stanley K. Stowers, *Letter Writing in Greco-Roman Antiquity* (Philadelphia: Westminster, 1989); on the rhetorical shaping of Paul's letter to the Romans, Stowers, *Rereading of Romans*, 16–21, 292–93, and the index for entries on "speech-in-character"; on that of Galatians, the Hermeneia commentary by H. D. Betz. More generally on the adversarial conventions of ancient rhetoric, Margaret M. Mitchell, "Patristic Rhetoric on Allegory: Origen and Eustathius Put 1 Samuel 28 on Trial," *JR* 85 (2005): 414–45. On Paul's level of education and rhetorical training—estimates of which swing between extremes—Ryan S. Schellenberg, *Rethinking Paul's Rhetorical Education: Comparative Rhetoric and 2 Corinthians 10–13* (Atlanta, GA: Society of Biblical Literature, 2013), reviews the arguments, and settles on a minimalist view.

5. The term *Ioudaïsmos* is a misery to translate. The RSV gives "Judaism," thereby entailing a host of problems, not least of which is the implication that Paul left one religion ("Judaism") for another ("Christianity"). See Nongbri, *Before Religion*, 49ff. and notes; Mason, "Jews, Judaeans," 457–512; Novenson, "Paul's Former Occupation," 24–39; and Thiessen, *Paul and the Gentile Problem*, 37–41, specifically applying Mason's idea relating the word to gentile "Judaizing."

6. Scholarship is long familiar with the inclusive Jewish traditions of conversion through circumcision: see, e.g., Fredriksen, "Judaism, the Circumcision of Gentiles," 535–39; Cohen, *Beginnings of Jewishness*, 198–238; Gary G. Porton, *The Stranger within Your Gates: Converts and Conversion in Rabbinic Judaism* (Chicago: University of Chicago Press, 1994). In several recent works, however, Matthew Thiessen has importantly called attention to a countervailing position that disallowed entry (at least for males) into the Jewish people: see *Contesting Conversion*; "Paul's Argument against Gentile Circumcision in Romans 2:17–29," *NovT* 56 (2014): 373–91; *Paul and the Gentile Problem*; "Paul's So-Called Jew and Lawless Lawkeeping," in *The So-Called Jew in Paul's Letter to the Romans*, ed. R. Rodriguez and M. Thiessen (Minneapolis, MN: Fortress, 2016), 59–84. Thiessen develops several ideas on genealogical purity introduced by Hayes, *Gentile Impurities*. Further on the problem of using "conversion" to indicate a human's realignment of his or her celestial allegiances, see Zeba A. Crook, *Reconceptualising Conversion: Patronage, Loyalty, and Conversion in the Religions of the Ancient Mediterranean* (Berlin: Walter de Gruyter, 2004).

7. For a discussion of rabbinic opinions on conversion, see *HJP* 3: 175 and nn. 93–101; also Cohen, *Beginnings of Jewishness*, 198–238, on rabbinic conversion ceremony; Porton, *The Stranger*. For the earlier period, see further on this

inclusive attitude toward incomers in, e.g., Philo, *De virt.* 20.103; Josephus, *c. Ap.* 2.210, 261; also *BJ* 2.388, where Agrippa II refers to the princes of Adiabene as *homophyloi*; *Judith* 14.10 on Anchior as "joined to the house of Israel"; cf. Justin's lament in *Trypho* 122.

8. Hayes, *Divine Law*, 142–43; quotation from p. 143 n. 8.

9. Eleven copies of Jubilees have been recovered in the Qumran library, evidence that this was an important text for the community. On the way that the genealogical paradigm of Jewish identity weighs against a concept of outsiders joining, see Thiessen, *Contesting Conversion*, 67–86 (Jubilees), 89–94 (on the "Animal Apocalypse" in 1 Enoch 85–90).

10. As did Helene of Adiabene, *AJ* 20.34. On gentile women becoming Jews, see Cohen, *Beginnings of Jewishness*, 169–71; and on the related issue of the "matrilineal principle" in rabbinic thought, pp. 263–307. As for "Timothy's" Jewishness as presented in Acts, Cohen votes nay, pp. 363–77. "It is becoming for a wife to worship and to know only those gods whom her husband esteems," opined Plutarch, *Moralia* 140D — a social fact that makes Herod's insistence that foreign men marrying into his family observe Jewish customs that much more striking (*AJ* 16.226). Even Paul was prepared to tolerate a Christ-following wife's necessary subordination to her pagan husband in matters of domestic cult: see the important essay by Caroline E. Johnson Hodge, "'Married to an Unbeliever': Households, Hierarchies and Holiness in 1 Corinthians 7:12–16," *HTR* 103 (2010): 1–25.

11. See Fredriksen, "Judaism, the Circumcision of Gentiles," 536 nn. 11–12, for a review of the older secondary literature on circumcision, as well as for primary references in Jewish and pagan sources; also Cohen, *Beginnings of Jewishness*, 39–49, 140–74; most recently, Thiessen, *Contesting Conversion*, index, p. 245, with many entries for "circumcision."

12. On this question, see the arguments by Neil J. McEleny, "Conversion, Circumcision and the Law," *NTS* 20 (1974): 319–41; and Peder Borgen, "Observations on the Theme 'Paul and Philo': Paul's Preaching of Circumcision in Galatia (Gal. 5: 11) and Debates on Circumcision in Philo," in *Die paulinische Literatur und Theologie*, ed. Sigfred Pedersen (Aarhus, Denmark: Aros, 1980), 85–102, esp. pp. 85–89, on circumcision as optional; refuted by John Nolland, "Uncircumcised Proselytes?" *JSJ* 12 (1981): 173–94.

Paul's letter to the Romans is often read to support this position against circumcision, in effect redefining Jewish identity. "True circumcision" is inward; being a "true Jew" is a matter of the spirit, of having the law in one's heart, not in one's flesh (Rom 2.1–29). For criticisms of the RSV translation of this specific chapter, see Thiessen, *Gentile Problem*, 54–68; sharpened and augmented in "Paul's So-Called Jew and Lawless Lawkeeping," pp. 59–83. Paul (so goes the anticircumcision argument), like Philo's allegorizers, by understanding the Law's spiritual meaning, renounced its fleshly practice for gentiles (and by implication for Jews as well). Gentile spiritual allegiance to the god of Israel was enough to make them "Israel" — the "Israel of God" (Gal 6.16). Paul has been read this way for almost two millennia: for a recent expression of such a reading, e.g., Barclay, *Paul and the Gift*, 470–71, taking the "heart-circumcision" of Rom 2 as radically relativizing fleshly circumcision; see too his earlier essay, "Paul and Philo on Circumcision: Romans 2.25–9 in Social and Cultural Context," *NTS* 44 (1998): 536–56. Much of this construal hangs upon how one reads the rhetorical "you" addressed by Paul in Rom 2, on which now see esp. Runar M. Thorsteinsson, *Paul's Interlocutor in Romans 2: Function and Identity in the Context of Ancient Epistolography* (Stockholm: Almqvist and Wiksell, 2003). Barclay dismisses Thorsteinsson's interpretation without argument, *Paul and the Gift*, 469 n. 51. We will revisit all of these issues in the course of the present study.

   The story that Josephus relates about King Izates and the royal house of Adiabene also complicates our picture (*AJ* 20.17–48 and 96). The women of Izates' household in Charax Spasini became committed to Jewish practices through contact with a Jewish merchant named Ananias: the story fails to reveal whether they became sympathizing pagans or all-the-way "converts." Independently, Helene, Izates' mother back in Adiabene, also takes up Jewish customs and laws. Izates himself then resolves to "cross over" (*metathesthai*) to the point of becoming circumcised, in order to become a Jew (20.38). Alarmed at the potential consequences of his affiliating to a foreign people and thus alienating his own kingdom, Helene objects (20.39), and Ananias advises Izates to forgo circumcision: it is enough (for what?) if Izates fears God (*sebein; AJ* 20.41). Enter Eleazar (*AJ* 20.43), another Jew sojourning in Adiabene who, seeing Izates reading the Jewish *nomos*, chides him for *not* going all the way and being circumcised (*AJ* 20.44–45). The story ends with Izates summoning a physician, becoming circumcised, and thus becoming a Jew (the point being that, *before receiving circumcision*, Izates would *not* be considered a Jew). On Izates and Paul, see Mark D. Nanos, "The Question of Conceptualization: Qualifying Paul's Position on Circumcision in Dialogue with Josephus's Advisors to King Izates," in *Paul within Judaism: Restoring the First-Century Context to the Apostle*, ed. Mark D. Nanos and Magnus Zetterholm (Minneapolis, MN: Fortress, 2015), 105–52.

13. From the other side, Philo confirms these points of pagan critique, praising "incomers" for "forsaking the ancestral customs [τὰ πάτρια] in which they were bred" (*Spec. Laws* 1.309; cf. 1.52).

14. "From Britain to Syria, pagan cults aimed to honour the gods and avert the misfortunes which might result from the gods' own anger at their neglect," notes Robin Lane Fox. "Any account of pagan worship which minimizes the gods' uncertain anger and mortals' fear of it is an empty account," *Pagans and Christians*, 39; see further his chap. 2, on the gods' social context, and chap. 3, on cult. Roman piety combined with patriotism, since the proper execution of traditional cult "is not only of concern to religion, but also to the well-being of the state," Cicero, *De legibus* 1.12.30. See Isaac, *Invention of Racism*, 467 and nn. 121–27, for citations to many Roman expressions of this view; also n. 62 below.

15. The emperor Domitian represents a notable exception to this general picture of grudging tolerance: he executed some members of the Roman aristocracy for

"atheism," that is, for spurning their own gods on account of treasonable loyalty to "the customs of the Jews," Dio, *Roman History* 67.14.1–2. Aristocrats in particular had civic, thus religious, obligations to the gods; those less socially elevated were in this regard freer. Peter Lampe, *From Paul to Valentinus: Christians at Rome in the First Two Centuries,* trans. Michael Steinhauser (Minneapolis, MN: Fortress, 2003), 198–205, speculates that Flavius Clemens, Domitilla, and unnamed others were condemned not for Judaizing but for becoming Christian, but his reconstruction rests in part on the later story in Eusebius, *EH* 3.18.4.

16. Some of these inscriptions are discussed in chap. 2 above.

17. Most secondary scholarship identifies these "weak" brethren squeamish about contact with idol-foods as Jewish Christ-followers, whether in Corinth or in Rome. I see Paul's letters as addressing ex-pagan Christ-followers in both communities (a position that I will argue further on); and I see his ex-pagan pagans—the Judaizing gentile Christ-followers—as the ones who might feel that eating (or drinking) such things effected a real exchange with their old gods. For a recent example of seeing these issues as tied up with Jewish attachments to kashrut, see Barclay, *Paul and the Gift,* 511 (used also as a plumb-line for reconstructing the incident at Antioch, Gal 2.11–14, pp. 365–70); on the contrary, for reading Rom 14 as concerning solely gentile Christ-followers, Thorsteinsson, *Paul's Interlocutor,* 92–97. Also, while the Mishnah (*Avodah Zara* 2:3) is perfectly clear—meat coming from pagan temples is strictly forbidden—its teaching is (a) specifically rabbinic, (b) Palestinian, and (c) early third century C.E. Paul—whatever he might have meant by claiming to be a Pharisee and zealous for *Ioudaïsmos*—lived in the mid-first century as a native of the western Diaspora. Practices varied, and diaspora cities would certainly have offered many occasions for Jewish flexibility and for varieties of practice, on which see Anders Runesson, "Entering a Synagogue with Paul: First-Century Torah Observance," in *Torah Ethics and Early Christian Identity,* ed. Susan J. Wendel and David M. Miller (Grand Rapids, MI: Eerdmans, 2016), 11–26; on flexibility around food specifically, also E. P. Sanders, *Jewish Law from Jesus to the Mishnah* (Philadelphia: Trinity Press International, 1990), 281; also David Rudolph, "Paul and the Food Laws: A Reassessment of Romans 14.14, 20," in *Paul the Jew,* ed. Boccaccini and Segovia, 151–81.

18. The following several paragraphs recapitulate and condense my arguments in "What 'Parting of the Ways'? Jews, Gentiles, and the Ancient Mediterranean City," in *The Ways That Never Parted: Jews and Christians in Late Antiquity and the Early Middle Ages,* ed. Adam H. Becker and Annette Yoshiko Reed (Tübingen: Mohr Siebeck, 2003), 48–56. The three great scholars of the first half of the twentieth century who proposed Jewish missions are James Parkes, *The Conflict of the Church and the Synagogue: A Study in the Origins of Antisemitism* (London: Soncino, 1934); Bernhard Blumenkranz, *Die Judenpredigt Augustins: Ein Beitrag zur Geschichte der jüdisch-christlichen Beziehungen in den ersten Jahrhunderten* (Basel: Helbing & Lichtenhahn, 1946); and Marcel Simon, *Verus Israël: Études sur les relations entre Chrétiens et Juifs dans l'empire romain (135–425)* (Paris: E. de Boccard, 1948). Against Adolf Harnack's description of Jewish desuetude after

the temple's destruction in 70 C.E. ("Die *Altercatio Simonis Iudaei et Theophili Christiani* nebst Untersuchungen über die antijüdische Polemik in der alten Kirche," in *Texte und Untersuchungen zur Geschichte der altchristlichen Literatur,* ed. Oscar von Gebhardt and Adolf Harnack, vol. 1.3.1 [Leipzig, 1883], 1–136), these later scholars offered a reconstruction of robust and self-confident Jewish communities energetically pursuing missions to pagans. For a review of this historiography, see Fredriksen, *Augustine and the Jews,* xv–xviii and 384–87 nn. 4–8; for an exhaustive review of the historiography on the whole question, Rainer Riesner, "A Pre-Christian Jewish Mission?" in *The Mission of the Early Church to Jews and Gentiles,* ed. J. Ådna and H. Kvalbein (Tübingen: Mohr Siebeck, 2000), 211–50.

On actual Jewish missions as the historical context for Mt 23.15 and Gal 5.11, see John G. Gager, *Reinventing Paul* (Oxford: Oxford University Press, 2000); on Gal 5.11 in particular as indicating that Paul, pre-Damascus, missionized pagans to turn them into Jews, Terence L. Donaldson, *Paul and the Gentiles: Remapping the Apostle's Convictional World* (Minneapolis, MN: Fortress 1997), 275–84; Donaldson, more recently, "Paul within Judaism: A Critical Evaluation from a 'New Perspective' Perspective," in Nanos and Zetterholm, *Paul within Judaism,* 299 n. 39; taken up by Thiessen, *Gentile Problem,* 37–41. The current chapter argues against such reconstructions.

19. Louis Feldman has based his defense of this idea of Jewish missions on what he deems "demographical evidence"—this supposed explosion in Jewish populations—in *Jew and Gentile,* 293 and 555–56: only aggressive proselytizing, he explains, can account for such an extreme rise. See the criticisms of these "numbers" in James Carleton Paget, "Jewish Proselytism at the Time of Christian Origins: Chimera or Reality?" *JSNT* 18 (1996): 65–103, at p. 70 (his article provides a road map for the historiographical controversy); also Leonard V. Rutgers, *The Hidden Heritage of Diaspora Judaism: Essays on Jewish Cultural Identity in the Roman World* (Louvain: Peeters, 1998), 200–205. On the hazards of staking *any* argument about ancient populations on "numbers" and demography, Roger S. Bagnall and Bruce W. Frier, *The Demography of Roman Egypt* (Cambridge: Cambridge University Press, 1994), 53–57 (with bibliography). See too Brian McGing, "Population and Proselytism: How Many Jews Were There in the Ancient World?" in *Jews in the Hellenistic and Roman Cities,* ed. John R. Bartlett (London: Routledge, 2002), 88–106.

20. "This Jewish literature was aimed at a target within its own religious community," notes Johannes Munck. "Its public [was] the educated Jews and its object . . . to confirm them in the religion of the fathers," *Paul and the Salvation of Mankind,* 267–68.

21. Justin identifies members of gentile churches other than his own as "atheists, impious, unrighteous and sinful, confessors of Jesus in name only . . . yet they style themselves 'Christians'! . . . Some are called Marcians, some Valentinians . . . others by other names" (*Trypho* 35). On Justin's community as the true holders of the scriptures, *Trypho* 29; on his own church as the "true Israel," 123.

22. On the second-century gentile Christian trifecta between Valentinians, Marcionites, and Justin's group that generated the main lines of Christian invective *contra Iudaeos*, see Fredriksen, *Augustine and the Jews*, 41–78; earlier, the fundamental article by David P. Efroymson, "The Patristic Connection," in *Anti-Semitism and the Foundations of Christianity*, ed. Alan T. Davis (New York: Paulist Press, 1979), 98–117. On the ways that Jewish sectarian writings transmuted into gentile anti-Jewish writings, John W. Marshall, "Apocalypticism and Anti-Semitism: Inner-Group Resources for Inter-Group Conflicts," in *Apocalypticism, Anti-Semitism and the Historical Jesus: Subtexts in Criticism*, ed. John S. Kloppenborg with John W. Marshall (London: T. & T. Clark, 2005), 68–82.

23. Christian anti-Jewish rhetoric and theology undergo a second great period of perfervid development in the decades following Constantine's conversion: the awareness and even the generation of difference within the *catholica* can be attributed to the imperial consolidation itself, with "Jews" once again standing in for the loathed false Christian insider, Fredriksen, *Augustine and the Jews*, 290–324; also, Paula Fredriksen, "Jewish Romans, Christian Romans, and the Post-Roman West: The Social Correlates of the *contra Iudaeos* Tradition," in *Conflict and Religious Conversation in Latin Christendom: Studies in Honour of Ora Limor*, ed. Israel Jacob Yuval and Ram Ben-Shalom (Turnhout, Belgium: Brepols, 2014), 17–38.

24. For the argument that Mt 23.15 implies intra-Jewish missionizing, see Martin Goodman, *Mission and Conversion: Proselytizing in the Religious History of the Roman Empire* (Oxford: Clarendon Press, 1994), 73; for the proposal that Jewish Pharisees are reacting (locally) to Christian missions, Edouard Will and Claude Orrieux, *"Prosélytisme juif"? Histoire d'une erreur* (Paris: Les Belles Lettres, 1992). Donaldson comments, rightly, "This little verse has had an influence all out of proportion to its size," *Judaism and the Gentiles*, 413.

25. In personal correspondence, Larry Hurtado has suggested to me that Paul indeed worked previously as an intra-Jewish missionary. "Paul refers to his former activity in 'Ioudaïsmos' (Gal 1:13), which I take to mean that as a Pharisee he actively promoted observance of Torah among Jews. In the diaspora setting, there were likely many Jews who in varying ways failed in this, or who accommodated pagan life in ways unacceptable to a more rigorist Pharisee. It seems to me there may well have been Jews who did not circumcise their sons, for example. So, Paul (like the Mitzvah-vans in NYC) may have been involved in promoting Jewishness among such." This is possible, of course, though such a construal seems an odd fit with the context of Gal 1, which focuses on *gentiles* receiving circumcision.

26. For speculations on Paul's being a missionary to gentiles even prior to his vision of Christ, see Thiessen, *Gentile Problem*, 37–41, following Donaldson; see n. 37 below.

27. A point persistently emphasized in Riesner's review of the historiography on this question, "Pre-Christian Missions?"

28. Ananias and Eleazar both seem to be freelancers. The differences between them demonstrate that Jews had no fixed "missionary" protocol or policy.

29. Much later rabbinic texts imply that conversions occur at the initiative of the gentile: "When a man comes in these times seeking to convert, he is asked, 'What is your motive? Do you not know that Israel is now afflicted, distressed, downtrodden . . .?' If he answers, 'I know,' they accept him at once," bYeb 47a. But cf. Marc Hirshman, "Rabbinic Universalism in the Second and Third Centuries," *HTR* 93 (2000): 101–15. Hirshman points to some passages in early rabbinic texts that express an open attitude toward gentile involvement with Torah as evidence for a "missionizing outlook" (pp. 102, 112, 114); but he does not argue the case, nor does he adduce evidence for actual missions.

30. "[T]he belief in the future universality of the true religion, the coming of an age when 'the Lord shall be king over the whole earth,' led to efforts to convert the Gentiles . . . and made Judaism the first great missionary religion of the Mediterranean world. *When it is called a missionary religion, the phrase must, however, be understood with a difference. The Jews did not send out missionaries.* . . . They were themselves settled by thousands in all the great centres and in innumerable smaller cities. . . . Their religious influence was exerted chiefly through the synagogues, which they set up for themselves, but which were open to all whom interest or curiosity drew to their services." Thus George Foot Moore, *Judaism in the First Centuries of the Christian Era: The Age of the Tannaim*, 3 vols. (Cambridge, MA: Harvard University Press, 1927–30), here quoted 1: 323–24 (my emphasis).

   As with Mediterranean paganism, much Jewish community activity and celebration took place out of doors, which also invited and accommodated the interest of outsiders: Philo, *Life of Moses* 2.41–42 (Jews and pagans mix at the "inter-faith" picnic at Pharos celebrating the translation of the LXX); Tertullian, *On Fasting* 16 (Jews on fast days worship outside, by the sea); Chrysostom, *Against the Judaizers* 2.3 (Jews dancing—and attracting Christians—on Rosh haShanah); 7.1 (visiting neighbors' sukkot); 1.4 (walking barefoot through the agora on Yom Kippur); also cf. *CTh* 16.8, 18 (the public celebration of Purim).

31. Cf. John P. Dickson, *Mission-Commitment in Ancient Judaism and in the Pauline Communities: The Shape, Extent and Background of Early Christian Mission* (Tübingen: Mohr Siebeck, 2003), 1–84, who sees in the Jewish critique of idol worship as well as the hopes for eschatological inclusion a "missionary mindset."

32. Cohen, *Beginnings of Jewishness*, 162.

33. Terence Donaldson disputes this definition of "god-fearers" as active pagans, asserting that there is "considerable evidence indicating that many did abandon polytheistic worship"; but he then produces only two examples, the fictional father of Juvenal's satire who "worships nothing but the clouds" (*Sat.* 14.96), and King Izates, precircumcision (*AJ* 20.34–38; "Paul within Judaism," at p. 295). The mass of inscriptional evidence, however, as Donaldson in the same paragraph acknowledges, "reflects a considerable range." No amount of evidence can prove a negative—that is, that *no* male god-fearers *ever* made an exclusive commitment to Israel's god, without undergoing circumcision—but neither do these two

examples provide "considerable evidence" that many male god-fearers did so commit. And Izates, as a ruler, presents a unique and therefore exceptional case (see above, p. 210 n. 12). I therefore stand by my generalization, distilled from the inscriptional and literary evidence reviewed *infra*: god-fearers were sympathetic pagans who added Israel's god to their native pantheons, and/or who sponsored Jewish activities while continuing in their own.

34. For the argument, with Hebrew and Greek texts, see Fredriksen, "Judaism, the Circumcision of Gentiles," 545 and n. 39.

35. There is no such thing as a "biblical doctrine" on this issue as on so many others, as Donaldson rightly observes ("Paul within Judaism," 287; amply substantiated in *Judaism and the Gentiles*). Isaiah elsewhere — like Paul — speaks also of the eschatological punishment and of the exclusion of the nations. And occasional End-time prophecies foresee the gentile adoption of some Jewish practices: Zech 14.16 looks forward to eschatological gentiles observing Sukkot annually; Isa 66.21, to some of them serving as priests and as Levites in the End-time temple. But, as Paul's cento in Rom 15.9–12 evinces, redeemed gentiles remain gentiles, and are saved as such. On the ways that Isaiah LXX fundamentally shapes Paul's vision in Romans, see esp. Wagner, *Heralds*; see also, for this same point about gentile inclusion but not conversion, Schweitzer, *Mysticism of Paul*, 186; Nils Alstrup Dahl, "The Story of Abraham in Luke-Acts," in *Studies in Luke-Acts: Essays Presented in Honor of Paul Schubert*, ed. Leander E. Keck and J. Louis Martyn (Nashville, TN: Abingdon Press, 1966), 151 ("Gentiles are saved as Gentiles").

36. This is one of the reasons why I cannot imagine Paul as having a motive for running a mission to gentiles before his conversion to the apocalyptic Christ movement; see too the following note.

37. In two major works, *Paul and the Gentiles* and *Judaism and the Gentiles*, and frequently elsewhere, Terence L. Donaldson has insisted that Paul both pre- and post-Damascus had been intensely committed to proselytizing gentiles: Paul thought that gentiles could be "saved" — included in God's Kingdom — only if they turned to him in the period *before* the Kingdom came (e.g., *Paul and the Gentiles*, 78, 149, 187–307; repeated in "Paul within Judaism," 289–93, 299–301, esp. n. 39). There are several problems, I think, with this proposal. The first is that such a belief (that is, that pagans are "saved" only if they cease being pagans at some point before the End) is attested *nowhere* in ancient Jewish texts: on the contrary, the pagans' "turning" coincides with Israel's in-gathering, as we have seen in Isaiah, Zechariah, Tobit, etc. Further, the normal ethnicity of "religions" in antiquity, which Paul himself presumes (e.g., Jews are Jews "by nature," *physei*, Gal 2.15, translated as "by birth" in the RSV; gentiles are grafted into the tree of Israel *para physin*, "against nature," Rom 11.24), combined with the absence of evidence for Jewish missions to gentiles to turn them into Jews, weighs against this reconstruction. And finally, outside of an apocalyptic mindset, it would be difficult to account for the urgency of such a mission on the part of the pre-Damascus Paul.

38. Commodian criticizes Jews for *not* trying to convert the *medius Iudaeus* who sprints between traditional altars and the synagogue ("They [the Jews] ought to tell you whether it is right to worship the gods," *Instructions* 1.37, 10); and Chrysostom, even in his most vituperative sermons, never accuses Jews of attempting such "outreach."

39. Shaye Cohen, in chap. 4 of *Beginnings of Jewishness* ("From Ethnos to Ethnos-Religion," 109–39), named the Maccabean period as the point at which *Ioudaismos* moved from ethnic indicator to ethno-"religious" indicator, meaning that outsiders (non-*Ioudaioi*) were able to join the community. "The Hasmonean period attests for the first time the idea of religious conversion: by believing in the God of the Jews and following his laws, a Gentile can become a Jew," 137. I wonder if this characterization is true. First, in antiquity, all gods exist, and all humans (except perhaps the doughtiest philosophers) knew this ("believed" this) to be the case: the question was what god(s) one showed respect to, and how. And, second, given that family structures generally governed relations between heaven and earth, *all* ethnicities were "ethno-religions" (which is why theology was mobilized to negotiate and maintain diplomatic relations between different groups, antiquity's kinship-diplomacy). Outsiders usually joined in showing respect to the gods of others (diplomacy, again, offering a premier occasion). It was the Jews' principle of cultic exclusiveness that singled out their particular "ethno-religion"; but "ethno-religion" characterizes Mediterranean divine-human relations generally.

40. Cf., for example, how Jesus at his second coming appears very similarly in 1 Thes 4.13–18 and in Mk 13.26–27 (cf. Dan 7.13–14).

41. For the ways that Mark's gospel functions within a two-generation framework (that of the narrative, c. 30, and that of Mark's contemporaries, post-70), and the ways that the temple's destruction serves as the sign to Mark's generation of the coming return of the Son of Man (that is, as the indicator of Christ's approaching Parousia), see Fredriksen, *From Jesus to Christ*, 48–52, 178–87.

42. According to the Synoptic gospels, the earliest disciples performed various charismata during their own missions, precrucifixion: see p. 242 n. 33 below for many references.

43. Mark's Syro-Phoenician woman seeks out Jesus for a cure; Jesus encounters the Gerasene demoniac on his travels in the territories of the Decapolis (Mk 7.24–30, 5.1–20): to neither does he "preach the kingdom." The centurion in Capernaum— within Antipas's territory—should likely be understood as Jewish (Mt 8.5–13/Lk 7.1–10). The most important pagan in the gospel stories with whom Jesus interacts is, of course, Pilate, who is also not a focus of Jesus's efforts. Schweitzer speculates that Jesus's *not* preaching to gentiles was an issue of eschatological principle, not only of opportunity: Jesus's "eschatological universalism forbids a mission among the Gentiles" because, according to prophetic paradigm, Jews are to be called first, *Mysticism of Paul*, 178–83.

44. I assume that members of these *ekklēsiai*—a small collectivity of wandering Jewish apostles, local Jews, and god-fearers-turned-Christ-followers—would have

continued to frequent the synagogue. Why wouldn't they? The synagogue was, first, the venue to pray in community to Israel's god and, second, the place to hear the scriptures. Also, had these people withdrawn from the synagogue, it would be difficult to account for Paul's both giving and getting "persecution."

45. See E. P. Sanders, *Paul, the Law, and the Jewish People* (Philadelphia: Fortress, 1983), 174.

46. Who are these circumcising apostles teaching in Galatia? Identifications range from their being Jews *tout court*, to Christ-following Jewish missionaries (which is my assumption), to gentile Judaizers. Any commentary will review these options; see too the collection of varying viewpoints assembled by Mark D. Nanos in *The Galatians Debate: Contemporary Issues in Rhetorical and Historical Interpretation* (Peabody, MA: Hendrickson Publishers, 2002), 321–433.

47. So too Barclay, "Mirror-Reading," 78: "We must acknowledge the possibility that Paul's lengthy self-defense in Gal 1–2 may not be a reply to a number of specific allegations . . . but may simply pick up almost incidental remarks about his personal credentials."

Paul's characterization of his pre-Christophany self as "zealous" has moved some scholars to see in his words a subtle allusion to the biblical Phineas (Num 25.6–15), whose violent "zeal" for the Law is commended by God. This "allusion" (is it really there?) then serves to provide a context and motivation for Paul's own persecuting activity: Paul, like Phineas, reacts violently against fellow Jews (*qua* Christ-followers) whom he sees as endangering the religious integrity of the Jewish people. See Terence L. Donaldson, "Zealot and Convert: The Origin of Paul's Christ-Torah Antithesis," *Catholic Biblical Quarterly* 51 (1989): 655–82; Torrey Seland, *Establishment Violence in Philo and Luke: A Study of Non-Conformity to the Torah and Jewish Vigilante Reactions* (Leiden: Brill, 1995). I think that this hangs a mountain of speculative reconstruction from the very slender hair of a putative allusion, constructed from a single word ("zealous"), that may exist only in the mind of the interpreter. For calmer thoughts on Paul, zeal, and Pharisaism, see Sanders, *Paul: Life, Letters and Thought*, 76–82.

Ioudaïsmos, a word that I have so far resisted translating, also complicates historical reconstruction. The RSV renders it as "Judaism," which in turn conjures familiar binary oppositions and the "social history" that they encode: law/gospel, Jews/gentiles, and finally, those two abstract bodies of competing religious doctrine, Judaism/Christianity. Paul's having "preached circumcision" (Gal 5.11) and his zeal for his ancestral customs/his life "in *Ioudaïsmos*" (Gal 1.14; Phil 3.6) can then be parsed two ways: either he took an intensified form of Judaism—that is, Pharisaic Judaism—to his own people, "persecuting" those who were less strict in Law observance than he; or he energetically pursued missions to gentiles to turn them into (strictly observant) Jews.

Ioudaïsmos "is rare in early Jewish and Christian literature, and nonexistent outside of it" (Thiessen, *Gentile Problem*, 38). The word made its literary debut in 2 Macc, where it served as a sort of counterterm to *Hellenismos* (cf. 2 Macc 2.21,

8.1, 14.38). Both verbal umbrellas cover a wide range of behaviors—linguistic, cultural, religious, political (the last three terms on a tight continuum of meaning)—that we might identify as "way of life," in this specific instance the Judean way of life as opposed to the Greek way of life. Within the narrative context of 2 Macc, it also implies a political program, "what Jews who reject Hellenism do. . . . [N]ot all Jews practice *Ioudaïsmos*, because Ioudaismos is the name not of an ancestral religion but of a cause, a political movement, a program of activism," Novenson, "Paul's Former Occupation in *Ioudaïsmos*," 34, referring to Elias J. Bickerman, *The God of the Maccabees: Studies on the Meaning and Origin of the Maccabean Revolt*, trans. Horst R. Moehring (Leiden: Brill, 1979). Thiessen, similarly to Donaldson, takes *Ioudaïsmos* in Gal 1.14 to mean that Paul was engaged in a Judaizing mission to gentiles before his exposure to the Jesus movement. Novenson argues that the word indicates an intensification of Jewishness practiced by Jews. I think that Paul was simply indicating his own excellence in living according to his interpretation of his ancestral practices, no outreach to anyone else, Jew or pagan, implied or required.

48. Sanders, *Paul, the Law, and the Jewish People*, 192. See his whole discussion, pp. 186–92, on the difficulties of construing this passage in Paul in a way that plausibly coheres with a realistic first-century diaspora social setting; so similarly Anthony Ernest Harvey, "Forty Strokes Save One: Social Aspects of Judaizing and Apostasy," in *Alternative Approaches to New Testament Study*, ed. Anthony Ernest Harvey (London: SPCK, 1985), 79–96, at pp. 80–81 and 92–93.

I find Sanders's exhortation to a certain historical agnosticism (p. 188) honest, realistic, and all too rare among scholarly commentators, myself included. For this reason, and belatedly, I repent of my own efforts to strive for greater clarity than I should have done by interpreting the "forty lashes less one," *ma'akot arba'im*, by appeal to the later rabbinic penalty of *ma'akot mardut*, discretionary lashing (see, e.g., *From Jesus to Christ*, 145; "Judaism, the Circumcision of Gentiles," 549 and n. 50; and frequently elsewhere). It is simply too hazardous to retroject later rabbinical practices back into first-century diaspora contexts; and our desire for clarity must cede, where we simply lack enough evidence, to historical modesty. Absent evidence, we can only speculate, and I will offer and defend my current speculation above. (For my moral exemplar, see the admirably forthright Sanders, *PLJP*, 189 top.) Were these various diaspora synagogue communities who disciplined Paul asserting a proto-rabbinic prerogative? Were they improvising from the biblical text, Deut 25.3? (Forty lashes *less* one is the halachic, that is, rabbinic, prescription; this customary practice, however, clearly precedes them.) Paul received a judicial punishment, to which he submitted, but for what trespass(es) we cannot know, though I will speculate below; see too the remarks of Martin Goodman, "The Persecution of Paul by Diaspora Jews," in *The Beginnings of Christianity*, ed. Jack Pastor and Menachem Mor (Jerusalem: Yad Ben-Zvi Press, 2005), 379–87. I thank Larry Hurtado, Oded Irshai, Avraham Isaacs, Jay Pomrenze, and especially Ishay Rosen-Zvi for helping me to reconcile myself to the limits of what I can know.

49. Again, I speculate: the number "forty lashes less one" in the context of Mishna Makkot 3 is statutory, contingent upon the physical constitution of recipient. Josephus, our other prerabbinic source apart from Paul, speaks of the "forty-less-one" strokes of the "public lash," for the offender's violating laws of charitable giving, *AJ* 4.238. This suggests that, in the first century and in the Diaspora, the charges sustained to merit this punishment were very interpretable.

50. Minucius Felix, *Octavius* 29.2, echoing a pagan sentiment. On Rome's "criminals" being perceived by its subject peoples as heroes, S. G. F. Brandon notes, "The cross was a symbol of Zealot sacrifice before it was transformed into the Christian sign of salvation," *Jesus and the Zealots: A Study of the Political Factor in Primitive Christianity* (Manchester: Manchester University Press, 1967), 145; cf. Martin Hengel's treatment of Jewish attitudes toward crucifixion, *Crucifixion in the Ancient World and the Folly of the Message of the Cross* (Philadelphia: Fortress, 1977), 84–90 and passim.

51. "The answer [of Gal 3.13] is introduced because of the *Stichworte* which lead the argument from 'Gentiles' to 'blessing' to its opposite, 'curse.' Thus Gal 3.13 is not the keystone of the argument, but has a subsidiary place in explaining how the curse (3.10) is removed," Sanders, *PLJP*, 25. Larry Hurtado suggests to me that the scandal would be a *dead* messiah, although a dead "anointed one" already appears in Dan 9.24–25, and would reappear in 4 Ezra 7.28–29. Besides, the law-observant members of the *ekklēsia* in Jerusalem obviously had no problem of cognitive dissonance proclaiming a crucified messiah, nor did the larger city "persecute" them for so proclaiming: by and large, the community lived peacefully within Jerusalem, unmolested by Romans and by other Jews, until the outbreak of the First Revolt. Alas, the idea that a messiah killed by crucifixion—"not just a death, but a cursed and scandalous execution" (Gal 3.13, 5.11)—would be shocking to first-century Jews is still alive and well: Barclay, *Paul and the Gift*, 386; so too Andrew Chester, "The Christ of Paul," in *Redemption and Resistance: The Messianic Hopes of Jews and Christians in Antiquity*, ed. Markus Bockmuehl and James Carleton Paget (London: T. & T. Clark, 2009), 120.

52. These last quotations come from Barclay, *Jews in the Mediterranean Diaspora*, 393. That the Hellenists from Jerusalem were lax in Torah observance is a leitmotif of the work of Martin Hengel, *Between Jesus and Paul: Studies in the Earliest History of Christianity* (London: SCM, 1983), and, earlier, *Acts and the History of Earliest Christianity* (London: SCM, 1979); so also John G. Gager, "Some Notes on Paul's Conversion," *NTS* 27 (1981): 697–704, at p. 700. These less-than-observant Hellenistic Jews are then imagined as the apostles who reached Paul's community in Damascus: he "persecuted" them, and then became like them himself.

53. The gentile membership in the *ekklēsia*; the scandal of a crucified messiah; no longer living according to the Law: these "explanations" for Paul's initial hostility, projected forward as descriptive of his own mission, message, and later persecution, embody theological principles of later majoritarian gentile Christianity. As we have seen above, gentiles *qua* pagans already participated in synagogue life; the message of a crucified messiah may have seemed unlikely, but it was not *eo ipso*

religiously offensive; and—as we will shortly see—we have small reason to think that Paul himself was not Law-observant. Plus, diversity of Jewish practice was the norm, not the exception, then (in antiquity) as now. See also the following note.

54. The quotation is from Martin Goodman's excellent article "Persecution of Paul," 381. My argument above is immediately indebted to Goodman's. On the internal diversity of first-century Judean Judaism, see Josephus, *AJ* 17.41 and 18.12–15 (Sadducees, Pharisees, and Essenes, described as *haireises*, "schools"). For discussion with much bibliography, see *HJP*, vol. 2 (for these "three philosophies") and vol. 3 (Diaspora); for a concise overview, Sanders, *Historical Figure of Jesus*, 33–48. Paul's letters, of course, testify to the vigorous disagreements around practices within the first generation of this new and tiny Jewish movement. The gospels also witness to telling distinctions of behavior even within two small and aligned indigenous groups, John the Baptizer's and Jesus of Nazareth's (e.g., Mt 11.18–19/Lk 7.33 on eating, drinking, and abstaining; Mk 2.18 and parallels, John's disciples fast and Jesus's do not; cf. Mk 7.1–6 and parallels, a dispute about purifying hands before eating). And as Mt 7.21–23 attests, already by the turn of the first century, differences between varieties of Christ-followers were extremely highly charged: the evangelist looked forward to the eschatological validation of his own views and the eternal repudiation of the others ("I never knew you," the returned Christ will say to these other Christ-followers. "Go away, you evil doers," 7.23).

55. So too Harvey: "Now it is important to notice that (at least in the diaspora) the jurisdiction of a Jewish court *extended only so far as it was willingly accepted*," "Forty Strokes Save One," 80 (emphasis mine).

56. His thinking of public cult means that Paul is speaking mainly about men. His expectations of Christ-following women whose spouses are still pagan is much more flexible and circumspect: see Johnson Hodge, "Married to an Unbeliever."

57. For the definition of ἀρχή as a demonic cosmic power, see *BAGD*, definition 3 (c); δύναμις, definition 5; ἐξουσία, definition 5 (b); στοιχεῖα, definition 2; cf. the "principalities and powers" of Eph 6.12. For Paul's many references to other gods, James D. G. Dunn, *The Theology of the Apostle Paul* (Grand Rapids, MI: Eerdmans, 1998), 33–38, 104–10. Further on the genealogy of these lower divinities, Martin, "When Did Angels Become Demons?" John K. Goodrich has recently (and, I think, plausibly) argued that Paul intends by these terms not only cosmic powers, but current earthly political ones as well, "After Destroying Every Rule, Authority, and Power: Paul, Apocalyptic, and Politics in 1 Corinthians," in *Paul and the Apocalyptic Imagination*, ed. Ben C. Blackwell, John K. Goodrich, and Jason Maston (Minneapolis, MN: Fortress, 2016), 275–95. Paul's passage of famous political quietism in Rom 13.1–7 (where he clearly has earthly authorities in mind) is also eschatologically resolved, 13.11.

58. Martyrdom as "discursive practice"—identity-confirming Christian narratives—currently dominates historical scholarship, and the historicity of events retailed by martyr stories, absent Roman evidence for persecution, "means that a historical narrative of legal persecution and prosecution cannot be re-created," Candida R. Moss, *Ancient Christian Martyrdom: Diverse Practices, Theologies,*

and Traditions (New Haven, CT: Yale University Press, 2012), 12; see also her remarks on pp. 1–22 for a good critical introduction to the historical and historiographical problems. Around 247 C.E., Origen of Alexandria claimed that the number of Christians martyred "could easily be counted," *c. Cel.* 3.8. However few the episodes of actual pagan persecution of Christians, then, the *idea*, amplified in martyriological literature, dominates ancient constructions of Christian identity, on which see Judith M. Lieu, *Image and Reality: The Jews in the World of the Christians in the Second Century* (Edinburgh: T. & T. Clark, 1996), s.v. "martyrs" and "persecution."

59. See esp. Goodman, "Persecution of Paul." "The best that humans could hope for was that they could keep the gods in a good mood," notes David S. Potter, "Roman Religion: Ideas and Actions," in Potter and Mattingly, *Life, Death and Entertainment*, 113–67, at p. 134. Cult went far toward assuaging divine egos. Early Jewish apostles of Christ, once in the Diaspora and, thus, speaking to pagans as well as to Jews, would run afoul of this deep and abiding—and commonsense—construal of human obligations toward the divine.

One century after our period, gentile Christians no less than pagans were aware that divine wrath was the consequence of neglecting cult, and for this reason they blamed these gods, *qua* evil *daimones*, for inspiring persecution against them, Reed, "Fallen Angels." For fear of divine anger as a root cause of the "Great Persecution" begun under Diocletian (303–311 C.E.), Elizabeth DePalma Digeser, *A Threat to Public Piety: Christians, Platonists, and the Great Persecution*. (Ithaca, NY: Cornell University Press, 2012); cf. the reconstruction by James Rives, "The Persecution of Christians."

60. For a different reconstruction of the meaning of Paul's remark, which also takes seriously the ethnic specificity of his commitments, see Anders Runesson, "Inventing Christian Identity: Paul, Ignatius, and Theodosius I," in *Exploring Early Christian Identity*, ed. Bengt Holmberg (Tübingen: Mohr Siebeck, 2008), esp. 80–84.

61. See Acts 13.50; 14.2, 4–6, 19; 16.20–24; 17.5–9; 18.12–17 (before Gallio in Corinth); 19.23–41 (the tumult in Ephesus). Cf. Paul's description of his woes, inflicted variously by Jews, gentiles, and Romans, 2 Cor 4.8–9; 6.4–5; 11.24–26; also Mk 13.6, 11. In the thirties and forties, this unprecedented and disruptive policy of separating gentiles-in-Christ from their native ethnic/urban cults gives the measure of the apocalyptic mindset, and indeed of the timeframe, of the earliest apostles.

62. This idea that heaven presided over the well-being of cities and, most particularly, of the empire endured well into the post-Constantinian period, though heaven's denomination had changed and the *pax deorum* had ceded to the *pax dei*. "Why has the spring renounced its accustomed charm? Why has the summer, barren of its harvest, deprived the laboring farmer? . . . Why all of these things, unless nature has transgressed the decree of its own law, to avenge impiety?" Thus Theodosius II, in his constitution against pagans, Samaritans, and Jews (*NTh* 3; 438 C.E.). Cf. his convening the Third Ecumenical Council in 429, so that "the condition of the church might honor God *and contribute to the safety*

of the Empire," *Acta consiliorum oecumenicorum* I.1, 1, 114. As Wolf Liebeschuetz rightly observed, "The basic conception [of this late imperial religious legisla- tion] was Roman rather than Christian. Constantine wished to maintain the *pax deorum* as his predecessors had done; but he looked to a new divinity and for new [ritual] procedures to maintain it," *Continuity and Change in Roman Religion* (New York: Oxford University Press, 1979), 292. Deviant religious practices, how- soever defined, risked divine wrath.

63. "Since they were neither Jew nor pagan, they were isolated, without a recogniz- able social identity," Sanders, "Paul's Jewishness," 67; see too n. 26. For the same reason, we have no Jewish term for these people either: they fit no actual (as opposed to optative) social category. Paul calls them either *hagioi* ("sanctified" or "set-apart" ones), or *adelphoi* ([adopted] "brothers"), or (since this is what they are), *ethnē*, which translates both as "pagans" and as "gentiles"; Paula Fredriksen, "Judaizing the Nations: The Ritual Demands of Paul's Gospel," *NTS* 56 (2010): 242–44, 247–50; cf. Johnson Hodge, *If Sons, Then Heirs*, 43–66, 202 n. 1.

64. Historians of Rome seem to have an easier time seeing this than do historians of Christianity: see, e.g., Timothy D. Barnes, "Legislation against the Christians," *JRS* 58 (1968): 32–50; Fergus Millar, "The Imperial Cult and the Persecutions," in *Le culte des souverains dans l'empire romain*, ed. Elias J. Bickerman and Willem de Boer (Vandœuvres-Genève: Fondations Hardt, 1973), 145–65; Lane Fox, *Pagans and Christians*, 419–34.

65. "If Paul's converts joined . . . communities [separate from the synagogue] the Jewish authorities need not ever have come across them. The problem for Paul's fellow Jews lay in the hostile reaction to the conversion of gentiles to Christianity to be expected from unconverted *gentiles* [I would say "pagans"], in particular the civic and Roman authorities, and the possibility that, because Paul portrayed himself as a Jew, *they as Jews might be blamed for his behavior*. . . . From the point of view of pagan polytheists, this attitude [toward the traditional gods] was incom- prehensible, offensive, dangerous insofar as it might alienate the traditional dei- ties, and disloyal," Goodman, "Persecution of Paul," 384–85 (emphasis mine).

66. Goodman, "Persecution of Paul," 385.

67. These are Josephus's numbers, so the usual cautions obtain. On the slaughter in Caesarea, see *BJ* 2.457; 7.361–362; in Ptolemais, 2.477; in Damascus, 2.559–61; cf. 7.367 ("There is not a city in Syria which has not slain its Jewish inhabitants"); 7.368. These same books give casualty figures for other violent outbreaks in Gaza, Anthedon, Ascalon, Hippus, Garada, and Scythopolis; for discussion, *HJP* 2: 85–183. For the earlier anti-Jewish riot in Alexandria, Philo's *In Flaccum* and *Legatio ad Gaium*; Josephus, *AJ* 18.257.

4. PAUL AND THE LAW

1. Acts 10 offers a mannered narrative about Peter's discomfort over baptizing the god-fearer Cornelius who, as a Roman officer, would perforce be understood by Luke's ancient audience as actively pagan; cf., too, the abrupt transition

announced in Acts 11.20–22, when Barnabas is sent from Jerusalem to investigate the situation of "mixed preaching" in Antioch. Earlier in the story, Philip, by contrast, has no problems baptizing an Ethiopian eunuch—perhaps to be understood, then, as a Jewish convert, though Luke does not identify him as a "proselyte." (The Ethiopian seems, to me, to "read" as a god-fearer, Acts 8.26–39.) In any case, and despite the risen Jesus's instructions to the disciples in Acts 1.8 to start a world mission, principled outreach to pagans does not occur until 11.20.

2. On Titus's role in the collection from pagan *ekklesiai* for the Jerusalem community: 2 Cor 2.13; 7.6, 13, 14; 8.6, 16, 23; 12.18.
3. What kind of meals are under consideration here—simple community commensality or, specifically, eucharistic meals? Any commentary on Galatians will weigh the options; see also Magnus Zetterholm, *The Formation of Christianity in Antioch: A Social-Scientific Approach to the Separation between Judaism and Christianity* (London: Routledge, 2003), 129–77.
4. For a similar construal of James's men simply as (Christ-following) "Jews" and not a "circumcision faction," see Francis Watson, *Paul, Judaism, and the Gentiles: Beyond the New Perspective*, rev. ed. (Minneapolis, MN: Eerdmans, 2007), 106 and n. 16.
5. For discussion of this idea of gentile impurity, see p. 53.
6. Johnson Hodge proffers vivid "snapshots" of the god-laden Greco-Roman household in "Married to an Unbeliever," 5–9. She further conjectures that Paul expects that slaves or wives in the household of a nonbelieving *dominus* "will continue to worship the gods of the slaveholder" or of the husband. "What choice do they have?" 17 n. 63; cf. 24 n. 88, on 1 Pet 3.1 and 6.
7. Was the issue, for these visiting Jerusalemites, the "gentileness" of the wine? See the fascinating essay by Sacha Stern, "Compulsive Libationers: Non-Jews and Wine in Early Rabbinic Sources," *JJS* 64 (2013): 19–44. Cf. the recent argument of Barclay, *Paul and the Gift*, 365–87, who sees the fundamental problem at Antioch that Peter did not acknowledge, together with Paul, that ever since "the Christ event," the value of the Torah in general (thus, I imagine, of the food laws in particular) had been overthrown (cf. 383, the Torah is like a "defunct currency"; 385, the "authority of the Torah *has been demolished*," author's emphasis). I cannot see how Barclay's position does not make nonsense of Paul's statement in Rom 3.31, "Do we overthrow the Law with this faith? On the contrary, we uphold the Law!"
8. See the similar speculations by Munck, *Paul and the Salvation of Mankind*, 107; Sanders, *PLJP*, 19.
9. Watson offers a nice list of these binary terms shaping Paul's rhetoric, *Paul, Judaism and the Gentiles*, 97–98.
10. Munck identified these competitors as Judaizing gentile Christians, *Paul and the Salvation of Mankind*, 87–134; so also Lloyd Gaston, *Paul and the Torah* (Vancouver: University of British Columbia Press, 1987), and Gager, *Origins of Anti-Semitism*. By contrast, Hans Dieter Betz, *Galatians: A Commentary on Paul's Letter to the Churches in Galatia* (Philadelphia: Fortress, 1979), takes them

to be Jews. My discussion assumes that they are other Jewish Christ-following apostles who are also, like Paul, going to pagans.

11. Marcion held that Galatians was Paul's "premier letter against Judaism," and Tertullian (through gritted teeth, one imagines), despite the context of his five-book refutation of Marcion, agrees with him on this point (*Adversus Marcionem* 5.2). The most recent iterations of this argument known to me appear in N. T. Wright's *Paul and the Faithfulness of God* (wherein Paul realizes that the Law was, and had always been, a curse, 1,032–37), and Barclay's *Paul and the Gift* (wherein Paul realizes that in Christ the Law is nullified, and that living according to the Law is "in the *same* category of subjection to the *stoicheia* of the world" (409).

12. See Munck's analysis of the Tübingen school, *Paul and the Salvation of Mankind*, 69–86; also Magnus Zetterholm, *Approaches to Paul: A Student's Guide to Recent Scholarship* (Minneapolis, MN: Fortress, 2009), 33–40; Benjamin White, *Remembering Paul* (Oxford: Oxford University Press, 2014) situates Baur's historiography in its nineteenth-century German intellectual context, 20–33. John Gager presents Paul as hounded from city to city by the same group of circumcising opponents within the movement, *Who Made Early Christianity? The Jewish Lives of the Apostle Paul* (New York: Columbia University Press, 2015), 25–28. I am less sure about the translocal stability of the identities of Paul's rivals.

13. See, for example, H. D. Betz's Hermeneia commentary on Galatians, 82; Bengt Holmberg, *Paul and Power: The Structure of Authority in the Primitive Church as Reflected in the Pauline Epistles* (Lund: Liber Läromedel/Gleerup, 1978), 18–32; for review of the arguments, Sanders, *PLJP*, 17–27, and, more recently, Sanders, *Paul: Life, Letters and Thought*, 475–574.

14. Hence, as Munck long ago observed, the mission *to gentiles* is a belated novelty both within the Christ movement and within Second Temple Judaism, *Paul and Salvation*, 207, 265 ("It was with Christianity that a mission to the Gentiles begins").

15. We see this linkage already in Paul's letters, where Christ's return comes together with the establishment of the Kingdom (1 Cor 15 being his fullest description); cf. Mk 13.26–31, where these eschatological events follow after the temple's destruction (13.2–3). On the evolving tradition's provision of a classically Davidic messianic near-future for a figure whose "first coming" had not been messianic, Paula Fredriksen, "'Are You a Virgin?' Biblical Exegesis and the Invention of Tradition," in *Jesus and Brian: Exploring the Historical Jesus and His Times via Monty Python's "Life of Brian,"* ed. Joan E. Taylor (London: Bloomsbury, 2015), 151–65.

16. Belief in the imminent End of the world and the coming of the Kingdom is, paradoxically, one of the longest-lived of Christian traditions. For a review of the systole and diastole of millenarian expectations in the first four Christian centuries, see Paula Fredriksen, "Apocalypse and Redemption in Early Christianity: From John of Patmos to Augustine of Hippo," *Vigiliae Christianae* 45 (1991): 151–83; on the persistent recalculations of the millenarian date in Western Christianity, Richard A. Landes, "Lest the Millennium Be Fulfilled: Apocalyptic

Expectations and the Pattern of Western Chronography 100–800 CE," in *The Use and Abuse of Eschatology in the Middle Ages*, ed. Werner Verbeke, Daniel Verhelst, and Andries Welkenhuysen (Louvain: Leuven University Press, 1988), 137–211, and, more recently (with scope through the 20th century), Landes, *Heaven on Earth: The Varieties of Millennial Experience* (New York: Oxford University Press, 2011). For a considered counterargument, maintaining that when Paul said "soon" he did not mean "right away"—in other words, that expectation of Christ's imminent return does not characterize Paul's letters and the earliest movement—see Ben Witherington, *Jesus, Paul, and the End of the World* (Downers Grove, IL: InterVarsity Press, 1992), 22–35 and endnotes, 258–61.

17. Whether before the crucifixion of Jesus or shortly thereafter in light of the resurrection experiences of some of his followers: Fredriksen, *Jesus of Nazareth*, 235–66.

18. This understanding of the ten "lost" tribes as "scattered among the nations" draws on the original suggestion of Staples, "What Do the Gentiles Have to Do with 'All Israel'?" In that essay, Staples argues that this idea served to stimulate *Paul's* gentile mission (pp. 378–90); I use it here to speculate about the motivations, midcentury, of Paul's circumcising opponents.

19. Abraham serves both as Philo's model of the convert and as the rabbis': *On the Virtues* 20.102–4; cf. *Spec. Laws* 1.9.51–55; cf., e.g., *Mekhilta de-Rabbi Ishmael, Nezikin* 18; and the discussion in Thiessen, *Gentile Problem*, 27–32. In personal correspondence, Larry Hurtado has suggested: "I think a key text is Sirach 44:19–21, which emphasizes that Abraham kept the Torah and 'established the covenant in his flesh,' and 'therefore' God blessed him. Note the sequence, which Paul reverses by cleverly citing the order of blessing/promise and then covenant and circumcision in the Genesis narrative. In short, Paul's line of argument seems to me explained if we see it as a direct answer to people arguing along the lines of the Sirach passage." Further on this interpretation of the figure of Abraham, George W. E. Nickelsburg, "Abraham the Convert: A Jewish Tradition and Its Use by the Apostle Paul," in *Biblical Figures outside the Bible*, ed. Michael E. Stone and Theodore A. Bergren (Harrisburg, PA: Trinity Press International, 1998), 151–75.

20. The proof that the Galatian gentiles-in-Christ have already received Christ's spirit is empirical: not only have they turned from idols, but they are also able to do *dynameis*, "works of power" or "miracles," Gal 3.5.

21. Paul calls his usage of the Hagar-Sarah story "allegorizing" (*allēgoroumena*), Gal 4.24. On this passage as an internal polemic, characterizing two types of missions-in-Christ, see e.g., Thiessen, *Gentile Problem*, 87–91.

22. For the same reason, in Galatians, where Paul says that "neither circumcision counts for anything, nor foreskin, but a new creation" (Gal 6.15), he is *not* referring to Jews in the first instance and to gentiles in the second: he says, rather, that circumcision (in light of Christ) is an irrelevant issue *for gentiles*, who are, again, both the recipients and the rhetorical focus of the letter. See further William S. Campbell, "'As Having and Not Having': Paul, Circumcision, and Indifferent

Things in 1 Corinthians 7.17–32a," *Unity and Diversity in Christ: Interpreting Paul in Context: Collected Essays* (Eugene, OR: Wipf and Stock Publishers, 2013), 106–26.

23. For recent statements of this position—namely, that Paul as a Christian theologian who, as part of his new mode of being, repudiates his former ethnic (and thus, religious) allegiances—see, e.g., Love L. Sechrest, *A Former Jew: Paul and the Dialectics of Race* (Edinburgh: T. & T. Clark, 2009); Wright, *Paul and the Faithfulness of God* (but the idea repeats in all his writings on Paul—and, for that matter, on Jesus); Barclay, *Paul and the Gift*.

24. *CTh* 16.8.19, a statute from the year 409, vilifies gentile god-fearing; *CTh* 16.9.5 specifies exile and confiscation of property if a Jew facilitates the conversion to Judaism of a Christian. Linder, *Jews in Roman Imperial Legislation*, conveniently collects and comments on all legislation relevant to Jews in book 16 of the Codex Theodosianus. For a recent estimation of the situation on the ground, John G. Gager, "Who Did What to Whom? Physical Violence between Jews and Christians in Late Antiquity," in *A Most Reliable Witness: Essays in Honor of Ross Shepard Kraemer*, ed. Susan Ashbrook Harvey et al. (Providence, RI: Brown Judaic Studies, 2015), 35–48.

25. On the Christianizing sea-change in the legal status of Jewish Romans after Constantine, see Amnon Linder, "The Legal Status of the Jews in the Roman Empire," in *The Cambridge History of Judaism*, vol. 4: *The Late Roman-Rabbinic Period*, ed. Steven T. Katz (Cambridge: Cambridge University Press, 2006), 128–73; and, in the same volume, on the intensifying interactions between episcopal ideology, imperial politics, and mixed urban populations, Paula Fredriksen and Oded Irshai, "Christian Anti-Judaism: Polemics and Policies," 977–1,034, at 998–1,007; also P. Fredriksen, "Jewish Romans, Christian Romans, and the Post-Roman West: The Social Correlates of the *contra Iudaeos* Tradition," in *Conflict and Religious Conversation in Latin Christendom: Studies in Honour of Ora Limor*, ed. Israel Yuval and Ram Ben-Shalom (Turnhout, Belgium: Brepols, 2014), 17–38.

26. Two notable exceptions, to either side of Constantine's conversion of Christianity: Origen of Alexandria (185–254), and Augustine of Hippo (354–430). Both theologians maintained that Paul as well as the original disciples continued to live according to Jewish ancestral custom. Origen's arguments appear chiefly in his commentary on Romans; Augustine makes this case against Jerome in *Ep.* 82.2, 8–15 (on Paul and the other Jewish apostles), and in 82.2, 19 (on Jesus's own Law-observance), arguments incorporated into his anti-Manichean magnum opus *Against Faustus*. See Paula Fredriksen, "Lawless or Lawful? Origen and Augustine on Paul and the Law," in *Law and Lawlessness in Early Judaism and Christianity: Essays from the Oxford Manfred Lautenschläger Colloquium 2015*, ed. D. Lincicum, R. Sheridan, and C. Stang (Tübingen: Mohr Siebeck, 2018); and Fredriksen, *Augustine and the Jews*, 298–319.

27. For Barclay's musings on theological usability and historical reconstruction, see *Paul and the Gift*, 7, 350, 573.

28. The grace/race sound bite comes from N. T. Wright, *The Climax of the Covenant: Christ and the Law in Pauline Theology* (Minneapolis, MN: Fortress, 1993), 247. The idea that Paul worked to erase "ethnic difference" is gospel in a wide swathe of Pauline studies, uniting the work of scholars as different as John Barclay, Daniel Boyarin, James D. G. Dunn, Richard Hays, Alan F. Segal, and Wright. For the contrary argument—namely, that Paul's resistance to gentile circumcision precisely preserves ethnic distinctions κατὰ σάρκα—see, e.g., Johnson Hodge, *If Sons, Then Heirs*; Fredriksen, "Judaizing the Nations"; Kathy Ehrensperger, *Paul at the Crossroads of Cultures: Theologizing in the Space Between* (London: Bloomsbury T. & T. Clark, 2013), esp. 105–39; and the essays assembled in Campbell, *Unity and Diversity in Christ.*

29. For patristic writers from Marcion to Tertullian through Jerome and well beyond, Paul's conversion is defined by his repudiation of Jewish Law. For an overview of this terrain, specifically as it touches on readings of Romans 9–11, see Karl Hermann Schelkle, *Paulus, Lehrer der Väter: Die altkirchliche Auslegung von Römer 1–11* (Düsseldorf: Patmos Verlag, 1956). Many modern scholars still hew to the patristic line: on Paul's personal repudiation of Jewish practice, Sanders, *Paul and Palestinian Judaism*, 500 (in turning to Christ, Paul in effect turned from the Law); Dunn, *Theology of Paul* and the essays gathered by him in *Paul and the Mosaic Law: The Third Durham-Tübingen Research Symposium on Earliest Christianity and Judaism (Durham, September, 1994)* (Tübingen: Mohr Siebeck, 1996); and the literature cited in n. 22 above. *Sonderweg* scholars, despite holding that Paul's negative remarks about Torah refer only to gentiles and nowhere to Jews, still maintain that he himself was no longer Law-observant, e.g., Gaston, *Paul and the Torah*, 76–79; Gager, *Reinventing Paul*, 86; cf. Stowers, *Rereading of Romans*, 156, 329.

30. Alan F. Segal, *Paul the Convert: The Apostolate and Apostasy of Saul the Pharisee* (New Haven, CT: Yale University Press, 1990), 205. This imagined scenario has been a leitmotif of Martin Hengel's work when reconstructing the history of the movement, e.g., *Between Jesus and Paul.*

31. Oftentimes, these Jewish apostles are simply assumed to be lax about Torah observance because of a presumption that Jesus of Nazareth had himself taught against the Law. This presupposition founders particularly against the argument described in Gal 2.11–12: if the historical Jesus had taught against the food laws (Mk 7.14ff. is pressed into service here), apparently (as the incident at Antioch attests) his own followers knew nothing about it. On the question of Jesus and the Law, see esp. John P. Meier's *Law and Love*, vol. 4 of *A Marginal Jew: Rethinking the Historical Jesus* (New Haven, CT: Yale University Press, 2009).

32. On the diversity of Jewish practice, see most recently Karin Hedner Zetterholm, "The Question of Assumptions: Torah Observance in the First Century," in Nanos and Zetterholm, *Paul within Judaism*, 79–103; further on internal Jewish diversity of practice, Goodman, "The Persecution of Paul by Diaspora Jews."

33. "There may also have been many points on which Paul and his opponents agreed, but which are submerged by the polarizing effect of his polemic," Barclay correctly notes, "Mirror-Reading a Polemical Letter," 78.

34. If "Christian" is a term to be avoided as distortingly anachronistic for this population of socially anomalous ex-pagan pagans, what term can we use? See Caroline E. Johnson Hodge, "The Question of Identity: Gentiles as Gentiles—but Also Not—in Pauline Communities," in Nanos and Zetterholm, *Paul within Judaism,* 153–74; Joshua D. Garroway, *Paul's Gentile-Jews: Neither Jew nor Gentile, but Both* (New York: Palgrave Macmillan, 2012); on the problem of anachronism with designating these people as "Christians," see p. 230. n. 43. "Judaizing" in the context of even Paul's mission, however, is not an "etic" term: above, p. 58, contra John M. G. Barclay, *Pauline Churches and Diaspora Jews* (Tübingen: Mohr Siebeck, 2011), 18 n. 48. On Paul's fulminations against pagan idolatry, and thus his debt to traditions of Jewish Law, Peter J. Tomson, *Paul and the Jewish Law: Halakha in the Letters of the Apostle to the Gentiles* (Assen, Netherlands: Van Gorcum, 1990), esp. 187–220.

35. Already in the early second century, Paul was misinterpreted in this way, that is, as teaching against Judaism *to Jews*: see, e.g., Acts 21.21 (Luke disavows the accusation). On the author of Ephesians, and the way that he as a deutero-Pauline author collapses the ethnic distinctions that Paul himself upheld, see J. Albert Harrill, "Ethnic Fluidity in Ephesians," *NTS* 60 (2014): 379–402.

36. John Barclay assumes that the intended audience for Paul's "no longer preaching circumcision" (Gal 5.11) was Jews (e.g., "Paul and the Hidden Circumcision of the Heart," *Pauline Churches and Diaspora Jews*; on this verse, p. 73). Paul the Christian theologian "radically redefines" Jewish identity and thinks that fleshly circumcision is of no consequence for Jews as well as for gentiles, Barclay maintains (ibid., 68–79, a theme repeated in *Paul and the Gift*). Further, Barclay's Paul likewise holds Torah to represent a sort of defunct currency (*Paul and the Gift,* 383) whose authority has been "demolished" (p. 385), and he (that is, Barclay's Paul) self-consciously rethinks the identity of Israel (p. 520). Barclay's Paul, like Wright's, is a Christian theologian.

37. Judith M. Gundry, in a paper delivered at the 2016 meeting of the SNTS in Montreal, has pointed to a supporting reason why Paul would have urged Corinthian Christ-followers to avoid procreative sex: "procreative sex to obtain heirs and secure one's family line and memory caused strife among men and should be abandoned," "Becoming 'One Flesh' and the Politics of Procreation: 1 Corinthians 7.29B and the Corinthian *Schismata*"; the quotation is from MS p. 35. I thank her for her permission to cite this as-yet unpublished paper.

38. 1 Cor 9.20–21 is sometimes adduced in proof of the contrary: "To the Jews I became as a Jew, in order to win Jews; to those under the Law I became as one under the Law—though not being myself under the Law—so that I might win those under the Law. To those outside the Law I became as one outside the Law—not being without the Law of God but under the law of Christ . . . I have been all things to all men." For my interpretation of these verses, see above, p. 165. Augustine's remarks in his correspondence with Jerome (c. 397 C.E.), when he upheld his view that Paul continued to live sincerely—not merely strategically—as a Torah-observant Jew his entire life, bear repeating here.

If Paul had observed those *sacramenta* [this is Augustine's term for Jewish rites] because he *pretended* that he was a Jew in order to gain the Jews, why did he not also offer sacrifice with the gentiles since he became like someone without the Law for those who were without the Law, in order that he might gain them, too? But instead, he acted as someone who was a Jew by birth, and he said all these things not so that he might deceitfully pretend to be what he was not, but because he thought that he might mercifully help these people in that way. (Augustine to Jerome, Letter 40.4, 6)

Therefore, concluded Augustine, this passage in 1 Cor 9 attested to the apostle's compassion as well as to his integrity. Becoming "like a Jew" and "like a gentile" did not mean "pretending" to be either a Jew or a gentile.

39. Gal 6.16 ("Peace and mercy be upon all who walk by this rule, and on the Israel of God," καὶ ὅσοι τῷ κανόνι τούτῳ στοιχήσουσιν, εἰρήνη ἐπ᾽ αὐτοὺς καὶ ἔλεος, καὶ ἐπὶ τὸν Ἰσραὴλ τοῦ θεοῦ) has long been read by many (though not all) commentators as indicating the Christian church rather than ethnic Israel. Against such a construal, see most recently the essay by Susan Grove Eastman, "Israel and the Mercy of God: A Re-reading of Galatians 6.16 and Romans 9–11," *NTS* 56 (2010): 367–95; see too Krister Stendahl, *Final Account: Paul's Letter to the Romans* (Minneapolis, MN: Fortress, 1995), 5, 40.

40. On this point, and the ways in which Paul's letters stand on an arc of developing *Jewish* discourse, see the two major essays by Ishay Rosen-Zvi and Adi Ophir, "Goy: Toward a Genealogy," *Diné Israel* 28 (2011): 69–112, and "Paul and the Invention of the Gentiles," *JQR* 105 (2015): 1–41.

41. Thus the NRSV translation of Deut 32.8. On the slippage between *benei elohim* ("sons of God," 4QDeut[j]), *benei Israel* (the MT), and *angeloi* (LXX), see above, p. 14, and notes.

42. On God's Sabbath-keeping, the angel in Jubilees tells Moses, "He [God] gave us a great sign, the Sabbath day, so that we might work six days and observe a Sabbath from all work on the seventh day. And he told us—all the angels of the presence and all the angels of sanctification, these two great kinds"—who are themselves circumcised (15.27)—"that we might keep the Sabbath with him in heaven and on earth. And he said to us, 'Behold, I will separate for myself a people from among all the nations. And they will also keep the Sabbath. And I will sanctify them for myself, and I will bless them. . . . And they will be my people and I will be their god. And I have chosen the seed of Jacob from among all that I have seen. And I have recorded them as my firstborn son, and have sanctified him for myself forever and ever. And I will make known to them the Sabbath day . . .," Jub 2.17–20. See further Kugel, "4Q369 'Prayer of Enosh,'" esp. 123–26. On practices, place, language, and family relationships as markers of ethnic identity, see chap. 2 above. The emphasis on Hebrew as the "Jewish" tongue probably accounts for the anxious authorizations through miracle retailed in Hellenistic Jewish legend about the LXX. Paul too, as we will see, will pick up *glōssa* as an ethnic indicator. For more on the divine ethnicity in Paul, my essay, "How Jewish Is God?" (forthcoming).

43. On the anachronism of the term "Christian" for this first generation of the movement, see especially the arguments by William Arnal, "The Collection and Synthesis of 'Tradition' and the Second-Century Invention of Christianity," *Method and Theory in the Study of Religion* 23 (2011): 193–215; Runesson, "Inventing Christian Identity," further developed in "The Question of Terminology: The Architecture of Contemporary Discussions on Paul," in Nanos and Zetterholm, *Paul within Judaism*, 53–78; John W. Marshall, "Misunderstanding the New Paul: Marcion's Transformation of the *Sonderzeit* Paul," *JECS* 20 (2012): 1–29. Marshall notes, p. 6:

> Using a category of "Christianity" is fundamentally erroneous when interpreting Paul. It exercises transformative influence on his writings in the same way the [later] pseudepigraphical Pastoral epistles do. . . . By reading Paul's writings as instances of "Christianity," the new, but later, religion is already retrojected onto the letters, the force of Paul's eschatological conviction is blunted, and the specificity of his address to Gentiles is effaced. These effects of the term "Christianity" are largely distorting in the way it takes over and transforms, Christianizes, or simply eradicates Paul's conviction at Rom 11.26 that "all Israel" would be saved.

It is perhaps worth noting that two of the most recent—and longest—works arguing that Paul is a Christian theologian who repudiates Judaism, Wright (2013, 1,660 pages) and Barclay (2015, 656 pages)—do not bring Paul's vivid eschatology into view at all in their respective depictions. Wright denies forthrightly that Paul thought in terms of an imminent end, and he mocks scholars who think otherwise as a guild "who wear their fringes long and their phylacteries wide"—hypocrites? Pharisees? "Jews"?—if they disagree with his nonapocalyptic construction of the Parousia (*Paul and the Faithfulness of God*, 165). Barclay considers "apocalyptic" solely as a term that other scholars—D. A. Campbell, Ernst Käsemann, and Louis Martyn—use; it nowhere figures in his presentation of his own views. Unsurprisingly, both scholars fit Marshall's paragraph above exactly: seeing Paul's letters as examples of "Christianity," they fail to consider eschatology as an important factor shaping Paul's message, and they see him as addressing his theology to Jews as well as to gentiles. The Israel that is saved (Rom 11.25–26), they conclude, is the Christian Israel. So also Christopher Zoccali, "'And So All Israel Will Be Saved': Competing Interpretations of Romans 11.26 in Pauline Scholarship," *JSNT* 30 (2008): 289–318.

44. *Hagioi* mobilizes the language of temple imagery and the sacrificial protocols of Leviticus; *adelphoi* is the language of lineage, kinship, and inheritance. We will look at both sets of associations closely in chap. 5 below.

45. Joshua Garroway proposes "Gentile-Jews" as Paul's term for these people: given their hybrid ethno-religious status—gentiles whose *pistis* in the god of Israel's messiah has grafted them into Israel (cf. Rom 11.17–24)—the hyphenated term, he argues, is apt. But Paul's metaphor of the olive tree does not overcome, to my mind, the distinction between Israel and the *ethnē* that he insists on, even as he

hymns their common redemption, at the letter's end, 15.9–12, quoted above, p. 163. (And the "wild" branches remain "wild," ingrafted *para physin*, "against nature.") Through Abraham/Christ, these gentiles do indeed *become* God's *adopted* sons (Gal 4); but Jews are Jews "by nature" (Gal 2.15), through being of the same *genos* of the patriarchs, blood-descendants of Abraham, Isaac, and Jacob (Rom 9.4–5); and, quite apart from Christ, they already count as God's sons (Rom 9.4): the two groups are eschatologically conjoined, but nevertheless distinct. Cf. Garroway, *Paul's Gentile-Jews*.

46. See Fredriksen, *Sin*, 6–49, on this common content between John, Jesus, and Paul.

47. Fredriksen, "Judaizing the Nations," emphasizes the ritual aspects of Paul's instruction to his ex-pagan pagans; see too Fredriksen, "The Question of Worship: Gods, Pagans, and the Redemption of Israel," in Nanos and Zetterholm, *Paul within Judaism*, 175–202.

48. On the continuities and contrasts between these terms as used by pagan writers, by the translators of the LXX, and by Paul, see Morgan, *Roman Faith and Christian Faith*, 212–306.

49. Sanders gives a lengthy consideration of the defects of English for translating Paul's δικαιοσύνη vel sim. in *Paul: A Very Short Introduction* (Oxford: Oxford University Press, 1991), 52–90; see esp. 54–55. I adopt his awkward neologism "righteoused" above since, for the reasons that he gives, it is preferable to "justified."

50. Krister Stendahl's classic 1963 essay "Paul and the Introspective Conscience of the West," *Harvard Theological Review* 56 (1963): 199–215, was mobilized precisely against this construal of individual "justification." Käsemann's work stands as Stendahl's theological antipode: see Stendahl's closing comments in *Final Account*, 76.

51. For a thoughtful critique of both of these positions, see Thiessen, *Gentile Problem*, 4–7 ("Judaism and the Quagmire of Pauline Studies") and passim.

52. Three great mid-20th-century Scandinavian scholars, Johannes Munck, Nils Dahl, and Krister Stendahl, insisted on this issue of Paul's gentile addressees; it was adopted, emphasized, and interpreted as meaning that Paul intended two different modes of salvation, Torah for Jews and Christ for gentiles, by Lloyd Gaston and by John Gager, as well as, with specific reference to Romans, Stanley Stowers (the so-called *Sonderweg* interpretation). Most recently, and refracted differently, the argument has been carried forward in the work of Matthew Thiessen and Christine Hayes. The present argument makes my case for taking this fact—that in the letters we have from him, Paul addresses gentiles and only gentiles—in tandem with Paul's commitment to an imminent eschatology, as the necessary point of orientation when interpreting Paul's epistles.

53. Werner Georg Kümmel, *Römer 7 und das Bild des Menschen im Neuen Testament* (Munich: Kaiser, 1974; first published in 1929), 139–160, argued exhaustively against taking the "I" of Rom 7 as Paul's description of his preconversion self. Munck built on Kümmel's position, urging that the word "conversion" be

dropped in favor of Paul's own phrasing as having received a (prophetic) "call," *Paul and Salvation*, 11–35. Munck's points were in turn picked up and promulgated by Stendahl, "Paul and the Introspective Conscience of the West," a reprint of his important 1963 article: Stendahl drew attention to the contributions of Augustine and Luther to this misreading of Rom 7.

It was Augustine's late interpretation of Paul, in the context of the Pelagian controversy, that bequeathed the apostolic identification to Rom 7: *Contra ii epistulas Pelagianorum* 1.8, 13–14, and *De predestinatione sanctorum* 1.2,4, thereby foregrounding Paul's "conversion" from the Law to Christ; see Fredriksen, "Paul and Augustine." For a recent defense of the Augustinian-Lutheran sensibility when reading Paul, see Barclay, *Paul and the Gift*, 85–116 (emphasizing constructs of "grace"). For recent arguments identifying the speaker in Rom 7 as Paul, Watson, *Paul, Judaism, and the Gentiles*, 290; Hayes, *Divine Law*, 153–56 (Paul, she argues, speaks this way strategically, to make the Law less attractive to gentiles).

54. And indeed, this is how most ancient interpreters—including Augustine in one of his early commentaries on Romans—read Rom 7: *Propp.* 41.1–46.7; see also Fredriksen, "Conversion Narratives," 20–26; Stowers, *Rereading of Romans*, 16–41. On the entire epistle's address explicitly and solely to gentile Christ-followers, see esp. Thorsteinsson's *Paul's Interlocutor in Romans* 2; and the volume of essays exploring all of Romans from this vantage point of the implied gentile reader, *The So-Called Jew in Paul's Letter to the Romans*, ed. Rafael Rodriquez and Matthew Thiessen (Minneapolis, MN: Fortress, 2016). In that volume's first chapter, Thiessen provides a pellucid summary of Thorsteinsson's argument, 7–37.

55. On Rom 7 and its resonances with Euripides' *Medea* 1,077–80 as addressing gentile problems of self-mastery, see Stowers, *Rereading of Romans*, 258–84; further on this theme of self-mastery and moral philosophy, Emma Wasserman, *The Death of the Soul in Romans 7: Sin, Death, and the Law in Light of Hellenistic Moral Psychology* (Tübingen: Mohr Siebeck, 2008).

56. How do we translate *arsenokoitēs* (which I render as "sexual exploiter") and *malakos* (effeminate or "soft" male)? Do the conjoined terms indicate active and passive male homosexuality (so Sanders, *Paul: A Very Short Introduction*, 128–33), or some sort of exploitation, together with excessive primping (so Dale B. Martin, *Sex and the Single Savior: Gender and Sexuality in Biblical Interpretation* [Louisville, KY: Westminster John Knox Press, 2006], 37–50)? I do not know, but gave my best guess above.

57. "How miserable are those, their hopes set on dead things, who give the name 'gods' to the works of human hands," chides the (Alexandrian?) author of Wisdom of Solomon, sometime in the first century B.C.E. (Wis 13.10; cf. 14.23–28, on infanticide, reveling, adultery, murder, and perjury). Especially in his long indictment, Rom 1.18–32, Paul repeats and amplifies Wisdom's themes. We see here the reuse of the old anti-Canaanite biblical polemic, wherein the worship of idols invariably leads to bad sex and murder. Like any ethnic stereotype, the "gentiles" of

Jewish antipagan rhetoric serve an identity-confirming function for Jews: *they behave in these ways, we don't.* For a review of such vice lists in Hellenistic Jewish literature, see Ernst Käsemann, *Commentary on Romans,* trans. and ed. Geoffrey W. Bromiley (Grand Rapids, MI: Eerdmans, 1980), 49f.; in Paul's letters specifically, Sanders, *PLJP* s.v. "porneia"; see also John T. Fitzgerald's article on virtue/vice lists in *ABD* 6: 857–59. Despite its resonance with Wisdom, and Paul's explicit reference to idol-worship, Barclay takes Rom 1.18–32 as indicting all humanity, Jew and pagan both, *Paul and the Gift,* 461–66.

58. See Shaye J. D. Cohen, "Respect for Judaism by Gentiles in the Writings of Josephus," *HTR* 80 (1987): 409–30; Cohen, "Crossing the Boundary and Becoming a Jew," where he distinguishes seven degrees of gentile affiliation/support for or interest in things Jewish, up to and including conversion, *Beginnings of Jewishness,* 140–62, with copious primary references to both Hellenistic and rabbinic sources. The traditions that eventually coalesce into the rabbinic "Noachide laws" feature the abandonment of idolatry as the measure of gentile righteousness: b Sanh. 56b; AvZar 8(9):4–6; cf. Jub 7.20ff.; "James's" rulings in Acts 15.20. On gentile righteousness, see also the discussion in Sanders, *PPJ,* 206–12, further developed in *Jesus and Judaism,* 212–21; *HJP* 3: 150–79; comprehensively, David Novak, *The Image of the Non-Jew in Judaism: An Historical and Constructive Study of the Noahide Laws,* Toronto Studies in Theology 14 (New York: Mellen Press, 1983). Donaldson concludes his careful study with the observation: "There simply was no unified view whatsoever on the religious status of non-Jews, either now or in the future. The range of diversity is striking," *Judaism and the Gentiles,* 512.

59. This (unsuccessfully) Judaizing gentile, who has "the written Law and circumcision," is the comparandum to the gentiles "who do naturally what the Law requires." Rom 2.26–28, in other words, speaks not about a Jew compared to a Christ-following gentile, but about the self-consciously Judaizing gentile compared to a naturally Judaizing pagan (those who, in Donaldson's categories, are "ethical monotheists"? *Judaism and the Gentiles,* 493–98).

60. So too, e.g., Munck, *Paul and Salvation,* 120; Watson, *Paul, Judaism, and the Gentiles,* 70–74; Wagner, *Heralds,* 35. This reconstruction of course corresponds to the picture presented in Acts, where Luke constantly registers the pagans' presence while discreetly omitting to mention their continuing engagement with their own gods: 13.16, 26; 14.1; 17.4, 12; 18.4. My conjecture here about Paul's access through the diaspora synagogue to pagans familiar with Jewish ideas is supported by Acts but not generated by it. (Or, as Munck notes, "the evidence of Acts may serve as a historical source where it does not contradict Paul's letters," ibid., 120, also 78–81.) For the view that Paul contacted gentiles independently of the synagogue, the work of Hock and of Sanders, cited at chap. 3, n. 1, above.

61. Which is not to say that his letters were not occasionally misunderstood, "for there are some things in them hard to understand," 2 Pet 3.16.

62. Cf. 2 Cor 11.1–23. We know nothing of the content of these apostles' "different gospel," but they share Paul's ethnic identity as well as his commitment to

spreading the good news of redemption in Christ, however they may interpret that message.

63. For a review of these scholarly interpretations, "antilegalistic" (the more traditional, so-called Lutheran reading, e.g., Barrett, Bornkamm, Käsemann, et al.) and "anti-ethnocentric" (the New Perspective, e.g., Dunn, Hayes, Wright, et al.), see Thiessen, *Gentile Problem*, 4–7 and passim.

64. This interpretation is most associated with Lloyd Gaston (*Paul and the Torah*) and John Gager (*Origins of Anti-Semitism* and *Reinventing Paul*). I have learned much and take much from the work of both scholars, but cannot follow them so far. First, Christ as the messiah son of David could never be of null import for Israel. And, second, Paul states that Jews as well as gentiles are "under sin" (Rom 3.9–20), and that the blessing of Abraham as the model of *pistis* is pronounced on "the circumcised" as well as "on the uncircumcised" (4.1–9). Christ as God's eschatological champion redeems the whole cosmos, of which Israel is certainly a part (Rom 8–15); Christ's Parousia coincides with the raising of the dead, among whom certainly number Jews. And Paul himself supported James, Peter, and John's mission to Jews, something that would be nonsensical if he were a *Sonderweg* thinker himself.

   Paul's concentration on the Law's negative effects for gentiles does not, in my view, diminish his conviction that Christ comes to redeem Israel as well as the nations (Rom 15.8–9). See too the measured remarks of Novenson, *Christ among the Messiahs*, 25ff., and Pamela M. Eisenbaum, *Paul Was Not a Christian: The Real Message of a Misunderstood Apostle* (New York: HarperOne, 2009), 250–55.

65. On the complications in Pauline scholarship caused by thinking with the concepts "religion" and "salvation," see the remarks of Brent Nongbri, "The Concept of Religion and the Study of the Apostle Paul," *JJMJS* 2 (2015): 1–26. On the complications of importing the idea of "religion"—a relationship with the divine predicated upon individual choice irrespective of ancestral protocols of worship—to antiquity more generally, besides Nongbri's own earlier monograph *Before Religion* (2013), see the essays by William Arnal, "What Branches Grow out of the Stony Rubbish? Christian Origins and the Study of Religion," *SR* 39 (2010): 549–72, and Annette Y. Reed's rejoinder, "Christian Origins and Religious Studies," *SR* 44 (2015): 307–19.

66. See esp. the foundational study by Johnson Hodge, *If Sons, Then Heirs*, and her more recent consideration of these issues in "The Question of Identity."

67. For these arguments from closed-ethnic genealogies, see the work of Christine E. Hayes, *Gentile Impurities* (2002) and *Divine Law* (2015), specifically with reference to Paul; Matthew Thiessen, *Contesting Conversion* (2011), on Acts, and *Paul and the Gentile Problem* (2016), specifically on Paul.

68. Hayes, *Divine Law*, 143.

69. Hayes, *Divine Law*, 162–63. I am not persuaded by this argument on its face: Paul also tells his gentiles that he himself *did* achieve righteousness under the Law (Phil 3.6; Hayes does not consider this verse). Also, such a theory of reading puts

us in the position of holding that Paul said (to his gentiles) something that he essentially did not really mean (because he personally did esteem Law). Finally, I query Hayes's phrasing in her n. 42: in my view, Paul never thought that gentiles could become part of Israel, even "spiritually." On the contrary, their ethnic status perdures even after they have become "sons by adoption." But Hayes is unquestionably correct as she continues on the page following: if Paul's negative rhetoric was *"a strategic accommodation to his audience"* (p. 164, italics in the original), its negative force lived on long afterward in later theology *adversus Iudaeos*, when gentile Christians came to vilify the "particularism" of the Law and the "fleshly" Jewish practices that express it. Further on the ethical consequences of echoing "ethnic reasoning" in modern interpretations of ancient works, Denise K. Buell, "God's Own People: Spectres of Race, Ethnicity and Gender in Early Christian Studies," *Prejudice and Christian Beginnings*, 159–190.

70. In view of the antiquity of the LXX, the Samaritan Pentateuch, and Jubilees, it is possible that *Hebrew* texts of Gen 17.14 that retained "on the eighth day" were circulating, pre-MT, early in the Hellenistic period. See the careful study by Matthew Thiessen, "The Text of Genesis 17:14," *JBL* 128 (2009): 625–42. These textual points need not be dwelled on, since the diaspora Jewish communities no less than later rabbinic ones clearly practiced proselyte circumcision: "determined readers could find support in either text for either view." I thank my anonymous colleague for emphasizing this observation in his or her critical reading of my earlier manuscript.

71. Thiessen, *Paul and the Gentile Problem*, 19–101, argues this interpretation with clarity and conviction. The idea is so new to me that I am still thinking about it. One of many interesting results of Thiessen's view is the way that it alters the meaning usually ascribed to Gal 5.3: "Every man who receives circumcision is bound to keep the whole Law." Rather than making a statement of principle about the behavioral requirements assumed by the convert, Paul would be saying that "the whole law" about circumcision—circumcision *on the eighth day*—is what is required; see ibid., 91f.

72. Cf. Barclay, who reads Gal 4.9–10 as Paul's correlating Torah observance and circumcision—implausibly, in my view—to worship of the *stoicheia, Paul and the Gift*, 408–9. The tangle of Paul's pronominal referents—whom does he think of when he says "we"? Who are his "you"? Jews, Christ-following Jews, Christ-following ex-pagans, Christ-following ex-pagans now persuaded by the circumcisers' arguments?—makes tracking his thought in Galatians that much harder. I assume that Paul's use of "we" in this letter is usually his way of rhetorically identifying himself with his gentile auditors (e.g., Gal 4.5, "so that we might receive adoption as sons" can only refer to gentiles, since ethnic Israel, according to Paul—and quite apart from Christ—already has "sonship," Rom 9.4). For a different consideration of this same issue, see Andrew A. Das, *Paul and the Stories of Israel: Grand Thematic Narratives in Galatians* (Minneapolis, MN: Fortress, 2016), 33–63.

5. CHRIST AND THE KINGDOM

1. A point insisted on already by Schweitzer, *Mysticism of Paul*, 52–65 and passim. "From his first letter to his last, Paul's thought is always uniformly dominated by the expectation of the immediate return of Jesus," p. 52.

2. Paul's equally strong assertion in Galatians that, before receiving his apostolic call, he "persecuted the assembly of God to the utmost and tried to destroy it" (Gal 1.13) somewhat compromises his claim to radical independence: this early assembly (ekklesia) in Damascus obviously first mediated the *evangelion* to him.

3. Collins, *The Scepter and Star*, notes that "the concept of a Davidic messiah as the warrior king who would destroy the enemies of Israel and institute an era of unending peace constitutes the common core of Jewish messianism around the turn of the era," p. 68; cf. pp. 136–53 on the dim figure of a heavenly redeemer. Collins, too, speculates that Jesus's so-called Triumphal Entry might have led to his Roman execution (pp. 204–7); for my own reconstruction on the relation of the Triumphal Entry to Jesus's identification as messiah, and Pilate's subsequent move against him, see *Jesus of Nazareth*, 235–59.

4. Novenson, *Christ among the Messiahs*, 103.

5. To Novenson's pellucid study goes the credit for dismantling this argument, *Christ among the Messiahs*. The quotation about honorifics comes from p. 95.

6. Compare the descent from heaven of the returning Christ, 1 Thes 4.13–18, Paul's warnings about the Day of the Lord coming like a "thief in the night" (5.1–4), and his description of the sequence of final events in 1 Cor 15.22–26, with passages about the apocalyptic Son of Man in Mk 8.31 and 13; see too Fredriksen, *Jesus of Nazareth*, 78–89, for analysis of apocalyptic traditions shared between gospel sources and Paul, some perhaps tracing back to Jesus of Nazareth; further on retrospective constructions of Jesus's Davidic messiahship, Fredriksen, "'Are You a Virgin?'"

7. Dahl, in his classic essay "The Crucified Messiah," closes the gap between Jesus's nonmessianic public mission and his followers' post-crucifixion acclamation of him as messiah with the crucifixion itself, *The Crucified Messiah, and Other Essays* (Minneapolis, MN: Augsburg Publishing House, 1974), 38. Israel Knohl has proposed that one Menachem, an Essene teacher, modeled a suffering and dying messiah in the generation before Jesus; but much of his argument depends upon filling in lacunae within tattered fragments from Cave 4. So far, his reconstruction has not persuaded most scholars: *The Messiah before Jesus* (Berkeley: University of California Press, 2000).

8. On this Davidic bracketing of his letter to Rome, and the ways that it affects Paul's understanding of his gentile mission, see Fredriksen, *Jesus of Nazareth*, 125–37; also Matthew V. Novenson, "The Jewish Messiahs, the Pauline Christ, and the Gentile Question," *JBL* 128 (2009): 373–89; before him, Christopher C. Whitsett, "Son of God, Seed of David: Paul's Messianic Exegesis in Romans 2 [sic]:3–4," *JBL* 119 (2000): 661–81.

9. On which see the classic study by Donald H. Juel, *Messianic Exegesis: Christological Interpretations of the Old Testament in Early Christianity*

(Philadelphia: Fortress, 1988); see also Novenson, *Christ among the Messiahs*, 136–73.

10. Scholarly consensus holds that this hymn represents pre-Pauline tradition. I am not certain that this is the case. If Paul chose to use it, however, it must relate to its new context. The same holds true for Rom 1.3–4: that passage also is often identified as pre-Pauline tradition, though, as we will see, it resonates deeply with key "Pauline" themes. Or, as Novenson has noted, "Pre-Pauline traditions, once used by Paul, become functionally Pauline and must be interpreted as meaningful parts of the texts in which they fall," "Jewish Messiahs," 370 n. 56.

11. As clear an exposition as one could hope for of the meanings of *morphē* in this difficult passage may be found in M. Bockmuehl, *The Epistle to the Philippians* (London: A. & C. Black, 1997), 126–29; for his interpretation of this whole "hymn," pp. 114–48.

12. Taking ancient Jewish thought as strictly "monotheistic" (in the modern sense, that only one god exists), Richard Bauckham accordingly reads this passage in Philippians as establishing this sort of radical identification, one of the "deepest insights of New Testament Christology," which had to wait for Martin Luther to be adequately theologically appropriated, *Jesus and the God of Israel* (Grand Rapids, MI: Eerdmans, 2009), 59; for his entire discussion, pp. 1–17 (early Jewish monotheism), pp. 18–31 ("Christological monotheism"), pp. 37–45 (specifically on Phil 2.6–11). For a recent problematizing of this sort of claim to divine identification (that is, of Christ with God), M. W. Martin, "ἁρπαγμὸς Revisited: A Philological Reexamination of the New Testament's 'Most Difficult Word," *JBL* 135 (2016): 175–94. Cf. too the classic article by C. H. Talbert, "The Problem of Pre-existence in Philippians 2.6–11," *JBL* 86 (1967): 141–53, arguing that these verses actually speak to the human Christ.

13. Here is the full text of Phil 2.5–11: τοῦτο φρονεῖτε ἐν ὑμῖν ὃ καὶ ἐν Χριστῷ Ἰησοῦ, (6) ὃς ἐν μορφῇ θεοῦ ὑπάρχων οὐχ ἁρπαγμὸν ἡγήσατο τὸ εἶναι ἴσα θεῷ, (7) ἀλλὰ ἑαυτὸν ἐκένωσεν μορφὴν δούλου λαβών, ἐν ὁμοιώματι ἀνθρώπων γενόμενος· καὶ σχήματι εὑρεθεὶς ὡς ἄνθρωπος (8) ἐταπείνωσεν ἑαυτὸν γενόμενος ὑπήκοος μέχρι θανάτου, θανάτου δὲ σταυροῦ· (9) διὸ καὶ ὁ θεὸς αὐτὸν ὑπερύψωσεν, καὶ ἐχαρίσατο αὐτῷ τὸ ὄνομα τὸ ὑπὲρ πᾶν ὄνομα, (10) ἵνα ἐν τῷ ὀνόματι Ἰησοῦ πᾶν γόνυ κάμψῃ ἐπουρανίων καὶ ἐπιγείων καὶ καταχθονίων, (11) καὶ πᾶσα γλῶσσα ἐξομολογήσηται ὅτι κύριος Ἰησοῦς Χριστὸς εἰς δόξαν θεοῦ πατρός.

Rom 9.5, likewise, can be read (I think, implausibly) as correlating *ho Christos* (v. 9a) with *ho theos* (v. 9b). I understand these two clauses as two sentences, with the break between *sarka* and *ho* marking the end of Paul's characterization of the messiah as "of the Israelite *genos*," and the concluding sentence as a doxology praising the biblical high god (cf. Rom 11.36, 16.27: God is distinguished from, and in 16.27 superior to, Christ). Further on Christ in this Philippians passage as "being in the form of a god," Camille Focant, "La portée de la formule τὸ εἶναι ἴσα θεῷ en Ph 2.6," *NTS* 62 (2016): 278–288, esp. at 285.

14. On the role of "messiah" and other such "chief agent" figures in Second Temple Judaism (divine attributes, important angels, etc.), especially as these relate to

YHWH's eschatological activities of judgment and salvation, see Hurtado, *One God, One Lord*, 41–92; also, by the same author, "Monotheism, Principal Angels, and the Background of Christology," *Oxford Handbook of the Dead Sea Scrolls*, ed. T. H. Lim and John J. Collins (Oxford: Oxford University Press, 2010), 546–64. One century after Paul, Justin Martyr will comfortably use all three terms—*christos, (heteros) theos, angelos*—to characterize Jesus, *1 Apol.* 63; *Trypho* 52; see Postscript above.

15. In Isa 45.23 LXX, "every knee shall bow" to God. When Paul refers to or uses the verse (Phil 2.10; Rom 14.11), he envisages knees bending to God as a consequence of the appearance of the victorious Christ of the Parousia. But calling Jesus "Lord" does not attest to unique divinity: as Paul says to his Corinthians, there are "many gods and many lords," by which he means other superhuman powers. Jesus's "lordship," I will argue shortly, functions primarily as an eschatological-messianic designation, not as a theistic one.

In his important book *Lord Jesus Christ* (Grand Rapids, MI: Eerdmans, 2003), Larry Hurtado has argued on the basis of early praxis—these Christ assemblies *worship* Jesus in a way formerly reserved, in Jewish circles, for the high god—that a claim for Jesus's uniquely elevated divinity was being made. "There is simply no parallel for this in any other group in this period in the Jewish tradition" (p. 143). This is a true statement, but I think that it rests on an absence of evidence. We have little idea about ancient Jewish liturgical practices outside of the temple. What happened in synagogues other than hearing the Law? Prayer? Probably, given that the Jewish gathering place is sometimes referred to as a *proseuchē* ("prayer house"). What else? What kind of synagogue liturgies marked the manumission ceremony whose commemorative inscription ends by invoking the lower gods of the pagan pantheon? What acts of obeisance did the Jewish adept perform when, touring heaven, he bowed down before the Sun and addressed him as "Lord" (*Kuriē*; *Sefer ha-Razim* 4.61–63, a third-century Jewish magical text)? How, liturgically, did Jewish exorcisms proceed? And finally, this prayer-language notwithstanding, Paul never advocates that believers offer actual sacrifice to Jesus, which was the premier liturgical marker of divinity, for pagans no less than for Jews. On this last point, see James M. McGrath, *The Only True God: Early Christian Monotheism in Its Jewish Context* (Urbana: University of Illinois Press, 2009), 54.

Conjuring Jewish magic within a Christological context leads to another question: how some LXX Greek within the ekklesia's gatherings might have been *heard*. In a communal ritual setting, Jesus-as-Lord does indeed sit on top of the LXX's God-as-Lord, especially in terms of the community's devotional practice, "calling upon the name of the Lord to be saved." Paul refers to such practices at, e.g., 1 Cor 1.2, "calling on the name of our Lord Jesus Christ." In Rom 10.9–13, "Jesus is Lord" (v. 9) is called upon (v. 12); then Paul directly quotes the statement from LXX Joel 3.5 (MT 2.32), "whoever calls upon the name of the Lord shall be saved" (v. 13). But here I would shift our gaze from *kurios* to *epikaloumai*, "call upon," the middle-voice form of *epikaleo*. The verb has another extremely common ritual context: magic. Frequently in magical recipes the adept or supplicant "calls upon" the name of the god in order to bring the god down, to establish effective contact between the deity and his human: so, for example, *PGM* VII.601; XII.67, 216; IV.987 (Horus-Harpocrates); XIII.1018 (Io); XIII.618 (Sarapis); V.187 (Hermes); V.469 (Zeus). I thank my colleague Joseph Sanzo for providing me with these *PGM* references. The charismata that Paul lists in 1 Cor 12—utterances, healings, working miracles, prophecy, distinguishing between spirits, tongue-speaking, and interpretation—index the effects of the "calling down" of Jesus's spirit. The cultic use of *kurios* thus has at least a double context: not only that of the biblical echo chamber, but also that of common protocols of Mediterranean adjuration. Given all the gods, lords, and demons that populate Paul's universe, then (e.g., 1 Cor 8.5, 10.21), I hesitate to infer, as Hurtado does, a clear "binitarian" theology from these performative utterances.

16. Bert Harrill cautions against "over-hearing" the significance of the term *kurios*: "Doesn't Paul calling Jesus Lord challenge and ultimately overturn the supreme lordship of the Roman emperor? My reply points to the ancient context of the term. 'Lord' was an epithet common of all deities in the ancient Mediterranean world, not unique to Roman emperor worship. . . . Moreover, in Rome's fundamentally hierarchical society, *kurios* had regular use in the daily speech of slaves to masters, commoners to aristocrats, soldiers to commanders—as illustrated even in the New Testament (Luke 7:6–8); virtually all ancient people spoke this way to their social betters. . . . [T]he term specified not the emperor alone but was a commonplace epithet of respect for both noble society and deities. . . . Rather than subverting the logic of Roman imperialistic thinking, Paul's letters provide instances of it," Harrill, *Paul the Apostle*, 88. His observation supports the point made by Dahl more than sixty years ago: when applied to Christ, *kurios* signals not a divine status so much as a royal, Davidic one; see below, n. 31.

17. See, for only one example, Chester's comments, "Christ of Paul," 119, for both an emphasis on a single down-and-up cycle, and a contradistinction between *kurios* and *Christos*: I will argue that, for Paul, the two terms function as synonyms.

18. Even though "messiah" does not appear in these lines, it occurs four times in the lines immediately preceding. As Novenson concludes, "The Davidic messiahship of Jesus is not the point of 1 Cor 15.20–28, but it is axiomatic for the argument," *Christ among the Messiahs*, 146.

19. For the *BAGD* definitions of these subordinate divine entities, see p. 220 above, n. 57.

20. Novenson, *Christ among the Messiahs*, 143–46, on the resonances of this eschatological-messianic passage with Dan 7.27.

21. See Wagner, *Heralds*, 225 n. 25, on Deut 32.8–9: God keeps Israel for himself, but parcels out the nations among the heavenly court, a story that echoes in Sirach 17.17 and Jub 15.30–32 (these spirits lead the nations "astray").

22. Novenson, *Christ among the Messiahs*, 146.

23. Lucidly, and with generous bibliographical annotation, Nathan Carl Johnson reviews the interpretive history of these verses, and their antecedents in other late Second Temple Jewish texts, in "Romans 1.3–4: Beyond Antithetical Parallelism,"

JBL 136 (forthcoming). By a different pathway, Johnson comes to the same conclusion that I will urge here, namely, "that the Davidic seed and the son of God are equivalent," MS p. 2. I thank him warmly for sharing his prepublication text with me.

24. Here is the corresponding Greek: "Paul, slave of Jesus Christ, called to be apostle, set apart for the gospel of God . . . concerning his son":

περὶ τοῦ υἱοῦ αὐτοῦ,
   τοῦ γενομένου <u>ἐκ σπέρματος Δαυὶδ</u> κατὰ σάρκα
   τοῦ ὁρισθέντος υἱοῦ θεοῦ ἐν δυνάμει κατὰ πνεῦμα ἁγιωσύνης <u>ἐξ</u>
   <u>ἀναστάσεως νεκρῶν</u>
   Ἰησοῦ Χριστοῦ τοῦ κυρίου ἡμῶν

25. Even by writers, such as Bart Ehrman, who can hardly be regarded as promoting a theological agenda: see *How Jesus Became God* (New York: HarperOne, 2014), 218–25, on Rom 1.3–4. (And cf. 254–66, a "two-stage cycle" interpretation of Philippians.) So, similarly, Chester, "Christ of Paul," 111, who consequently, in my view, overdistinguishes between "messiah" and "lord" in this passage. This mistranslation of *ez anastaseōs nekrōn* as "by *his* resurrection *from* the dead" goes back at least as far as Martin Luther, "von den Toten." See too the examples brought by S. H. Hooke, "The Translation of Romans 1:4," *NTS* 9 (1963): 370–71; also the remarks by Robert Jewett, *Romans: A Commentary* (Minneapolis, MN: Fortress, 2007), 105 ("there is no reason to provide a less than literal translation").

26. The absence of the *ek* from Paul's verses did not suffice to prevent this misrendering. But Rom 1.4 is the *only* place where the RSV superimposes a preposition where none exists. Consider these other examples:

1 Cor 15.42: So [it is] also [with] the resurrection *of* the dead [ἡ ἀνάστασις τῶν νεκρῶν].

Phil 3.8–11: . . . I count all things as refuse in order that I may gain Christ . . . that I may know him and the power of his resurrection . . . so that somehow I might attain resurrection *from* the dead [ἐξ ἀνάστασιν τὴν ἐκ νεκρῶν].

Mk 6.14: Some said, "John the Baptizer has been raised *from* the dead [ἐκ νεκρῶν]."

Acts 17.31–32: Of this [God] has given assurance to all men by raising [Christ] *from* the dead [ἀναστήσας αὐτὸν ἐκ νεκρῶν]. Now when they heard of the resurrection *of* the dead [ἀνάστασιν νεκρῶν], some mocked. . . .

Acts 23.6: Brethren, I am a Pharisee, the son of Pharisees; and it is about the hope and the resurrection *of* the dead [περὶ ἐλπίδος καὶ ἀναστάσεως νεκρῶν] that I am being judged.

27. True for ancient commentators, e.g., Augustine, *Inch. Exp.* 4.6–5.8; true for (some) modern ones, e.g., James Dunn, *Theology of Paul*, 242–44; A. Hultgren, *Paul's Letter to the Romans* (Grand Rapids, MI: Eerdmans, 2011), 49.

28. Dunn, *Theology of Paul*, 242–60, segueing to Rom 9.5 and whether or to what degree Paul considers Jesus to be or identifies him as "God." Hurtado too is "binitarian," but he argues from the perspective of devotional practices, not textual hermeneutics as such. N. T. Wright, cheerfully Nicene, states simply that Paul considers Jesus "God," e.g., *Paul and the Faithfulness of God*, 2: 707, and frequently elsewhere.

29. Cf. Philo, *De vita Mosis* 1.158, who comments that, on account of his moral and spiritual excellence, Moses "was named god [*theos*] and king of the whole nation" (said with reference to Exod 20.21). Similarly, Origen in his commentary on Romans designates both David "the prophet" and the apostle Paul as "gods" (*sine dubio non erant homines sed dii, Comm. Rom.* II.10, 18 [SC 532, p. 438]).

    On imperial divinity in the early empire, Peppard, *Son of God*, 31–49; on the sanctity and *numen* both of the emperor (whether pagan or Christian) and of his image, Jan Elsner, *Imperial Rome and Christian Triumph* (Oxford: Oxford University Press, 1998), 53–87; further, Keith Hopkins, "Divine Emperors, or the Symbolic Unity of the Roman Empire," *Conquerors and Slaves* (Cambridge: Cambridge University Press, 1978), 197–226. Emperor worship continued under Constantine and his successors, A. H. M. Jones, *The Later Roman Empire, 284–602: A Social, Economic, and Administrative Survey*, 2 vols. (Norman: University of Oklahoma Press, 1964), 1: 93 (with comments on Constantine's personal approval of various dedicated cultural competitions and gladiatorial games under the supervision of an imperial priest); G. Bowersock, "Polytheism and Monotheism in Arabia and the Three Palestines," *Dumbarton Oaks Papers* 51 (1997): 1–10; Ramsay MacMullen, *Christianity and Paganism in the Fourth through Eighth Centuries* (New Haven, CT: Yale University Press, 1997), 34–39, on the cult of the Christian Roman emperor; Douglas Boin, "Late Antique *Divi* and Imperial Priests in the Late Fourth and Early Fifth Centuries," in *Pagans and Christians in Late Antique Rome: Conflict, Competition, and Coexistence in the Fourth Century*, ed. M. Salzman, R. L. Testa, and M. Sághy (New York: Cambridge University Press, 2015), 139–61. The point about the (robust) post-Constantinian imperial cult is that even the man who convened and oversaw the Council of Nicea was perfectly happy—*as were his bishops*—to regard himself, and to be regarded, as endowed with *numen*, as in some special way divine. Long story short: divinity is an extremely flexible category and concept in Mediterranean antiquity, and it is applied to humans (even Jewish and Christian ones!) as well as to superhumans.

30. See Novenson, *Christ among the Messiahs*, 98–173, on Christ-phrases and Christ-passages in Paul; further, Wagner, *Heralds*, who adduces many other late Second Temple Jewish texts that use "Isaiah 11 . . . to stoke the fires of messianic and eschatological hopes," 320–40. On the functional synonymy of "son of God" and "messiah" specifically with reference to Galatians, Adela Yarbro Collins, "Jesus as Messiah and Son of God in the Letters of Paul," *King and Messiah*, 101–22, at p. 106; with reference to Phil 2, p. 114; on the Hellenistic run-up to these associations of divine sonship with the messiah, John J. Collins, "Messiah and Son of God in the Hellenistic Period," *King and Messiah*, 48–74.

31. Nils Alstrup Dahl, "The Messiahship of Jesus in Paul," in *Jesus the Christ: The Historical Origins of Christological Doctrine*, ed. Donald H. Juel (Minneapolis, MN: Fortress, 1991), 20.

32. "The appearing of the future Messiah before the Messianic Age, His dying and rising again, nothing of which was foreseen in the traditional eschatology, gave a problematical character to the period between the Resurrection of Jesus and His Return," Schweitzer, *Mysticism of Paul*, 98.

33. Mk 3.15 and 6.7: Jesus gives "authority over unclean spirits" and over "demons" to the Twelve, enabling them to work exorcisms and cures (3.13), though not always (9.18, 28); Matthew's parallel section (Mt 10.1–42) expands the followers' repertoire to "cure every disease and every sickness" (v. 1), raising the dead and cleansing lepers (v. 8), and prophesying (v. 41; cf. 7.22, prophecy, exorcism, and acts of power); so similarly Luke's commissioning of the Twelve (Lk 9.1, exorcisms and cures; cf. 10.9, 17, the seventy work cures and exorcisms); Acts 3.1–7, Peter cures a paralytic; 5.1–11, Peter has lethal charismatic authority over Ananias and Sapphira; 5.12, the apostles work "many signs and wonders"; 8.13, signs and great miracles; 8.14–17, Peter and John call down the holy spirit; 11.39–40, Philip charismatically tesseracts; 9.36–40, Peter raises the dead Tabitha; 10.9–16, Peter's heavenly vision; 11.28, inspired prophecy; 13.10–11, Paul charismatically blinds Elymas; 14.8–10, Paul cures a paralytic; 15.32, prophecy; 16.9, Paul's vision; 16.16–18, Paul exorcises a demon; 18.9, Paul has a heavenly vision; 19.6, Paul calls down the holy spirit and subsequently works "extraordinary miracles" (vv. 11–12); 20.7–12, Paul (more or less) raises the (mostly) dead; 21.9, prophecy; 27.1–44, a combination of surviving a tempest and making accurate prophecies; 28.3–5, Paul survives a viper's bite; 28.8–10, charismatic cures. For the charismata of Paul and of his communities as reported in Paul's own letters, see above, p. 165.

34. This was so because of the demand of no *latreia* to native gods. Again, Acts well catches the social consequences of this demand, 16.21: pagans complain to Roman magistrates about Paul and Silas, "They are Jews, and are advocating customs that are not lawful for us to adopt or observe."

35. "The *requirement* of circumcision for gentile converts to Christianity was not part of the Christian mission from the beginning, and regarding it as essential would invalidate the numerous conversions of gentiles ... and Paul's own mission," Sanders, *Paul: Life, Letters and Thought*, 498, author's emphasis.

36. Cf., for only one example of the classic NT "explanation" of Jewish "anti-Christian persecutions" as having to do with Jewish "zeal for the Law" and fear of gentile contagions, Dunn, *Theology of Paul*, 346–79, and the many citations he gives in support of this position.

37. Whence Paul's irritation and anathematizing of some of his apostolic colleagues as "false brothers" (Gal 2.4), hypocrites (Gal 12–13, said of Peter and Barnabas), "dogs, evil-workers, and mutilators of the flesh" (Phil 3.2), "super-apostles, boasters, false apostles, deceitful workers, ministers of Satan" (2 Cor 5.13–14).

38. Cf. Richard B. Hays, *First Corinthians* (Louisville: Westminster John Knox Press, 1997), 95, concerning the translation of 1 Cor 6.1–11; so too M. Peppard, "Brother

against Brother: *Controversiae* about Inheritance Disputes and 1 Corinthians 6.1–11," *JBL* 133 (2014): 179–92, at p. 180f. On this particular point—Paul's male-specific language and ideas about inheritance—Johnson Hodge, *If Sons, Then Heirs*, 19–42; cf. pp. 72–82 on the transformative effect of spirit in making the *ethnē* "sons."

39. Peppard, *Son of God*, 50–60, who quotes Cicero (202 n. 7) that the laws of adoption concern "the inheritance of the name and of the property and of the sacred rites of the family," *Oration on His House (Dom.)*, 35. Further on the Roman legal and cultural context of adoption: Suzanne Dickson, *The Roman Family* (Baltimore, MD: Johns Hopkins University Press, 1992); Jane F. Gardner, *Family and Familia in Roman Law and Life* (Oxford: Clarendon Press, 1998); Christine Kunst, *Römische Adoption: Zur Strategie einer Familienorganisation* (Hennef: Marthe Clauss, 2005). James M. Scott pulls together a tremendous amount of material, both Greco-Roman and (chiefly) biblical, around issues internal to Paul's letters, in *Adoption as Sons of God* (Tübingen: Mohr Siebeck, 1992).

40. On Philemon as a letter that "did not so much proclaim Messiah Jesus as discuss a private business transaction about a slave," see Harrill, *Paul the Apostle*, 18.

41. On this distinction between "the promise to Abraham" (in the singular) that benefits gentiles and the irrevocable "many promises" to Israel, Stanley Stowers notes, "for Israel, there were many promises, not one. Because Romans is about gentiles, the promises peculiar to Jews bear only a mention [i.e. at 9.4 and at 15.8]. . . . In 15.8, Paul speaks of the fathers (plural), who include Jacob, Joseph, Moses, and many others who are not fathers of the gentiles in the same way as Abraham. Only Abraham received the promise that in his seed the gentiles would be blessed. This promise does not lessen the significance of the other fathers for the Jews (9.5)," *Rereading of Romans*, 133.

42. For this reason, I am persuaded by Richard Hays on the question of how to translate Rom 4.1. The text runs: Τί οὖν ἐροῦμεν εὑρηκέναι Ἀβραὰμ τὸν προπάτορα ἡμῶν κατὰ σάρκα. The RSV translates: "What then should we say about Abraham, our forefather according to the flesh?" But Paul addresses *gentiles* in the assembly at Rome (1.5–6), and the whole point of "adoption" via Abraham is that the gentiles do *not* have a connection *kata sarka*: if they did, they would not be candidates for "adoption" (Rom 8.23; made sons through spirit, 8.14; cf. Gal 4.5–7). Hays proposes instead: "What then shall we say? Have we found Abraham [to be] our forefather according to the flesh?" *The Conversion of the Imagination* (Grand Rapids, MI: Eerdmans, 2005), 61–84. For a (brief) counterargument, Barclay, *Paul and the Gift*, 483 n. 88.

43. The following draws on my argument in "Judaizing the Nations," 244–49; see also Kathy Ehrensperger, " 'Called to Be Saints': The Identity-Shaping Dimension of Paul's Priestly Discourse in Romans," in *Reading Paul in Context: Explorations in Identity Formation; Essays in Honour of William S. Campbell*, ed. Kathy Ehrensperger and J. Brian Tucker (London: T. & T. Clark, 2010), 90–109.

44. Paul thinks with the sacrificial protocols of the temple both metaphorically (he is applying them to humans, and to his work as apostle to gentiles, Rom 15) *and*

"realistically" (gentiles truly have received holy spirit, and are thus "sanctified"). This is one of the reasons why his meaning is difficult to track.

"Pure" (*katharos*) and "holy" (*hagios*) are two distinct concepts, but in the late Second Temple period the Greek *koinos*, "common," begins to function as a synonym for *akatharos* in some Hellenistic Jewish texts. Thus, e.g., 1 Macc 1.62, where people refuse to eat "unclean" food; Mk 7.2, 5; Acts 10.14–15; Rom 14.14. I thank my colleague Daniel Schwartz for bringing the example from 1 Macc to my attention.

45. "The use of purity language for correct behavior and impurity terms for transgression, highly visible in Paul, is what leads so many New Testament scholars to confuse the entire issue," E. P. Sanders, personal correspondence, June 29, 2009. For Paul's lists of gentile vices, see, e.g., Rom 1.18–31; cf. Gal 5.19–21, there as "works of the flesh"; 1 Cor 6.9–11 (personal, not abstract nouns: "idolaters, adulterers, sexual malefactors . . . and such were some of you"); cf. 1 Thes 4.4–6. For a discussion of such vice lists in Hellenistic Jewish literature, Käsemann, *Commentary on Romans*, 49f.; on Paul's lists of vices and virtues, the chart in Dunn, *Theology of Paul*, 662–63.

46. See above, pp. 49–54.

47. These views on "holy seed" and ancient ideas of (realistically conceived) genealogical purity inform the arguments of Hayes, *Gentile Impurities* and *Divine Law*, and Thiessen's reconstruction of Acts and of Paul on the question of conversions to Judaism, *Contesting Conversion* and *Paul and the Gentile Problem*.

48. Klawans, "Notions of Gentile Impurity," 292; cf. p. 298.

49. Jewish Christ-followers are likewise empowered by *pneuma*, Paul being one of Paul's premier examples of this (1 Cor 14.18; 2 Cor 12.13–14; cf. the *hagioi* of the Jerusalem community, Rom 15.25).

I doubt, in light of their pneumatic adoption, that Paul would have imagined eschatological gentiles as still segregated from the inner courts of the temple in Jerusalem once the Kingdom came; cf. Hayes's description of—I think—my views ("delimited inclusion"), *Divine Law*, 147. On the contrary, and as I have said elsewhere, I imagine Paul walking with the gentile-in-Christ into Jerusalem's inner temple area in anticipation of the Kingdom, "Apocalyptic Hope," 564. But was Paul envisaging a terrestrial Kingdom at all? Where does the raised *pneumatikon sōma* go? Why is the *politeuma* of the redeemed "in the heavens" (Phil 3.20)? See Thiessen, *Paul and the Gentile Problem*, 129–60, for the sidereal possibilities.

50. On Paul's analogy of eucharist as sacrifice in this passage, Klawans (*Purity, Sacrifice and the Temple*, 221) notes how Paul draws a contrast "between proper worship on the one hand and idolatry on the other. This contrast—which is drawn elsewhere (1 Cor 8:4–6, 13; 2 Cor 6:16)—is instructive, and it allows us to juxtapose the picture of early Christian worship in a Pauline, Diaspora community with Acts' picture of the apostles' [temple] worship in Jerusalem. In Acts 2, we are presented with a picture of early Christians performing both eucharistic and sacrificial rituals. In 1 Corinthians 10, we are presented with a different

picture: that of Gentile Christians in Corinth who do not have the option of performing sacrificial rites and eucharistic rites. Jewish sacrificial devotion outside of Jerusalem is out of the question. Other local forms of sacrifice are equally out of the question, because they are idolatrous. And what is Paul's message? That early [Gentile] Christians must choose one or the other: it's either idolatry or the worship of God, either sacrifice or eucharist. . . . [But] Paul himself did not articulate a broadly antisacrificial perspective. In his view, the Jewish cult is proper and effective, though it refers primarily to the people of Israel (cf. Rom 9:4). *The sacrificing that he does reject . . . is idolatry.* But to a Gentile in the Diaspora, rejecting all sacrifice but the Jerusalem cult is little different from rejecting all sacrifice whatsoever. The origin of the idea that the eucharist is a replacement for sacrifice is likely to be found in this kind of social reality, among those who—unlike the disciples in Jerusalem—actually had to choose between two distinct options: eucharist or sacrifice" (author's emphasis). See too Ehrensperger on "Cult Practice and the Translatability of Rituals," *Crossroads*, 175–213.

51. Friedrich Wilhelm Horn, "Paulus und die Herodianische Tempel," *NTS* 53 (2007): 184–203, esp. pp. 191 and 196.

52. Commenting on Paul's conceptual breakthrough in Romans—his using priestly language to describe his mission and his using temple imagery to describe gentile Christ-followers—Horn remarks on the temple's notional commodiousness, whereby not only Jews and Jewish Christ-followers *but also* gentile Christ-followers stand "inside": in Paul's view, the temple plays the role of an "identity-marker" over-against pagans, thus paganism, "Paulus und der Tempel," 203; also p. 201 n. 65.

53. In what way does Paul see Christ himself as some sort of sacrifice? On this issue, Paul's language and his conceptualization become hard to track. Paul's reference to Christ as a paschal lamb in 1 Cor 5.7, for example, seems less Christological than hortatory: in this passage, he urges his gentiles to cleanse themselves of the "leaven" of pride in view of the fact that redemption is already under way. The paschal image, in other words, refers to Jewish timekeeping (no leaven in the house by 14 Nisan!), not to a sacrificial death on the part of Christ.

   2 Cor 5.21 and Rom 8.3—Christ as *hattat/harmartia* or as *peri harmartias*—also seem confusing, especially if scholars have rightly understood the temple's own dynamics of purity: sin sacrifices cleanse the sancta, not the sinner. See on this issue J. Milgrom, *Leviticus 1–16* (New York: Doubleday, 1991), 254–58; also J. Klawans, *Impurity and Sin in Ancient Judaism* (Oxford: Oxford University Press, 2000), 3–20, for a succinct review of various scholarly perspectives.

   The *hilastērion* of Rom 3.25, finally, has often been taken to mean a sacrifice of expiation; but again, the image is extremely confusing (and, I think, confused). In Leviticus, such a sacrifice is brought by penitent humans; in Romans, it is God who brings Jesus. The closest analogy to a sacrifice in Paul's time that would bear away a sinner's sin would be the scapegoat of Yom Kippur. But Paul nowhere uses this image and, besides—a nod to the eucharistic traditions—you do not eat scapegoats. Dunn, *Theology of Paul*, 212–23, labors to transform the intrinsic messiness of Paul's sacrificial references into coherence, but he confuses all sacrifices with atonement (p. 217, on the Pesach offering) and imputes "sinlessness" to the animal offering (pp. 217, 221). As Klawans notes, the sacrificial animal is neither sinful nor sinless, neither "innocent [n]or guilty. The animal is food," *Purity, Sacrifice and the Temple* (New York: Oxford University Press, 2006), 44.

Stowers, *Rereading of Romans*, proposes a nonsacrificial understanding of *hilastērion*, arguing instead for an interpretation as "conciliation, appeasement" (pp. 206–13)

54. Wagner notes that "citations from Isaiah account for nearly half of Paul's explicit appeals to scripture in Romans," *Heralds*, 2; see also the important charts on pp. 342–43.

55. On this point—Paul's focus on the ultimate redemption of his own people—see also James M. Scott, "And Then All Israel Will Be Saved (Rom 11.26)," *Restoration: Old Testament, Jewish and Christian Conceptions*, ed. James M. Scott (Leiden: Brill, 2001), 490–527.

56. Commentators, combining Suetonius's report that Claudius expelled Jews from Rome who were constantly making disturbances *impulsore Chresto* ("at the instigation of Chrestus," perhaps meaning "of *Christus*," that is, of Christ? *Claud.* 25.4), the mention in Acts 18.2 of a similar edict ("Claudius had ordered all the Jews to leave Rome"), and an identification of the "weak" in Rom 14 as Jewish Christ-followers, the "strong" as the gentile ones, have confected a social history for the letter to the Romans, thus a motivation for Paul's writing. The church by late midcentury, so goes the argument, had become predominantly gentile during the years when the Jews had gone missing; now that the Jews were back, the community was riven with ethnic division. Paul, on this hypothesis, writes to reconcile both groups to each other, and in so doing redefines "Jewishness" as spiritual, that is, "Christian." Ergo, the letter is addressed to both Jewish and gentile members of the assembly at Rome. For a concise demolition of this reconstruction, see Thorsteinsson, *Paul's Interlocutor*, 92–97.

57. I follow Thorsteinsson's important study, *Paul's Interlocutor*, in this view. For a careful exegetical working through of sequential chapters of Romans with Thorsteinsson providing the plumb line, see also the essays assembled by Rafael Rodriguez and Matthew Thiessen, *The So-Called Jew in Paul's Letter to the Romans* (Minneapolis, MN: Fortress, 2016).

58. See Stowers, *Rereading of Romans*, 21–22, on the implicit reader; pp. 22–41, on the interpretive consequences of confusing empirical readers with the rhetorical implicit reader. See too Wagner's remarks, *Heralds*, 34f.

59. Two ready examples: Augustine, explaining the Jews' "blindness" to (his construction of true) Christianity as their punishment for some "secret sin, known only to God," brings as a proof text Rom 1.24: *Contra Faustum*, 13.11 (written c. 399 C.E.). Barclay argues that Rom 1.18–32 addresses the problem of *universal* sin, thus that these verses indict both Jews and gentiles, *Paul and the Gift*, 463–66 (written c. 2014). Thiessen, by contrast, brings examples of ancient Christian commentators who took Paul's indictment as targeting pagans specifically and,

pointing to various pagan authors aware of Judaism's aniconism, argues that even ancient *gentile* hearers (like those whom Paul addresses!) would have recognized in Paul's opening salvo a critique of specifically pagan practices and ethics, *Paul and the Gentile Problem*, 43–52. Cf. Krister Stendahl's conclusion to *Final Account*: "The issue at hand in Romans is the justification of Paul's Gentile converts, not of sinners in general," p. 76. See now too M. Novenson, "The Self-Styled Jew of Romans 2 and the Actual Jews of Romans 9–11," in Rodriguez and Thiessen, *The So-Called Jew in Paul's Letter to the Romans*, 133–62.

60. Thus Barclay, most recently in *Paul and the Gift*, 467–74. He dismisses without argument Thorsteinsson's interpretation of the questioner in Rom 2 as a Judaizing gentile, p. 469 n. 51. Thus "true Jewishness," maintains Barclay, is about "heart circumcision," and so on. (This view makes Paul's continuation in Rom 3.1–2—"Then what advantage has the Jew? Or what is the value of circumcision? Much in every way"—a little awkward, to my mind.) Against this interpretation, and maintaining that Paul in Rom 2 does *not* redefine Jewishness, besides Stowers and Thorsteinsson, see Thiessen's remarks, "Paul's Argument," 375–76.

61. On a Jewish proselyte as one who "calls himself a Jew" (Rom 2.17), see Thorsteinsson, *Paul's Interlocutor*, 233–34; for the whole argument, pp. 151–242; Thiessen, *Paul and the Gentile Problem*, 43–71.

62. Thorsteinsson, *Paul's Interlocutor*, 151.

63. In my view, Paul thought that this redemption of all Israel—the eschatological ingathering of the 12 tribes—would be effected by the second coming of Christ. In the (brief) time remaining before that event, the *pistis* of Israel's "remnant"— their confidence in or loyalty to this message—enables their *dikaiosynē* (right-acting toward their fellows, whether Jews or gentiles, within the Christ-assemblies). Christ-following Jews no less than Christ-following gentiles, in other words, are "righteoused by *pistis*," Rom 3.9, 29–30; cf. 10.12–13.

Paul knows that those Jews who trust in this good news are currently a minority, "a remnant chosen by grace" (11.5; Paul is a conspicuous member thereof, 11.1–2). This remnant language itself matters. Even if Paul had not stated plainly that "all Israel will be saved" (11.26, on account of God's irrevocable promises, v. 29), his mobilization of this idea of the remnant would have implied as much: Sanders, *Jesus and Judaism*, 95; expanded and illumined in Wagner, *Heralds*, 106–17.

64. See esp. Thiessen, *Gentile Problem*, 43–52.

65. This reading presupposes the continuity of the rhetorical gentile's persona: Paul here argues against this man's proselyte circumcision as having had any morally transformative effect, since the man still acts as his fellow noncircumcised *ethnē* do. Others, however, Paul continues, who have not "become" Jews can and do act Jewishly, thus with "circumcised hearts." The RSV translation, wed to the traditional interpretation of Rom 2 as a condemnation and a spiritualizing redefinition of Judaism, completely masks this reading. On understanding all of Rom 2 as an indictment of the gentile Judaizer, see Thorsteinsson, *Paul's Interlocutor*;

Thiessen, *Paul and the Gentile Problem*, 56–59; "Paul's Argument against Gentile Circumcision," 375–78; and, yet more forcefully, "Paul's So-Called Jew and Lawless Lawkeeping," in *The So-Called Jew in Paul's Letter to the Romans*, 59–83, esp. pp. 76–81. Stealing, adultery, and sacrilege—the three "gentile" sins that Paul emphasizes in Rom 2.21–23—are also named as such in Wis 14.23–27. Rom 2, in short, contains no indictment of the *Jewish* practice of Jewish tradition.

66. Stowers, *Rereading of Romans*. Aaron Glaim has illumined and substantiated Stower's interpretation in "Sin and Sin Sacrifices in the Pauline Epistles," a paper delivered at the 2013 SBL Annual Meeting. I hope for the publication of Glaim's essay, speedily and in our days.

67. Though I would insist on Hays's translation of Rom 4.1; see above, p. 243, n. 42.

68. Hence Paul's focus on self-mastery: see Stowers, *Rereading of Romans*, 42–82.

69. Presumably, this "bondage" has something to do with those powers that Christ, at his Parousia, overcomes, Rom 8 passim. Do "sin," "flesh," and "death" themselves number among these apocalyptic opponents? For a "yes" answer to this question, see Beverly Roberts Gaventa, "Thinking from Christ to Israel: Romans 9–11 in Apocalyptic Context," in *Paul and the Apocalyptic Imagination*, 239–55. Emma Wasserman challenges this interpretation in "Myths of Victory: The Case of Sin and Apocalyptic Battle in Paul's Letters," a paper delivered at the 2013 SBL annual meeting.

70. Of Isaiah in Romans, Wagner notes, "Even where he is not named, the ancient prophet's words are a weighty and palpable presence," *Heralds*, 2.

71. It's important to see what Paul does *not* say here, as well as what he does. He does *not* say that gentiles, through *pistis*, have attained righteousness but that Israel, pursuing righteousness through the Law, did *not* attain righteousness. Attaining righteousness through the Law is a genuine possibility, one that Paul thinks he himself had "blamelessly" realized (Phil 3.6); presumably, the rest of Israel may have done so too. But Israel did not "arrive at Law" (cf. the RSV's "succeed in fulfilling that law"), since the Law's goal is Christ, for righteousness (Rom 10.4). See too Wagner, *Heralds*, 157–65.

72. "Paul does not ultimately collapse Israel into the remnant or call 'the elect' by the name 'Israel.' Rather, as the rest of the chapter [11] will make clear, 'Israel' is an eschatological category for Paul. . . . The existence of an elect remnant in the present is thus for Paul a sign of God's continuing election of Israel, for ultimately, God's redemptive purpose encompasses 'all Israel' (11.26)," Wagner, *Heralds*, 237; further on this idea in post-Exilic Judaism, pp. 108–16.

73. Scott, *Paul and the Nations*, 5–6 n. 2, and his chart on p. 7; also pp. 73, 133, 135 n. 3; cf. Donaldson, *Judaism and Gentiles*, "The inclusion of the Gentiles in the final consummation was an essential part of Israel's expectations and self-understanding," 505, also p. 509. We might also note that Genesis begins at chap. 1, not at chap. 12.

74. Note: there is no "of God" in Paul's text here, despite the usual (and unconscionable) English translation of both the RSV and the NRSV 11.28: "They are enemies *of God* for your sakes."

75. J. Ross Wagner suggests a subtly different translation: "The Christ has become a servant of the circumcision on behalf of the truthfulness of God, in order to confirm the promises made to the patriarchs; and a [servant] with respect to the gentiles on behalf of his mercy [of God] in order to glorify God," "The Christ, Servant of Jew and Gentile: A Fresh Approach to Romans 15.8–9," *JBL* 116 (1997): 473–85, at p. 481f.

76. So Scott's suggestion, *Paul and the Nations*, 179; cf. 13.

77. See too Schweitzer, *Mysticism of Paul*, 196.

78. In light of the absence of evidence, before the midcentury Jesus movement, for Jewish missions to gentiles to turn them into Jews, I assume that if Paul once "preached circumcision" (Gal 5.11), it would have been in the context of *encouraging* pagan god-fearers already associated with his own synagogue community in Damascus to accept proselyte circumcision. This is a guess, not an argument.

79. In *Paul and the Gentiles* and frequently elsewhere, Terry Donaldson has objected to framing Paul's message with these Isaianic traditions of "the eschatological pilgrimage of the nations" for the simple reason that Paul rarely quotes these verses in his letters. See, e.g., pp. 100–106, 187–210, 222; reprised in his recent response to essays in Nanos and Zetterholm, *Paul within Judaism*, 277–301. Donaldson conjectures, rather, that Paul—who, he maintains, had been a missionary to gentiles to turn them into Jews *before* joining the Christ movement, p. 299 n. 39—believed that the period for the gentiles' incoming *would come to an end* with the return of Christ: the Parousia shuts the door on gentile salvation (e.g., "Paul within Judaism," 290, 299). Additionally, he points out, in the traditional biblical sequence, Israel is saved first, the nations second, whereas Paul seems to have the gentiles (in Christ) preceding the turning of Israel (pp. 290–91).

     To these points, I can only respond: (1) that Wagner, *Heralds*, has established, exhaustively, the import and impact of Isaiah on Paul's thinking; (2) that our *only* secure evidence for Jewish missions to gentiles comes in the mid-first century, and from *within* the Jesus movement; ergo, Paul cannot have been such a missionary in the decades before; (3) that Donaldson's extremely circumscribed view of gentile salvation leaves room for the eschatological redemption of, *at most*, a few thousand people. This seems an improbably meager return on the impending events that Paul envisages: the resurrection of the dead, the transformation of the living, the conquest and rehabilitation of pagan gods, and, thus, the transformation of the cosmos (see ibid., p. 290 n. 25, where Donaldson says that he "recognizes[s] the force of Fredriksen's objection" on these points, without altering his conceptualization); and (4) that Paul's reordering of the traditional sequence—Israel first, then the nations, ceded first to a remnant of Israel, then to some of the nations, then to the fullness of the nations and *all* Israel (Rom 11.25–26)—itself attests to the force of the original paradigm (so too Sanders, *PLJP*, 185). But see Scott's view in the following note.

80. On this last point, James Scott has asked, "Did Paul reverse the traditional order of events in Rom 11.25–26, or did he find scriptural warrant for this reversal? A more likely explanation is that the apostle entertained a two-stage process of

Israel's restoration. In the first phase, the gospel began in Jerusalem and came first and foremost to Israelites (cf. Rom 1.16). . . . Therefore, from Paul's perspective, the restoration of Israel had *already* been inaugurated in Jerusalem. . . . The initial stage of Israel's restoration was already in full progress. In the second phase . . . all Israel would be saved after the full number of the nations comes in. . . . [I]t is unnecessary to suppose that Paul has reversed the traditional expectation of the eschatological pilgrimage of the nations to Zion," "And Then All Israel Will Be Saved," 494–96.

81. Paul's apocalyptic eschatology is trained on the near *future*; this present inbreaking of the spirit serves simply to confirm the nearness (in his own lifetime) of the coming cosmic fulfillment. Wright's "inaugurated eschatology," by comparison, relocates Paul's emphasis from the future to the present, *Paul and the Faithfulness of God*, 1,047–89; cf. pp. 1,138 and 1,251, for a de-eschatologized reading of Rom 11—no small feat.

82. Perhaps it had been initially such reformed ex-pagan god-fearers within the Damascus synagogue that first drew Paul's attention to the diaspora Christ movement.

83. This view—that Paul the apostle continued to be Law-observant during his missions to pagans—is repudiated by centuries of traditional interpreters of Paul (though not by Luke/Acts), by the so-called New Perspective scholars, and by the *Sonderweg* scholars. Those associated with interpreting "Paul within Judaism," on the other hand, envisage Paul's keeping Jewish tradition (see the various essays collected in Nanos and Zetterholm, *Paul within Judaism*; in Boccaccini and Segovia, *Paul the Jew*; and in Rodriguez and Thiessen, *The So-Called Jew in Paul's Letter to the Romans*). Schweitzer back in 1931, however, had already made the same assertion: "[Paul] himself—we must not allow his protestations that he had become a Greek to the Greeks to introduce any confusion on this point—continued to live as a Jew," *Mysticism of Paul*, 196. So also, despite their own contributions to Christian theology *contra Iudaeos*, two ancient and premier interpreters of the Pauline corpus, Origen of Alexandria (185–254) and Augustine of Hippo (354–430), who based their arguments particularly on their readings of Galatians and of Romans.

84. For a Jew, recognizing Jesus as the eschatological messiah is not the same thing as "converting." Unlike Christ-following ex-pagans, Jews continue to worship their same god, to esteem his books, and to follow their ancestral practices. What was required was more like a shift of perspective than like the commitment to a radically different world view and set of ritual/cultic behaviors, such as Christ-following gentiles had to sustain. Brent Nongbri puts it clearly:

> Consider the following scenario as a possibility: Paul claims that Jesus is the messiah. He further claims that other *Ioudaioi* should acknowledge that Jesus is indeed the messiah, and thus acknowledge that these are the last days, and that non-*Ioudaioi*, having been made pure by the newly available *pneuma* of the messiah, are now to join together with *Ioudaioi* in worshipping their

ancestral god, who expressed this desire for joint worship in the book of Isaiah. *Ioudaioi* would still carry out their ancestral traditions; they would have to change their behavior only in regard to interacting with these newly purified non-*Ioudaioi*. To characterize those kinds of behavioral changes as "conversion to Christ" would be baffling. (*JJMJS* 2 [2015]: 1–26, at 14 n. 43)

See too the helpful animadversions on the use of the word and the concept "conversion" for this early period by Moisés Mayordomo, "'Conversion' in Antiquity and Early Christianity: Some Critical Remarks," in *Religiöse Grenzüberschreitungen*, ed. C. Lienemann-Perrin and W. Lienemann (Wiesbaden: Harrassowitz, 2012), 211–26; also Daniel Boyarin, "Another Response to Gabriele Boccaccini," *Paul the Jew*, 26–29 ("Unless we adopt, from outside, the notion that conversion is defined by a conversion experience . . . there is no sense in which Paul's adherence to a radical Jewish apocalyptic sect constitutes a conversion at all," pp. 26–27).

85. "It is therefore to save Israel that Paul exercises his calling as the Apostle to the Gentiles!" Schweitzer, *Mysticism of Paul*, 84. "For God the salvation of the Gentiles is bound up with the salvation of Israel, just as Israel's salvation is of importance to all the Gentiles," Munck, *Paul and Salvation*, 259. "Paul could become the apostle to the Gentiles because the crucified and risen Jesus was the Messiah of Israel; his work as the apostle to the Gentiles aimed, in turn, at the salvation of Israel," Dahl, "The Messiahship of Jesus in Paul," 22. "Romans is Paul's account of how his mission to the Gentiles fit into God's total mission to the world, the *tikkun*, the mending of creation (cf. Romans 8.18–25), and hence particularly the redemption of Israel," Stendahl, *Final Account*, ix.

POSTSCRIPT

1. Barclay, *Paul and the Gift*, 561.
2. Scholars have noted that ancient pagan observers do not seem to have confused "Jews" with "Christians" (*Christianoi*), a Latin-based term denoting "followers of Christ"; see John Barclay, "'Jews' and 'Christians' in the Eyes of Roman Authors c. 100 CE," in *Jews and Christians in the First and Second Centuries: How to Write Their History*, ed. Peter J. Tomson and Joshua Schwartz (Leiden: Brill, 2014), 313–26; also, e.g., Pliny's famous *Ep.* 10.96. The mid-first-century synagogues' self-distancing from the disruptive cultic exclusiveness of god-fearers-turned-Christ-followers might account for this surprising, and early, clarity (though these institutions had no problem continuing to engage gentiles whether as pagans or, eventually, as Christians in later centuries: see Fredriksen, "What Parting?"). Philippa Townsend speculates that the term *Christianoi* grew out of Paul's specific designation for his gentiles as *hoi tou Christou* ("those of Christ"), "Who Were the First Christians? Jews, Gentiles, and the Christianoi," in *Heresy and Identity in Late Antiquity*, ed. Eduard Iricinschi and Holger M. Zellentin (Tübingen: Mohr Siebeck, 2008), 212–30. The early synagogue abreaction to the first generation's mission might explain this surprising island of clarity.

3. James's and Peter's and John's no less than Paul's, I assume: the gentiles' engagement as ex-pagan pagans would be much-needed encouragement as these others pursued their mission to Israel (Gal 2.7–10).

4. On which, see esp. Harrill, "Ethnic Fluidity in Ephesians."

5. Campbell, *Framing Paul,* has recently argued that Paul is indeed the author of 2 Thessalonians, Colossians, and Ephesians. He resequences this fuller corpus (pp. 412–14), placing 2 Thessalonians before Ephesians ("Laodiceans") and Colossians, which in turn come before 1 and 2 Corinthians, Galatians, and Romans; Philippians is sandwiched between the last two letters. Campbell's exiguous considerations of "eschatology" urge that the expanded scenarios in, for example, 2 Thessalonians are "compatible" with those of the undisputed letters; and he implies that Paul's eschatology is not particularly "futurist." (I note that his index lacks entries for "apocalyptic," "Parousia," "Kingdom of God," etc.)

I continue to see these letters as more likely deutero-Pauline than not; and the degree to which they differ from the unquestionably authentic letters on the issue of Christ's *imminent* second coming is a key datum informing my assessment. On this question of the chronology of the Pauline corpus (and of its make-up), I favor Tatum's project, *New Chapters,* esp. 126–30. Tatum focuses on relative sequence rather than on chronology per se; for the latter, see Sanders's adaptation of Lüdermann's outline, *Paul: Life, Letters and Thought,* xxxiii (on the sequence of the letters); 158–61 (chronology).

Further on the second-century reception of Paul: for the related issue of early Christian pseudepigraphy, Bart D. Ehrman, *Forgery and Counterforgery: The Use of Literary Deceit in Early Christian Polemics* (New York: Oxford University Press, 2013), esp. 155–237 on Pauline forgeries dealing with the problem of (unrealized) eschatology. White, *Remembering Paul,* provides a fascinating overview and analysis of the complex reception (and creation) of images(s) of Paul ("the work of reputational entrepreneurs," p. 173) in the second century; so too, though differently, Daniel Marguerat, "Paul après Paul: Une histoire de reception," *NTS* 54 (2008): 317–37, who traces Paul's "complex and multiform" literary afterlives in terms of his letters (thus, the deutero-Paulines), his biography (thus, Acts of the Apostles, and the apocryphal Acts of Paul), and his posthumous authority. See also Richard I. Pervo, *The Making of Paul: Constructions of the Apostle in Early Christianity* (Minneapolis: Fortress Press, 2010), who considers anti-Paulinist traditions as well as Paulinist ones, up through Irenaeus.

6. Marguerat, "Paul après Paul," 318–20, sees Luke's depiction of Paul's Torah observance as a "rupture" with the theology of the historical Paul; I see it as consonant. See too Thiessen's closing remarks on the consonance of Luke and Paul on the issue of Jewish Law observance, *Gentile Problem,* 161–69; also Isaac W. Oliver, "The 'Historical Paul' and the Paul of Acts," in *Paul the Jew,* 51–71.

7. Wright, *Paul and Faithfulness,* at 1,660 pages, is literally a monument to this sort of reading: see his index, p. 1,651, on the "curse of Torah." For the de-eschatologized Paul whose message is not apocalyptic, ibid., 173–75 and passim. Barclay's Paul, *qua* Christian theologian of universal sin—a continuation of an Augustinian/

Lutheran reading of the apostle—is also a post-Torah Jew, *Paul and the Gift*, passim. Such reconstructions are not a Protestant monopoly: Paul's post-Damascus self as anti-Torah also characterizes the readings of Alan F. Segal, *Paul the Convert*, and of Daniel Boyarin, *A Radical Jew: Paul and the Politics of Identity* (Berkeley: University of California Press, 1994).

8. See above, p. 196 and n. 21, for Tacitus (early second century), Origen (mid-third century, reporting pagan opinion), and the emperor Julian (mid-fourth century) on Israel's god as the high god; also Belayche's remarks, "Deus deum," 145, on the Jews' god "as an ethnic god, as indeed he also was."

9. Michael F. Bird and Joseph R. Dodson, eds., *Paul and the Second Century* (London: T. & T. Clark, 2011), contains useful essays discussing how Paul was read by Valentinus (Nicholas Perrin), by Justin (Paul Forster), and by Marcion (Todd D. Still). Middle Platonism obviously framed Philo's theology too, whence his introduction of the divine Logos as God's mediator. Two excellent introductions to ancient philosophical theology: John M. Dillon, *The Middle Platonists: A Study of Platonism 80 B.C. to A.D. 220* (Ithaca, NY: Cornell University Press, 1977), and Richard T. Wallis, *Neoplatonism* (London: Duckworth, 1972). E. R. Dodds's graceful classic, *Pagan and Christian*, narrates the afterlives of Plato's cosmogony, the *Timeaus*, in various Roman Christian and pagan theologies and practices. More recently, with much relevant bibliography, Frederick E. Brent, "Plutarch's Middle-Platonic God," in *Gott und die Götter bei Plutarch*, ed. Rainer Hirsh-Luipold (Berlin: Walter de Gruyter, 2005), 27–49; and Jan Opsomer, "Demiurges in Early Imperial Platonism," in *Gott und Götter*, 51–99. I thank Stephen Young for bringing these last two essays to my attention.

10. For a lucid introduction to Valentinian Christian sensibilities—and texts—see Einar Thomassen, *The Spiritual Seed: The Church of the "Valentinians"* (Leiden: Brill, 2008), and the entry on Valentinus by Ismo Dunderberg, "The School of Valentinus," in *A Companion to Second-Century Christian "Heretics,"* ed. Antti Marjanen and Petri Luomanen (Leiden: Brill, 2005), 64–99. I thank David Brakke for guiding my reading.

11. On which see White, *Remembering Paul*; also, incisively and exhaustively, Judith M. Lieu, *Marcion and the Making of a Heretic: God and Scripture in the Second Century* (New York: Cambridge University Press, 2015).

12. Lieu, *Marcion*, 438.

13. Ibid. 323–439.

14. For an overview of these different ideas of redemption, see Fredriksen, *Sin*, 66–92 and notes. With respect to the apocalyptic diminuendo sounded in these later gentile Christian theologies, John Gager notes, "What we call Christianity is not just post-Pauline; it is un-Pauline," *Jewish Lives of Paul*, 13.

BIBLIOGRAPHY

PRIMARY SOURCES

JEWISH AND EARLY CHRISTIAN TEXTS

Where noted, I have cited biblical texts (both Old Testament and New Testament) and Apocrypha according to the Oxford Annotated Revised Standard Version (RSV) or New Revised Standard Version (NRSV); otherwise, the translations are my own. The Greek text of Jewish scriptures is conveniently available in *The Septuagint* (Grand Rapids, MI: Zondervan Publishing House, 1970). For the Greek and Latin NT texts, *Novum Testamentum Graece et Latine*, ed. Eberhard Nestle and Kurt Aland (Stuttgart: Deutsche Bibelgesellschaft, 1984).

Pseudepigrapha are translated in *The Old Testament Pseudepigrapha*, 2 vols., ed. James H. Charlesworth (New York: Doubleday, 1985). For texts from Qumran, *The Dead Sea Scrolls in English*, trans. Geza Vermes, 3rd ed. (Harmondsworth, UK: Penguin, 1987). A universe of texts, translations, and academic essays on this ancient library is available through the website of the Orion Center at the Hebrew University, Jerusalem.

I availed myself of the Loeb Classical Library editions and translations for the works of Philo (LCL, 10 vols. and 2 supplementary vols., Cambridge, MA: Harvard University Press, 1929–1936) and of Josephus (LCL, 10 vols., Cambridge, MA: Harvard University Press, 1927–1965).

LATER CHRISTIAN TEXTS

Athenagoras. *Apologia pro Christianos, Legatio,* and *De Resurrectione.* Edited and translated by W. Schoedel. Oxford Early Christian Texts. Oxford: Clarendon Press, 1972.
Augustine. *City of God.* Translated by H. Bettenson. New York: Penguin, 1972.
——. *Reply to Faustus the Manichaean.* Translated by R. Stothert. Nicene and Post-Nicene Fathers, ser. 1, vol. 4, 155–345. Grand Rapids, MI: Eerdmans, 1974.

——. *Augustine on Romans: Propositions from the Epistle to the Romans and Unfinished Commentary on the Epistles to the Romans*. Translated and edited by Paula Fredriksen. Society of Biblical Literature Texts and Translations Series 23. Chico, CA: Scholars Press, 1982.

——. *The Works of St. Augustine: Answer to the Pelagians*. Vols. 2 and 4. Translation, introduction, and notes by Roland J. Teske. Hyde Park, NY: New City Press, 1998–1999.

——. *The Works of St. Augustine: Letters*. Vol. 1. Translation, introduction, and notes by Roland J. Teske. Hyde Park, NY: New City Press, 2001.

John Chrysostom. *Discourses against Judaizing Christians*. Translated by Paul W. Harkins. Fathers of the Church 69. Washington, DC: Catholic University of America Press, 1999.

Eusebius. *The History of the Church from Christ to Constantine*. Translated by G. A. Williamson. Revised and edited by Andrew Louth. New York: Penguin, 1989.

——. *Preparation for the Gospel*. Translated by Edwin Hamilton Gifford. 2 vols. Eugene, OR: Wipf and Stock, 2002.

Justin. *Dialogue with Trypho*. Translated by Thomas P. Halton. Fathers of the Church 3. Washington, DC: Catholic University of America Press, 2003.

——. *Justin, Philosopher and Martyr: Apologies*. Edited and translated by Denis Minns and Paul Parvis. Oxford Early Christian Texts. Oxford: Oxford University Press, 2009.

Minucius Felix. *Octavius*. Translated by Gerald H. Rendall. Loeb Classical Library, 315–437. Cambridge, MA: Harvard University Press, 1984.

Origen. *Contra Celsum*. Translated by Henry Chadwick. Cambridge: Cambridge University Press, 1953.

——. *Contre Celse*. 5 vols. Edited and translated by Marcel Borret. Sources chrétiennes. Paris: Les Éditions du Cerf, 1965–1976.

——. *Commentary on the Epistle to the Romans*. 2 vols. Translated by Thomas P. Scheck. Washington, DC: Catholic University of America Press, 2001–2002.

——. *Homilies on Genesis and Exodus*. Translated by Robert E. Heine. Fathers of the Church. Washington, DC: Catholic University Press of America, 2002.

——. *Homilies on Leviticus, 1–16*. Translated by Gary Wayne Barkley. Fathers of the Church. Washington, DC: Catholic University of America Press, 2005.

——. *Commentaire sur l'Épître aux Romains*. 4 vols. Edited by Caroline Hammond Bammel. Translated by Luc Brésard. Sources chrétiennes. Paris: Les Éditions du Cerf, 2009–2012.

Ptolemy. *Letter to Flora* apud Epiphanius, *Panarion*. In *Gnosis: A Selection of Gnostic Texts*. Edited by W. Foerster. 1: 155–61. Oxford: Oxford University Press, 1972.

Tertullian. *Adversus Marcionem*. Translated by Ernest Evans. 2 vols. Oxford: Clarendon Press, 1972.

——. *To the Nations*. Translated by S. Thelwall. In *The Ante-Nicene Fathers*. Vol. 3, 109–47. Edited by Alexander Roberts and James Donaldson. Grand Rapids, MI: Eerdmans, 1978.

——. *Apology* and *De spectaculis*. Translated by T. R. Glover. Loeb Classical Library. Cambridge, MA: Harvard University Press, 1984.

——. *On Fasting*. Translated by S. Thelwall. In *The Ante-Nicene Fathers*. Vol. 4, 102–14. Edited by Alexander Roberts and James Donaldson. Grand Rapids, MI: Eerdmans, 1986.

——. *De idololatria/On Idolatry*. Edited and translated by J. H. Waszink and J. C. M. van Winden. Leiden: Brill, 1987.

OTHER ANCIENT TEXTS

Herodotus. *The Histories*. Translated by A. D. Godley. Loeb Classical Library. 4 vols. Cambridge, MA: Harvard University Press, 1981.

Julian. *Imp. Caesaris Flavii Clavdii Ivliani epistvlae, leges, poemata, fragmenta varia*. Edited by Joseph Bidez and Franz Cumont. Paris: Les Belles Lettres, 1922.

Pliny the Younger. *The Letters of the Younger Pliny*. Translated with an introduction by Betty Radice. Harmondsworth, UK: Penguin, 1977.

Plutarch. *Moralia*. Translated by Frank Cole Babbitt et al. Loeb Classical Library. Cambridge, MA: Harvard University Press, 1969.

Sallustius. *Concerning the Gods and the Universe*. Edited and translated by A. D. Nock. Hildesheim: Georg Olms, 1966.

Tacitus. *The Histories*. Translated by Clifford H. Moore. Loeb Classical Library. Cambridge, MA: Harvard University Press, 1969–1980.

COLLECTIONS OF ANCIENT TEXTS

Corpus of Jewish Inscriptions: Jewish Inscriptions from the Third Century BC to the Seventh Century CE. Edited and translated by J.-B. Frey. New York: Ktav, 1975. First published 1936.

Greek and Latin Authors on Jews and Judaism. Edited and translated by Menachem Stern. 3 vols. Jerusalem: Dorot Press, 1974–1994.

Greek Magical Papyri, including the Demotic Spells. Edited and translated by H. D. Betz. Chicago: University of Chicago Press, 1986.

Inscriptiones Judaicae Orientis. Vol. 2. Edited and translated by Walter Ameling. Tübingen: Mohr Siebeck, 2004.

Jews among the Greeks and Romans: A Diasporan Sourcebook. Edited and translated by Margaret Williams. Baltimore, MD: Johns Hopkins University Press, 1998.

The Jews in Roman Imperial Legislation. Edited and translated by Amnon Linder. Detroit: Wayne State University Press, 1997.

SECONDARY SOURCES

Adams, Edward. "First-Century Models for Paul's Churches: Selected Scholarly Developments since Meeks." In *After the First Urban Christians*, edited by Todd D. Still and David G. Horrell, 60–78. London: T. & T. Clark, 2009.

Ahuvia, Mika. "Israel among the Angels: A Study of Angels in Jewish Texts from the Fourth to Eighth Century CE." Ph.D. diss., Princeton University, 2014.

Allison, Dale C., Jr. *Jesus of Nazareth: Millenarian Prophet.* Minneapolis, MN: Fortress Press, 1998.

——. *Constructing Jesus: Memory, Imagination, and History.* Grand Rapids, MI: Baker Academic, 2010.

Ameling, Walter. *Inscriptiones Judaicae Orientis.* Vol. 2: *Kleinasien.* Texts and Studies in Ancient Judaism 99. Edited by Martin Hengel and Peter Schäfer. Tübingen: Mohr Siebeck, 2004.

Arnal, William. "What Branches Grow out of the Stony Rubbish? Christian Origins and the Study of Religion." *SR* 39 (2010): 549–72.

——. "The Collection and Synthesis of 'Tradition' and the Second-Century Invention of Christianity." *Method & Theory in the Study of Religion* 23, nos. 3–4 (2011): 193–215.

Athanassiadi, Polymnia, and Michael Frede, eds. *Pagan Monotheism in Late Antiquity.* Oxford: Clarendon Press, 1999.

Bagnall, Roger S., and Bruce W. Frier. *The Demography of Roman Egypt.* Cambridge: Cambridge University Press, 1994.

Baker, Cynthia M. "'From Every Nation under Heaven': Jewish Ethnicities in the Greco-Roman World." In Nasrallah and Fiorenza, *Prejudice and Christian Beginnings,* 79–99.

Barclay, John M. G. "Mirror-Reading a Polemical Letter: Galatians as a Test Case." *JSNT* 31 (1987): 73–93.

——. *Jews in the Mediterranean Diaspora: From Alexander to Trajan (323 BCE–117 CE).* Edinburgh: T. & T. Clark, 1996.

——. "Paul and Philo on Circumcision: Romans 2.25–9 in Social and Cultural Context." *NTS* 44 (1998): 536–56.

——. *Pauline Churches and Diaspora Jews.* Tübingen: Mohr Siebeck, 2011.

——. "'Jews' and 'Christians' in the Eyes of Roman Authors c. 100 CE." In *Jews and Christians in the First and Second Centuries: How to Write Their History,* edited by Peter J. Tomson and Joshua Schwartz, 313–26. Leiden: Brill, 2014.

——. *Paul and the Gift.* Grand Rapids, MI: Eerdmans, 2015.

Barnes, Timothy D. "Legislation against the Christians." *JRS* 58 (1968): 32–50.

Bauckham, Richard. *Jesus and the God of Israel: God Crucified and Other Studies on the New Testament's Christology of Divine Identity.* Grand Rapids, MI: Eerdmans, 2008.

Belayche, Nicole. "*Deus deum . . . summorum maximus* (Apuleius): Ritual Expressions of Distinction in the Divine World in the Imperial Period." In Mitchell and van Nuffelen, *One God,* 141–66.

Betz, Hans Dieter. *Galatians: A Commentary on Paul's Letter to the Churches in Galatia.* Hermenia Commentary Series. Philadelphia: Fortress Press, 1979.

——. *The Sermon on the Mount: A Commentary of the Sermon on the Mount, including the Sermon on the Plain (Matthew 5:3–7:27 and Luke 6:20–49),* edited by

Adela Yarbro Collins. Hermenia Commentary Series. Minneapolis, MN: Fortress Press, 1995.

Bickerman, Elias J. "The Warning Inscriptions of Herod's Temple." *JQR*, n.s. 37 (1947): 387–405.

———. *The God of the Maccabees: Studies on the Meaning and Origin of the Maccabean Revolt*. Translated by Horst R. Moehring. Studies in Judaism in Late Antiquity 32. Leiden: Brill, 1979.

Bird, Michael F., and Joseph R. Dodson, eds. *Paul and the Second Century*. Library of New Testament Studies 412. London: T. & T. Clark, 2011.

Blackwell, Ben C., John K. Goodrich, and Jason Maston, eds. *Paul and the Apocalyptic Imagination*. Minneapolis, MN: Fortress Press, 2016.

Bloch, René S. *Moses und der Mythos: Die Auseinandersetzung mit der griechischen Mythologie bei jüdisch-hellenistischen Autoren*. Leiden: Brill, 2011.

Blumenkranz, Bernhard. *Die Judenpredigt Augustins: Ein Beitrag zur Geschichte der jüdisch-christlichen Beziehungen in den ersten Jahrhunderten*. Basler Beiträge zur Geschichtswissenschaft 25. Basel: Helbing & Lichtenhahn, 1946.

Boccaccini, Gabriele, and Carlos A. Segovia, eds. *Paul the Jew: Rereading the Apostle as a Figure of Second Temple Judaism*. Minneapolis, MN: Fortress Press, 2016.

Bockmuehl, Markus N. A. *The Epistle to the Philippians*. London: A. & C. Black, 1997.

Bodel, John, and Saul M. Olyan, eds. *Household and Family Religion in Antiquity*. Malden, MA: Blackwell, 2008.

Bohak, Gideon. "Ethnic Continuity in the Jewish Diaspora in Antiquity." In *Jews in the Hellenistic and Roman Cities*, edited by John R. Bartlett, 175–92. London: Routledge, 2002.

———. "The Ibis and the Jewish Question: Ancient 'Anti-Semitism' in Historical Context." In *Jews and Gentiles in the Holy Land in the Days of the Second Temple, the Mishnah and the Talmud: A Collection of Articles*, 27–43. Jerusalem: Yad Ben-Zvi Press, 2003.

Boin, Douglas. "Late Antique *Divi* and Imperial Priests in the Late Fourth and Early Fifth Centuries." In *Pagans and Christians in Late Antique Rome: Conflict, Competition, and Coexistence in the Fourth Century*, edited by Michelle Renee Salzman, Marianne Sághy, and Rita Lizzi Testa, 139–61. New York: Cambridge University Press, 2015.

Borgen, Peder. "Observations on the Theme 'Paul and Philo': Paul's Preaching of Circumcision in Galatia (Gal. 5:11) and Debates on Circumcision in Philo." In *Die paulinische Literatur und Theologie*. Teologiske Studier 7, edited by Sigfred Pedersen, 85–102. Aarhus, Denmark: Aros, 1980.

———. "'Yes,' 'No,' 'How Far?': The Participation of Jews and Christians in Pagan Cults." In *Paul in His Hellenistic Context*, edited by Troels Engberg-Pedersen, 30–59. Edinburgh: T. & T. Clark, 1994.

Bowden, Hugh. *Classical Athens and the Delphic Oracle: Divination and Democracy*. New York: Cambridge University Press, 2005.

Bowersock, G. W. "Polytheism and Monotheism in Arabia and the Three Palestines." *Dumbarton Oaks Papers* 51 (1997): 1–10.

Boyarin, Daniel. *A Radical Jew: Paul and the Politics of Identity.* Berkeley: University of California Press, 1994.

——. "Another Response to Gabriele Boccaccini," in Boccaccini and Segovia, *Paul the Jew*, 26–29.

Brandon, S. G. F. *Jesus and the Zealots: A Study of the Political Factor in Primitive Christianity.* Manchester: Manchester University Press, 1967.

Brent, Frederick E. "Plutarch's Middle-Platonic God." In *Gott und die Götter bei Plutarch*, edited by Rainer Hirsh-Luipold. Religionsgeschichtliche Versuche und Vorarbeiten 54, 27–49. Berlin: Walter de Gruyter, 2005.

Büchler, Adolf. "The Levitical Impurity of the Gentile in Palestine before the Year 70." *JQR* 17 (1926): 1–81.

Buell, Denise Kimber. "Race and Universalism in Early Christianity." *JECS* 10 (2002): 429–68.

——. *Why This New Race? Ethnic Reasoning in Early Christianity.* New York: Columbia University Press, 2005.

——. "God's Own People: Spectres of Race, Ethnicity and Gender in Early Christian Studies." In Nasrallah and Fiorenza, *Prejudice and Christian Beginnings*, 159–90.

Buxton, Richard, ed. *Oxford Readings in Greek Religion.* New York: Oxford University Press, 2000.

Campbell, Douglas A. *The Deliverance of God: An Apocalyptic Rereading of Justification in Paul.* Grand Rapids, MI: Eerdmans, 2009.

——. *Framing Paul: An Epistolary Biography.* Grand Rapids, MI: Eerdmans, 2014.

Campbell, William S. "Gentile Identity and Transformation in Christ According to Paul." In *The Making of Christianity: Conflict, Contacts, and Constructions: Festschrift for Bengt Holmberg*, edited by M. Zetterholm and S. Byrskog, 22–55. Winona Lake, IN: Eisenbrauns, 2012.

——. "'As Having and Not Having': Paul, Circumcision, and Indifferent Things in 1 Corinthians 7.17–32a." In Campbell, *Unity and Diversity in Christ*, 106–26.

——. "No Distinction or No Discrimination? The Translation of Διαστολὴ in Romans 3:22 and 10:12." In *Erlesenes Jerusalem: Festschrift für Ekkehard W. Stegemann*, edited by Lukas Kundert and Christina Tuor-Kurth, 146–71. Basel: Friedrich Reinhart Verlag, 2013.

——. *Unity and Diversity in Christ: Interpreting Paul in Context. Collected Essays.* Eugene, OR: Wipf and Stock Publishers, 2013.

——. "Paul, Antisemitism, and Early Christian Identity Formation." In Boccaccini and Segovia, *Paul the Jew*, 301–40.

——. "Reading Paul in Relation to Judaism: Comparison or Contrast?" In *Earliest Christianity within the Boundaries of Judaism: Essays in Honor of Bruce Chilton*, edited by Alan Avery-Peck, Craig Evans, and Jacob Neusner, 1–21. Leiden: Brill, 2016.

Carleton Paget, James. "Jewish Proselytism at the Time of Christian Origins: Chimera or Reality?" *JSNT* 18 (1996): 65–103.

Chadwick, Henry. "Oracles of the End in the Conflict of Paganism and Christianity in the Fourth Century." In *Mémorial André-Jean Festugière: Antiquité païenne et chrétienne*, edited by E. Lucchesi and H. D. Saffrey, 125–29. Geneva: P. Cramer, 1984.

Chaniotis, Angelos. "The Jews of Aphrodisias: New Evidence and Old Problems." *SCI* 21 (2002): 209–42.

——. "Megatheism: The Search for the Almighty God and the Competition of Cults." In Mitchell and van Nuffelen, *One God*, 112–40.

——. "Greek Ritual Purity: From Automatisms to Moral Distinctions." In Rösch and Simon, *How Purity Is Made*, 123–39.

Charlesworth, James H. "Paul, the Jewish Apocalypses, and Apocalyptic Eschatology." In Boccaccini and Segovia, *Paul the Jew*, 83–105.

Chester, Andrew. "The Christ of Paul." In *Redemption and Resistance: The Messianic Hopes of Jews and Christians in Antiquity*, edited by Markus Bockmuehl and James Carleton Paget, 109–21. London: T. & T. Clark, 2009.

Clark, Elizabeth A. *The Origenist Controversy*. Princeton, NJ: Princeton University Press, 1992.

Cohen, Shaye J. D. "Respect for Judaism by Gentiles in the Writings of Josephus." *HTR* 80, no. 4 (1987): 409–30.

——. *The Beginnings of Jewishness: Boundaries, Varieties, Uncertainties*. Hellenistic Culture and Society 31. Berkeley: University of California Press, 1999.

Collins, Adela Yarbro. "Jesus as Messiah and Son of God in the Letters of Paul." In Collins and Collins, *King and Messiah as Son of God*, 101–22.

Collins, Adela Yarbro, and John J. Collins. *King and Messiah as Son of God: Divine, Human, and Angelic Messianic Figures in Biblical and Related Literature*. Grand Rapids, MI: Eerdmans, 2008.

Collins, John J. *The Scepter and the Star: Messianism in Light of the Dead Sea Scrolls*. Anchor Bible Reference Library. New York: Doubleday, 1995.

——. *The Apocalyptic Imagination: An Introduction to Jewish Apocalyptic Literature*. 2nd ed. Grand Rapids, MI: Eerdmans, 1998.

——. "Powers in Heaven: God, Gods and Angels in the Dead Sea Scrolls." In *Religion in the Dead Sea Scrolls*, edited by John J. Collins and Robert A. Kugler, 9–28. Grand Rapids, MI: Eerdmans, 2000.

——. "The 'Apocryphal' Old Testament." In *The New Cambridge History of the Bible*. Vol. 1: *From the Beginnings to 600*, edited by James Carleton Paget and Joachim Schaper, 165–89. Cambridge: Cambridge University Press, 2013.

Crook, Zeba A. *Reconceptualising Conversion: Patronage, Loyalty, and Conversion in the Religions of the Ancient Mediterranean*. Berlin: Walter de Gruyter, 2004.

Dahl, Nils Alstrup. "The Story of Abraham in Luke-Acts." In *Studies in Luke-Acts: Essays Presented in Honor of Paul Schubert*, edited by Leander E. Keck and J. Louis Martyn, 139–58. Nashville, TN: Abingdon Press, 1966.

——. "The Messiahship of Jesus in Paul." In *The Crucified Messiah, and Other Essays*. Augsburg Publishing House, 1974.

——. *Jesus the Christ: The Historical Origins of Christological Doctrine*. Edited by Donald H. Juel. Minneapolis, MN: Fortress Press, 1991.

Das, Andrew A. *Paul and the Jews*. Peabody, MA: Hendrickson Publishers, 2003.

——. *Solving the Romans Debate*. Minneapolis: Fortress Press, 2007.

——. *Paul and the Stories of Israel: Grand Thematic Narratives in Galatians*. Minneapolis, MN: Fortress Press, 2016.

Davies, J. P. *Paul among the Apocalypses? An Evaluation of the "Apocalyptic Paul" in the Context of Jewish and Christian Apocalyptic Literature*. Library of New Testament Studies 562. London: Bloomsbury T. & T. Clark, 2016.

Dickson, John P. *Mission-Commitment in Ancient Judaism and in the Pauline Communities: The Shape, Extent and Background of Early Christian Mission*. Tübingen: Mohr Siebeck, 2003.

Digeser, Elizabeth DePalma. *A Threat to Public Piety: Christians, Platonists, and the Great Persecution*. Ithaca, NY: Cornell University Press, 2012.

Dillon, John M. *The Middle Platonists: A Study of Platonism 80 B.C. to A.D. 220*. Ithaca, NY: Cornell University Press, 1977.

Dixon, Suzanne. *The Roman Family*. Baltimore, MD: Johns Hopkins University Press, 1992.

Dodd, C. H. *The Bible and the Greeks*. London: Hodder & Stoughton, 1935.

Dodds, E. R. *Pagan and Christian in an Age of Anxiety: Some Aspects of Religious Experience from Marcus Aurelius to Constantine*. Cambridge: Cambridge University Press, 1965.

Donaldson, Terence L. "The 'Curse of the Law' and the Inclusion of the Gentiles: Galatians 3:13–14." *NTS* 32 (1986): 94–112.

——. "Zealot and Convert: The Origin of Paul's Christ–Torah Antithesis." *Catholic Biblical Quarterly* 51 (1989): 655–82.

——. *Paul and the Gentiles: Remapping the Apostle's Convictional World*. Minneapolis, MN: Fortress Press, 1997.

——. *Judaism and the Gentiles: Jewish Patterns of Universalism (to 135 CE)*. Waco, TX: Baylor University Press, 2007.

——. "Paul within Judaism: A Critical Evaluation from a 'New Perspective' Perspective." In Nanos and Zetterholm, *Paul within Judaism*, 277–302.

Douglas, Mary. *In the Wilderness: The Doctrine of Defilement in the Book of Numbers*. Journal for the Study of the Old Testament Supplemental Series 158. Sheffield, UK: JSOT Press, 1993.

——. *Purity and Danger: An Analysis of the Concept of Pollution and Taboo*. London: Routledge, 2002.

Dunderberg, Ismo. "The School of Valentinus." In *A Companion to Second-Century Christian "Heretics,"* edited by Antti Marjanen and Petri Luomanen, 64–99. Leiden: Brill, 2005.

Dunn, James D. G. *The Theology of the Apostle Paul*. Grand Rapids, MI: Eerdmans, 1998.

Dunn, James D. G., ed. *Paul and the Mosaic Law: The Third Durham-Tübingen Research Symposium on Earliest Christianity and Judaism (Durham, September, 1994)*. WUNT 1, 89. Tübingen: Mohr Siebeck, 1996.

Eastman, Susan Grove. "Israel and the Mercy of God: A Re-reading of Galatians 6.16 and Romans 9–11." *NTS* 56 (2010): 367–95.

Efroymson, David P. "The Patristic Connection." In *Anti-Semitism and the Foundations of Christianity*, edited by Alan T. Davis, 98–117. New York: Paulist Press, 1979.

Ehrensperger, Kathy. "'Called to Be Saints': The Identity-Shaping Dimension of Paul's Priestly Discourse in Romans." In *Reading Paul in Context: Explorations in Identity Formation. Essays in Honour of William S. Campbell*, edited by Kathy Ehrensperger and J. Brian Tucker, 90–109. London: T. & T. Clark, 2010.

——. *Paul at the Crossroads of Cultures: Theologizing in the Space Between*. Library of New Testament Studies 456. London: Bloomsbury T. & T. Clark, 2013.

Ehrman, Bart D. *Jesus: Apocalyptic Prophet of the New Millennium*. Oxford: Oxford University Press, 1999.

——. *Forgery and Counterforgery: The Use of Literary Deceit in Early Christian Polemics*. New York: Oxford University Press, 2013.

——. *How Jesus Became God: The Exaltation of a Jewish Preacher from Galilee*. New York: HarperOne, 2014.

Eisenbaum, Pamela Michelle. *Paul Was Not a Christian: The Real Message of a Misunderstood Apostle*. New York: HarperOne, 2009.

Eliav-Feldon, Miriam, Benjamin Isaac, and Joseph Ziegler, eds. *The Origins of Racism in the West*. Cambridge: Cambridge University Press, 2010.

Elsner, Jas. *Imperial Rome and Christian Triumph: The Art of the Roman Empire*. Oxford: Oxford University Press, 1998.

Engberg-Pedersen, Troels. *Cosmology and Self in the Apostle Paul*. Oxford: Oxford University Press, 2010.

Esler, Philip F. *Conflict and Identity in Romans: The Social Setting of Paul's Letter*. Minneapolis, MN: Fortress Press, 2003.

Feldman, Louis H. *Jew and Gentile in the Ancient World: Attitudes and Interactions from Alexander to Justinian*. Princeton, NJ: Princeton University Press, 1993.

Fitzgerald, John T. "Virtue/Vice Lists." In *The Anchor Bible Dictionary*, edited by David Noel Freedman, 6: 857–59. New York: Doubleday, 1992.

Flusser, David. "The Ten Commandments and the New Testament." In *The Ten Commandments in History and Tradition*, edited by Ben-Zion Segal and translated by Gershon Levi. Jerusalem: Magnus Press, 1990.

Focant, Camille. "La portée de la formule τὸ εἶναι ἴσα θεῷ en Ph 2.6." *NTS* 62 (2016): 278–288.

Fredriksen, Paula. "Paul and Augustine: Conversion Narratives, Orthodox Traditions, and the Retrospective Self." *JTS* 37 (1986): 3–34.

——. "Apocalypse and Redemption in Early Christianity: From John of Patmos to Augustine of Hippo." *Vigiliae Christianae* 45, no. 2 (1991): 151–83.

——. "Judaism, the Circumcision of Gentiles, and Apocalyptic Hope: Another Look at Galatians 1 and 2." *JTS* 42 (1991): 532–64.

——. "What You See Is What You Get: Context and Content in Current Research on the Historical Jesus." *Theology Today* 52 (1995): 195–204.

——. *Jesus of Nazareth, King of the Jews: A Jewish Life and the Emergence of Christianity.* New York: Alfred A. Knopf, 1999; Vintage, 2000.

——. *From Jesus to Christ: The Origins of the New Testament Images of Jesus.* 2nd ed. New Haven, CT: Yale University Press, 2000. First published 1988.

——. "What 'Parting of the Ways'? Jews, Gentiles, and the Ancient Mediterranean City." In *The Ways That Never Parted: Jews and Christians in Late Antiquity and the Early Middle Ages,* edited by Adam H. Becker and Annette Yoshiko Reed. Texte und Studien zum Antiken Judentum 95, 35–63. Tübingen: Mohr Siebeck, 2003.

——. "Mandatory Retirement: Ideas in the Study of Christian Origins Whose Time Has Come to Go." *SR* 35 (2006): 231–46.

——. "Gospel Chronologies, the Scene in the Temple, and the Crucifixion of Jesus." In *Redefining First-Century Jewish and Christian Identities: Essays in Honor of Ed Parish Sanders,* edited by Fabian E. Udoh, Susannah Heschel, Mark Chancey, and Gregory Tatum. Christianity and Judaism in Antiquity 16, 246–82. Notre Dame, IN: University of Notre Dame Press, 2008.

——. *Augustine and the Jews: A Christian Defense of Jews and Judaism.* New Haven, CT: Yale University Press, 2010.

——. "Judaizing the Nations: The Ritual Demands of Paul's Gospel." *NTS* 56 (2010): 232–52.

——. *Sin: The Early History of an Idea.* Princeton, NJ: Princeton University Press, 2012.

——. "How Later Contexts Affect Pauline Content, or: Retrospect Is the Mother of Anachronism." In *Jews and Christians in the First and Second Centuries: How to Write Their History,* edited by Peter J. Tomson and Joshua Schwartz, 17–51. Leiden: Brill, 2014.

——. "Jewish Romans, Christian Romans, and the Post-Roman West: The Social Correlates of the *contra Iudaeos* Tradition." In *Conflict and Religious Conversation in Latin Christendom: Studies in Honour of Ora Limor,* edited by Israel Jacob Yuval and Ram Ben-Shalom. Cultural Encounters in Late Antiquity and the Middle Ages 17, 17–38. Turnhout, Belgium: Brepols 2014.

——. "Paul's Letter to the Romans, the Ten Commandments, and Pagan 'Justification by Faith,'" *JBL* 133 (2014): 801-8.

——. "'Are You a Virgin?' Biblical Exegesis and the Invention of Tradition." In *Jesus and Brian: Exploring the Historical Jesus and His Times via Monty Python's "Life of Brian,"* edited by Joan E. Taylor, 151–65. London: Bloomsbury, 2015.

——. "If It Looks Like a Duck, and It Quacks Like a Duck . . .: On *Not* Giving Up the Godfearers." In *A Most Reliable Witness: Essays in Honor of Ross Shepard Kraemer,* edited by Susan Ashbrook Harvey, Nathaniel DesRosiers, Shira L. Lander, Jacqueline Z. Pastis, and Daniel Ullucci, 25–34. Providence, RI: Brown Judaic Studies, 2015.

——. "The Question of Worship: Gods, Pagans, and the Redemption of Israel." In Nanos and Zetterholm, *Paul within Judaism,* 175–202.

——. "Why Should a 'Law-Free' Mission Mean a 'Law-Free' Apostle?" *JBL* 134 (2015): 637-650.

———. "Lawless or Lawful? Origen and Augustine on Paul and the Law." In *Law and Lawlessness in Early Judaism and Christianity: Essays from the Oxford Manfred Lautenschläger Colloquium 2015*, edited by D. Lincicum, R. Sheridan, and C. Stang. Tübingen: Mohr Siebeck, 2018.

———. "How Jewish Is God? Divine Ethnicity in Paul's Theology" (forthcoming, *JBL*).

———. "Paul the 'Convert'?" In *The Oxford Handbook of Pauline Studies*, edited by R. Barry Matlock. New York: Oxford University Press (forthcoming).

Fredriksen, Paula, and Oded Irshai. "Christian Anti-Judaism: Polemics and Policies." In *The Cambridge History of Judaism*. Vol. 4: *The Late Roman-Rabbinic Period*, edited by Steven T. Katz, 977–1,034. Cambridge: Cambridge University Press, 2006.

———. "'Include Me Out': Tertullian, the Rabbis, and the Graeco-Roman City." In *Identité à travers l'éthique: Nouvelles perspectives sur la formation des identités collectives dans le monde gréco-romain*, edited by K. Berthelot, R. Naiweld, and D. Stoekl ben Ezra. Bibliothèque de l'École des Hautes Études, Sciences Religieuses 168, 117–32. Turnhout, Belgium: Brepols, 2015.

Gager, John G. "Some Notes on Paul's Conversion." *NTS* 27 (1981): 697–704.

———. *The Origins of Anti-Semitism: Attitudes toward Judaism in Pagan and Christian Antiquity.* New York: Oxford University Press, 1983.

———. *Reinventing Paul.* Oxford: Oxford University Press, 2000.

———. "Who Did What to Whom? Physical Violence between Jews and Christians in Late Antiquity." In *A Most Reliable Witness: Essays in Honor of Ross Shepard Kraemer*, edited by Susan Ashbrook Harvey, Nathaniel P. DesRosiers, Shira L. Lander, Jacqueline Z. Pastis, and Daniel Ullucci, 35–48. Providence, RI: Brown Judaic Studies, 2015.

———. *Who Made Early Christianity? The Jewish Lives of the Apostle Paul.* New York: Columbia University Press, 2015.

Gardner, Jane F. *Family and Familia in Roman Law and Life.* Oxford: Clarendon Press, 1998.

Garroway, Joshua D. *Paul's Gentile-Jews: Neither Jew nor Gentile, but Both.* New York: Palgrave Macmillan, 2012.

Gaston, Lloyd. *Paul and the Torah.* Vancouver: University of British Columbia Press, 1987.

Gaventa, Beverly Roberts. "Rhetoric of Violence and the God of Peace in Paul's Letter to the Romans." In *Paul, John, and Apocalyptic Eschatology: Studies in Honor of Martinus de Boer*, edited by Jan Krans et al., 61–75. Leiden: Brill, 2013.

———. "Thinking from Christ to Israel: Romans 9–11 in Apocalyptic Context." In *Paul and the Apocalyptic Imagination*, edited by Ben C. Blackwell, John K. Goodrich, and Jason Maston, 239–55. Minneapolis, MN: Fortress Press, 2016.

Glaim, Aaron. "Sin and Sin Sacrifices in the Pauline Epistles." Paper presented at the Annual Meeting of the Society of Biblical Literature, Baltimore, MD, November 2013.

Goodenough, Erwin R. *Jewish Symbols in the Greco-Roman Period.* 13 vols. Bollingen Series 37. New York: Pantheon Books, 1953–1968.

Goodman, Martin. *Mission and Conversion: Proselytizing in the Religious History of the Roman Empire*. Oxford: Clarendon Press, 1994.

——. "The Persecution of Paul by Diaspora Jews." In *The Beginnings of Christianity: A Collection of Articles*, edited by Jack Pastor and Menachem Mor, 179–87. Jerusalem: Yad Ben-Zvi Press, 2005.

Goodrich, John K. "After Destroying Every Rule, Authority, and Power: Paul, Apocalyptic, and Politics in 1 Corinthians." In *Paul and the Apocalyptic Imagination*, edited by Ben C. Blackwell, John K. Goodrich, and Jason Maston, 275–96. Minneapolis, MN: Fortress Press, 2016.

Gradel, Ittai. *Emperor Worship and Roman Religion*. Oxford: Clarendon Press, 2002.

Graf, Fritz. "Roman Festivals in Syria Palaestina." In *The Talmud Yerushalmi and Graeco-Roman Culture*, edited by Peter Schäfer. Texts and Studies in Ancient Judaism 93, 435–51. Tübingen: Mohr Siebeck, 2002.

Gray, Rebecca. *Prophetic Figures in Late Second Temple Jewish Palestine*. Oxford: Oxford University Press, 1993.

Gruen, Erich S. *Heritage and Hellenism: The Reinvention of Jewish Tradition*. Berkeley: University of California Press, 1998.

——. "Jewish Perspectives on Greek Ethnicity." In *Ancient Perceptions of Greek Ethnicity*, edited by Irad Malkin, 347–73. Washington, DC: Center for Hellenic Studies, 2001.

——. *Diaspora: Jews amidst Greeks and Romans*. Cambridge, MA: Harvard University Press, 2002.

Gundry, Judith M. "Becoming 'One Flesh' and the Politics of Procreation: 1 Corinthians 7.29b and the Corinthian *Schismata*." Paper presented at the 71st general meeting of the Studiorum Novi Testamenti Societas, Montreal, Canada, August 2016.

Hanson, Ann E. "The Roman Family." In Potter and Mattingly, *Life, Death and Entertainment*, 19–66.

Harland, Philip A. *Associations, Synagogues and Congregations: Claiming a Place in Ancient Mediterranean Society*. Minneapolis, MN: Fortress Press, 2003.

——. "Acculturation and Identity in the Diaspora: A Jewish Family and 'Pagan' Guilds at Hierapolis." In *The Religious History of the Roman Empire: Pagans, Jews, and Christians*, edited by J. A. North and S. R. F. Price, 385–418. Oxford: Oxford University Press, 2011.

Harnack, Adolf. "Die *Altercatio Simonis Iudaei et Theophili Christiani* nebst Untersuchungen über die antijüdische Polemik in der alten Kirche." In *Texte und Untersuchungen zur Geschichte der altchristlichen Literatur*, edited by Oscar von Gebhardt and Adolf Harnack, vol. 1.3.1. Leipzig, 1883.

Harrill, J. Albert. *Paul the Apostle: His Life and Legacy in Their Roman Context*. Cambridge: Cambridge University Press, 2012.

——. "Ethnic Fluidity in Ephesians." NTS 60 (2014): 379–402.

Harvey, Anthony Ernest. "Forty Strokes Save One: Social Aspects of Judaizing and Apostasy." In *Alternative Approaches to New Testament Study*, edited by Anthony Ernest Harvey, 79–86. London: SPCK, 1985.

Hayes, Christine E. *Gentile Impurities and Jewish Identities: Intermarriage and Conversion from the Bible to the Talmud.* Oxford: Oxford University Press, 2002.

——. *What's Divine about Divine Law?* Princeton, NJ: Princeton University Press, 2015.

Hayman, Peter. "Monotheism—a Misused Word in Jewish Studies?" *JJS* 42 (1991): 1–15.

Hays, Richard B. *Echoes of Scripture in the Letters of Paul.* New Haven, CT: Yale University Press, 1989.

——. *First Corinthians: Interpretation: A Bible Commentary for Teaching and Preaching.* Louisville, KY: Westminster John Knox Press, 1997.

——. *The Conversion of the Imagination: Paul as Interpreter of Israel's Scripture.* Grand Rapids, MI: Eerdmans, 2005.

Heiser, Michael S. "Monotheism, Polytheism, Monolatry, or Henotheism? Toward an Assessment of Divine Plurality in the Hebrew Bible." *Bulletin for Biblical Research* 18, no. 1 (2008): 1–30.

Hengel, Martin. *Crucifixion in the Ancient World and the Folly of the Message of the Cross.* Philadelphia: Fortress Press, 1977.

——. *Acts and the History of Earliest Christianity.* London: SCM, 1979.

——. *Between Jesus and Paul: Studies in the Earliest History of Christianity.* London: SCM, 1983.

Hirshman, Marc. "Rabbinic Universalism in the Second and Third Centuries." *HTR* 93 (2000): 101–15.

Hock, Ronald F. *The Social Context of Paul's Ministry: Tentmaking and Apostleship.* Minneapolis, MN: Fortress Press, 1980.

Holmberg, Bengt. *Paul and Power: The Structure of Authority in the Primitive Church as Reflected in the Pauline Epistles.* Lund: LiberLäromedel/Gleerup, 1978.

Hooke, S. H. "The Translation of Romans 1:4." *NTS* 9 (1963): 370–71.

Hopkins, Keith. *Conquerors and Slaves.* Sociological Studies in Roman History 1. Cambridge: Cambridge University Press, 1978.

Horbury, William. "Biblical Interpretation in Greek Jewish Writings." In *The New Cambridge History of the Bible.* Vol. 1: *From the Beginnings to 600,* edited by James Carleton Paget and Joachim Schaper, 289–320. Cambridge: Cambridge University Press, 2013.

Horn, Friedrich Wilhelm. "Paulus und der Herodianische Tempel." *NTS* 53 (2007): 184–203.

Hultgren, Arland J. *Paul's Letter to the Romans: A Commentary.* Grand Rapids, MI: Eerdmans, 2011.

Hurtado, Larry W. *One God, One Lord: Early Christian Devotion and Ancient Jewish Monotheism.* 2nd ed. London: T. & T. Clark, 1998.

——. *Lord Jesus Christ: Devotion to Jesus in Earliest Christianity.* Grand Rapids, MI: Eerdmans, 2003.

——. "Monotheism, Principal Angels, and the Background of Christology." In *The Oxford Handbook of the Dead Sea Scrolls,* edited by Timothy H. Lim and John J. Collins, 546–64. Oxford: Oxford University Press, 2010.

Isaac, Benjamin H. *The Invention of Racism in Classical Antiquity*. Princeton, NJ: Princeton University Press, 2004.

———. "Racism: A Rationalization of Prejudice in Greece and Rome." In *The Origins of Racism in the West*, edited by Miriam Eliav-Feldon, Benjamin Isaac, and Joseph Ziegler, 32–56. Cambridge: Cambridge University Press, 2009.

Jeremias, Joachim. *Jesus' Promise to the Nations*. Studies in Biblical Theology 24. London: SCM, 1967.

Jewett, Robert. *Romans: A Commentary*. Minneapolis, MN: Fortress Press, 2007.

Johnson, Nathan. "Romans 1:3–4: Beyond Antithetical Parallelism." *Journal of Biblical Literature* 136 (forthcoming).

Johnson Hodge, Caroline E. *If Sons, Then Heirs: A Study of Kinship and Ethnicity in the Letters of Paul*. Oxford: Oxford University Press, 2007.

———. "'Married to an Unbeliever': Households, Hierarchies and Holiness in 1 Corinthians 7:12–16." *HTR* 103 (2010): 1–25.

———. "The Question of Identity: Gentiles as Gentiles—but Also Not—in Pauline Communities." In Nanos and Zetterholm, *Paul within Judaism*, 153–74.

Jones, A. H. M. *The Greek City from Alexander to Justinian*. Oxford: Clarendon Press, 1940.

———. *The Later Roman Empire, 284–602: A Social, Economic and Administrative Survey*. 3 vols. Norman: University of Oklahoma Press, 1964.

Jones, Christopher P. *Kinship Diplomacy in the Ancient World*. Cambridge, MA: Harvard University Press, 1999.

———. "The Fuzziness of 'Paganism.'" *Common Knowledge* 18 (2012): 249–54.

Juel, Donald H. *Messianic Exegesis: Christological Interpretation of the Old Testament in Early Christianity*. Philadelphia: Fortress Press, 1988.

Kahlos, Maijastina. *Debate and Dialogue: Christian and Pagan Cultures c. 360–430*. Ashgate New Critical Thinking in Religion, Theology and Biblical Studies. Aldershot, UK: Ashgate, 2007.

Käsemann, Ernst. *Commentary on Romans*. Translated and edited by Geoffrey W. Bromiley. Grand Rapids, MI: Eerdmans, 1980.

Kerkeslager, Allen. "'Maintaining Jewish Identity in the Greek Gymnasium: A Jewish Load' in *CPJ* 3.519 (= P. Schub. 37 = P. Berol. 13406)." *JSJ* 28 (1997): 12–33.

Klawans, Jonathan. "Notions of Gentile Impurity in Ancient Judaism." *AJS Review* 20 (1995): 285–312.

———. *Impurity and Sin in Ancient Judaism*. Oxford: Oxford University Press, 2000.

———. "Interpreting the Last Supper: Sacrifice, Spiritualization, and Anti-Sacrifice." *NTS* 48 (2002): 1–17.

———. *Purity, Sacrifice and the Temple: Symbolism and Supersessionism in the Study of Ancient Judaism*. Oxford: Oxford University Press, 2006.

Knohl, Israel. *The Messiah before Jesus: The Suffering Servant of the Dead Sea Scrolls*. Translated by David Maisel. Berkeley: University of California Press, 2000.

Knox, John. *Chapters in a Life of Paul*. New York: Abingdon-Cokesbury Press, 1950.

Knust, Jennifer W. *Abandoned to Lust: Sexual Slander and Ancient Christianity*. New York: Columbia University Press, 2006.

Knust, Jennifer Wright, and Zsuzsanna Várhelyi, eds. *Ancient Mediterranean Sacrifice*. New York: Oxford University Press, 2011.

Kraemer, Ross S. "Jewish Tuna and Christian Fish: Identifying Religious Affiliation in Epigraphic Sources." *HTR* 84 (1991): 141–62.

——. "Giving Up the Godfearers." *Journal of Ancient Judaism* 5 (2014): 61–87.

Kugel, James. "4Q369 'Prayer of Enosh' and Ancient Biblical Interpretation." *Dead Sea Discoveries* 5 (1998): 119–48.

Kümmel, Werner Georg. *Römer 7 und das Bild des Menschen im Neuen Testament. Zwei Studien*. Theologische Bücherei 53. Munich: Kaiser, 1974. First published 1929.

Kunst, Christiane. *Römische Adoption: Zur Strategie einer Familienorganisation*. Frankfurter althistorische Beiträge 10. Hennef, Germany: Buchverlag Marthe Clauss, 2005.

Lampe, Peter. *From Paul to Valentinus: Christians at Rome in the First Two Centuries*. Translated by Michael Steinhauser. Minneapolis, MN: Fortress Press, 2003.

Landes, Richard A. "Lest the Millennium Be Fulfilled: Apocalyptic Expectations and the Pattern of Western Chronography 100–800 CE." In *The Use and Abuse of Eschatology in the Middle Ages*, edited by Werner Verbeke, Daniel Verhelst, and Andries Welkenhuysen, 137–211. Louvain: Leuven University Press, 1988.

——. *Heaven on Earth: The Varieties of Millennial Experience*. New York: Oxford University Press, 2011.

Lane Fox, Robin. *Pagans and Christians*. New York: Viking, 1987.

Law, Timothy M. *When God Spoke Greek: The Septuagint and the Making of the Christian Bible*. New York: Oxford University Press, 2013.

Lenowitz, Harris. *The Jewish Messiahs: From the Galilee to Crown Heights*. New York: Oxford University Press, 1998.

Levine, Lee I. *Jerusalem: Its Sanctity and Centrality to Judaism, Christianity, and Islam*. New York: Continuum, 1999.

——. *The Ancient Synagogue: The First Thousand Years*. New Haven, CT: Yale University Press, 2000.

Levinskaya, Irina. *The Book of Acts in Its Diaspora Setting*. The Book of Acts in Its First Century Setting 5. Grand Rapids, MI: Eerdmans, 1996.

Liebeschuetz, J. H. W. G. *Continuity and Change in Roman Religion*. New York: Oxford University Press, 1979.

——. "The Influence of Judaism among Non-Jews in the Imperial Period." *JJS* 52 (2001): 235–52.

Lieu, Judith M. *Image and Reality: The Jews in the World of the Christians in the Second Century*. Edinburgh: T. & T. Clark, 1996.

——. *Marcion and the Making of a Heretic: God and Scripture in the Second Century*. New York: Cambridge University Press, 2015.

Linder, Amnon. "The Legal Status of the Jews in the Roman Empire." In *The Cambridge History of Judaism*. Vol. 4: *The Late Roman-Rabbinic Period*, edited by Steven T. Katz, 128–73. Cambridge: Cambridge University Press, 2006.

Linder, Amnon, ed. and trans. *The Jews in Roman Imperial Legislation*. Detroit, MI: Wayne State University Press, 1987.

Litwa, M. David. *Iesus Deus: The Early Christian Depiction of Jesus as a Mediterranean God*. Minneapolis, MN: Fortress Press, 2014.

Llewelyn, Stephen R., and Dionysia van Beek. "Reading the Temple Warning as a Greek Visitor." *JSJ* 42, no. 1 (2011): 1–22.

Ma, John. "Relire les *Institutions des Séleucides* de Bickerman." In *Rome, a City and Its Empire in Perspective: The Impact of the Roman World through Fergus Millar's Research*, 59–84. Leiden: Brill, 2012.

MacMullen, Ramsay. *Christianity and Paganism in the Fourth to Eighth Centuries*. New Haven, CT: Yale University Press, 1997.

Malherbe, Abraham J. *Paul and the Popular Philosophers*. Minneapolis, MN: Fortress Press, 1989.

Malkin, Irad, ed. *Ancient Perceptions of Greek Ethnicity*. Center for Hellenic Studies Colloquia 5. Washington, DC: Center for Hellenic Studies, Trustees for Harvard University, 2001.

Marguerat, Daniel. "Paul après Paul: Une histoire de réception." *NTS* 54 (2008): 317–37.

Markschies, Christoph. "The Price of Monotheism: Some New Observations on a Current Debate about Late Antiquity." In Mitchell and van Nuffelen, *One God*, 100–111.

Marshall, John W. "Apocalypticism and Anti-Semitism: Inner-group Resources for Inter-group Conflicts." In *Apocalypticism, Anti-Semitism and the Historical Jesus: Subtexts in Criticism*, edited by John S. Kloppenborg with John W. Marshall. *Journal for the Study of the New Testament* Supplemental Series 275, 68–82. London: T. & T. Clark, 2005.

——. "Misunderstanding the New Paul: Marcion's Transformation of the *Sonderzeit* Paul." *JECS* 20 (2012): 1–29.

Martin, Dale B. *The Corinthian Body*. New Haven, CT: Yale University Press, 1995.

——. *Inventing Superstition: From the Hippocratics to the Christians*. Cambridge, MA: Harvard University Press, 2004.

——. *Sex and the Single Savior: Gender and Sexuality in Biblical Interpretation*. Louisville, KY: Westminster John Knox Press, 2006.

——. "When Did Angels Become Demons?" *JBL* 129 (2010): 657–77.

Martin, Michael Wade. "ἁρπαγμός Revisited: A Philological Reexamination of the New Testament's 'Most Difficult Word.'" *JBL* 135 (2016): 175–94.

Mason, Steve. "Jews, Judaeans, Judaizing, Judaism: Problems of Categorization in Ancient History." *JSJ* 38 (2007): 457–512.

Maurizio, Lisa. "Delphic Oracles as Oral Performances: Authenticity and Historical Evidence." *Classical Antiquity* 16 (1997): 308–34.

Mayordomo, Moisés. "'Conversion' in Antiquity and Early Christianity: Some Critical Remarks." In *Religiöse Grenzüberschreitungen: Studien zu Bekehrung, Konfessions- und Religionswechsel*, edited by Christine Lienemann-Perrin and Wolfgang Lienemann, 211–26. Wiesbaden: Harrassowitz Verlag, 2012.

McEleny, Neil J. "Conversion, Circumcision and the Law." *NTS* 20 (1974): 319–41.

McGing, Brian. "Population and Proselytism: How Many Jews Were There in the Ancient World?" In *Jews in the Hellenistic and Roman Cities*, edited by John R. Bartlett, 88–106. London: Routledge, 2002.

McGrath, James F. *The Only True God: Early Christian Monotheism in Its Jewish Context.* Urbana: University of Illinois Press, 2009.

Meeks, Wayne. *The First Urban Christians: The Social World of the Apostle Paul.* New Haven, CT: Yale University Press, 1983.

——. "Taking Stock and Moving On." In *After the First Urban Christians*, edited by Todd D. Still and David G. Horrell, 134–46. London: T. & T. Clark, 2009.

Meier, John P. *A Marginal Jew: Rethinking the Historical Jesus.* Vol. 2: *Mentor, Message and Miracles.* Anchor Bible Reference Library. New York: Doubleday, 1994.

——. *A Marginal Jew: Rethinking the Historical Jesus.* Vol. 4: *Law and Love.* Anchor Bible Reference Library. New Haven, CT: Yale University Press, 2009.

Mélèze-Modrzejewski, Joseph M. "How to Be a Jew in Hellenistic Egypt?" In *Diasporas in Antiquity.* Brown Judaic Studies 288, edited by Shaye J. D. Cohen and Ernest S. Frerichs, 65–91. Atlanta, GA: Scholars Press, 1993.

Miles, Richard. *Carthage Must Be Destroyed: The Rise and Fall of an Ancient Civilization.* New York: Viking, 2011.

Milgrom, J. *Leviticus 1–16: A New Translation with Introduction and Commentary.* Anchor Bible 3. New York: Doubleday, 1991.

Millar, Fergus. "The Imperial Cult and the Persecutions." In *Le culte des souverains dans l'empire romain*, edited by Elias J. Bickerman and Willem de Boer, 145–65. Vandœuvres-Geneva: Fondations Hardt, 1973.

——. "The Jews of the Graeco-Roman Diaspora between Paganism and Christianity." In *The Jews among Pagans and Christians in the Roman Empire*, edited by Judith Lieu, John North, and Tessa Rajak, 97–123. London: Routledge, 1992.

Miller, D. "The Meaning of *Ioudaios* and Its Relationship to Other Group Labels in Ancient Judaism." *Currents in Biblical Research* 9 (2010): 98–126.

——. "Ethnicity Comes of Age: An Overview of Twentieth-Century Terms for *Ioudaios.*" *Currents in Biblical Research* 10, no. 2 (2012): 293–311.

Mitchell, Margaret M. "Patristic Rhetoric on Allegory: Origen and Eustathius Put 1 Samuel 28 on Trial." *JR* 85 (2005): 414–45.

——. "Paul's Letter to Corinth: The Interpretive Intertwining of Literary and Historical Reconstruction." In *Urban Religion in Roman Corinth: Interdisciplinary Approaches*, edited by Daniel N. Showalter and Steven J. Friesen, 307–38. Cambridge, MA: Harvard University Press, 2005.

——. "Gift Histories: A Review of John M. G. Barclay, *Paul and the Gift.*" *JSNT* (forthcoming).

Mitchell, Stephen. "Further Thoughts on the Cult of Theos Hypsistos." In Mitchell and van Nuffelen, *One God*, 167–208.

Mitchell, Stephen, and Peter van Nuffelen, eds. *One God: Pagan Monotheism in the Roman Empire.* Cambridge: Cambridge University Press, 2010.

Momigliano, Arnaldo. *Alien Wisdom: The Limits of Hellenization.* Cambridge: Cambridge University Press, 1975.

Moore, George Foot. *Judaism in the First Centuries of the Christian Era: The Age of the Tannaim.* 3 vols. Cambridge, MA: Harvard University Press, 1927–1930.

Morgan, Teresa. *Roman Faith and Christian Faith: Pistis and Fides in the Early Roman Empire and Early Churches.* Oxford: Oxford University Press, 2015.

Moss, Candida R. *Ancient Christian Martyrdom: Diverse Practices, Theologies, and Traditions.* New Haven, CT: Yale University Press, 2012.

Munck, Johannes. *Paul and the Salvation of Mankind.* Translated by Frank Clarke. Richmond, VA: John Knox Press, 1959.

Najman, Hindy. "The Vitality of Scripture Within and Beyond the 'Canon.'" *JSJ* 43 (2012): 497–518.

Nanos, Mark D. *The Galatians Debate: Contemporary Issues in Rhetorical and Historical Interpretation.* Peabody, MA: Hendrickson Publishers, 2002.

——. "Paul and Judaism: Why Not Paul's Judaism?" In *Paul Unbound: Other Perspectives on the Apostle*, edited by Mark Douglas Given, 117–60. Peabody, MA: Hendrickson, 2010.

——. "Paul's Non-Jews Do Not Become 'Jews,' But Do They Become 'Jewish'? Reading Romans 2.25–29 within Judaism, alongside Josephus." *JJMJS* 1 (2014): 26–53 (www.jjmjs.org).

——. "The Question of Conceptualization: Qualifying Paul's Position on Circumcision in Dialogue with Josephus's Advisors to King Izates." In Nanos and Zetterholm, *Paul within Judaism*, 105–52.

Nanos, Mark D., and Magnus Zetterholm, eds. *Paul within Judaism: Restoring the First-Century Context to the Apostle.* Minneapolis, MN: Fortress Press, 2015.

Nasrallah, Laura. *Christian Responses to Roman Art and Architecture: The Second-Century Church amid the Spaces of Empire.* Cambridge: Cambridge University Press, 2010.

Nasrallah, Laura, and Elizabeth Schüssler Fiorenza, eds. *Prejudice and Christian Beginnings: Investigating Race, Gender and Ethnicity in Early Christian Studies.* Minneapolis, MN: Fortress Press, 2009.

Neusner, Jacob. "The Idea of Purity in Ancient Judaism." *JAAR* 43 (1975): 15–26.

Nickelsburg, George W. E. "Abraham the Convert: A Jewish Tradition and Its Use by the Apostle Paul." In *Biblical Figures outside the Bible*, edited by Michael E. Stone and Theodore A. Bergren, 151–75. Harrisburg, PA: Trinity Press International, 1998.

Noam, Vered. "'The Gentileness of the Gentiles': Two Approaches to the Impurity of Non-Jews." In *Halakhah in Light of Epigraphy*, edited by Albert I. Baumgarten, Hanan Eshel, Ranon Katzoff, and Shani Tzoref, 27–41. Göttingen: Vandenhoeck & Ruprecht, 2011.

——. "Another Look at the Rabbinic Conception of Gentiles from the Perspective of Impurity Laws." In *Judaea-Palaestina, Babylon and Rome: Jews in Antiquity*, edited by Benjamin Isaac and Yuval Shahar, 89–110. Tübingen: Mohr Siebeck, 2012.

Nock, Arthur Darby, ed. *Sallustius: Concerning the Gods and the Universe.* Hildesheim: G. Olms, 1966.

Nolland, John. "Uncircumcised Proselytes?" *JSJ* 12 (1981): 173–94.

Nongbri, Brent. *Before Religion: A History of a Modern Concept.* New Haven, CT: Yale University Press, 2013.

———. "The Concept of Religion and the Study of the Apostle Paul." *JJMJS* 2 (2015): 1–26 (www.jjmjs.org).

Novak, David. *The Image of the Non-Jew in Judaism: An Historical and Constructive Study of the Noahide Laws.* Toronto Studies in Theology 14. New York: Mellen Press, 1983.

Novenson, Matthew V. "The Jewish Messiahs, the Pauline Christ, and the Gentile Question." *JBL* 128 (2009): 357–73.

———. *Christ among the Messiahs: Christ Language in Paul and Messiah Language in Ancient Judaism.* New York: Oxford University Press, 2012.

———. "The Messiah ben Abraham in Galatians: A Response to Joel Willitts." *Journal for the Study of Paul and His Letters* 2 (2012): 163–69.

———. "Paul's Former Occupation in *Ioudaismos.*" In *Galatians and Christian Theology: Justification, the Gospel, and Ethics in Paul's Letters,* edited by Mark W. Elliott, Scott J. Hafemann, N. T. Wright, and John Frederick, 24–39. Grand Rapids, MI: Baker Academic, 2014.

———. "The Self-Styled Jew of Romans 2 and the Actual Jews of Romans 9–11." In Rodriguez and Thiessen, *The So-Called Jew in Paul's Letter to the Romans,* 133–62.

Oliver, Isaac W. "The 'Historical Paul' and the Paul of Acts." In Boccaccini and Segovia, *Paul the Jew,* 51–71.

Olyan, Saul M. "Purity Ideology in Ezra-Nehemiah as a Tool to Reconstitute the Community." *JSJ* 35 (2004): 1–16.

Opsomer, Jan. "Demiurges in Early Imperial Platonism." In *Gott und Götter bei Plutarch: Götterbilder-Gottesbilder-Weltbilder,* edited by Rainer Hirsch-Luipold. Religionsgeschichtliche Versuche und Vorarbeiten 54, 51–99. Berlin: Walter de Gruyter, 2005.

Parker, Robert. *Miasma: Pollution and Purification in Early Greek Religion.* Oxford: Clarendon Press, 1983.

Parkes, James. *The Conflict of the Church and the Synagogue: A Study in the Origins of Antisemitism.* Philadelphia: Jewish Publication Society of America, 1961. First published 1934.

Pearce, Sarah. "Jerusalem as 'Mother-City' in the Writings of Philo of Alexandria." In *Negotiating Diaspora: Jewish Strategies in the Roman Empire,* edited by John M. G. Barclay. Library of Second Temple Studies 45, 19–36. London: T. & T. Clark, 2004.

Pearson, Birger A. "1 Thessalonians 2:13–16: A Deutero-Pauline Interpolation." *HTR* 64 (1971): 79–94.

Peppard, Michael. *The Son of God in the Roman World: Divine Sonship in Its Social and Political Context.* Oxford: Oxford University Press, 2011.

——. "Brother against Brother: *Controversiae* about Inheritance Disputes and 1 Corinthians 6:1–11." *JBL* 133 (2014): 179–92.

Pervo, Richard I. *The Making of Paul: Constructions of the Apostle in Early Christianity*. Minneapolis, MN: Fortress Press, 2010.

Porton, Gary G. *The Stranger within Your Gates: Converts and Conversion in Rabbinic Judaism*. Chicago: University of Chicago Press, 1994.

Potter, David S. "Entertainers in the Roman Empire." In Potter and Mattingly, *Life, Death and Entertainment*, 256–325.

——. "Roman Religion: Ideas and Actions." In Potter and Mattingly, *Life, Death and Entertainment*, 113–67.

Potter, D. S., and D. J. Mattingly, eds. *Life, Death and Entertainment in the Roman Empire*. Ann Arbor: University of Michigan Press, 1999.

Price, Simon R. F. *Rituals and Power: The Roman Imperial Cult in Asia Minor*. Cambridge: Cambridge University Press, 1984.

Pucci Ben Zeev, Miriam. *Jewish Rights in the Roman World: The Greek and Roman Documents Quoted by Josephus Flavius*. Texte und Studien zum antiken Judentum 74. Tübingen: Mohr Siebeck, 1998.

Rajak, Tessa. *Translation and Survival: The Greek Bible of the Ancient Jewish Diaspora*. Oxford: Oxford University Press, 2009.

Reed, Annette Y. "The Trickery of the Fallen Angels and the Demonic Mimesis of the Divine: Aetiology, Demonology, and Polemics in the Writings of Justin Martyr." *JECS* 12 (2004): 141–71.

——. *Fallen Angels in the History of Judaism and Christianity: The Reception of Enochic Literature*. Cambridge: Cambridge University Press, 2005.

——. "Christian Origins and Religious Studies." *SR* 44, no. 3 (2015): 307–19.

Reynolds, Joyce, and Robert Tannenbaum. *Jews and God-Fearers at Aphrodisias: Greek Inscriptions with Commentary*. Cambridge: Cambridge Philological Society, 1987.

Riesner, Rainer. "A Pre-Christian Jewish Mission?" In *The Mission of the Early Church to Jews and Gentiles*, edited by J. Ådna and H. Kvalbein, 211–50. Tübingen: Mohr Siebeck, 2000.

Rives, James B. "Human Sacrifice among Pagans and Christians." *JRS* 85 (1995): 65–85.

——. "The Persecution of Christians and Ideas of Community in the Roman Empire." In *Politiche religiose nel mondo antico e tardoantico: Poteri e indirizzi, forme del controllo, idee e prassi di tolleranza*. Atti del convegno internazionale di studi (Firenze, 24–26 settembre 2009), edited by A. Cecconi and Ch. Gabrielli, 199–216. Bari: Edipuglia, 2011.

Rodriguez, Rafael. *If You Call Yourself a Jew: Reappraising Paul's Letter to the Romans*. Eugene, OR: Cascade Books, 2014.

Rodriguez, Rafael, and Matthew Thiessen, eds. *The So-Called Jew in Paul's Letter to the Romans*. Minneapolis, MN: Fortress Press, 2016.

Rösch, Petra, and Udo Simon, eds. *How Purity Is Made*. Wiesbaden: Harrassowitz Verlag, 2012.

Rosen-Zvi, Ishay, and Adi Ophir. "Goy: Toward a Genealogy." *Diné Israel* 28 (2011): 69–112.

———. "Paul and the Invention of the Gentiles." *JQR* 105 (2015): 1–41.

Runesson, Anders. "Inventing Christian Identity: Paul, Ignatius, and Theodosius I." In *Exploring Early Christian Identity*, edited by Bengt Holmberg, 59–92. WUNT 1, 226. Tübingen: Mohr Siebeck, 2008.

———. "The Question of Terminology: The Architecture of Contemporary Discussions on Paul." In Nanos and Zetterholm, *Paul within Judaism*, 53–78.

———. "Entering a Synagogue with Paul: First-Century Torah Observance." In *Torah Ethics and Early Christian Identity*, edited by Susan J. Wendel and David M. Miller, 11–26. Grand Rapids, MI: Eerdmans, 2016.

Runesson, Anders, Donald D. Binder, and Birger Olsson. *The Ancient Synagogue from Its Origins to 200 C.E.: A Source Book*. Leiden: Brill, 2008.

Rutgers, Leonard V. "*Dis Manibus* in Jewish Inscriptions from Rome." In *Jews in Late Ancient Rome: Evidence of Cultural Interaction in the Roman Diaspora*. Religions in the Graeco-Roman World 126, 269–72. Leiden: Brill, 1995.

———. *The Hidden Heritage of Diaspora Judaism: Essays on Jewish Cultural Identity in the Roman World*. Contributions to Biblical Exegesis and Theology 20. Louvain: Peeters, 1998.

Salvesen, Alison G., and Timothy M. Law. *The Oxford Handbook of the Septuagint*. Oxford: Oxford University Press (forthcoming).

Sanders, E. P. *Paul and Palestinian Judaism: A Comparison of Patterns of Religion*. Philadelphia: Fortress Press, 1977.

———. *Paul, the Law, and the Jewish People*. Philadelphia: Fortress Press, 1983.

———. *Jesus and Judaism*. London: SCM, 1985.

———. "Jewish Association with Gentiles and Galatians 2:11–14." In *The Conversation Continues: Studies in Paul and John in Honor of J. Louis Martyn*, edited by Robert T. Fortna and Beverly R. Gaventa, 170–88. Nashville, TN: Abingdon Press, 1990.

———. *Jewish Law from Jesus to the Mishnah: Five Studies*. London: SCM, 1990.

———. *Paul: A Very Short Introduction*. Oxford: Oxford University Press, 1991.

———. *Judaism: Practice and Belief, 63 BCE–66 CE*. Philadelphia: Trinity Press International, 1992.

———. *The Historical Figure of Jesus*. London: Allen Lane, Penguin, 1993.

———. *Paul: The Apostle's Life, Letters and Thought*. Minneapolis, MN: Fortress Press, 2015.

Sanzo, Joseph Emanuel. "'For Our Lord Was Pursued by the Jew . . .': The (Ab)Use of the Motif of 'Jewish' Violence against Jesus on a Greek Amulet (P. Heid. 1101)." In *One in Christ Jesus: Essays on Early Christianity and "All That Jazz" in Honor of S. Scott Bartchy*, edited by David Lertis Matson and K. C. Richardson, 86–98. Eugene, OR: Pickwick Publications, 2014.

Schäfer, Peter. *Judeophobia: Attitudes toward the Jews in the Ancient World*. Cambridge, MA: Harvard University Press, 1997.

Scheid, John. *Quand faire, c'est croire: Les rites sacrificiels des Romains*. Collection historique. Paris: Aubier Flammarion, 2011.

Schelkle, Karl Hermann. *Paulus, Lehrer der Väter: Die altkirchliche Auslegung von Römer 1–11*. Düsseldorf: Patmos Verlag, 1956.

Schellenberg, Ryan S. *Rethinking Paul's Rhetorical Education: Comparative Rhetoric and 2 Corinthians 10–13*. Early Christianity and Its Literature 10. Atlanta, GA: Society of Biblical Literature, 2013.

Schremer, Adiel. "'The Lord Has Forsaken the Land': Radical Explanations of the Military and Political Defeat of the Jews in Tannaitic Literature." *JJS* 59 (2008): 183–200.

Schürer, Emil. *The History of the Jewish People in the Age of Jesus Christ*. 3 vols. Edited by Geza Vermes, Fergus Millar, Matthew Black, and Martin Goodman. Edinburgh: T. & T. Clark, 1973–1987.

Schweitzer, Albert. *The Mysticism of Paul the Apostle*. Translated by William Montgomery, with an introduction by Jaroslav Pelikan. Baltimore, MD: Johns Hopkins University Press, 1998. First published 1931.

———. *The Quest of the Historical Jesus*. Edited by John Bowden and translated by W. Montgomery. Minneapolis, MN: Fortress Press, 2001. First published as *Geschichte der Leben-Jesu-Forschung* (Tübingen: J. C. B. Mohr, 1906).

Scott, Alan. *Origen and the Life of the Stars: A History of an Idea*. Oxford: Clarendon Press, 1991.

Scott, James M. *Adoption as Sons of God: An Exegetical Investigation into the Background of huiothesia in the Pauline Corpus*. WUNT 2, 48. Tübingen: Mohr Siebeck, 1992.

———. *Paul and the Nations: The Old Testament and Jewish Background of Paul's Mission to the Nations with Special Reference to the Destination of Galatians*. WUNT 1, 84. Tübingen: Mohr Siebeck, 1995.

———. "And Then All Israel Will Be Saved (Rom 11:26)." In *Restoration: Old Testament, Jewish, and Christian Perspectives*, edited by James M. Scott. Supplements to the *Journal for the Study of Judaism* 72, 489–527. Leiden: Brill, 2001.

Sechrest, Love L. *A Former Jew: Paul and the Dialectics of Race*. Edinburgh: T. & T. Clark, 2009.

Segal, Alan F. *Paul the Convert: The Apostolate and Apostasy of Saul the Pharisee*. New Haven, CT: Yale University Press, 1990.

Seland, Torrey. *Establishment Violence in Philo and Luke: A Study of Non-Conformity to the Torah and Jewish Vigilante Reactions*. Biblical Interpretation Series 15. Leiden: Brill, 1995.

Simon, Marcel. *Verus Israël: Études sur les relations entre Chrétiens et Juifs dans l'empire romain (135–425)*. Paris: E. de Boccard, 1948.

Smith, Jonathan Z. "Here, There, and Anywhere." In *Relating Religion: Essays in the Study of Religion*, 323–39. Chicago: University of Chicago Press, 2004.

Sourvinou-Inwood, Christiane. "Further Aspects of *Polis* Religion." In *Oxford Readings in Greek Religion*, edited by Richard Buxton, 38–55. New York: Oxford University Press, 2000.

Stanley, Christopher D. *Arguing with Scripture: The Rhetoric of Quotations in the Letters of Paul.* New York: T. & T. Clark, 2004.

Staples, Jason A. "What Do the Gentiles Have to Do with 'All Israel'? A Fresh Look at Romans 11:25–27." *JBL* 130 (2011): 371–90.

Stendahl, Krister. "Paul and the Introspective Conscience of the West." In *Paul among Jews and Gentiles,* 78–96. Philadelphia: Fortress Press, 1976. First published in *HTR* 56 (1963): 199–215.

——. *Paul among Jews and Gentiles.* Minneapolis, MN: Fortress Press, 1976.

——. *Final Account: Paul's Letter to the Romans.* Minneapolis, MN: Fortress Press, 1995.

Stern, Menachem, ed. and trans. *Greek and Latin Authors on Jews and Judaism.* 3 vols. Jerusalem: Israel Academy of Sciences and Humanities, 1974–1984.

Stern, Sacha. "Compulsive Libationers: Non-Jews and Wine in Early Rabbinic Sources." *JJS* 64 (2013): 19–44.

Steudel, Annette. "אחרית הימים in the Texts from Qumran." *Revue de Qumrân* 16 (1993): 225–46.

Still, Todd D., and David G. Horell, eds. *After the First Urban Christians: The Social-Scientific Study of Pauline Christianity Twenty-Five Years Later.* London: T. & T. Clark International, 2009.

Stowers, Stanley K. *Letter Writing in Greco-Roman Antiquity.* Philadelphia: Westminster, 1989.

——. *A Rereading of Romans: Justice, Jews, and Gentiles.* New Haven, CT: Yale University Press, 1994.

Sumney, Jerry L., ed. *Reading Paul's Letter to the Romans.* Atlanta, GA: Society of Biblical Literature, 2012.

Talbert, C. H. "The Problem of Pre-existence in Philippians 2:6–11." *JBL* 86 (1967): 141–53.

Tatum, Gregory. *New Chapters in the Life of Paul: The Relative Chronology of His Career.* Catholic Biblical Quarterly Monograph Series 41. Washington, DC: Catholic Biblical Association of America, 2006.

Taylor, Joan E. *The Immerser: John the Baptist within Second Temple Judaism.* Grand Rapids, MI: Eerdmans, 1997.

Thiessen, Matthew. "The Text of Genesis 17:14." *JBL* 128, no. 4 (2009): 625–42.

——. *Contesting Conversion: Genealogy, Circumcision, and Identity in Ancient Judaism and Christianity.* Oxford: Oxford University Press, 2011.

——. "Revisiting the προσήλυτος in the LXX." *JBL* 132 (2013): 333–50.

——. "Paul's Argument against Gentile Circumcision in Romans 2:17–29." *NovT* 56 (2014): 373–91.

——. *Paul and the Gentile Problem.* Oxford: Oxford University Press, 2016.

——. "Paul's So-Called Jew and Lawless Lawkeeping." In Rodriguez and Thiessen, *The So-Called Jew in Paul's Letter to the Romans,* 59–84.

Thomassen, Einar. *The Spiritual Seed: The Church of the "Valentinians."* Nag Hammadi and Manichaean Studies 60. Leiden: Brill, 2008.

Thorsteinsson, Runar M. *Paul's Interlocutor in Romans 2: Function and Identity in the Context of Ancient Epistolography.* Coniectanea Biblica New Testament Series 40. Stockholm: Almqvist and Wiksell, 2003.

Thorsteinsson, Runar, Matthew Thiessen, and Rafael Rodriguez, "Paul's Interlocutor in Romans: The Problem of Identification." In Rodriguez and Thiessen, *The So-Called Jew in Paul's Letter to the Romans,* 1–37.

Tomson, Peter J. *Paul and the Jewish Law: Halakha in the Letters of the Apostle to the Gentiles.* Compendia Rerum Iudaicarum ad Novum Testamentum sec. 3, Jewish Traditions in Early Christian Literature 1. Assen, Netherlands: Van Gorcum, 1990.

Tomson, Peter J., and Joshua Schwartz, eds. *Jews and Christians in the First and Second Centuries: How to Write Their History.* Leiden: Brill, 2014.

Tov, Emanuel. *The Text-Critical Use of the Septuagint in Biblical Research.* 2nd ed. Jerusalem Biblical Studies 8. Jerusalem: Simor, 1997.

———. *Textual Criticism of the Hebrew Bible.* 2nd rev. ed. Minneapolis, MN: Fortress Press, 2001.

Townsend, Philippa. "Who Were the First Christians? Jews, Gentiles, and the Christianoi." In *Heresy and Identity in Late Antiquity,* edited by Eduard Iricinschi and Holger M. Zellentin, 212–30. Tübingen: Mohr Siebeck, 2008.

Trebilco, Paul R. *Jewish Communities in Asia Minor.* Society for New Testament Studies Monograph Series 69. Cambridge: Cambridge University Press, 1991.

———. "The Christian and Jewish Eumeneian Formula." In *Negotiating Diaspora: Jewish Strategies in the Roman Empire,* edited by John M. G. Barclay. Library of Second Temple Studies 45, 66–88. London: T. & T. Clark, 2004.

Ulrich, Eugene. "Isaiah, Book of." In *Encyclopedia of the Dead Sea Scrolls,* edited by Lawrence H. Schiffman and James C. VanderKam, 384–88. Oxford: Oxford University Press, 2000.

Urbach, Ephraim E. *The Sages, Their Concepts and Beliefs.* Translated by Israel Abrahams. Jerusalem: Magnes, 1975.

van der Horst, Pieter W. "'Thou Shalt Not Revile the Gods': The LXX Translation of Ex. 22: 28 (27), Its Background and Influence." *Studia Philonica Annual* 5 (1993): 1–8.

———. "The Myth of Jewish Cannibalism: A Chapter in the History of Antisemitism." In *Studies in Ancient Judaism and Early Christianity,* 173–87.

———. *Studies in Ancient Judaism and Early Christianity.* Ancient Judaism and Early Christianity 87. Leiden: Brill, 2014.

van Henten, Jan Willem. "The Hasmonean Period." In *Redemption and Resistance: The Messianic Hopes of Jews and Christians in Antiquity,* edited by Markus Bockmuehl and James Carleton Paget, 15–28. London: T. & T. Clark, 2009.

Wagner, J. Ross. "The Christ, Servant of Jew and Gentile: A Fresh Approach to Romans 15:8–9." *JBL* 116 (1997): 473–85.

———. *Heralds of the Good News: Isaiah and Paul "in Concert" in the Letter to the Romans.* Supplements to Novum Testamentum 101. Leiden: Brill, 2002.

Walbank, Frank W. *The Hellenistic World.* Cambridge, MA: Harvard University Press, 1992.

Wallis, Richard T. *Neoplatonism.* London: Duckworth, 1972.

Wander, Bernd. *Gottesfürchtige und Sympathisanten: Studien zum heidnischen Umfeld von Diasporasynagogen.* Tübingen: Mohr Siebeck, 1998.

Ware, James. "Paul's Understanding of the Resurrection in 1 Corinthians 15:36–54." *JBL* 133 (2014): 809–35.

Wasserman, Emma. *The Death of the Soul in Romans 7: Sin, Death, and the Law in Light of Hellenistic Moral Psychology.* Tübingen: Mohr Siebeck, 2008.

———. "'An Idol Is Nothing in the World' (1 Cor 8:4): The Metaphysical Contradictions of 1 Corinthians 8:1–11:1 in the Context of Jewish Idolatry Polemics." In *Portraits of Jesus: Studies in Christology,* edited by Susan E. Meyers, 201–27. Tübingen: Mohr Siebeck, 2012.

———. "Myths of Victory: The Case of Sin and Apocalyptic Battle in Paul's Letters." Paper presented at the Annual Meeting of the Society of Biblical Literature, Baltimore, MD, November 2013.

Watson, Francis. *Paul, Judaism, and the Gentiles: Beyond the New Perspective.* Rev. ed. Minneapolis, MN: Eerdmans, 2007.

Weiss, Johannes. *Jesus' Proclamation of the Kingdom of God.* Translated by Richard Hyde Hiers and David Larrimore Holland. Philadelphia: Fortress Press, 1971. First published as *Die Predigt Jesu vom Reiche Gottes* (Göttingen, 1892).

Weiss, Zeev. *Public Spectacles in Roman and Late Antique Palestine.* Cambridge, MA: Harvard University Press, 2014.

White, Benjamin. "Reclaiming Paul? Reconfiguration as Reclamation in 3 Corinthians." *JECS* 17 (2009): 497–523.

———. *Remembering Paul.* Oxford: Oxford University Press, 2014.

Whitsett, Christopher G. "Son of God, Seed of David: Paul's Messianic Exegesis in Romans 2:3–4." *JBL* 119 (2000): 661–81.

Will, Edouard, and Claude Orrieux. *"Prosélytisme juif"? Histoire d'une erreur.* Paris: Les Belles Lettres, 1992.

Williams, Margaret H. *The Jews among the Greeks and Romans: A Diasporan Sourcebook.* Baltimore, MD: Johns Hopkins University Press, 1998.

Witherington, Ben. *Jesus, Paul, and the End of the World.* Downers Grove, IL: InterVarsity Press, 1992.

Wright, N. T. *The Climax of the Covenant: Christ and the Law in Pauline Theology.* Minneapolis, MN: Fortress Press, 1993.

———. *Paul and the Faithfulness of God.* 2 vols. Minneapolis, MN: Fortress Press, 2013.

Young, Frances M. *Biblical Exegesis and the Formation of Christian Culture.* Cambridge: Cambridge University Press, 1997.

Zetterholm, Karin Hedner. "The Question of Assumptions: Torah Observance in the First Century." In Nanos and Zetterholm, *Paul within Judaism,* 79–103.

Zetterholm, Magnus. *The Formation of Christianity in Antioch: A Social-Scientific Approach to the Separation between Judaism and Christianity.* London: Routledge, 2003.

———. *Approaches to Paul: A Student's Guide to Recent Scholarship.* Minneapolis, MN: Fortress Press, 2009.

——. "'Will the Real Gentile-Christian Please Stand Up!': Torah and the Crisis of Identity Formation." In *The Making of Christianity: Conflicts, Contacts, and Constructions: Essays in Honor of Bengt Holmberg*, edited by Magnus Zetterholm and Samuel Byrskog, 373–93. Winona Lake, IN: Eisenbrauns, 2012.

——. "The Non-Jewish Interlocutor in Romans 2.17 and the Salvation of the Nations: Contextualizing Romans 1.18–32." In Rodriguez and Thiessen, *The So-Called Jew in Paul's Letter to the Romans*, 39–58.

Zoccali, Christopher. "'And So All Israel Will Be Saved': Competing Interpretations of Romans 11.26 in Pauline Scholarship." *JSNT* 30 (2008): 289–318.

Names and Places

Aaron, 189n23
Abram/Abraham, 10, 14–15, 17, 24, 37, 71, 84, 105–6, 107, 126, 129–30, 148–51, 153, 158, 161, 164, 171, 172, 175, 188nn14 and 15, 192–93n11, 205n48, 225n19, 231n45, 234n64, 243nn41 and 42
Adiabene, 67, 73, 209nn7 and 10, 210n12
Aeneas, 36, 37
Aeschylus, 48
Africa, 33
Agrippa II, 209n7
Ahuvia, Mika, 206n48
Akko/Ptolemais, 206n50
Alexander Janneus, 84
Alexander the Great, 19, 26, 31, 32, 33, 190n2
Alexandria, 46, 48–49, 67, 92, 222n67
Allison, Dale C., Jr., 184n11
Ameling, Walter, 200n30
Ananias, 67, 73, 210n12, 213n28, 242n33
Anchior, 209n7
Anthedon, 222n67
Antioch, 5, 29, 57, 58, 79, 81, 92, 95–98, 111, 127, 152, 198n23, 211n17, 223n1, 223n7, 227n31
Antiochus Epiphanes, 27
Antiochus the Great, 190n1
Antipas, 216n43
Aphrodisias, 11, 55–56, 59, 205n46

Apion, 46, 199n29
Apollo, 36
Apollos, 192n10
Apuleius, 187n10
Aristobulus, 201n32
Arnal, William, 230n43, 234n65
Artapanus, 48, 199n27, 201n32
Ascalon, 222n67
Asia Minor, 2, 33, 43, 57, 190n1, 199nn28–29
Assyria, 20, 25, 104
Athens, 11
Augustine, 12, 90, 143, 177, 183n8, 199n26, 226n26, 228–29n38, 232n53, 246n59, 250n83
Augustus, 38, 43, 50, 193n12, 197n23, 202n35

Babylon, 20, 21, 25, 26, 32, 104
Bagnall, Roger S., 212n19
Baker, Cynthia, 201n33
Barclay, John M. G., 191n2, 194n13, 196n19, 197n23, 199n28, 199–200n29, 201n32, 208n2, 210n12, 211n17, 217n47, 219nn51 and 52, 223n7, 224n11, 226nn23 and 27, 227nn28 and 33, 228nn34 and 36, 230n43, 232n53, 233n57, 235n72, 243n42, 246n59, 247n60, 251n2, 252–53n7

ANCIENT DOCUMENTS AND AUTHORS

SUBJECTS

adoption (*huiothesia*): and Abraham, 243n42; and ethnicity, 235n69; as legal creation of "sonship," 37, 148; as Paul's model for End-time integration of gentiles through Christ, 148–51, 154, 159; and Roman law, 243n39; through spirit, not flesh, 148–51, 159; status of Israel apart from being "in Christ," 37, 235n72 (*see also entries for* Rom 9.4 *in Ancient Documents index*)

ancestral custom. *See* ethnicity

aniconism: and Jewish cult, 16, 41, 43, 195n19, 197n21, 247n59; and paideia, 41

apocalyptic eschatology: and "eschatological gentiles," 73–77, 88; foreshortened timeframe (expecting the End soon), 9, 28, 88, 185n3; and the gentile nations, 28–30, 76, 116, 161–64 (Table of Nations), 190n24; and Isaiah, 25, 29, 75, 80, 116, 136, 150, 155, 160–64, 215nn35 and 37, 241n30, 249n79; and Jesus' message, 6, 9, 29, 101, 184n11; Jewish traditions of, xii, 5–7, 9, 26–31, 73, 103, 189n21; and other superhuman beings, 89, 140, 162; and Paul's message, xi, 9, 102, 132; relation to

Babylonian exile, 20–22; and significance of Christophanies, 77, 135, 141–43. *See also* Kingdom of God; Messiah; resurrection

baptism, and reception of divine spirit, 151. *See also* separation

Bible: Latin text of, 143; as library, 8; and Qumran, 8, 185n2; and Septuagint (LXX), 9, 32, 39, 191n3, 194n14, weekly readings of, 196n20, 204n44

Christian, Christianity: and accusations of cannibalism, 45, 193n13, 198n26; anachronism of term for first generation, 117, 127–28, 173, 219n53, 228n34, 230n43; and Christian anti-Jewish persecutions, 109–10, 226nn24 and 25; and delay of the End, 102, 224n16; and distinction between ethnicity and religion, 34, 192n6; divinity of Christian emperors, 144, 241n29; as gentile movement, xii, 30–31, 251n2; inter-Christian competition ("heresy"), 45, 71–72, 198n26, 212n21, 213nn22 and 23; and magic, 205n48; and pagan gods, 12; presence in Roman-period diaspora synagogues, 85, 205n46, 206n51,

69, 200n31; as sign of kinship
(*syngeneia*), 37, 65, 103, 192nn7 and
8; and temple at Leontopolis, 42,
196n20; valued by Paul, 154, 163–65
(Romans)

cult (*latreia*), pagan: abandoned by
Christ-following ex-pagan pagans,
80, 89–91, 104; and cult statues, 41,
194n15 ("idolatry"); and divine
anger, 68, 104, 210n14, 221n59,
222n64; as expression of people-
hood/ethnicity/ancestral tradition
(inheritance), 34–36, 44; family cult
(*gens*, patrilineal *genius*), 148, 150
(responsibility of adopted son),
191n4, 193 n.12, 209n10 and 220n56
(Paul tolerating); honored by
Judaizing god-fearers (*theosobeis*),
59–60, 87, 201n1; imperial cult, 55,
144 (Christian), 193n12, 241n29; as
medium of Hellenization, 32; as
prime function of polis culture, 33,
191n4; and ritual purity, 51; as sign
of kinship (*syngeneia*), 37, 103. *See
also* ethnicity

David: called "god" by Origen, 241n29;
descendants as also God's sons, 36;
eternity of Davidic dynasty, 18, 20,
25 (restoration); as God's son, 18, 19;
and Jerusalem, 17–18, 42; king of
Israel, 17, 234n64; as messiah, 17–18,
19, 134; progenitor of eschatological
messiah, 1, 25, 27, 28, 75, 133–145
(Paul, on Jesus), 151, 163, 165, 166,
236n3, 239n18; in Qumran, 134;
varieties of Davidic messiah, 189n23

demons (*daimonia*): associated with evil
(by Jews and Christians), 194n15,
221n59; distinguished from idols, 40;
enabling LXX to express divine
multiplicity, 39; identified in Jewish
tradition with pagan gods, 40, 76,
89; as lower cosmic gods, 39–40,

194n15; and sacrifices, 69, 111, 164
(renounced by Christ-following
gentiles)

Diaspora: and competing gospel
missions, 30, 74, 94, 100, 104; and
diversity of Jewish practice, 85–86,
197n23 (Sabbath), 211n17, 220n54,
254n50 (Jews as only nonsacrificing
population in Diaspora); and gospel
missions to gentiles, 29–30, 79, 94,
146; and Jewish encounter with
foreign gods, 68–69, 87, 98,
199–201nn27–32; as Jewish "father
land" (Philo), 33, 48; as Jews'
voluntary relocation, 32, 48; site of
Roman, Greek, and Jewish
resistance to Christ-missions, 91–93,
103, 168, 221n59, 227n32; and temple
tax, 42

divinity: and Christ, 137–145; of
(Christian) emperor, 144, 241n29;
conveyed through spirit, 151–54; and
daimonia, 40; of David and Paul
(Origen), 241n29; and demiurge,
171; divine agents, 92, 186n5 (in
creation), 189n23 (messianic
figures); and ethnicity, 115 (Jewish
god), 199n28, 229n42; and family
(*genius*), 34, 151, 191n4, 193n12; on a
gradient, spanning heaven and
earth, 39–40, 69; of heavenly bodies,
197n21, 220n57; and high god of
paideia, 170–71; and kinship
diplomacy, 37; as localized in
people(s) 18, 19 (divine descent), 36
(divine descent), 54, 117 (ethnic
embeddedness); as localized in
place (lands, city, temples, altars),
18, 19; as marked by sacrifice,
238n15; of Moses (Philo), 241n29;
and multiplicity, 39 (in LXX), 162
(Paul), 187n9, 238n15; of Octavian,
192n9, 193n12, 241n29. *See also*
gods

idolatry (*continued*)
228n34, 232n57, 244n50 (and
sacrifice); as root of pagan moral
failings, 38, 53, 64, 124–25, 156,
232n57; in the Talmud, 195n17; and
Ten Commandments, 112, 118
Israel (people-group): and cultic
exclusivism, 16, 68, 92; designation
appropriated by gentile Christian
tradition, 71, 150, 156; as distinct
from "the nations" (*ethnē*), 114–16
(Paul), 150, 153, 159–66 (Paul); and
eschatological gentiles, 75, 77, 88,
92 (within ekklesia), 94; and ethnic
language, 151 ("Abba"), 192n7
(Hebrew in Paul); Exile and return,
20–26, 30; as focus of Jesus's
mission, 1, 79, 146; as focus of
post-resurrection movement, 79,
94–95, 101; God's covenant with,
15–17, 52 (*torah*), 64 (Paul), 86, 107,
113–14; God's creation of, 14–17;
God's promises to, 5, 9, 107, 149,
160, 163; as God's son, 18, 37, 150
(Paul); and lineage, 65, 149; and
locality (Land, Jerusalem, temple),
15–20, 33, 50; and ritual impurity,
52–53, 152; and Sabbath, 10;
theology of, 10 (ethnicity of God),
115; as 12 tribes, 15, 76, 102, 104–105,
130 ("all Israel"), 150, 157 ("all
Israel"), 161 ("all Israel"); western
Diaspora, 32–49. *See also* aniconism; conversion; covenant; law

Jesus of Nazareth: announcing coming
Kingdom of God (apocalyptic
expectation), 2, 5, 6, 9, 77, 101, 135,
145, 167; and call to repentance, 2,
118; and gentiles, 29–30, 146; and
inter-Jewish arguments, 71; mission
to Israel in Galilee and Judea, 1,
79–80, 103, 135; and significance of
resurrection, 4–6, 77, 135–36,

141–42, 145, 168; superhuman status,
138, 141, 144; and temple, 19; and
Torah-observance, 2, 118; and
traditions about his End-time return
(*Parousia*), 78, 79, 89, 101, 116, 132,
140, 145. *See also* messiah
Judaizing (the gentile assumption of
some Jewish behaviors and
customs)/Judaizers: advocated by
Paul, 86, 111–12, 117, 125, 127, 147,
228n34, 247n65; Christian Judaizing
condemned by Chrysostom, 206n51,
214n30; combined with pagan
practice, 56–60, 74, 94; condemned
by Christian emperors, 109; as
corruptors of NT manuscripts
(Marcion), 172; criticized by pagans,
43, 57, 68; criticized by Paul, 58, 125
(if attempted without Christ), 126
(the persona of the "I" of Romans
7), 129 (and eighth-day
circumcision), 157–58, 233n59 (if
attempted without Christ); and
"god-fearing," 59; as Paul's
competitors in Galatia, 81, 223n10;
Paul's complaint to Peter in
Antioch, 58, 96–99, 127; and
persona of interlocutor in Romans
2, 156–57, 247nn60–62; as recipients
for gospel message, 80, 126, 211n17.
See also conversion; god-fearers

Kingdom of God: and charismata, 6,
146, 165, 183n10; and Christophanies,
78–79, 135–36, 142, 147, 167; and
delay, xi–xii, 78, 102–103, 154–155,
160, 169, 224n16; dethroning of
pagan gods, 12, 89, 140, 143, 145, 168;
and end of idolatry, 80, 88, 94;
established by returning Christ, 8,
89, 94, 101, 126–27, 132–36, 139, 141,
146, 224n15; gentile Christian
reconceptualizations of, 173; and
gospel of Mark, 78; and inclusion of